Although much has b........ ....ture suffers
from a lack of histor...... ....ing theoretical
frameworks. Through case studies drawing on the rich historical experience of
crisis diplomacy, James Richardson offers an integrated analysis based on a
critical assessment of the main theoretical approaches. Due weight is given to
systemic and structural factors, but also to the specific historical factors of each
case, and to theories which do not presuppose rationality as well as those
which do. Crisis diplomacy – the major political choices made by decision
makers, as well as their strategies, judgments and misjudgments – is found to
play a crucial role in each of the case studies. This broad historical inquiry is
especially timely when the ending of the Cold War has removed the settled
parameters within which the superpowers conducted their crisis diplomacy.

CAMBRIDGE STUDIES IN INTERNATIONAL RELATIONS

Series list continues after index

CRISIS DIPLOMACY
THE GREAT POWERS
SINCE THE
MID-NINETEENTH
CENTURY

JAMES L. RICHARDSON

Australian National University

CAMBRIDGE
UNIVERSITY PRESS

Published by the Press Syndicate of the University of Cambridge
The Pitt Building, Trumpington Street, Cambridge CB2 1RP
40 West 20th Street, New York, NY 10011–4211, USA
10 Stamford Road, Oakleigh, Melbourne 3166, Australia

First published 1994

Printed in Great Britain at the University Press, Cambridge

A catalogue record for this book is available from the British Library

Library of Congress cataloguing in publication data

Richardson, J. L. (James L.), 1933–
Crisis diplomacy: the Great Powers since the mid-nineteenth century /
James L. Richardson.
    p.   cm. – (Cambridge Studies in International Relations: 35)
Includes bibliographical references.
ISBN 0 521 45392 5 (hc) – ISBN 0 521 45987 7 (pb)
1. Great powers.   2. World politics – 19th century.
3. World politics – 20th century.
I. Title.   II. Series.
D363.R46   1994
327'.09'03 – dc20   93-41564   CIP

ISBN 0 521 45392 5 hardback
ISBN 0 521 45987 7 paperback

CE

CONTENTS

PART IV

TABLES

ACKNOWLEDGMENTS

During the research and writing of this work I have accumulated many intellectual and personal debts. In particular, I would like to thank those who commented extensively on the manuscript: Richard Ned Lebow, John Ravenhill and Glenn Snyder. John Dunbabin, John Groom, Robert Jervis, Ian Nish and Paul Schroeder offered valuable comments on specific chapters or issues, and the reports of the two readers for the publisher contributed very substantially to the final revision of the whole. Many of the chapters were presented at seminars, not only at the Australian National University but also during visits to Columbia, Cornell, Frankfurt and the Universities of Kent (Canterbury) and Illinois (Urbana/Champaign). I am grateful to those who arranged the seminars and to the many participants for helpful comments and reactions. An earlier version of Chapter 3 was presented at the XIIIth World Congress of the International Political Science Association in a panel organised by Gilbert Winham, and was included in his edited volume *New Issues in International Crisis Management*.

A grant from the Australian Research Grants Committee supported the early stages of the research, and an individual grant from the Ford Foundation enabled me to undertake travel in the USA and Europe at a later stage. Research assistance was provided by Luu Tuong Quang, Janet Penny and Robin Ward, who also assisted with the final preparation of the manuscript. The typing of the whole of the manuscript was undertaken by Barbara Owen-Jones, who coped with handwriting, numerous revisions and pressing deadlines with good humour as well as efficiency. My greatest debt is to Ursula Vollerthun, for her support for the project from the outset; her attention to detail as well as to the larger argument has contributed immeasurably to the quality of the final product.

PART I

1 INTRODUCTION: AIMS AND APPROACH

In the nuclear age, and more especially since the Cuban missile crisis of 1962, international crises have become a major focus of study. The reasons are evident: crises between nuclear powers confront whole societies with the spectre of their sudden destruction and require decision makers to contemplate choices of intolerable consequence, sometimes under extreme time pressure. From an earlier era, the example of Sarajevo stands as an awesome warning of the way in which governments can lose control over events. Analysts have examined many crises, drawing on a wide range of theoretical approaches, and there have been some outstanding works. However, the literature on crises shows serious limitations. Many studies are narrowly based, being restricted to the decisions of a single actor; relatively few crises have been studied in depth; and persisting differences over theoretical assumptions stand in the way of agreed findings. Above all, there is no accepted answer to the question: under what conditions do crises lead to war, and when are they resolved peacefully? Since the diversity of international conflicts may preclude any general answer, however, the starting point for the present inquiry is a reformulation of the question: to what extent does the outcome depend on the gravity of the underlying conflict – on what may be termed 'structural' factors – and to what extent on crisis diplomacy – on decisions and interactions during the crisis itself?

The work has several objectives. First, it seeks to correct a tendency to generalise from a few well-known examples by examining less familiar cases which bring out the diversity of crises. Second, it seeks nonetheless to identify central features of crisis diplomacy, examining each case within a common analytical framework. The third aim is to evaluate the competing theories of crisis behaviour in the light of this analysis, and the final task is to draw out the study's implications for policy thinking, pointing to a need to go beyond familiar assumptions concerning 'crisis management'.

The cases are chosen to illustrate the diversity of great-power crises and their settings from the mid-nineteenth to the mid-twentieth century. One important reason for studying cases from earlier periods, despite the evident contrasts with the strategic and technological environment of the present, is that the interaction between the crisis adversaries can be traced adequately only in cases for which documentation of the decisions of all major parties is available, that is, those before 1945. Direct evidence of the perceptions and intentions of the Soviet government after 1945 has only begun to become available, and its assessment is at a very early stage. The element of speculation in the reconstruction of Soviet policy is different in kind from the problems of interpretation where ample documentation is available. A second reason is that pre-1945 experience offers a rich source of great-power crises which led to war, and thus the opportunity to compare them with those which were resolved peacefully – a comparison which thankfully cannot be made since 1945. The diversity of circumstances in the different periods is conducive to the testing of generalisations.

The work focuses on the political aspects of crises, where earlier experience can illuminate the present, not the technological aspects, where discontinuities between past and present are most evident, and which have been addressed in a number of important studies.[1] Many of the essential problems of crisis decision making have changed little, if at all, especially those which bear on the processes by which conflicts become so acute as to generate crises, and crises move towards 'confrontations', or this is avoided. Among the problems common to all periods are those of confusion and division over objectives, of achieving sound perception and judgment under pressure, of seizing or missing diplomatic opportunities, and of constraints on rational choice such as the impact of conflicting political 'imperatives'.

The evaluation of theories is approached indirectly: that is to say, it is undertaken only after the completion of the prior tasks of interpreting and comparing the cases in terms of a common framework of analysis which can be used to assess a range of theories, not just a single theory. The comparative analysis of multidimensional phenomena such as international crises presents problems for which the methodologies of social science or history do not have ready answers. Social scientists tend to interpret the complex 'reality' as a case of a particular kind – for some, a case of bargaining and rational choice, for others a case of stress or cognitive distortion. Historians, while never free from theoretical assumptions, tend to emphasise the particular: the individual decision maker, the rich contextual detail. And their interpretations differ, not only over the explanation of important events but also over which were the important events – over consequences as well as explanations, and over whether the important choices occurred during a crisis or predated it.

The interpretation of the cases, then, is a major task in itself. Even the barest outline of events is open to challenge: which are to be included, which omitted? Already, judgments of the significance of events are presupposed. Different interpretations are always possible, and are usually present in the literature. The case studies must come to terms with the relevant historical debates: the chosen interpretation always requires justification. In view of the overall aims of the work, however, these justifications are presented briefly, the relevant debates being noted in the references.

The cases

Preliminary reading suggested that the circumstances and the problems experienced in crises are more diverse than is generally recognised. But which cases should be chosen from the experience of a century and a quarter? In accordance with the concerns over nuclear crises which are central to crisis studies, the cases are limited to serious crises among great powers. Since 1815 the great powers have seen themselves as actors of a special kind, the 'managers' of the international system, the 'great responsibles'.[2] Viewing one another as long-term associates as well as rivals, and mindful of the risk of major war, they have normally been reluctant to go to war with one another. In this their conduct differs from that of many smaller states – for which the continued existence of an adversary may not be presupposed – just as it differs from their own conduct in relation to lesser states. Most of the decision makers studied here were reluctant to go to war, yet all the crises were 'serious': participants and historians concur that a serious risk of war was present. Whether the conclusions from this study would hold for non-great-power crises would require further investigation.

Since one of the aims is to inquire into what distinguishes crises that lead to war from those which do not, these outcomes are represented equally (four led to war, four were resolved peacefully, and one offered only a brief respite from war). In order to take account of changes in the international system, cases are chosen from successive phases: the Concert of Europe (to 1854); the years of Italian and German unification; the era of alliances and imperialism preceding World War One; the interwar period; and the Cold War. Among the crises of the multipolar system – a context which will become more relevant if the global power structure moves in that direction – some

5

are chosen from those involving several powers, some from those with only two protagonists. Most of the crises chosen were of relatively long duration – at least several months. Only one, the Franco-Prussian crisis, was a confrontation measured in days. Relatively few of the serious great-power crises take this form. The two crises most fully studied by social scientists, Cuba and July 1914, both of them short crises, are not included. Little could be added to the study of the Cuban case though its 'lessons' form the starting point for the discussion of policy implications; and the interpretation of July 1914 remains so contested that its inclusion would require an elaborate interpretive chapter, yet would still provide a questionable basis for assessing theories.[3]

The first two cases (the Eastern and Crimean crises), the most serious in the Concert period, permit a close comparison of cases with many similarities but opposite outcomes. The Franco-Prussian case provides the sole instance of the short crisis and, as a clash between the two potentially dominant continental powers, is of greater interest than the other crises during the second phase. The Russo-Japanese case, a characteristic 'imperialist' crisis, brings in the extra-European world, as well as an instructive instance of an unfamiliar path to war. An alternative to Agadir could readily be found in the pre-World War One years, but it was arguably the most serious of those crises, the one in which brinkmanship came closest to escaping from control. The Sudeten crisis was the most serious of the European interwar crises, the only one which came close to war. The Rhineland crisis, a possible alternative, had major strategic consequences, but the term 'crisis' is almost a misnomer in that there was no real risk of war.[4] The crisis between the United States and Japan in 1940–41 brings in the non-European powers. The Berlin crises – after Cuba the most serious of the Cold War – offer a further close comparison. Within the respective time periods there are no cases which better satisfy the criteria that they be 'serious' great-power crises divided evenly between war and peaceful outcomes. The selection may appear Eurocentric, but this is inevitable for the nineteenth century, and the later selections strike a more even balance.

Four of the cases are presented extensively: the Eastern, Crimean, Russo-Japanese and Sudeten. These include a narrative followed by sections on six aspects of the cases, discussed below: the setting, goals, perception, bargaining, internal politics and the outcome. They demonstrate the methods used in interpreting the cases and employing the analytical framework. The remaining five cases are presented more briefly, as narratives sufficiently detailed to provide a basis for the interpretations which are drawn upon in the comparative chapters that follow. While the case studies are not based on archival research, they are more than mere syntheses of existing sources. As Alexander George has observed, asking new questions requires a thorough re-examination of the sources[5] – in this instance, in addition to the major secondary literature, primary sources readily available in English, supplemented by certain French and German sources, including older studies which often include valuable information, later neglected.

The analytical scheme

Six aspects of crises are examined, first in the case studies and then in the comparative/analytical chapters in Part III: the setting; the actors' goals; perception and misperception; bargaining (and also non-bargaining); internal politics; and the outcome. Given the theoretical assumptions outlined in Chapter 2, below, each of these appear to be necessary for an adequate reconstruction of any crisis, and for explaining its outcome. Only two of them – perception and bargaining – have been the subject of extensive theoretical analysis. Some aspects of the setting are often noted, and bureaucratic politics sometimes figures prominently, but internal politics as a whole is usually neglected. Goals are often assumed, not studied in depth. In view of these lacunae, explanations of crisis outcomes tend to be incomplete. Further research may reveal a need to extend or reformulate the framework, but it seems safe to say that an interpretation of a crisis 'in the round' must include the above 'dimensions', in some form, as a basis for explaining the outcome.[6]

The discussion of *the setting* includes an account of the international system at the time of the crisis and also the essential background – the goals and capabilities of the protagonists and the development of the conflict up to the point where it is deemed to have reached the level of crisis. This permits a broad judgment of the seriousness of the initial conflict and the extent to which the final outcome can plausibly be regarded as 'predetermined' or 'prefigured' at the outset.

The actors' *goals* are broken down into long-term (values) and short-term (crisis objectives), the linkage between which is found to be problematic. The prevalence of differences among decision makers over goals is evident in the case studies, raising questions for the later theoretical discussion. Since it is, prima facie, governments' immediate objectives which shape crisis strategies and decisions, some character-istics of objectives are examined, but the limitations of such an analysis are also acknowledged. That is to say, the extent to which crisis behaviour is intentional, calculated – 'rational' – is a matter to be investigated in each particular case, not one to be resolved by prior assumption.

The discussion of *perception* also inquires into differences among decision makers – in their perception of capabilities and intentions, of the effects of their own actions and of the risk of war. Numerous examples of these are to be found in the cases, as are frequent instances of misperception. The consequences of misperception, however, are not so well understood: the study seeks to identify which of the many misperceptions proved to have important consequences, and why this was so.

The discussion of *bargaining*, similarly to that of goals, proceeds from the premise that while there is a great deal of apparent bargaining behaviour in most of the cases, it cannot be assumed in advance that the actions of the adversaries amount to genuine strategies or that their interactions constitute first and foremost a bargaining process. Rather, these are questions to be investigated. Imperfections in the bargaining process, and unintended interactions, need to be taken seriously, as do alternative models of interaction such as the 'hostility spiral'.

Internal political processes determine who will be the decision makers whose goals will be pursued, and whether governments will be cohesive or divided, stable or unstable. The analysis of internal politics inquires especially into those cases where its 'logic' or 'pressures' were at odds with those of foreign policy, or where internal political instability tended to impair the quality of crisis diplomacy.

The discussion of *determinants of the outcome* distinguishes between the long term – 'structural' changes and constraints, clashes over fundamental values and goals – and the short term – policy choices, strategies and tactics, misperceptions, diplomatic mishaps and the like. This provides a way of approaching the question whether there is a common pattern in the case of those crises which lead to war as against those which are resolved peacefully, or a variety of patterns.

The comparative chapters examine the findings of the case studies in terms of this framework. These findings, for the most part in the form of distinctions and contingent generalisations, provide the basis for the final evaluation of theories which is attempted in Chapter 16.

There is no precise model for the evaluation of multiple theories by means of multiple case studies. The approach followed here is adapted from the method of 'structured, focused comparison' outlined by Alexander George, according to which theories may be tested or refined by comparing appropriate cases in terms of carefully specified variables.[7] Although George's own application of the method is concerned with a single theory, he allows for the possibility of a broad-ranging historical study such as the present (his example is war termination). The present task is quite different from the precise testing of a specific theory, and has different criteria which are summed up by Glenn Snyder and Paul Diesing as 'fruitfulness and relevance'.[8] The two principal criteria used in this study are *relevance*, that is to say, whether the theory addresses the main problems exemplified in the cases, and *fit* – whether its explanations are well supported by the evidence. These issues are taken up at the end of Chapter 2.

The work is divided into four parts. Part I includes an outline of the theories which are selected for closer examination and a discussion of the policy assumptions associated with the notion of 'crisis management'. Part II includes the case studies, and Part III the comparative chapters on the six aspects of crises discussed above. Part IV presents the overall conclusions: an assessment indicating which of the theories are found to be well supported and illuminating, and which prove of limited relevance; and also some conclusions for policy thinking. It is argued that 'crisis management' is an unattainable aspiration, and that the more modest concept of crisis diplomacy offers greater potential for constructive thought about policy.

2 THEORIES OF CRISIS BEHAVIOUR

The discussion of international crises reflects a bewildering kaleido-scope of theories. In public comment and even in policy making these may remain at the level of assumption, but one of the tasks of social science is to articulate the theories which underlie such assumptions. The aim of this chapter is to identify the most significant theories for the understanding of international crises – those which, in the light of previous research, still need to be taken into account – and the extent of their incompatibility or complementarity. 'Understanding' is used here to refer to the role of concepts in description as well as expla-nation, providing a theoretical language as well as a set of hypotheses.[1] Initially, however, in view of the looseness with which the term is often used, it is necessary to formulate a definition of 'crisis' which is appropriate to the present study.

The definition of 'crisis'

The term has been used in such varied ways by social scientists, historians and commentators that a common definition appears unat-tainable.[2] It is necessary to find one which is appropriate to the particular subject matter, and for the most part, this is what students of international crises have attempted. Even so, they have offered several different types of definition.[3] In particular, crises have been defined in terms of abrupt systemic change, a certain class of decisions or a high risk of war, with a tendency to converge on the third of these. The problems associated with the other types of definition suggest that this is well founded.

A systemic definition sees a crisis as a brief phase in which the breakdown or transformation of a system (a pattern of relationships) is threatened. Coral Bell, for example, drawing on the original Greek meaning of the term, defines international crises as 'the turning points or decision points in relations between states', when conflicts 'rise to a level which threatens to transform the nature of the relationship'.[4]

However, turning-points are more difficult to recognise than crises. Extensive study may be necessary to identify a true decision point, but not to determine the presence or absence of an international crisis. More fundamentally, the definition is too wide: not all turning-points take the form of crises. Gradual changes may transform relationships more surely and inexorably than sudden crises – thus may represent the true turning-points. Or sudden turning-points – the death of a crucial actor, a change of government – may provide no opportunity for engaging in conflict, thus no crisis.

Decision making definitions avoid this error by adopting a clearer focus: a crisis is defined as a particular type of governmental decision. Michael Brecher, for example, defines crises in terms of three perceptions of top-level decision makers: 'a threat to basic values; high probability of involvement in military hostilities; and finite time for response to the external value threat'.[5] Such definitions, in terms of the decision making process, draw attention to the fact that a particular crisis may be more acute for some governments than for others – indeed, a situation may be a crisis for one government but not for another. The problem, however, is that they define a relationship – an interaction – in terms of only one of the actors involved. Just as a conflict, a dispute, a settlement or a war must be defined by reference to more than one actor, so must an international crisis: it is something more than a foreign policy crisis for one state.[6] Decision making definitions may identify some essential features of crises, but nonetheless amount to a misclassification.

There remain the definitions which identify international crises as situations involving a heightened risk of war. For Snyder and Diesing, for example, an international crisis is 'a sequence of interactions between the governments of two or more sovereign states in severe conflict, short of actual war but involving the perception of a dangerously high probability of war'.[7] This type of definition points directly to what the generally acknowledged examples of international crises have in common, that is to say, they are conflicts in which the possibility of war appears real and immediate, not just remote and abstract. And it points to the concerns which have led to the study of international crises, in particular the concern to understand the relationship between crisis and war.

One issue requires clarification: should the definition refer to the actual probability of war or to the perceived probability, and if the latter, then whose perception? Unless this is explicit, it is not clear whether the actual probability is implied, or whether it is assumed that the perception of the risk of war is uniform. However, decision makers

11

may perceive risks of which the public is not yet aware, or there may be cases of needless public alarm. And even among decision makers there can be major variations in the perception of the risk of war, some of which survive among scholars. On balance, it is best that the definition refer to the perceptions of decision makers – those directly involved in crisis diplomacy.

The definition adopted in the present study is as follows:

> An international crisis is an acute conflict between two or more states, associated with a specific issue and involving a perception by decision makers of a serious risk of war.

The term 'serious risk' is taken to refer to a psychological threshold: war comes to seem a real possibility, directly affecting policy choices. Although the onset of a crisis, the transition from 'tension' to 'crisis', is rarely perceived at the same moment in different capitals, this does not present major problems. Cases such as the Russo-Japanese crisis, in which for most of the time one side failed to perceive the risk of war which was clear to the other, are very rare. In this case the risk was perceived by most of the other powers, thus it is reasonable to treat the whole of the interaction as a crisis. At the opposite extreme, there may be a war scare in one capital which is soon perceived to be without foundation: such an episode would not count as a crisis. However, if the war scare were to generate a 'hostility spiral', a dangerous sequence of hostile interactions and a perceived threat of war, this would, of course, amount to a crisis.

The reference to a specific issue is intended to distinguish a crisis from a period of high tension such as the early years of the Cold War. Everyday usage distinguishes crises from general background tension, not because of their short duration but because the conflict becomes focused on a particular issue which requires crucial decisions. One of the earliest writers on contemporary crises, Alistair Buchan, included in his definition a defined or definable issue, and indeed crises are often named after the principal issue at stake.[8] This is not to imply that the issue is the principal reason for the conflict, but without an issue, there is no crisis, though there may in exceptional cases be a war. The proposed definition is narrower than everyday usage. Some so-called 'crises' do not involve a perception by decision makers of a serious risk of war. Drawing on the language of diplomacy, we may define such cases as 'incidents' – sudden conflicts of lesser magnitude than crises, which require urgent attention but do not pose the question of war or peace.

Theoretical perspectives

The study of international crises may be seen as falling into two phases. During the first, lasting for about a decade after the Cuban missile crisis, two theoretical schools coexisted but did not interact. For one school, associated with strategic studies, crises were the supreme occasion for strategic bargaining – for attempted coercion and manipulation. The problems of deterrence could be reformulated as problems of crisis management. This school retained the strategists' assumption of rationality, and the influence of strategic analysts, in particular Thomas Schelling, was widely acknowledged.[9] A second school found its inspiration in psychological studies of conflict. Its natural affinity was with the peace research movement and with those critics of strategic studies who had long contested its postulate of rationality. Drawing on the behavioural sciences, this school emphasised the psychology of stress, threat perception and hostile interaction, leading to an entirely different view of crisis decision making.[10] There was little recognition by either school of the problems and perspectives opened up by the other.

The publication which marks the change to the second phase is the symposium edited by Charles F. Hermann, *International Crises: Insights from Behavioral Research* (1972).[11] Crisis studies since that time have sought to come to terms with differing theoretical perspectives. They have also been influenced by developments in the field of foreign policy decision making, in turn influenced by developments in public policy and in organisation theory. However, the original dichotomy between 'rational actor' and 'behavioural/psychological' approaches, though now more clearly articulated, was not resolved. Subsequent studies, despite their recognition of competing theories, still tend to fall broadly within one or other of the original schools, as do studies of deterrence, escalation and the causes of war.

For example, Phil Williams, *Crisis Management* (1976), develops a rational-actor perspective within which he takes account of psychological and bureaucratic theories.[12] Snyder and Diesing's *Conflict Among Nations* (1977) remains the principal theoretical statement of the rational-actor school: while its focus is on bargaining, it incorporates a range of cognitive and decision making theories. On the other hand, in the works of Michael Brecher and of Richard Ned Lebow the psychological dimension of decision making predominates, along with organisational or domestic political pressures.

Theories relating to international crises have been classified in

13

various ways, sometimes by level of analysis, sometimes by distinguishing among theories of decision making. The following breakdown is advanced for convenience of exposition. The greater theoretical differentiation at the decision making level is reflected in the breakdown, without implying that this should have priority over other levels.

Theories are grouped as follows:

1 rational-choice theories;
2 psychological theories of decision making;
3 political theories, including bureaucratic politics;
4 theories of adversary interaction;
5 systemic and deterministic theories.

Theories of rational choice

We may follow Graham Allison in seeing rational-actor theories as the typical mode of explaining foreign policy decisions, by scholars and laymen alike, and in identifying their 'trademark' as 'the attempt to explain international events by recounting the aims and calculations of nations and governments'.[13] For Allison, the rational actor is a state or government, considered as a unitary decision maker, but he allows for variants of his basic model, including one – especially relevant for the present study – in which the rational-actor is the individual decision maker.[14] In the social sciences more generally, rational-choice theory is taken to apply to individuals rather than collective actors, but in view of the 'state-as-actor' focus in international relations theory, it should not be prejudged in advance which level of analysis, state or individual, will prove most relevant for the study of crises.

According to this first theoretical perspective, decision making is a rational process of choosing, from among the available alternatives, the course of action whose expected consequences best promote the actor's goals or preferences. Decision makers act purposefully and prudently in the light of the information available to them. Misperception and misunderstanding may result from the incompleteness or the ambiguity of the information, but do not imply any diminution of rationality. Departures from rationality require special explanation.

We may distinguish two broad types of rational-actor theories, formal and those here termed informal. Formal (or mathematical) theories such as those developed in economics and game theory are increasingly prominent in international relations. Formal modelling assumes that highly simplified descriptions can identify the basic patterns, structures or causal mechanisms which underlie complex phenomena: formal theories have the attractions of explicitness, analytical rigour, parsimony and generality.[15] Snyder and Diesing's development of formal bargaining theory, discussed in Chapter 13, is clearly a major contribution to the theoretical analysis of crises. Whether formal modelling offers a fruitful approach to theory at the decision making level, however, is problematic. It is true that a concept of decision making as that which best promotes the actor's goals can be construed, in the language of formal theory, as the maximisation of utility.[16] But the appropriateness of the 'utility' concept, with its assumption that the relevant values are sufficiently homogeneous to be ranked in a common scale, is widely questioned when the choices involve war and peace, national survival and perhaps the decision maker's own survival.

Such questioning leads to claims that the formal models are either unrealistic or else tautological – decisions are assumed or deemed to be utility maximising. This is countered by the response that the models do not seek to reproduce the complexities of actual cases but to isolate key variables for general explanatory theory. The historical study of particular decisions – necessarily complex and contextual – should not be confused with theory which, it is maintained, is necessarily abstract and general.

Decision making studies, however, need not be limited to the individual case but can examine institutions, procedures, perception, information flows and the like, in general terms. Some of these studies presuppose rationality in various everyday senses – that actions are intentional, beliefs are consistent with the relevant evidence, and so forth. Others, discussed below, deny these assumptions. In other words, decision making studies concern themselves with what the formal theories take as given. Bruce Bueno de Mesquita, explaining utility theory, notes that 'the rationality assumption tells us nothing about how actors form their preferences, but rather how actors behave, given their preferences'.[17] Jon Elster dubs this the 'thin' theory of rationality and asserts the need for a 'broad' theory which will also address the rationality of the beliefs and desires which underlie actors' preferences, here termed the informal concept of rationality.[18]

Explanations of this informal kind – the characteristic rational explanations noted by Allison – recur in the sources drawn upon for the present case studies. Such explanations are at once more limited and more extensive in their claims than the formal theories. They lack the scope and generality of the formal theories, but can deepen the

15

understanding of decisions by examining what lies behind the 'givens' of those theories – the dimensions of rationality which, not being open to formal modelling, are perforce omitted.[19] Informal analysts have advanced criteria for the rationality of beliefs such as 'sensitivity to pertinent new information' – criteria whose application requires careful judgment.[20] The present work will pay special attention to this mode of analysis, undervalued in recent theoretical writing, including its concern for the rationality of the choice of goals as well as that of beliefs.

Informal rationality should be distinguished from Herbert Simon's theory of 'bounded rationality', according to which, in cases where there is insufficient information to permit the choice of an optimal policy, the actor adopts a principle of 'satisficing', choosing a policy which is merely acceptable.[21] Conceptually, this resembles utility maximising in being a 'thin' theory of rationality, not addressing the 'broader' issues of concern to informal rationality.

The informal rationality concept is compatible with the rational actor's being either the state or government, conceived as a unitary actor, or the individual decision maker, but has a more natural affinity with the latter. At the level of the state-as-actor, classical or neo-realist theories of the national interest, like utility maximising theories, tend to 'black-box' the decision making process: national interests are assumed to reflect the logic of the state's position in the international system. The decision making school tends to see greater variability and 'openness' in the definition of national goals and interests. Rationality assumptions can, however, be applied or questioned at either level.

Impaired rationality: psychological theories

According to the second theoretical perspective, the rational-actor approach is too complacent: under the pressures of intense crisis, behaviour is quite different from that which it postulates. The normal functioning of cognitive processes is such that rationality is seriously impaired, either because of the stress induced by crises or because the general conditions of foreign policy making are incompatible with the psychological assumptions of rationality theories.

The most prominent crisis studies in the 1960s saw psychological stress as the central problem, the most potent source of disastrous outcomes. Definining crisis in terms of restricted time for decision, they associated stress with the acute time pressures of this type of crisis. It was seen as undermining the capacity to form realistic judgments by

16

distorting perception in a number of major respects, summed up by Ole Holsti as follows:

> Evidence from the 1914 crisis revealed that with increasing stress there was a vast increase in communication; information which did not conform to expectation and preferences was often disregarded or rejected; time pressure became an increasingly salient factor in policy making; attention became focused on the immediate rather than the longer-range consequences of actions; and one's alternatives and those of others were viewed as limited and becoming more restricted with increasing stress, whereas those of the adversary were believed to be relatively free from constraints. As a consequence European statesmen felt a declining sense of responsibility for their actions...[22]

Subsequent case studies of nuclear-age crises cast doubt on the generality of these findings, even though their primary focus was on other issues.[23] More recently, the country studies in Michael Brecher's International Crisis Behavior series were designed specifically to test hypotheses on the effects of crisis-induced stress. The findings show that the pattern which Holsti discerned in 1914 does not recur widely.[24] However, it remains likely that under certain conditions it will be present, with the direst consequences. If stress is no longer a promising foundation for a general theory of crisis behaviour, it still represents a major issue. The present study will not attempt to replicate the work of the ICB project in this area, but certain instances of stress will be noted.

A more fundamental challenge to rational-actor theories is presented by a number of authors – John Steinbruner, Robert Jervis and Richard Ned Lebow – who offer an alternative general account of foreign policy decision making, based on well-established principles of cognitive psychology. Steinbruner presents these as constituting an alternative paradigm: while not denying that decision making ever proceeds along the lines postulated by rational-choice theory, he claims that cognitive processes are such that, under the conditions which are normal in foreign policy making and are accentuated in crises, it typically proceeds along different lines. These conditions, which he terms 'complexity', are the existence of incompatibilities among the goals to which the decision maker is committed, the presence of multiple uncertainties, and collective decision making.[25]

According to Steinbruner's cognitive paradigm, decision makers do not consciously integrate their competing values, that is, they do not rank them and seek an optimal trade-off among them. Uncertainty permits them to avoid facing up to incompatibilities among their goals. However, they do not adequately acknowledge uncertainty, but construe new situations in terms of past experience, holding their beliefs with much greater confidence than is justified by the relevant evidence, underestimating the range of potentialities before them. Individuals at lower organisational levels press for policies conducive to their particular values; the top leaders tend to oscillate between different policies and even between different beliefs supporting and rationalising them. Policy makers attend to few information channels and are resistant to new information except when it is consistent with their preconceptions.[26] Steinbruner acknowledges that it is difficult to obtain sufficient information about a sequence of decisions to apply or evaluate the paradigm in concrete cases, but illustrates it through a detailed case study of American policy towards the proposal for a multilateral force in Europe.

Robert Jervis offers a similar account of the principles of cognitive psychology and a wealth of examples of patterns of selective perception and misperception, which provide extensive support for the elements of Steinbruner's paradigm; in particular the reluctance to acknowledge incompatibilities among objectives, and the strength of images and expectations. But whereas Steinbruner's analysis points to the dysfunctional irrationality of the cognitive pattern as a whole, Jervis is concerned to emphasise the normality of its specific aspects, the continuum between rational and non-rational, sound and unsound judgments. The same processes which enable the mind to cope with the vast flow of incoming stimuli also lead to distorted perception.[27]

Richard Ned Lebow differs from Steinbruner and Jervis in emphasising motivational factors – the decision maker's conflicting emotions and needs – rather than purely cognitive processes. For Lebow, major foreign policies not only require painful choices among external goals but are potentially divisive and may endanger a political leadership's continuation in power. In such situations, decision makers engage in 'defensive avoidance' by 'bolstering' the preferred course of action, exaggerating its benefits and denying its risks. Distorted perception results not so much from the strength of past images as from the need for emotional reassurance.[28]

Subsequent works in political psychology have introduced further refinements,[29] but those noted here remain the most influential challenges to the rational actor theory at the level of the individual decision maker. The chapter on misperception will attempt a general assessment of their plausibility.

Impaired rationality: organisational and political theories

For the third perspective, the rationality of policies and outcomes is undermined by organisational and political conditions inherent in collective action. This perspective can also be glimpsed in the works of historians who are sceptical of larger patterns and impressed by the extent to which personal and institutional conflicts, accidents of timing and tactical manoeuvres give the policy making process an air of hectic confusion and improvisation. It has been formalised by the 'bureaucratic politics' school of analysts, in particular by Morton Halperin and Graham Allison, for whom 'a government consists of a conglomerate of semi-feudal, loosely allied organisations, each with a substantial life of its own ... governments act as those organisations enact routines'.[30] This was not yet the case in the mid-nineteenth century, but was becoming so in the years before 1914.[31] It has been widely noted that the plans ('routines') of military organisations constrain the options available to policy makers in crises, and Steinbruner notes that cognitive and organisational rigidities tend to reinforce one another.[32] The presumption that collective decision making leads to irrationality, however, is challenged by Snyder and Diesing's finding that collective decision making structures achieved greater rationality than decisions taken by a single leader, alone or in consultation with a key adviser.[33]

The 'bureaucratic politics' school also emphasises the political character of foreign policy making. Crisis decisions reflect the political weight of particular actors as well as the weight of the argument: their support may be essential to a government's survival, thus ensuring them great bargaining power. Knowing that crises may arouse intense emotion, decision makers may appeal to the larger public or may seek to anticipate its reaction. Lebow shows that the pressures of internal politics may lead governments to base their external policies on unrealistic assumptions and expectations.[34] More generally, according to this view, decision makers are to be understood first and foremost as protecting their political position.

Just as it is difficult to find conclusive evidence of irrational cognitive processes in any particular case, it may be difficult to substantiate hypotheses of political motivation. Direct evidence is often fragmentary, and there is a well-established fiction that national decision makers in crises consider only the larger national interest. Arguments couched in these terms tend to gain support and survive in the record. The 'political' reconstruction of a decision requires as much care as its cognitive reconstruction. Its plausibility will often derive from the difficulty of finding alternative explanations: it may 'fit' the case while attempts at explanation in terms of foreign policy rationality remain implausible.

Theories of adversary interaction

The fourth grouping consists of theories of interdependent decisions. The two most prominent theories, bargaining and the hostility spiral, are closely related to rational-choice theory and psychological theories of decision making, respectively. A third approach, implicit in some of the historical literature, would see these as ideal types, but would maintain that actual crises fall between the extremes of rationality and irrationality, and would highlight the contingent and unexpected – a view with a certain affinity with the third grouping of organisational and political theories.

Bargaining theory has been the most influential of these approaches – 'bargaining' in this context being the attempt to influence the decisions of others through strategies of coercion and accommodation.[35] Bargaining and game models, however, are at a level of abstraction far removed from the complex circumstances of crises, and the strategies which they generate may appear to have limited application. Nonetheless, Oran Young showed that crisis behaviour could be analysed in terms of bargaining hypotheses derived from Thomas Schelling, and bargaining has the central place in Snyder and Diesing's theoretical synthesis: for them, game models reveal the basic 'structure' of crises, and provide a schema for classifying them. Decision makers tend to misperceive this basic structure, but their experience in bargaining with their adversaries tends to correct their misperceptions.[36]

The concept of the hostility spiral is discussed in its most general form by Jervis in relation to the security dilemma – the tendency of states in an anarchic international system to take measures to enhance their own security which have the unintended consequence of threatening the interests and security of others.[37] The states thus threatened take counter-measures, in turn perceived as threatening, prompting further counter-measures; and so forth. Charles Hermann and Linda Brady's 'hostile interaction model' applies this idea to crises.[38] One party initiates a crisis because it perceives the actions of another as threatening: the other party, perceiving the initiator's actions as threatening, is likely to respond in ways which reinforce the original perception of hostility. Unless conditions are present which can counter these perceptions – which the authors postulate is often not the case – the spiral will continue. Essentially this is a theory of quasi-automatic interaction: the forces making for the escalation of crises are similar to those identified by the theories of stress, discussed above.

The contingent and the unexpected are not overlooked by theorists of bargaining or the hostility spiral. Schelling, for example, maintains that the essence of crisis is its unpredictability. 'The "crisis" that is confidently believed to involve no danger of things getting out of hand is no crisis, no matter how energetic the activity.'[39] A major form of interaction, communication, has been extensively examined by students of bargaining and of perception. The signalling of intentions is of central importance in crises, but the recipient of signals – actions and symbolic gestures as well as words – interpreting them in terms of a pre-existing image of the sender, may construe them quite differently from what was intended.[40] Kennedy's difficulty in communicating his intentions over Berlin to Khrushchev in 1961 illustrates one kind of problem; the difficulty of construing precisely what the German government was signalling in sending the *Panther* to Agadir illustrates another.

The case studies suggest that bargaining theory may be taken as the starting point for the analysis of crisis interaction: it alone offers the prospect of systematic theoretical explanation. By starting from intentions and strategies, it makes it possible to assess the importance of the unintended: the reverse process is difficult to envisage. The hostility spiral lacks plausibility as a general theory of crises, given that in so many cases the spiral is brought under control, permitting some form of diplomatic resolution. However, like the psychology of stress, it identifies a potentiality which may have disastrous consequences. The third approach is a reminder that unintended consequences may be of many kinds, not only those which lead to hostility spirals.

Systemic and deterministic theories

The approaches included under this heading do not examine particular aspects of crises but seek to place them in a larger setting – either the international system or the overall historical process. They may be deterministic, seeing crisis outcomes as predetermined by underlying structures or processes, or they may see significant scope for choice: the context provides opportunities as well as constraints.

Among systemic theories, we may distinguish between parsimonious theories of the system structure in Waltz's sense ('the number of major actors and the gross distribution of military power among them') and those which may be termed the historical sociology of international systems, developed by historians such as F.H. Hinsley and Paul Schroeder, which differentiate among systems in terms of multiple criteria, giving weight to normative as well as structural considerations.[41] Chapter 10 explores ways in which, according to these approaches, the systemic context may enhance or reduce the chances for effective crisis diplomacy.

Deterministic theories, in effect, question the appropriateness of crises as a focus of study. A crisis is seen as merely the 'tip of an iceberg', a phase in the working out of a larger conflict, the 'moment of truth' in which the inevitable outcome becomes clear. Structural-determinist versions of Marxism or power-politics realism provide the clearest examples of this approach. For example, the essential causes of World War One may be found in the domestic socio-economic determinants of German policy, not in the July crisis; or the Cold War may be explained in terms of American internal structures.[42] The geopolitical school of determinism, taking its cue from Thucydides' view that Sparta's fear of the growing power of Athens rendered the Peloponnesian War inevitable, seeks to explain wars as the outcome of such power imbalances.[43] Crises lead to war when, in view of their compelling national interests, the opposing powers are ready to resolve the contest by force: if not, they are resolved peacefully.

Not all structuralist interpretations are so deterministic. Many historians, even though they draw on geopolitical 'realist' theories or on Marxism, assume that leaders exercise genuine choice, thus aligning themselves with the 'decision making' rather than the 'state-as-actor' theorists. Not infrequently, however, the historian's narrative is presented as a 'seamless web' in which every move in a crisis is so deeply influenced by experiences from earlier periods that any separation of the crisis from its long-term context is seen as artificial and distorting.

In general, this perspective represents a challenge to crisis studies – a challenge to demonstrate that crises 'matter' and can be analysed as such, even while taking contexts into account. The problem of assessing the importance of long-term, 'underlying' or 'structural' determinants of the outcome of crises, as against immediate choices and diplomacy, is addressed in Chapter 15.

Incompatible or complementary?

Steinbruner articulates his paradigms as incompatible explanations of decision making; Allison treats his models as incompatible in some respects, complementary in others; Snyder and Diesing offer a theoretical synthesis. Lebow likens a crisis to a finely cut gem: 'to appreciate a crisis in its totality one must observe it from a variety of angles', drawing on theories and approaches as appropriate.[44]

The logical relationships among the theoretical perspectives, and levels of analysis, are not self-evident, and may depend on the precise

22

formulation of particular theories within each of the perspectives. Prima facie, the first three offer incompatible accounts of the normal process of crisis decision making. In the Snyder/Diesing analysis, the bargaining process brings the parties to confront the foreign policy realities, thus the second and third perspectives become little more than secondary perturbations. In Allison's analysis the third perspective is central, the first remains hazy, 'disembodied'.[45]

Certain affinities were noted between each of the three perspectives on decision making with certain of the competing theories at the level of crisis interaction, but there are possibilities of further combinations between these levels. For example, decision makers whose beliefs are formed in accordance with the cognitive paradigm may nonetheless engage in bargaining, and their misperceptions may not necessarily cumulate in ways predicted by the hostility spiral model. The deterministic version of the final perspective relegates all the others to a marginal role in explaining major events: they may illuminate the details, but not the larger outcomes. On the other hand, if the international system, and other 'structures', are understood as presenting decision makers with options as well as constraints, the fifth perspective represents a level of analysis, not a final determinant, and thus needs to be related to the other levels.

A historical narrative tends to presuppose a certain theoretical perspective. In using case studies to evaluate theories, it is necessary to avoid interpreting the cases in terms of any one of those theories. The danger of thus resolving the issue by assumption rather than by inquiry can best be averted by approaching the cases with a multiplicity of perspectives and hypotheses in mind.

The theories discussed in this chapter have at times been referred to as models or as perspectives: these terms are used in the sense of Graham Allison's models of decision making – sets of concepts and assumptions which structure a field of inquiry – and not in the sense of specific models within a particular field. The term 'paradigm' has been avoided because this has further connotations, not presupposed here, in particular the incommensurability of paradigms. The evaluation of theoretical models, understood in this sense, is not a straightforward matter of testing empirical hypotheses but, as noted in the Introduction, is a matter of satisfying two criteria: *relevance* to the cases and *fitting* the evidence. First, does the theory address the main issues raised by the case? A model may be highly relevant in one case, but not in another. Second, assuming its relevance, how well does it fit the evidence? Are its explanations satisfactory, or is crucial evidence unexplained, or difficult to reconcile with the theory? This is coming closer to empirical testing, but in a project designed to assess broad conceptual models it is not practicable to design rigorous tests of specific hypotheses – hence the inquiry remains at the level which has been termed the 'plausibility probe'. Snyder and Diesing's comments, although referring to formal models, are pertinent to the present inquiry:

> What we look for is not correct predictions but rather fruitfulness and relevance. Each of our models calls attention to certain factors, implicitly says that these are the important ones, and ties them together into a neat mathematical package. If we find (with the help of other models) that important factors have been omitted by some model and that when these are included the resulting package looks quite different, we are justified in saying that the model is superficial, incomplete, misleading, beside the point, but not false. The same model ... may be quite useful in other situations.[46]

The evaluation of the theories takes place in two stages, in the relevant sections of the case studies and in the corresponding comparative chapters. Rational-actor theories, and especially informal rationality assumptions, are assessed mainly in the discussions of goals and perceptions (Chapters 11 and 12). Psychological approaches to decision making are assessed in Chapter 12, political approaches in Chapter 14. For convenience of exposition, bargaining and other theories of interaction are discussed before internal politics, under the heading 'bargaining' (Chapter 13). The discussion of systemic and deterministic theories is subdivided: an account of the initial setting precedes the narrative in each of the cases and is linked to Chapter 10, on the systemic context, while a concluding section of each case study, on the outcome, is linked to Chapter 15, which draws together the long-term and short-term explanations of outcomes.

Before proceeding to the cases, however, the study will briefly examine policy thinking relating to crises, in particular the distinctive body of ideas on crisis management which emerged during the 1960s and still retains a large measure of acceptance. Although these ideas are sometimes linked with one or other theory, the linkages are loose and have been little studied. One of the aims of the present work is to bring policy thinking into a closer relationship with theory: questions for policy assumptions suggested by some of the theoretical approaches are noted in the next chapter, and policy implications of the study as a whole are discussed in the Conclusions.

3 'CRISIS MANAGEMENT' VERSUS 'CRISIS DIPLOMACY'

In view of the diversity of theoretical approaches to the study of crises there is a surprising degree of consensus in the discussion of 'crisis management' – an expression which came into use at the time of the Cuban missile crisis. It refers to a body of ideas which reflect the lessons of that crisis as perceived by Americans at that time. With minor variations these general principles have frequently been reaffirmed in the scholarly literature. One or other of the principles has occasionally been challenged by policy makers, but none has developed an alternative to the standard doctrine of crisis management.

The concept

The term was popularised by Robert McNamara's comment on the Cuban experience: 'There is no longer any such thing as strategy, only crisis management.'[1] The term is often taken to mean the exercise of restraint in order to reduce the risk of war.[2] However, this usage obscures the central problem confronting decision makers in nuclear-age crises – that each party seeks to pursue simultaneously two potentially incompatible goals: to prevail over the adversary, while at the same time avoiding nuclear war. 'Crisis management' must address the tension between the two goals, but this brings out the questionable character of the concept itself. The dilemmas of choice are glossed over by the use of the term 'management', with its overtones of technical rationality and efficiency.

Lebow comments that some officials and scholars search for 'the secret keys to nuclear crisis management' in 'organisational structures and decision making techniques', but that 'good crisis management cannot be fabricated from communication nodes, computer software, and special action groups', but depends on far more fundamental conditions.[3] Recent scholarly discussion, while not neglecting technical responses to the changing strategic environment, has addressed those political fundamentals, introducing a strong cautionary note.

25

For example, the editor of a recent study, Gilbert Winham, concludes that:

> It is sobering to observe analysts who approach nuclear crisis management from entirely different perspectives reach similarly pessimistic judgments about the capacity to avoid hostilities as a crisis intensifies ... If there is any one message to be taken from this volume, it is that we cannot be sanguine about the capacity of the superpowers to manage the kind of crises that the East–West rivalry could easily generate.[4]

Even though East–West relations have been transformed, the cautionary note remains pertinent, if and when tensions among the major powers should revive.

The present work will use the term 'crisis diplomacy' in preference to 'crisis management', except where commenting on discussions which use the latter term. The choice of terminology has consequences for thought and practice insofar as it influences what is regarded as significant. 'Diplomacy' is used in its broader sense – as in the diplomacy of Bismarck, Roosevelt or Kennedy – not in its narrower sense, the activity of professional diplomats. In the broad sense it includes the whole process of the formulation of goals and policies, the taking and implementing of decisions, and interaction and communication with other governments. It can serve as an appropriate all-encompassing term which retains within its focus all the dimensions of a complex sequence such as a crisis.

The terms 'crisis diplomacy' or 'management' are not restricted to the nuclear age, where the imperative to avoid war becomes near-categorical. They include the whole spectrum of cases of relative acceptance of, or aversion to, war, even the manoeuvring for a favourable pretext for war. Nonetheless, most of the great-power decision makers studied in this work were highly averse to war, accepting it only as an option of last resort. Thus, if the principles of crisis management formulated in relation to nuclear crises are valid, they should be relevant in the earlier case studies as clues to successes and failures of crisis diplomacy.

Principles

The standard doctrine of crisis management may be summed up in terms of the following seven principles, articulated during the Cuban crisis and frequently reaffirmed in the scholarly literature. Cautionary voices such as Winham's, noted above, or McGeorge Bundy's retrospective judgment that the Cuban outcome owed more to circumstances than to unusual management,[5] may have weakened confidence in the doctrine but have not led to any fundamental reappraisal. Individual authors have advanced a variety of further considerations, but the consensual doctrine does not appear to extend beyond these principles.[6]

The decision making process: multiple advocacy

I believe our deliberations proved conclusively how important it is that the President have the recommendations and opinions of more than one individual, of more than one department, and of more than one point of view. Opinion, even fact itself, can best be judged by conflict, by debate. There is an important element missing when there is unanimity of viewpoint.   Robert Kennedy[7]

The structuring of decision making to promote the serious canvassing of policy alternatives has been widely endorsed, and not only with respect to crisis management.[8] Questions have been raised about its feasibility or its compatibility with the styles of some decision makers, but its desirability is endorsed on a number of grounds: above all to correct the rigidities which are part of normal cognitive processes and organisational behaviour, and also as a check on the more pathological cognitive processes characteristic of high levels of stress.

The implementation of policy: close political control

The President was also determined to manage the crisis himself – and he did so, in all its exquisite detail. There was not going to be any possibility for someone down the line to push events any faster or further than he judged necessary. It was the President who decided what ships would be stopped and when, how the announcements would be made, what would be said publicly and privately.
                                                                 Hilsman[9]

The need to ensure that military operations serve well-defined political goals is a major theme in contemporary strategic studies. Acceptance of the principle does not, however, prevent sharp conflict between political and military leaders in specific cases, and military hostility to the detailed control over bombing exercised by President Johnson during the Vietnam war led subsequently to the granting of broad discretion to theatre commanders, as in the case of the Gulf war.[10] In the context of crises between nuclear powers, however, the general principle of close political control over operations remains

27

unchallenged, even though it might be expected to meet with resistance in practice.

The limitation of objectives

> Defining a clear and limited objective, he moved with mathematical precision to accomplish it. Schlesinger[11]

Kennedy's limitation of his objective to the withdrawal of the missiles was seen as a crucial choice. A well-defined, restricted objective can serve as a basis for a settlement in a way that diffuse, opportunistic objectives cannot. In the superpower context the logic of limiting crisis objectives in order to avoid challenging interests vital to the adversary has been regarded as compelling.

Maintaining flexible options

> McNamara helped the Attorney-General mightily with his now-celebrated argument on 'maintaining the options' ... The clinching argument in favor of the blockade was that it could be applied without losing the option to launch an air strike later. If, however, the air strike was to be the first step, other options would be closed.
> Abel[12]

The principle of flexible response is invariably included in discussions of crisis management. The blockade left both sides with a range of options, whereas the air strike would have posed a stark choice between a humiliating defeat or a hazardous escalation. Kennedy, like many commentators, had in mind the situation of July 1914, when rigid mobilisation plans had denied such a range of options to the decision makers. Some discussions emphasise the military aspect of the principle – proportionate or graduated response – others the political goal of maintaining freedom of manoeuvre.

Reducing time pressure

> Against the advice of many of his advisers and of the military, he decided to give Khrushchev more time. 'We don't want to push him to a precipitous action – give him time to consider ...'
> Robert Kennedy[13]

The goal of maintaining freedom of choice can be negated not only by actions that preclude a range of options but also by time pressure such that one or another party is unable to examine its options, either because of absolute time constraints or because the heightened stress imposed by time pressure tends to reduce the awareness of options. The contrast between July 1914 and the Cuban crisis has been discussed extensively from this point of view.[14]

Perception of the adversary: the need for insight

During the crisis President Kennedy spent more time trying to determine the effect of a particular course of action on Khrushchev or the Russians than on any other phase of what he was doing.

Robert Kennedy[15]

In order to judge the effects of their own actions, crisis decision makers must make every effort to see the situation through the eyes of the adversary. This may well be the most difficult of the principles to implement: as Holsti observes, achieving 'sensitivity to the adversary's frame of reference' is 'a skill in short supply'.[16] In the Cuban instance, great weight was placed on the advice of a former ambassador to Moscow, Llewellyn Thompson, but this technique presupposes that the ambassador has the requisite skill. There are many examples to the contrary. The principle is sometimes confused with the maxim that the adversary should be offered a face-saving line of retreat. To know what will prove face-saving, of course, presupposes insight into the adversary's frame of reference, but the maxim is dangerous insofar as it encourages policy makers to see themselves as potential victors, whereas many situations permit no clear-cut victor.

Maintaining communication

President Kennedy dedicated himself to making it clear to Khrushchev by word and deed – for both are important – that the United States had limited objectives and that we had no interest in accomplishing these objectives by adversely affecting the national security of the Soviet Union or by humiliating her.   Robert Kennedy[17]

Problems relating to communication in crises are among those most extensively studied. Although communication was relatively close in 1962, compared with many earlier crises, policy makers on both sides perceived a need for a more direct channel. Hence the agreement on the 'hot line' some months later. Among the important issues are the danger of communication overload and the difficulty of distinguishing the important signals from the mass of background 'noise'.[18] General remedies are not easily arrived at, but it is agreed that important

29

communications should be clear and precise, and supported by accompanying signals and actions, not inadvertently undermined by them.[19]

Critiques

The above consensus has been challenged by a number of scholars in other fields, such as history or peace research, as well as occasionally by policy makers.[20] Four themes are prominent in these criticisms: that the doctrine is overgeneralised and oversimplified; that it neglects the prior question, which crises are manageable?; that it overemphasises short-term considerations; and that it neglects fundamental political and psychological constraints.

Overgeneralised and oversimplified

The prescriptions, it is claimed, are 'about as useful as general advice to hospital emergency room personnel – keep calm, have equipment ready, make no premature diagnoses'.[21] The problem, however, is that they are not banal truisms but are specific enough to be dangerous if regarded as general rules to be applied universally, as the principle of graduated response appears to have been in US policy in the Vietnam war. They have been likened to traditional rules of statecraft which, like everyday maxims and homilies, need to be applied with discrimination and judgment: it is dangerous to neglect the rule, but there is no assurance that observing it will bring success.

At times it may be the opposite rule that is appropriate to the circumstances. Reducing time pressure is often appropriate, but it may be necessary to increase time pressure in order to prevent a slow but dangerous deterioration. Schelling's well-known discussion of the tactical advantages of commitment is at odds with the maxim of maintaining flexible options.[22] A striking formulation of an alternative to that maxim is offered by Henry Kissinger:

> In my view what seems 'balanced' and 'safe' in a crisis is often the most risky. Gradual escalation tempts the opponent to match every move; what is intended as a show of moderation may be interpreted as irresolution... A leader must choose carefully and thoughtfully the issues over which to face confrontation. He should do so only for major objectives. Once he is committed, however, his obligation is to end the confrontation rapidly. For this he must convey implacability. He must be prepared to escalate rapidly and brutally to a point where the opponent can no longer afford to experiment.[23]

This approach has won little support as a general guide to conduct. Other principles require similar qualification. The limitation of objectives, for example, represents only one dimension of a complex issue. The unconditional pursuit of a limited goal may introduce rigidities and unwanted side-effects. And how is comprehension of the adversary's frame of reference to be distinguished from 'softness' or appeasement?

In reflecting salient issues of a specific time and place, the principles may neglect issues that are central in other times and places. It has been argued that the Cuban crisis was atypical in important respects and may even be a 'profoundly misleading subject for reflection'.[24] The problems confronting Neville Chamberlain, for example, were in a sense prior to the kinds of choices to which the contemporary rules of crisis management are addressed: they included basic choices over values (what issue would justify going to war) and dilemmas over means (how, if at all, could Germany be induced to limit its objectives?).

Which crises are manageable?

According to the conventional usage a successfully managed crisis is one in which war is avoided at an acceptable cost. However, a crisis is unmanageable – war cannot be avoided – if one party sees advantage in fighting or if adversaries regard the issue as vital and the situation admits no compromise. Or a situation may be beyond control for less readily definable reasons. Decision makers cannot know whether a crisis is manageable, or with what degree of difficulty, and even with hindsight and with full documentation, historians' interpretations of some major crises such as the origins of the Crimean war or July 1914 differ to an extent that there is no agreement on how manageable they were.[25] The conditions for crisis manageability are not yet understood, but it is evident that in some contexts crisis management, however sound its principles, cannot achieve success and in others the margin for error, or bad luck, is perilously slight.

Too short-term a perspective?

A further limitation of crisis management doctrine is its preoccupation with the immediate outcome. Although it is arguable that in a crisis survival goals should come first, survival may reasonably be extended beyond the immediate crisis to the longer term. The case against the 1930s appeasers is that they unwittingly neglected this, and it is often

31

suggested that although the crises preceding World War One were resolved peacefully, they tended to exacerbate the tensions between the powers and thus increased the subsequent probability of war. Bell refers to such sequences as 'crisis slides', a concept which has received little attention, but which would raise questions concerning the relationship between systemic determinants of such 'slides' and policy choices.[26] Lebow compares the pre-1914 crises with two cases that opened the way towards improved relationships between the adversaries, Fashoda (1898) and Cuba (1962), in terms only of policy choices.[27] Despite this limitation, his discussion suggests a way of moving beyond the short-term focus of orthodox crisis management doctrine.

Psychological and political constraints

Finally, it is claimed that the doctrine suffers from a fundamental lack of realism in its neglect of the constraints which may render it impossible for decision makers to act in accordance with its principles. First, they may lack the unusual combination of intellectual and imaginative capacities that is required.[28] Second, the pressures of acute crisis may impair the performance even of decision makers who in other contexts show outstanding qualities of leadership. And third, the cognitive weaknesses induced by stress may be reinforced by acute domestic political pressures. In such situations unshakable commitment to a chosen course of action can become fatally attractive: because achievement of the goal is necessary, it must be possible. 'Those policy makers with the greatest need to learn from external reality appear the least likely to do so.'[29] Decision makers in this frame of mind are unlikely to be capable of the flexibility required by the principles of crisis management.

It is likely that there are crises that in principle are open to management (that is, the parties are strongly averse to war and their basic interests are not irreconcilable *ab initio*) but in which crisis management fails because of psychological and political pressures that lead decision makers to become committed to incompatible courses of action, unable to correct their misperceptions or reconsider their goals in the way that crisis management would require. Lebow makes a convincing interpretation of certain of his cases along these lines.

On the other hand, Snyder and Diesing's case studies show that the contrary is possible, that quite frequently the bargaining process during crises enables decision makers to correct their misperceptions or reformulate their goals in order to avoid becoming locked into a collision course.[30] The presence of even a few counter-examples, however, shows that the concerns do not lack foundation.

Theoretical issues

Taken as a whole, these four lines of criticism point to fundamental theoretical problems. The doctrine of crisis management exemplifies George and Smoke's dictum that policy-oriented theories in international relations tend to consist of 'free-floating generalisations and isolated insights'.[31] Such generalisations may be based on the 'lessons' of recent historical experience or may be loosely related to one or another of the theories relating to crisis behaviour. However, as we have seen in the previous chapter, there are competing theories at each level and there is a major tension between theories based on axioms of rationality and those which focus on non-rational processes. A firmer theoretical foundation for policy thinking requires not only that the free-floating generalisations be anchored in the relevant theories, but also a critical evaluation of the competing theories. George and Smoke argue that the goal of policy-oriented theory should not be to strive for hypotheses of the widest scope and generality, but to formulate contingent or differentiated generalisations which take account of the diversity of the conditions that affect policy and their outcomes.[32] It is theory of this kind which might identify the conditions under which the principles discussed above might be appropriate and effective.

This does not imply eclecticism, nor a synthesis of competing theories. The tensions between theories should be respected, as should tensions within them. One such tension has been widely noted in the psychological theories of crisis behaviour: whereas the analysis is in non-rational terms, the associated policy recommendations presuppose a level of rationality which the theories take to be atypical of actual decision making.[33]

Questions

The preceding discussion points to certain questions for further inquiry. Policy ideas for crisis diplomacy need to be reconsidered in the light of the reappraisal of theories which will be undertaken in later chapters. One of the specific issues which will need to be addressed is the dissonance between non-rational descriptive analyses and highly rational normative prescriptions.

Despite the critiques, the principles of crisis management may be taken as a starting point. Which of them remain persuasive in the light of broader historical experience? Under what conditions are they valid, and what qualifications need to be taken into account? If these questions can be answered, 'free-floating' generalisations will be replaced by more systematic contingent generalisations which may lend themselves more readily to theoretical explication. And are there additional principles – the 'lessons' of crises other than the Cuban missile case?

The discussion of manageability and constraints raises further questions. Insofar as 'manageability' relates to the actors' basic values – in particular their relative willingness to go to war – Snyder and Diesing's version of game theory will provide a foundation, while Lebow's discussion of preconditions for crisis management will provide a starting point for the broader political analysis of constraints.

PART II

4 THE EASTERN CRISIS, 1839–1841

The Eastern crisis, which arose from a long-expected threat to the survival of the Ottoman Empire, had a number of distinctive features, the most striking of which was that the risk of war which alarmed Europe in the autumn of 1840 arose not from the issue of vital concern to four of the powers – the control of Constantinople and the Straits – but from a dispute over a much lesser issue, whether or not the ruler of Egypt, Mehemet Ali, should be permitted to retain control of Syria. This was an implausible cause of war among the powers, but it would have caused the war only indirectly, through its effect on the volatile political situation in France, where revolution or a sudden upsurge of nationalism, as was to be experienced in 1870, could never be entirely discounted. The interpretation of the crisis has not given rise to major historical debates, but in reconstructing it there is a need to take account of the extent to which British diplomatic history of the period is limited by a national perspective: the Foreign Secretary, Palmerston, indeed played the central role, but his words cannot be taken at face value.

The crisis falls squarely within the period of the Concert of Europe, and is instructive in illustrating the way in which its loosely defined conventions assisted diplomacy, and also their limitations. Each of the powers sought to constrain others while minimising constraint on its own actions; frictions resulted both from the observance of the basic norm of acting in concert and from attempts to evade it. The reasons for the relative success of the Concert in this case and its failure in the Crimean war crisis are explored in the next chapter. As was characteristic of the period, there were loose alignments but no firm coalitions among the powers at the outset, and the development most surprising to contemporaries was the manner in which the main rivals in the 1830s, Britain and Russia, established a good working partnership for the duration of the crisis.

All four of the powers principally involved, Britain, France, Russia and Austria, followed unusually coherent strategies – in Britain's case

37

despite acute conflict among the decision makers, and in the French case with a change of strategy in order to avert the impending threat of war. This was not because the interests of each power logically permitted only one course of action – indeed the interests of each were open to a variety of interpretations – but because those in control of policy had developed clear conceptions of their goals and strategies, and were able to prevail in policy disputes. The crisis is thus a narrative of manoeuvre and bargaining, but one which illustrates the way in which the course of events could well have become unmanageable.

One of the most striking features of the confrontation in autumn 1840 was the difference in the perception of the risk of war among experienced decision makers. Palmerston and Nesselrode, the Russian Chancellor, who based their judgment on strategic rationality, were confident that there would be no war; Austrian Chancellor Metternich, his attention focused on political instability in France, shared the widespread public alarm. Good reasons could be advanced for either assessment. The significance of misperception in the crisis is difficult to determine because, rather similarly, good reasons could be advanced for what proved to be a series of misjudgments on the part of Thiers. Thus the case illustrates the conceptual problems of determining precisely what constitutes misperception.

The crisis did not disrupt the internal political balance in the case of the autocratic empires, Austria and Russia, but precipitated major conflict in the more open political systems of Britain and France. In the British case the opposition had remarkably little impact on policy, whereas in France there was not only a policy reversal but a threat to the continued existence of the regime, which posed the main risk of war. It was for this reason that the crisis became much more serious than might have been expected in the light of the initial conditions and the interests at stake.

The setting

Following the 1830 revolution in France, the powers formed two uneasy groupings, the 'liberal alliance' of France and England versus the informal alliance of the three eastern courts opposed to liberalism as well as revolution. But there was considerable friction between France and England over specific issues, such as Spain and especially Belgium.[1] In the Belgian settlement in 1838–39 Palmerston worked quite closely with the eastern powers in the later stages of the negotiations.

The most serious potential threat to the system was a French challenge to the 1815 treaties, should there be a new revolution in France. But a more immediate source of conflict was the 'Eastern question': the fear of a power vacuum in the Balkans and the Near East if the Ottoman Empire should collapse, and above all, the concerns over the future of Constantinople and the Straits. Russia feared that their control by England and/or France, opening the Black Sea to their navies, would leave it defenceless in the south. To England and France, Russian control of the Straits would threaten their interests in the Mediterranean and British communications with India. Austria feared Russian expansion into southeastern Europe. Four powers, then, had major stakes in the Eastern question. In order to avoid serious risks, they could agree to support the preservation of Ottoman rule in Constantinople, but fears of secret defection from these professions of agreement were never far beneath the surface.

Turkey had seemed close to collapse in the aftermath of Greek independence (1830) when much of the Empire was occupied by Russia and by the forces of Mehemet Ali, the Pasha of Egypt. Finally, Russia had supported the Empire against further encroachments by Mehemet Ali: under the Treaty of Kutaya of April 1833 the latter was to retain control of his newly occupied territories which included almost the whole of Syria, but only as the Sultan's vassal. Russia's price for this support and for the evacuation of its troops was the Treaty of Unkiar-Skelessi (July 1833), which reaffirmed the closing of the Dardanelles but also provided for Turkish consultation with Russia in the event of any future threat to the Empire. Palmerston had been extremely alarmed by this treaty, which he perceived as tantamount to a Russian protectorate over Turkey, but had been unable to persuade the British government to take action to prevent its entering into force. The navy was heavily committed elsewhere, and his perception of the strategic importance of Constantinople was not yet widely shared. However, Palmerston set himself the goal of preventing the renewal of the treaty at the end of its eight-year term.[2]

Anglo-Russian rivalry was becoming acute during the years preceding the crisis, as Russia sought to consolidate its newly acquired territory in the Caucasus and to use its dominant position in Persia to extend its influence into Afghanistan. Britain, perceiving for the first time a potential Russian threat to northwest India, began to prepare its own expedition into Afghanistan, at the same time contesting Russian primacy in Tehran as well as in Constantinople. Anti-Russian sentiment in England, dating from the suppression of the Polish revolution of 1830–31, was stimulated by inflammatory publications such as *The Portfolio*, edited by David Urquhart, a former British diplomat in Constantinople, the most prominent of a number of publicists who encouraged rebellion against Russian rule in the Caucasus.[3] Russian imperialism was not so much anti-English as unilateralist, but there was a continuing tension in Russian foreign policy between the 'nationalists', who sought to expand the empire with scant regard for the reactions of the other powers, and the 'Europeans' in the Foreign Ministry, led by Nesselrode, who sought a measure of restraint in general accordance with the Concert of Europe, above all in order to avoid the risk of war against a hostile coalition.[4]

This Anglo-Russian friction led to several near-crises during 1836–38. The first was precipitated by an attempt by an English merchant vessel, the *Vixen*, to trade with the Caucasian rebels, with the encouragement of Urquhart, still at the embassy in Constantinople. The *Vixen* was captured by the flagship of the Russian fleet blockading the Circassian coast – a blockade which Britain refused to recognise – and, in accordance with Nesselrode's policy of avoiding a crisis with Britain, its owner was charged with a violation of customs regulations.

The alternative, promoted by the commander of the Black Sea Fleet – to treat the *Vixen* as a prize of war – would have entailed a formal protest to Britain and would have precipitated a crisis over the status of the blockade and its implementation. Palmerston responded circumspectly, resisting public pressure for a 'strong' response, but before eventually acquiescing in Nesselrode's version of the issues he explored the possibility of a common front with France and Austria which might have challenged Russia's claims in Circassia.[5]

Nesselrode avoided a second crisis with Britain in January 1838, when the Minister of the Navy, Admiral Menshikov, induced the Tsar (Nicholas I) to order the transfer of two ships from the Baltic Fleet to the Black Sea. Nesselrode persuaded the Tsar to reverse his decision, reminding him that the move would contravene the provisions of the treaties which closed the Straits to foreign warships. If Turkey should insist on its legal rights, Russian prestige would suffer a severe blow; but if Turkey permitted the ships to pass, England and France would demand the same, and their presence in the Black Sea would greatly weaken Russian security and its influence in Constantinople.[6]

The two powers avoided a crisis in Persia in October 1838 by restraining their respective ministers in Tehran. The Russian minister had supported an unsuccessful Persian siege of Herat and his British counterpart proposed an invasion of southern Persia. Palmerston, however, did not respond to Nesselrode's overture for an agreement to establish buffer zones in central Asia, but on the contrary Britain endorsed an initiative of the Indian Viceroy to invade Afghanistan in order to replace pro-Russian rulers with supporters of Britain, this in turn prompting a Russian expedition to Khiva.[7]

A conflict between France and England over Egypt was becoming more significant by the late 1830s, though far less acute than the Anglo-Russian conflict. France, which had long-standing connections with Mehemet Ali, favoured an expansion of his influence. England, however, was determined to prevent Mehemet Ali from controlling the two routes to India which it was seeking to develop – the Red Sea route with a short overland stretch in Egypt, and the overland route through Mesopotamia. Britain also feared Mehemet Ali's expansion for its implications for the wider balance of power. In Palmerston's view it would weaken the main bulwark against Russia, the Ottoman Empire; and to the extent that Mehemet Ali was allied to, or dependent on, France it raised the spectre of French control of the route to India and French predominance in the Mediterranean, to the detriment of British commercial interests.

Prelude to the crisis

For several years before 1839 there was a sense that a crisis over the Eastern question could erupt without warning. The Sultan appeared ready to risk war with Mehemet Ali and the British ambassador, Ponsonby, privately advised Palmerston that this might be the only way to preserve the Empire.[8] Palmerston, however, vetoed any encouragement of war, as did the other powers, but the atmosphere of intrigue in Constantinople fostered suspicions that one or the other power might encourage the Sultan's ambitions for its own ends. Palmerston sought to bring about a diplomatic alignment which might negate the effectiveness of the Treaty of Unkiar-Skelessi, but his efforts to achieve an Anglo-French alliance with Turkey in 1835–36 failed to win sufficient support from the Cabinet or from the French themselves.[9] Until such an improvement in Britain's diplomatic position could be achieved, he sought to prevent any local outbreak.

The military situation of Constantinople was a source of tension. Both Russia and Britain planned to intervene in order to forestall intervention by the other. From 1836 Ponsonby was authorised to summon the fleet if the Sultan requested it, and if the admiral agreed that there was no naval risk, on the understanding that he would use this power only to pre-empt an impending Russian move.[10] On the Russian side, the Black Sea Fleet and a contingent in Sebastopol were intended to take possession of the Straits in order to prevent entry by England and France, and perhaps also if Mehemet Ali should attack the Empire. However, no moves were made which might have precipitated a pre-emptive occupation.[11] In May 1838 Palmerston rejected Ponsonby's proposal that British frigates should pass through the Straits to explore the Black Sea, and in September–October he denied him permission to summon the fleet to Constantinople.[12]

In May 1838 Mehemet Ali created a crisis atmosphere by informing the European consuls that he intended to declare his independence from the Sultan. Aged seventy, he was preoccupied with the position of his family and the maintenance of his reforms after his death.[13] He was persuaded to defer this move by notes from the four powers most involved (England, France, Austria and Russia), arranged by Palmerston and Metternich. Palmerston sought to revive his idea of an Anglo-French alliance with Turkey, but France was no more willing to enter into such a commitment than in 1835.

Nesselrode, while agreeing to the note to Mehemet Ali, advised the Russian ambassadors that there could still be circumstances under which Russia would intervene in Turkey under the Treaty of Unkiar-Skelessi. The communication of this message to Palmerston on 5 August reawakened his concern. He adopted the unorthodox procedure of inviting the ambassadors of the four powers (including Prussia, as well as the three other powers primarily involved) to a meeting at which, without prior warning, he proposed concerted action if Mehemet Ali were to defy the powers. Only the French ambassador was responsive, the Russian remaining silent. Nesselrode rejected Palmerston's proposal, arguing that the attempt to agree on such contingencies was likely to accentuate the differences among the powers.[14]

On receiving this reply, Palmerston warned the ambassador that unilateral Russian intervention could lead to war, and in a dispatch to be communicated to the Russian government he wrote that:

> Europe would never endure that the matter should be settled by the single independent and self-regulated interference of any one Power, acting according to its own will or without concert with any other Power ... the only way in which Turkey could be assisted without risking a disturbance of the peace would be by the establishment of that concert between the Five Powers which Her Majesty's Government have proposed.[15]

Webster maintains that 'there can be no doubt that Palmerston's explicit warning had great influence on Russian policy when the crisis came next year'.[16] This may, however, overstate its significance. Nesselrode, having been disturbed by Palmerston's earlier actions, found little more than a reiteration of familiar themes.[17]

Together with other English initiatives at this time, however, it led the Russians to conclude that they could not maintain a predominant position in Turkey.[18] In August 1838 England signed a Treaty of Commerce which opened the Ottoman market to British manufactured exports; later in the year the English and Turkish fleets exercised together, and there was speculation about an Anglo-Turkish alliance. Even though this was not achieved – England would not enter into an offensive alliance against Mehemet Ali – the effect of these initiatives was to enhance English influence at Constantinople.

Russia's restraint in the years preceding the crisis was in accordance with the norms of the Concert of Europe. Though imprecise, they were by no means meaningless or trivial. The great powers accepted a responsibility not only to maintain collectively the territorial status quo of 1815 but also to confer on major international issues as they arose: changes were not to be imposed unilaterally or by sheer assertion of the power of the stronger coalition, but required the consent of all five powers. There were no precise rules or understandings, however, as to how the necessary consultations were to be brought about: outright refusal to enter into a conference was ruled out, but there was scope for ingenuity in avoiding or postponing one. The application of the norms in each particular instance occasioned friction and animosity. As F.H. Hinsley notes, conferences were not easy to convene, 'each met only after a fierce struggle concerning its agenda as well as its venue', and 'the assembled Powers were never unanimously contented with the proceedings'.[19] The crisis was to subject the Concert to the utmost stress.

The phases of the crisis

Phase 1: The opening of the crisis (May–August 1839)

The crisis was precipitated by the Sultan's decision in May to attack Mehemet Ali's forces, despite attempts by the powers to dissuade him. However, the Ottoman forces were defeated at the battle of Nezib (24 June); the Sultan died (30 June); and the Turkish fleet deserted to Mehemet Ali (7 July). The collapse of the Ottoman Empire appeared imminent. France intervened to persuade Ibrahim, Mehemet Ali's son and commander-in-chief, not to cross the Taurus mountains and invade Turkey, but to remain within the boundaries agreed at Kutaya in 1833. In order to deter Russia from intervening at Constantinople, the British and French navies exercised together, under instructions to proceed through the Dardanelles to Constantinople in a number of contingencies: actual or threatened Russian intervention, a request by the Sultan or insurrection in Constantinople. They were also to discourage further hostilities between the Turkish and Egyptian forces.[20] Austria supported this joint initiative.

After Egypt's military successes, Mehemet Ali's representatives opened negotiations at Constantinople, and it appeared that the government of the new Sultan, Abdul Medjid, deprived of its bargaining leverage by the loss of its army and navy, would concede Mehemet Ali's demand for the hereditary rule of his possessions, above all Syria and Egypt.[21] However, France, England and Austria saw such a settlement as depriving the Empire of its effective independence. France and England sent a joint naval squadron to the eastern Mediterranean, and on Metternich's initiative the ambassadors of all five powers presented a joint note to the Turkish government on 27 July. They acted, in advance of formal instructions, on a formula agreed upon in Vienna. The Russian ambassador, Butenev, appears to have joined the others mainly to avoid isolation, since Russia had indicated that it was prepared to accept any settlement agreed between Turkey and Egypt. The note stated that 'an accord between the five governments on the Eastern Question is assured, and they are charged to engage it [Turkey] to abstain from any definitive deliberation without their support and to await the effect of the interest which they are extending'.[22] Thus the powers forestalled a direct settlement: since their intervention could only strengthen the position of the Ottoman government, it complied with their proposal to delay an agreement.

Metternich sought to follow up this success by calling for a conference of the five powers at Vienna to draw up the terms of a settlement. Russia refused: although it had not attempted to intervene unilaterally, it had been alarmed by the cooperation of the three powers (England, France and Austria), and the Tsar had been angered by Metternich's manoeuvre on the joint note. Nesselrode repeated his earlier argument that a conference would accentuate the differences among the powers, but the underlying fear appears to have been that Russia might be isolated against a common front by the others.[23]

The first sign of a rift between England and France appeared by the end of July, when France rejected Palmerston's proposal that the two fleets compel Mehemet Ali to return the Turkish fleet to Constantinople. The two governments also differed over the extent of territory to be retained by Mehemet Ali, Palmerston wishing to restrict him to Egypt, returning the whole of Syria to the Empire, while the French government, in accord with the public sympathy for Mehemet Ali, favoured granting him far more.[24] Metternich was silenced by Russia's rejection of his conference proposal, but in any case the mediating role which he adopted in the crisis precluded strong support for either position.

Phase 2: Realignment (September 1839–July 1840)

Russia's decision to send Brunnow to negotiate in London in September opened up the possibility of a realignment of the powers. Russia had been closer to France than to England on the issues in dispute: it had proposed the transfer of Orfa and Diarbekir in southeastern Turkey to Mehemet Ali, but this seems to have reflected a desire to achieve a quick settlement rather than any strong commitment to the cause of Mehemet Ali.

According to some interpretations, the Tsar's main objective in turning to England was to break up the Anglo-French alliance. This probably oversimplifies his concerns. Russia's immediate need was to escape the threat of diplomatic isolation. But why turn to England, rather than France? The immediate concurrence of views with France over Mehemet Ali cannot have counted for very much in view of the Tsar's long-standing hostility to Louis-Philippe and his lack of confidence in the stability of France's regime or its policy. Despite the serious friction with England in the preceding years, its policy was more predictable. Palmerston, for all his rhetoric and vigorous promotion of British interests, had shown a willingness to avoid war with Russia.[25] If these considerations counted in favour of a serious overture towards England, the outcome would depend on Palmerston's reponse.

The Russian proposal was to abandon the Treaty of Unkiar-Skelessi in favour of a general treaty of the European powers closing the Straits to warships. Russia would support any English action to compel Mehemet Ali to abandon Syria: if necessary, it would intervene to protect Turkey against Mehemet Ali's forces, but would do so not under the Treaty of Unkiar-Skelessi but as the mandatory of Europe. The proposal met Palmerston's primary objective of terminating Russia's special position in Turkey and also his immediate aim of strengthening the Empire against Mehemet Ali. He was willing to accept it but the Cabinet, reluctant to break with France, supported the French objection to allowing Russia to intervene separately at Constantinople. Brunnow had to return to Russia to consult the Tsar on the Cabinet's proposal that England and France should participate in any such intervention.[26]

In the later part of 1839 the situation remained tense. The powers

45

could not withdraw from their involvement but seemed unable to agree on a course of action. There was uncertainty over their alignment. The breach between England and France widened when the French government failed even to respond to a concession offered by Palmerston, that Mehemet Ali should, in addition to hereditary rule in Egypt, receive the Pashalik of Acre, without its fortress, for his lifetime.[27] France was becoming isolated, but many in London found it difficult to envisage a complete break between France and England, or agreement between England and Russia. The main danger was that Mehemet Ali might seek to resolve the issue by the use of force which could involve England, France and Russia in a naval confrontation at Constantinople. Though not as great as at the time of the Turkish defeats in June–July, tension remained at a high level.

The Tsar attempted to break out of the stalemate in November by accepting the British condition that the English and French fleets should participate in any intervention at Constantinople – a 'naval picnic'. Brunnow returned to London. Agreement, however, was long delayed. Russia eventually conceded two further demands by Palmerston, which emerged as soon as he began to draft a submission to the Cabinet based on Brunnow's proposals: first, as Metternich had proposed, that the Ottoman Empire should be a party to the agreement, and second, that England and France combined should have an equal number of ships to Russia if there should be a joint intervention. But the principal cause of the delay was the Cabinet's desire to include France in the agreement, which led Palmerston to withhold his submission until circumstances were more favourable. Austria also sought to include France in any agreement, and Metternich appeared to share the French view that it would be impossible to coerce Mehemet Ali.[28] Confident in this belief, the French government, from 1 March headed by Thiers, now maintained that Mehemet Ali should have the hereditary rule of Syria as well as Egypt. This was France's response to a further concession offered by Palmerston at Austria's urging, namely, that Mehemet Ali should have the whole of southern Syria as far as Beirut for his lifetime. In June, as frustration caused by the delay mounted, the Austrian representative, Neumann, privately offered Guizot (then French ambassador in London) the whole of Syria for Mehemet Ali's life. Thiers rejected even this, holding out for hereditary rule.[29]

Two developments in June hastened a decision. The Turkish Grand Vizier, Husrev – Mehemet Ali's leading opponent – was deposed, opening the way for the possibility of a direct agreement between Turkey and Egypt. Mehemet Ali sent a special emissary to Constantinople. It appears that Ponsonby's intervention was needed to prevent an agreement which might have ceded Syria to Mehemet Ali in exchange for the return of the Turkish navy.[30] At the same time, an insurrection in the Lebanon seemed to provide an opportunity for ousting his forces from Syria. Both developments pointed to the need for a quick decision.

Neumann continued to press for maximum concessions to Mehemet Ali in order to win French support. Only Thiers' continuing rejection of his proposal (Syria for life) prevented a Franco-Austrian alignment which would have led to a quite different outcome. It would have precluded the four-power agreement and would have been extremely embarrassing to Palmerston. Failing agreement with France, Austria was willing to offer a symbolic naval contribution to an English force acting under a four-power Convention. Palmerston was able to obtain Cabinet approval only by a threat to resign, as well as by making the most of France's rejection of his successive offers.

The four-power Convention of 15 July consisted of a long-term agreement closing the Straits in time of peace, and short-term agreements on joint Anglo-Russian intervention at Constantinople if it were necessary to protect the Empire. Mehemet Ali was to be offered the hereditary rule of Egypt and the Pashalik of Acre for life. If he did not accept within ten days the offer of the Pashalik would be withdrawn; if he did not accept the offer of Egypt within a further ten days it too would be withdrawn. In this case the English and Austrian navies would cut Egypt's naval communications with Syria and engage in operations to expel the Egyptian forces. France was not informed of the Convention until orders for its implementation had been dispatched.[31]

Phase 3: Military operations and the threat of a wider war (August–November 1840)

Although the naval and land operations against Mehemet Ali's forces in Syria were far more successful than was widely expected, there was unavoidable delay in initiating them and news took approximately three weeks to reach London. During the period of waiting there was mounting tension and opposition to Palmerston's policy. The ultimatum was presented on 16 August, and the British commander, Admiral Stopford, waited at Alexandria for Mehemet Ali's replies to the two deadlines. He refused to reply to the first and was ruled by the consuls to have rejected the second.[32]

The British ships, supported by a small Austrian squadron, bombarded Beirut (9–10 September) and troops landed from the fleets captured Djuni, Djebail and Batrun (10–15 September). Arms were supplied to the Lebanese insurgents. Turkish forces, strengthened by European leaders, won their first victory over Ibrahim on 24 September, followed by further successes; Beirut was captured on 9–10 October. On 29 October Stopford received Palmerston's orders to seize Acre, and its fortress was bombarded and captured on 3 November – a great prestige success as it had held out against Ibrahim for six months. This marked the effective victory of the European and Turkish forces.[33]

During the early part of this period Thiers hoped for a new offer from Britain, confident in Mehemet Ali's ability to hold out in a defensive position. He avoided challenging Britain, going so far as to withdraw the fleet, which enjoyed marginal superiority in the number and size of its ships, from the eastern Mediterranean shortly before the expiry of the ultimatum to Mehemet Ali.[34] By now he was prepared to accept Syria for Mehemet Ali's lifetime only. In September Palmerston was under pressure from the Cabinet, in particular Lord John Russell, to make a new approach to France. The diplomatic situation was exacerbated by the Sultan's deposing of Mehemet Ali after his rejection of the second ultimatum – it was widely thought at Ponsonby's instigation.

The public mood in France became increasingly bellicose. Even Louis-Philippe had joined in the initial expressions of outrage at France's exclusion from the four-power Convention, and in Paris there was 'a joyful warlike enthusiasm ... Except for the Legitimists, all Frenchmen have rallied round the tricolour, and their unanimous cry is: War on perfidious Albion!'[35] The army was expanded and fortifications were constructed. Thiers, believing that England would win any naval war, hinted that France might fight for the Rhine frontier or spread revolutionary war throughout Europe.[36] There was an outburst of nationalist feeling in Germany; French and German poets and journalists exchanged insults. Palmerston and Nesselrode remained confident that there would not be a European war, but many feared that it was imminent.

Thiers made public notes sent to England on 3 and 8 October, demanding the revocation of the Sultan's deposing of Mehemet Ali. Palmerston reduced the tension by conceding this. His decision signalled a turning point, but the decisive step was Louis-Philippe's decision to accept Thiers' resignation (21 October). The danger of a European war now receded. Louis-Philippe had rejected as too provocative the language which Thiers wished to insert in the speech from the throne opening the French parliament:

More than ever I am pleased to count on your patriotic support. You wish France to be strong and great, as I do. No sacrifice will be too great to keep her in her rightful place in the world ... France is strongly attached to peace, but she will not purchase it at a price unworthy of her and your King ... wishes to leave intact to his successors this sacred heritage of independence and national honour which the French revolution has placed in his hands.[37]

Until Thiers' successor, Guizot's successful defence of his more moderate policy and Thiers' loss of support in the debates in the Chamber it was not certain that the new government would prove stable, nor that Louis-Philippe could hold out against the forces of nationalism which Thiers had sought to evoke. By then, however, the fall of Acre and the defeat of Ibrahim's forces were known and the case for war correspondingly weakened.

Phase 4: Resolution (December 1840–July 1841)

The final settlement was delayed for seven months after Mehemet Ali submitted in December because Turkey, encouraged by Ponsonby and indirectly by Palmerston, took advantage of the difficulties of applying the concept of hereditary tenure to the office of Pasha, in principle a servant or even slave of the Sultan. In a *firman* of 13 February the Sultan retained the choice of a successor among Mehemet Ali's sons and restricted him to the normal powers of the office of Pasha. The Sultan would appoint all high-ranking officers, supervise the collection of revenue and receive one-quarter as tribute. Mehemet Ali rejected these terms.

On 15 March France initialled the new five-power Convention on the Straits but refused to sign it until the other powers pronounced the termination of the four-power Convention. This they in turn refused until agreement had been reached between Mehemet Ali and the Sultan: without the threat of coercion, they feared, Mehemet Ali might reject any agreement and the local conflict would remain unresolved. On 1 June the Sultan, advised by the European ambassadors, issued a new *firman* which conceded most of Mehemet Ali's demands: succession should go to the eldest direct heir; he would retain control over his army; and the tribute could be negotiated between the two. This opened the way for the signing of the Convention on the Straits on 13 July.

Under the Convention, Turkey undertook to maintain the ancient rule which excluded foreign warships from the Straits while the Sultan was at peace. Thus Russia was excluded from the Mediterranean but

49

the other powers were excluded from the Black Sea. There was no special provision for consultation between Turkey and Russia (the clause in the Treaty of Unkiar-Skelessi which had raised the principal difficulty). On the other hand, there was no guarantee of the integrity of the Ottoman Empire; nor could agreement be reached on other issues such as the position of Jews in the Empire. The Convention remained limited to the single issue of regulating the Straits.[38]

Values, interests and objectives

Foreign policy values of the powers were not fully articulated during the crisis, but their policies are consistent with the following three propositions:

1 All, even France, were committed to the stability of the European social order, and thus to the preservation of the existing international system and to the informal rules of the Concert.

2 At the same time, all four powers most involved were empires, sensitive to questions of prestige and, except for Austria, actively expanding their imperial frontiers, leading to pressures for more vigorous imperial self-assertion, contrary to the restraints of the Concert.

3 Except for the control of the Straits and of Constantinople, the issues at stake in the crisis were not perceived as vital interests: to the extent that there was a risk of war, it was for reasons other than a clash over basic values.

Britain

In Britain, the frictions of the 1830s led to a sharp increase in the perceived interest in containing Russia's southward expansion, which threatened Britain's capacity to influence developments in the eastern Mediterranean and its communications with India. In empowering the ambassador to summon the fleet, the Cabinet was prepared to risk war in order to prevent Russia from gaining control over Constantinople.[39] There was an increasing strategic interest in ensuring that no other great power should control the routes to India. Britain objected to the possibility that France might control Syria, and clashed with Mehemet Ali in Arabia and Mesopotamia for this reason.[40] Direct commercial interests in the Ottoman Empire had been limited, but the Commercial Convention of 1838 opened up a prospect for their expansion.

If the decision makers, by and large, shared this conception of British interests, several of them differed from Palmerston over the means by which they might best be secured. In Palmerston's view it was essential that the Ottoman Empire be preserved as a bulwark against further Russian advance, and this in turn pointed to the need to restrict to the minimum the territory that might have to be ceded to Mehemet Ali, even at the price of serious friction with France. His Cabinet critics placed greater value on the 'liberal alliance' with France and were not persuaded of the need to coerce Mehemet Ali in the interests of containing Russian expansion.[41] Palmerston also regarded Mehemet Ali's mercantilist economic system as hostile to Britain's interests, a point that was disputed in commercial circles but was not salient at the Cabinet level.[42]

Palmerston set himself two objectives. The first, achieved with surprising ease due to the course of action chosen by Russia in autumn 1839, was to terminate Russia's special position at Constantinople under the Treaty of Unkiar-Skelessi. His second objective, voiced as early as July 1839, was to strengthen the Ottoman Empire by depriving Mehemet Ali of all his territory except Egypt. It was Palmerston's insistence on this which set the scene for the more acute phase of the crisis. Few of his colleagues shared this determination, and the prevailing mood of the other powers was to patch up the status quo in the Near East rather than to seek to change it so drastically, at a time when Mehemet Ali had so recently demonstrated his military superiority over the Ottoman forces.

Russia

There was no question that the Tsar and his advisers deemed it vital that Constantinople should not fall into the hands of any other power and that foreign warships should be excluded from the Black Sea. As Brunnow expressed it to Palmerston:

> Suppose that the geographical position of England were similar to our own, and that your trading fleet was forced to pass through a narrow canal in order to maintain its relations with the rest of the world. And imagine to yourself that Russian warships would be stationed at the entrance to this canal. I leave it to you to imagine what your merchants would say! Do you, or do you not, wish to preserve the Ottoman Empire? If you value its existence, then leave Russia in peace, respect the closure of the Dardanelles, and do not force our Emperor to seize them. For, mark my words well, on the very day that you force a passage through the Straits, Russia will set her armies in motion and the final hour of the Ottoman Empire will have struck.[43]

51

Beyond this vital minimum, however, two schools of thought conten-
ded for the support of the Tsar, representing two incompatible conceptions of Russian interests, the European and the nationalist, which
reflected in an extreme manner the clash of values between the
European Concert and imperial self-assertion. As the French Ambassador, Barante, expressed it:

> Three things influence the course of policy ... first, the opinions and
> momentary impressions of the Emperor ... [which, second] were
> modified, corrected and guided by the prudent and well-calculated
> actions of M. de Nesselrode ... [and, third, subject to nationalistic
> pressure] which never troubles itself about European affairs and
> would prefer that the Tsar did not... [While Nicholas wants] to be
> Russian and to advance the development and progress of the
> national potential ... one idea that neither he nor cultivated Russians
> would be able to accept is to be isolated from Europe.[44]

Nesselrode had made it a condition of accepting office in 1825 that he
treat the Eastern question as 'a general European question beyond the
immediate interests of Russia',[45] and in 1829 the government had
resolved not to seek to gain possession of Constantinople because this
would probably bring the other powers permanently into the region.
Instead it would seek to preserve the Ottoman Empire as a buffer.[46]
This approach, however, remained ambivalent, as the Treaty of
Unkiar-Skelessi was to show.

Russia's objectives were not sharply defined in relation to the issues
in dispute, but related more generally to strengthening its security and
its diplomatic position. It abandoned its claim to a right of unilateral
intervention at Constantinople. Confronted by the appearance of a
potential naval threat to its vital interest there, its initial response, the
rejection of a conference at which it feared isolation, left it potentially
even more isolated. The successful overture to England removed these
major threats, leaving Russia in a favourable position to participate in
the diplomatic resolution of the crisis in a way which would secure its
defensive goal, the closing of the Straits by international agreement.

Beyond this, the Tsar and Nesselrode no doubt hoped for further
gains from the improvement in Russia's diplomatic position: perhaps
to achieve a more lasting breach between France and England, or a
broad partnership with England, or a greater role for Russia in a
revived European Concert. But these could be little more than aspirations. The main Russian crisis objectives derived from immediate
strategic and diplomatic imperatives. The subsequent delays were not
sufficiently costly to lead Russia, so well positioned diplomatically, to
reconsider its course of action. In the final phase, Nesselrode eventu-

ally overcame the Tsar's preference for maintaining French isolation, in the name of restoring the five-power Concert.[47]

France

France, like Britain, sought to contain Russia in the interests of remaining a major power in the Eastern Mediterranean. French prestige was associated with Mehemet Ali, who enjoyed popular sympathy because of his link with Napoleon. Some French leaders may have aspired to make France the dominant power in the Near East, but official policy was never committed to so costly and perhaps unattainable a goal. France sought a greater role in the Mediterranean, but with circumspection: while extending its control over Algeria, it complied with British demands not to move into Tunisia and Morocco. There was little prior indication that France might support Mehemet Ali's ambitions to the extent of causing a major breach in its relations with the other powers.

France's initial objectives, set out in the diplomatic correspondence, gave priority to preserving the Ottoman Empire – its collapse would mean war and perhaps even the nightmare of its partition between England and Russia. But it favoured a settlement which would leave Mehemet Ali the legitimate ruler of Syria as well as Egypt, the rest of his territory reverting to the Empire. France's role would be to support him within the general framework of preserving the Empire.[48]

When Mehemet Ali later resisted tentative French suggestions that he should settle for less than the hereditary rule of Syria, Thiers, in the light of French public sentiment, was unwilling to press him. Thus France became rigidly committed to the objective of Mehemet Ali's hereditary rule of the whole of Syria; the only acceptable alternative was that he should agree directly with the Sultan. Only after the four-power agreement to coerce Mehemet Ali did Thiers begin to press him to accept Syria only for his lifetime.

Austria

Austria also placed great value on preventing Russia from gaining control of Constantinople, and Metternich had on occasion indicated a readiness to go to war to this end. Yet, while deploring the weakness of the other powers in 1832–33, he had hastened to seek an accommodation with Russia, and through successive Eastern crises Austria was less ready to fight than Britain or France. In 1839–41 it was more interested in the wider systemic aim of maintaining a European concert than in the local outcome, provided always that Mehemet Ali was not permitted to undermine Turkey's effective independence. There were internal reasons, discussed below, for Austria's passive policy, and there was also an awareness that Russian support might be needed to maintain the Hapsburg regime, and that a major war would endanger it. Finally, so long as Britain and France were taking the lead against Russia they were safeguarding Austria's security interests, and Metternich's diplomacy could profit from this fortunate circumstance.

Austria initially set itself the ambitious objective of taking the lead in conference diplomacy, but this was defeated by Russia's refusal to attend. At the same time Austria succeeded through the joint note in achieving its related objective of ensuring great-power intervention in settling the conflict between Turkey and Mehemet Ali. This diplomatic *fait accompli* had the effect of circumventing any Russian intention of invoking the Treaty of Unkiar-Skelessi. In the later phases the promotion of agreement among all five powers took precedence over the details of a local settlement, but there was a limit to potential Austrian concessions to France and Mehemet Ali in that Metternich, although prepared to concede Syria for Mehemet Ali's life, thought that a permanent union of Syria and Egypt would destroy the local balance. Austrian objectives thus reflected a desire to avoid war and Metternich's general conceptions of balancing power.

The specific objectives sought by the powers derived from the ways in which the policy makers interpreted the particular circumstances of the crisis in the light of their individual conceptions of the 'national interest'. Certain key objectives played a crucial role in shaping the course of events. Metternich's promptness in concerting the actions of the three powers most concerned to avert unilateral Russian intervention warded off that threat, but Russia took the opportunity to transform a position of potential strategic weakness into one of great diplomatic strength. With the major threat of war averted, Palmerston and Thiers became increasingly committed to incompatible objectives over the control of Syria, and despite the uncertain political support for both, this structured the crisis in 1840 as a 'duel' between Britain and France.

Perception

The main questions to be considered are: first, how great was the range of perception among decision makers in each country?; and second, what was the extent of misperception and how significant was it?

54

Britain

There were major differences among British decision makers in their perception of the Ottoman Empire and Mehemet Ali, and later of the risk of war with France. In the public debate there were differences in the perception of a Russian threat to British interests, but only a small minority followed Richard Cobden in thinking that the control of Constantinople should be of no concern to Britain. Public anti-Russian feeling was such that there was considerable hostility to Palmerston's alignment with Russia in the crisis, but this had little impact on the decision makers.

With respect to the Ottoman Empire and Mehemet Ali there was no consensus. For Palmerston all talk of the decay of the Ottoman Empire was a myth; it could be reformed and strengthened, and offered the only satisfactory buffer against Russian expansion. On the other hand, he not only perceived Mehemet Ali as a threat to the peace and to British commerce, and a satellite of France, but also denied his claim to be a reformer, presenting him as an oppressive despot whose regime lacked moral foundation or political support. From this 'definition of the situation' it followed that there could be only one kind of lasting settlement, one which restored to the Empire most of the territory controlled by Mehemet Ali and restricted him to Egypt. This was an extreme position shared by no other major decision maker.[49]

Clarendon provided the most articulate statement of the alternative view. He doubted Turkey's value as a buffer, denying that the Empire was capable of reform or even survival, while he perceived Mehemet Ali's Egypt as a modern state which offered security of passage, which sought good relations with Britain and relied on France only because of British hostility. It was not, therefore, in Britain's interests to support the decrepit Empire against a more vigorous and orderly regime which could provide a better buffer against Russia. And it was doubtful whether military operations could bring about Mehemet Ali's defeat at tolerable cost.[50]

In the event, Palmerston's perception of the military prospects proved the sounder, but expert opinion had been extremely divided.[51] On neither side can one identify outright misperception: each perceived some aspects of the situation quite accurately, but selectively, omitting those aspects which were not in accordance with his overall conception. Each made extreme assumptions concerning the reform and survival of the Ottoman Empire, neither of which were fully borne out in the future.

Palmerston's confidence that France would not go to war was

grounded in strategic reasoning, and in his analysis of French attitudes. France *could* not go to war, he wrote in February 1840, because Britain was superior at sea and it would be isolated on the continent. It would be unwise to underrate France when a national interest and a just cause were at stake, 'but it would be equally inexpedient to be daunted by big words and empty vapouring'.[52] Moreover, the France of Louis-Philippe was very different from France of the revolutionary wars. 'There are in France a vast number of proprietors and industrialists who object decidedly to a useless war, and are determined opponents of the revolution...'.[53] In autumn 1840 he was less categorical: 'For the present at least the French will remain quiet and there will be no war', but he asked Bulwer (the chargé d'affaires in Paris) to continue sending his own differing view, 'for ... it is right that I should know what are the impressions made upon an able man observing things upon the spot'.[54] In October, acknowledging that France might make moves which could lead to war, he took the precaution of instructing the ambassador, Granville, to bring all the archives if he had to leave Paris.[55] Thus, while maintaining his basic analysis, Palmerston accepted uncertainty and sought new information as the situation changed. The extraordinary determination – or obstinacy – which characterised his policy was not associated with cognitive rigidity.

Palmerston's domestic critics did not perceive a risk of war with France until August–September. Clarendon's original objection was that Palmerston's policy did not serve British interests in the Near East, and that he lacked the means to implement it. In the statement dissenting from the Cabinet minute of 8 July 1840 which approved the four-power Convention, Clarendon and his supporters first stated that the means were insufficient, and that there might be war on the coasts and in the Asiatic provinces of Turkey and an interruption of commerce. The 'far more extensive and disastrous ... more remote and indirect ... tendency' of the policy is not described in terms of war with France but in generalities: 'a disturbance of that System of Policy and Alliance in Europe which ... has succeeded in preserving the Peace of the World'.[56]

Fear of war arose suddenly. As Lord John Russell's biographer expresses it, 'the country was suddenly awakened to the knowledge that war, and the worst of all wars, war with France, was not merely probable but imminent'.[57] Rebuked for his lack of concern in August, by 9 September Russell was writing to Melbourne of the 'great danger' of a European war 'which seems inevitable' unless Britain changed its policy.[58] On 8 October Russell saw the country unprepared 'on the brink of war', and remained unconvinced by evidence which Palmerston showed him that France was not preparing for war. 'I do not suppose that France is less prepared for war than she was in 1792. Pitt in that year said we should have no war; in 1793 he said we should have a short war.'[59] Two of the British ambassadors, Granville in Paris and Beauvale in Vienna, shared Russell's perception; on the other hand Bulwer reported increasing opposition to Thiers in Paris.[60]

The context of the alarmist perceptions is not well recorded, but whereas Palmerston offered substantial reasons for construing the French warnings as bluff, his critics reacted to the immediate appearances of events. The French government and public appeared outraged; the outcome would depend on the next British decisions, and to refuse all concession appeared to signify war. Palmerston's 'francophile' critics were also influenced by their view that the French reaction was quite legitimate and that the issues in dispute did not justify the slightest risk of war.

Russia

With the 'Russian nationalist' school excluded from policy making, there is no indication of important differences of perception between the two key decision makers, Nesselrode and the Tsar, during the earlier phases of the crisis. The initial changes in Russian policy represented adjustments to an unexpected situation, not an expression of differing views of the situation. Their lack of interest in the details of the territorial division between the Sultan and Mehemet Ali allowed the Russians greater flexibility than the other powers. There were no major misjudgments, and minor misperceptions such as the exaggeration of Anglo-French solidarity in July 1839 were rapidly corrected by events.

The two leaders differed in their perception of the war scare in the autumn of 1840, the Tsar taking it very seriously and envisaging assistance to England or to Prussia, Nesselrode perceiving it as a political manoeuvre. This led him to expect hints of a French desire for compromise, which were duly forthcoming. Nesselrode placed even greater weight than Palmerston on France's overall strategic weakness. France could not risk war against all four powers: it would be truly formidable on the Continent only if it were supported by England. Thus peace was secure so long as England was in the front line. A continental war might arouse French dreams and ambitions, but a naval war would be too destructive of its commerce and industry.[61]

France

There was little internal division over the Eastern question. A few individuals such as the ambassador in Constantinople, Roussin, sympathised with the Empire, but for historical reasons, as we have seen, the great majority sympathised with Mehemet Ali. Up to July 1840 the range of differences in perception was very narrow, between Thiers who saw little risk in giving Mehemet Ali unqualified public support and those who, like Guizot, perceived danger in this course and favoured a modest compromise.

Thiers misjudged the relations of the powers, the chances of a direct settlement between Mehemet Ali and the Sultan, and Mehemet Ali's military strength. He thought that a four-power agreement was unlikely, that a direct settlement could be achieved first, and that even if there were a four-power agreement, the powers could not defeat Mehemet Ali and force him to withdraw from Syria. Information on the various diplomatic manoeuvres was so ambiguous, and the outcomes so unpredictable, that it may be said that Thiers was unlucky, and Palmerston on the contrary rather fortunate. Thiers was well informed on differences in the English Cabinet, and Austria's preference for a compromise was evident in its increasing concessions to the French position. On the third point, Palmerston judged the military prospects correctly, Thiers incorrectly. Palmerston relied on expert advice from several sources on Mehemet Ali's military weakness, a view that was shared by Cochelet, the French consul. It is not clear why Thiers rejected Cochelet's appraisal, but his confidence was widely shared in France, and Metternich and Nesselrode similarly doubted that the four powers could succeed.[62] Essentially, Thiers gambled on the basis of plausible assumptions concerning matters outside his control. But he overestimated the strength of Palmerston's Cabinet opponents and failed to perceive that there was a limit to Austria's agreement to concessions to Mehemet Ali.

From the signing of the Convention in July until early October, the evidence suggests that Thiers did not misperceive the situation but followed a policy of bluffing, fomenting a war scare but with no intention of going to war. As late as 9 October he wrote to Cochelet that 'the wise and patriotic people desire peace ... and yet prefer war to dishonour ... in fact, we are not ready ... Our navy would win the first battle and lose the last ... we must not make war except for an absolutely obligatory reason'.[63] His biographers judge that Thiers was arming in order to strengthen his hand in negotiation, on the assumption that Mehemet Ali could hold out until the following spring.[64]

The news of the capture of Beirut in early October undermined this assumption and caused a new upsurge of anger in Paris. Now for the first time the decision makers had to confront the choice between war and humiliation.[65] Thiers proposed to intensify the war of nerves, but it was no longer evident that he could keep the risks under control. 'Many of his closest associates were convinced that he would eventually have fought if necessary.'[66] His own comments lend some support to this view, presenting war as something which might be imposed by events – 'if events drive France to it', 'if circumstances bring us to it' (*nous y amènent*);[67] and the language which he proposed for the speech from the throne might have proved sufficiently inflammatory to set in motion an irreversible spiral towards war.

Louis-Philippe's family were seriously alarmed. One of his daughters wrote of 'the most critical moment for the last ten years. Within the country opinion is in a nervous state, and some incitement to revolution; at our gates a foreign war, with all Europe against us. God alone can save us.'[68] An assassination attempt on Louis-Philippe on 15 October dramatised the precarious position of the monarchy and those supporting peace. He himself expressed greater confidence, remarking to his ministers, in a comment surprisingly similar to Palmerston's: 'I tell you, I am not nearly so pacific as the country. You do not know how far the yearning for peace can carry the country.'[69]

Austria

Subject to the internal constraint discussed below, which ruled out policies that risked war, Metternich was free to shape Austrian diplomacy in accordance with his perception of the issues. His primary concern was with the central balance, but he also had a distinctive perception of the local situation which allowed him greater flexibility than Palmerston or Thiers, but less than Nesselrode. He saw the Empire as very weak materially but possessing the major asset that it could grant or withhold the legitimacy of the claims of Mehemet Ali's heirs. Egypt's strength, he thought, was limited to the lifetime of Mehemet Ali unless legitimate succession was conferred on them. Metternich rejected the French view that he should have hereditary rule over Syria as well as Egypt, as this would create too great an imbalance. But he did not share Palmerston's view that there was only one correct settlement; thus he sought to bring France and England together to bargain for intermediate options, including Mehemet Ali's retaining Syria for his lifetime. Metternich perceived Palmerston and Thiers as lacking judgment, and was frequently alarmed by their language or tactics, hence he perceived a major role for Austria as a mediator.[70]

Further, Metternich did not think it would be possible to deprive Mehemet Ali of Syria without French help: naval operations would have limited value and large armies would be needed to defeat Mehemet Ali – and these of course were not available.[71] After Mehemet Ali's death the Sultan would retain the right to rule Syria, and Egypt would probably lose the power to dominate it. Thus there was a similar fusion of perception, analysis and policy preference as in the cases of Palmerston and Thiers: none perceived a need to make trade-offs.

Metternich took the danger of war more seriously than the other leading decision makers. He was alarmed over the instability of French politics and the unpredictable consequences of Thiers' leadership. The position of the monarchy was 'most dangerous' in August and Guizot's position 'highly dangerous' in November. Thiers had placed himself at the head of the party of revolution, the King was forced into the position of leading the party of conservatism. France was shaken to its foundations, and in a few months Thiers had brought about a situation in which the whole of Germany was ready to accept war, 'et cela *de peuple à peuple*'. But Thiers would be even more dangerous if he were dismissed from office.[72] Metternich's acute perception of irrational and revolutionary forces in France denied him the common-sense basis for confidence shared by Nesselrode and Palmerston. Experience of the sudden upsurge of popular nationalism in Germany heightened his fear of revolution, and this perception dominated his thinking on the risk of war. Although he misjudged the outcome, his was the most acute perception of the nature of the risk of war in autumn 1840.

Bargaining

Three aspects of bargaining in the crisis are of particular interest:

1 The alignments of the powers. Since these were more uncertain than in the other cases, and success depended on maintaining the support of others, the aim of much of the bargaining was to influence the composition of the informal coalitions.

2 The extent to which each of the powers followed clearly defined strategies, especially in the second and third phases.

3 The overall significance of bargaining in the crisis. That is to say, to what extent were the coalitions and the main actions an expression of

conscious bargaining, or to what extent should they be explained in other terms?

Informal coalitions and the risk of isolation

As was noted earlier, ideological affinities were not strong enough to determine the alignments of the powers in particular diplomatic conflicts. What was unusual was that the powers were in substantial agreement on the most important issue, the preservation of the Ottoman Empire, but differed so greatly over a secondary issue, the extent of the territory to be ruled by Mehemet Ali. Initial Russian ambiguity over the Ottoman Empire, however, led to the formation of the coalition between Austria, Britain and France, whose objective was as much to deter unilateral Russian intervention at Constantinople as to prevent a surrender by Constantinople to Mehemet Ali. Fearing diplomatic isolation if it accepted Metternich's invitation to concert further moves in Vienna, Russia sought to promote a more favourable coalition.

Russia broke out of isolation by its unexpected approach to Britain, offering a framework for a working partnership which was favourable to British interests and permitted effective diplomatic cooperation. Russian support for Palmerston was, however, in the last analysis tactical and conditional: it could accept a settlement negotiated directly between the new Sultan and Mehemet Ali, an outcome which would have amounted to a defeat for Palmerston. There was thus an asymmetry between the positions of the four powers most involved. Russia and Austria, both of which could accept a range of outcomes between the extremes supported by Britain and France, must form part of any coalition which would determine a settlement. Britain and France, on the other hand, risked isolation if either one could win the support of the other powers for its preferred solution. Britain, enjoying Russia's informal support, had an advantage over France in this respect: France would be isolated if Austria were to support Britain; Britain would not be immediately isolated if Austria were to support France.

In the event, France *was* isolated. Despite Austria's strong preference for a five-power over a four-power agreement, Thiers' holding out for a settlement beyond the limit of concession to Mehemet Ali which Metternich could accept led to Austria's accepting a four-power solution. As for Britain, Palmerston's policy risked not so much British but his own isolation. A direct settlement between Sultan and Pasha would have been welcomed by the other powers, and by many in the

British Cabinet. If Thiers had compromised to meet Austria's views, while Britain would not have been immediately isolated, it must be assumed that the Cabinet, so reluctant to support Palmerston's policy even when he could claim Austria's support, would have welcomed the compromise, leaving Russia with no option but to do the same.

Strategies and tactics

Russia's initial goal, to avert the risk of war against a superior coalition, was achieved rapidly, thanks to Palmerston's positive response to its proposals in September 1839. It was able to accommodate Britain's condition that the British and French fleets should take part in any naval intervention at Constantinople. Once these central provisions were agreed, Russia could afford to wait, lending Palmerston general support, since the Tsar preferred a four-power to a five-power agreement, but able to accept whatever might be agreed concerning Mehemet Ali, whether in a direct agreement with Turkey or as part of a four- or five-power settlement.

Austria, with its decided preference for a five-power agreement and its fear that delay might lead to a new upheaval, was the power most concerned to end the deadlock during the first half of 1840. It sought to persuade both Britain and France to compromise, its role as mediator being backed by the (mainly tacit) threat to support the power which proved more accommodating. Until French intransigence became clear, Metternich withheld the commitment of a token Austrian force for the coercion of Mehemet Ali.

Russia's approach to Palmerston provided him with an opportunity to achieve his objective with respect to Mehemet Ali, even though the obstacles remained formidable. His bargaining with Russia over joint naval intervention was due to the Cabinet's support for French demands. His offer of southern Syria to Mehemet Ali met certain French concerns, but was more a concession to his Cabinet adversaries than an attempt to reach agreement with France. Believing that France was unwilling to coerce Mehemet Ali, he sought a four-power agreement. The six-month delay was not due to a strategy of waiting on external events but reflected the constraints of internal politics, the need to wait for an opportunity to win Cabinet support for a four-power agreement. External developments eventually provided the opportunity. Seizing it, Palmerston succeeded in obtaining the rapid conclusion and implementation of the four-power Convention, just in time before winter would have prevented naval operations in the area.

Until Palmerston's discussions with Brunnow and Neumann at the end of 1839 it appeared that France's refusal to coerce Mehemet Ali might be sufficient to deny Palmerston his objective. Thiers continued the policy of his predecessors, seeking to persuade Mehemet Ali to compromise but refraining from pressure or threat. He made clear the limits of French support, in particular that there was no question of France's going to war with the other powers over Syria.[73] His rejection of all compromise proposals was not because he hoped for a better offer but because he was not willing to break with Mehemet Ali. Thiers' strategy, in contrast to Palmerston's, was one of deliberately waiting on events, on the assumption that there was a good chance that Palmerston would be thwarted, either by his colleagues, by the other powers, or by a local settlement. This was not unreasonable, but Thiers gambled in an exposed position.

During the third, military phase of the crisis the strategies of the parties to the Convention were in line with those of the previous phase. Palmerston pressed for its rapid implementation. His main efforts were directed, once again, to warding off demands from his colleagues for concessions to France in order to avert the threat of war, before the naval operations could be completed. His only significant concession was to deny support to the Sultan's deposition of Mehemet Ali. Russia continued to support Palmerston's policy, offering greater military assistance than appeared likely to be required; it, too, declined to support the deposition of Mehemet Ali, signalling this before it became an issue in London.[74] In September Metternich, showing some concern over the French threat of war and subject to domestic pressure, revived the suggestion that Syria remain under Mehemet Ali for his life.[75]

France's position in the third phase was far more complex. The four-power Convention signified the failure of the strategy of holding out for a satisfactory outcome. Three elements of a new strategy may be discerned in the period up to early October. The first was the policy of arming in order to improve France's negotiating position, on the assumption that Mehemet Ali could hold out until the next spring. The second was to inflame French anger and resentment over the Convention, fomenting a war scare which might improve France's immediate negotiating position. The third element was extreme caution with respect to actual military moves, in particular the decision to withdraw the fleet from the Eastern Mediterranean. This element, and Thiers' comments to his associates, justify the overall judgment that the strategy at this stage was essentially one of bluff.

By October, however, Britain's early military successes and its rejection of all proposed concessions to France suggested that the second strategy was also doomed to failure. Thiers sought to heighten the war scare, but complained that Louis-Philippe was undermining his efforts: 'If the King would let me act, I would prepare him an honourable peace, [but] if, when I speak firmly to the ambassadors ... the King talks peace, promising everyone that we shall have it ... he makes all favourable negotiation impossible'.[76]

It was now more difficult, however, for Thiers to convince the King and other conservatives that brinkmanship would remain bluff. It is true that he gained an apparent success through his 'threat' to Britain that the deposition of Mehemet Ali would amount to a change in the balance of power which France could not accept. This, however, was widely perceived as a safe threat: Thiers probably knew that Nesselrode as well as Metternich was unhappy over the deposition.[77] The inflammatory language which he proposed to include in the speech from the throne, whose rejection by Louis-Philippe led to the government's resignation, was more dangerous. Bury and Tombs argue that it would have been more prudent for Louis-Philippe to leave it to Parliament to bring down the government, but it may well be that this would have been the greater risk: if the speech had evoked the desired patriotic response, it might have been impossible to dismiss Thiers thereafter.[78] It is a matter of speculation how far Louis-Philippe's decision was influenced by Melbourne's threat to recall Parliament and increase Britain's armaments.

The final phase of the crisis, in which the parties edged towards the five-power agreement, is not further reviewed here. It may be concluded that the policies of the four powers can be characterised as strategies, consciously devised and modified in relation to objectives which were reasonably clearly defined. The main qualifications relate to the divided decision making authorities in Britain and France. There was no strategy of the British Cabinet as a whole, but rather an unusually well-defined strategy on the part of Palmerston. In the case of France, there was agreement among the decision makers on a course of action until this appeared to risk war. At this point the crucial difference between Louis-Philippe and Thiers could be resolved only by the King's acceptance of an increased risk, or by a change of government which amounted to a change of strategy, more dramatic in its public appearance than in the underlying intention.

The significance of bargaining

Although there was relatively little active bargaining, in the sense of exchange of major proposals and counter-proposals, offers and threats, the crisis can be seen as essentially a bargaining process in slow motion. The first phase can be construed as one in which Russia accepted the immediate 'proposal' of the three-power coalition concerning the diplomatic and naval support of the Ottoman Empire, but declined their additional proposal to concert further action in Vienna, instead offering a counter-proposal, which Britain accepted. This was followed by a lengthy phase of manoeuvre with little active bargaining. The pace of events was mainly determined by British internal politics: there was no genuine bargaining between Britain and France or between France and Austria, since the French strategy was to wait on events, and Palmerston's was to offer concessions just sufficient to retain the support of Austria and of his own colleagues. During the military phase France sought to use the threat of war to induce the four powers to reduce their demands on Mehemet Ali, but the effectiveness of the bluff was limited. It caused turmoil in the British Cabinet and a readiness to compromise in Vienna, but its eventual failure and Louis-Philippe's refusal, sustained by the Parliament, actually to risk war led France to acquiesce in the military outcome and introduced the final phase of bargaining over the details of a five-power agreement. The crisis, then, lends itself to explanation in terms of bargaining within constraints imposed by internal politics, especially in Britain and France.

Internal politics

Domestic political constraints were important for all the powers except Russia, where Nesselrode was temporarily in the ascendant. The Tsar had resolved against pressing any of the preceding conflicts with Britain to the point of war, and had recalled some of the key 'nationalist' officials. There was little conflict between Nesselrode and the Tsar until the final phase, when it occurred over the inclusion of France in the settlement.

The divisions in the British Cabinet played a major role during the second and third phases of the crisis, yet their eventual consequences were quite limited. This, however, was only due to the exceptional determination with which Palmerston pursued his objective. The slightness of the Whig government's parliamentary majority also worked in Palmerston's favour, since it strengthened Melbourne in his refusal to accept any resignations. The opposition delayed the Convention for several months and engaged in protracted Cabinet debates on the military operations, but in the end Palmerston wore it down. It reflected political rivalry as much as concern over the issues, but drew strength initially from two issues: the challenge to Palmerston's view of Mehemet Ali and the Ottoman Empire, and the pro-French sentiment of Holland and the supporters of the liberal alliance. A third group, roused by the sudden threat of war, strengthened the opposition when the policy was on the point of succeeding. The French government was fully aware of the opposition to Palmerston, but was unable to benefit from its knowledge – indeed, it may have been misled into faulty expectations. Public anti-Russian feeling was expressed in Parliament and in the Opposition press, but Cabinet dissidents did not, as later in the Crimean crisis, seek to exploit it, and the leading Conservatives gave substantial support to Palmerston's policy.[79]

The French regime as a whole, and its parliamentary governments, were much less stable, and thus highly exposed to public pressure. Neither Thiers nor his predecessors enjoyed a firm parliamentary majority. Thiers, as the spokesman for the parliamentary opposition to Louis-Philippe's dominance of politics, lacked a clearly defined ideological position and a body of firm supporters. His moderate domestic reforms and gestures, such as the return of Napoleon's ashes to Paris, won him some support, but his reliance on nationalist slogans rendered his government dependent on foreign policy successes. The temptation to gamble on the success of Mehemet Ali proved irresistible. Instead there was the humiliation of the four-power treaty followed by the crushing of Mehemet Ali's forces. The surge of popular anger was genuine, and the policy of bluff followed logically from the need to champion French honour, yet he was aware that powerful conservatives opposed the risk of war and might well regain a parliamentary majority. Nonetheless, most observers were surprised by the size of the majority (247 against 161) for his successor. While it is an overstatement to see Thiers as a prisoner of public opinion, the groundswell of public sentiment was a crucial constraint on any French government in this period, especially when the volatility of nineteenth-century French politics is taken into account.[80]

In the case of Austria, Metternich's hands were tied to a considerable extent by the division of power between himself and State Councillor Kolowrat, the minister responsible for domestic affairs. The decision making structure under the mentally retarded Emperor, Ferdinand, made for immobility, given the rivalry between Metternich and Kolowrat and the reluctance of Archduke Ludwig (the Emperor's uncle, presiding in his place over the Conference of State) to make decisions. Kolowrat had long opposed the cost of what he saw as Metternich's over-ambitious foreign policy, and financial constraints limited the size and effectiveness of the army.[81] Thus – quite apart from other reasons inclining him to caution – Metternich's diplomacy had to dispense with threats and rely heavily on the arts of manoeuvre. He could achieve a success such as that of July 1839 by exploiting all possibilities for reviving the Concert, but his mediating role of 1840 was forced on him as much as chosen. His tendency, deplored by Palmerston and his supporters, to seek further compromises during the 'war scare' period, may have been due to the political strength of Kolowrat.[82]

The risk of war: the outcome

How great was the risk of war? There is no basis for a precise judgment of probabilities, but in terms of several criteria the risk was quite high. A key decision maker, Thiers, was urging steps which could have brought war much closer, and there was no certainty in advance that Louis-Philippe could successfully overrule him. The combination of inflammatory language with war preparations was likely to 'escalate' the crisis, if Melbourne had indeed carried out his threat to summon Parliament and call for arms increases. Louis-Philippe's final authority in France remained nominal unless he dared to exercise it, in a way which some of his advisers thought hazardous. His judgment of parliamentary and public opinion proved sound, but if he had followed the contrary advice, or if he had been assassinated, the crisis might have been extremely difficult to bring under control.

The risk of war was far greater than might have been expected in the light of the interests at stake over the extent of Mehemet Ali's control in Syria. None of the decision makers considered this worth a major war: Thiers bluffed in order to secure the best possible outcome, and Palmerston's hard line was based on a correct perception of the bluff. In terms of game theory, both were playing Chicken: the rational outcome was the avoidance of war.[83] The risk of war arose, however, from the possibility that the decision makers would lose control over the sophisticated bargaining process – that political forces in France which were fundamentally irrational in terms of the decision makers' values and calculations would transform the nature of the game.

If the avoidance of war was one important outcome, a second was Palmerston's achievement of his objectives against the opposition of many of his colleagues and despite the scepticism of most of the leading diplomats. This must be attributed very largely to his personal qualities, his exceptional confidence in his own judgment and his determination not to make any of the compromises urged on him by the Prime Minister, his colleagues, the diplomats and even the Queen.

In Melbourne's words: 'Never, I will answer for it, was a great measure undertaken upon a basis of support so slender and so uncertain.'[84] Palmerston also enjoyed good fortune, not so much with respect to the decisive military outcome, but in profiting from Thiers' declining to bargain, Mehemet Ali's inability to reach agreement with the Sultan, and the timing of the four-power Convention. If it had been further delayed, the season would have been too far advanced to complete the operations.

The outcome also illustrated the strengths and limitations of the Concert of Europe as a mechanism for alleviating international conflict. An outcome acceptable to all the powers was eventually achieved without war, but in the process the difficulties of Concert diplomacy were exemplified and its norms were observed only in a rough and ready fashion. The early stages provided examples of jockeying for position such that if a conference were held at all, it would be under favourable auspices. Russia emerged from these manoeuvres in the strongest position, and supported Palmerston in isolating France, contrary to the norm that Concert diplomacy should involve all the powers. But France contributed greatly to its own isolation, seeking as it did to circumvent the joint offer of diplomatic support to the Sultan *vis-à-vis* Mehemet Ali. The final Convention was acceptable to all, but Nesselrode's larger ambitions for reconciliation with Britain proved illusory. The Russian nationalists regained influence in policy making, anti-Russian sentiment in Britain was little affected, and rivalries in Asia continued. Whatever its effectiveness in the crisis, the Concert did not address long-term relationships.

5 THE CRIMEAN WAR CRISIS, 1853–1854

This case offers the clearest example of lost opportunities: it is the case in which factors such as misunderstanding, inadvertently misleading signals and accidents of personality and timing played the greatest part in determining the outcome. The underlying tensions, though important, were not such as to necessitate a European war. Thus, the crisis is a rich source of negative lessons for crisis diplomacy, and for this reason its 'mismanagement' is given special emphasis. While this general view is endorsed by most historians, some significant differences over the interpretation of the crisis, especially over Britain's role, will be noted.[1]

At the level of the international system, the outstanding feature of the case, compared to the preceding Eastern crisis, was the decline in the efficacy of the Concert of Europe. Since there is no consensus on the reasons for this, nor on which of the actors, if any, bears the primary responsibility, these questions will need to be examined closely; but in view of the difficulties experienced in the successful Concert diplomacy of 1840–41, its breakdown in the next great Eastern crisis is not surprising. The alignment of the powers – a return to the 'relationship of major tension' between Britain and Russia – was less favourable to diplomacy than in 1840; the revival of old hostilities led British public opinion to adopt an extreme anti-Russian stance.

The adversaries' interests were not incompatible *ab initio*, but the crisis is notable for confusion over goals in the case of Russia and a government deeply divided over goals in Britain. These divisions were exacerbated by different perceptions of the Near Eastern issues: a government thus divided was vulnerable to pressure from a public increasingly hostile to Russia and perceiving the issues in terms of traditional stereotypes. The character of British internal politics at the time, it will be argued, was of central importance for the unintended escalation of the crisis.

But if Britain played a crucial role in the drift to war, the crisis had many other dimensions. The failure of negotiation reflected confusion

69

on all sides over the issues between Russia and Turkey, European insensitivity to the concerns of the Ottoman government, and a cumbersome negotiating process which allowed competing initiatives to negate one another. The negotiations never achieved the character of a clearly defined bargaining process, and few of the actors were able to devise strategies relevant to the intensifying crisis. There were many reasons for the failure of diplomacy: the case study will seek to identify the most important of them.

The setting

There was no clear pattern of alignments in Europe in the decade before the crisis. The liberal alliance had broken down in the previous Eastern crisis, and Britain's relations with France in the 1840s were seldom close; in a climate of reduced tensions, the Conservative government led by Peel and Aberdeen sought good relations with each of the powers. French policy was more conservative than in the 1830s, and the Holy Alliance was irrelevant to many of the new issues such as Austro-Prussian rivalry in Germany. The 1848 revolution brought Louis Napoleon to power in France and led to the major Russian counter-revolutionary intervention in Hungary, but had surprisingly limited repercussions on the general relations of the powers. France, Prussia and Austria were preoccupied with internal turmoil, and Britain was passive. Palmerston was far less radical in private than in public: where possible he worked for stability and moderation, and did nothing to discourage the counter-revolution in central and eastern Europe.

Napoleon's coming to power inevitably raised apprehension of a French attempt to overthrow the 1815 territorial settlement, but France did not pose a sufficient threat to unite the other powers. He did not challenge the Treaties directly, nor could the Empire appeal to European radicalism. However, as early as May 1850 he embarked on a diplomatic initiative on the control over the Holy Places in the Near East, in particular the sacred sites in Bethlehem. Over the centuries control had been disputed between monks of the Latin and Orthodox Churches, and the rights of both were enshrined in ancient treaties with the Ottoman Empire. Because Russia was seen as the external patron of the thirteen million Orthodox Christians in the Empire, however, the issue was of far greater significance to Russia than to France. French support for the demands of the Latin clergy was pressed by vigorous diplomacy – the despatch of the warship *Charlemagne* to Constantinople in violation of the 1841 Convention, and the offer of a defensive treaty of alliance against Russia – and the Sultan conceded the substance of French demands in December 1852. Napoleon's policy is sometimes explained in terms of his interest in winning clerical support for his new regime. Both he and his foreign minister, Drouyn de Lhuys, subsequently claimed that the initiative was part of a far-reaching diplomatic strategy, aimed at breaking up the continental alliance, in particular the Austro-Russian alignment, which provided the essential bulwark of the 1815 settlement.[2] Whether grand strategy or opportunism, his policy remains subject to different interpretations, but these are not crucial for an understanding of the course of events in the crisis which it precipitated.

The phases of the crisis

Phase 1: The Menshikov mission (February–May 1853)

In December–January Tsar Nicholas I considered his response to the blow to Russian prestige which France had inflicted. A note survives in which he surveyed his options. His objectives were to secure some form of redress, guarantees for the future and 'conservation of the position as it used to be', despite the doubt, 'is this probable?' He saw drawbacks in every course of action – negotiation, intimidation, the use of force – but did not record his choice. Despite undertaking military preparations, he appeared to conclude that the least bad of the options might be agreement among the powers to partition the Ottoman Empire.[3]

Nesselrode, however, invoking all the arguments for the traditional policy of preserving the Empire as a buffer, and fearing the consequences of the use of force, persuaded Nicholas to send a special emissary to Constantinople, whose mission would be to secure the restoration of Russia's traditional rights as protector of the Orthodox Church.[4] The Tsar chose for this difficult task not Count Orlov, recommended by Nesselrode, who had negotiated the Treaty of Unkiar-Skelessi, but Prince Menshikov, chief of the naval staff, who enjoyed Nicholas' confidence but had little diplomatic experience or (as events were to show) aptitude.

According to Nesselrode's letter of instructions, the two essential goals were to obtain satisfactory arrangements for the Holy Places and to secure guarantees for the future. The latter were referred to as Russia's traditional rights and privileges, but as set out in the accompanying draft convention, a general guarantee of the privileges of the Orthodox Church, they went far beyond the provisions of the relevant treaties. Whereas Article 7 of the Treaty of Kutchuk Kainardji (1774), on which Russia based its legal claims, authorised the Russian government to make representations 'on behalf of the new church at Constantinople... and its officiating ministers', the draft Convention would authorise it to make representations on behalf of all Orthodox churches and clergy: '... the right to make representations in favour of the churches of Constantinople and of other places and cities, as well as in favour of the clergy...'.[5] This attempt to broaden the interpretation of the treaty could be traced back to Catherine the Great.[6] Menshikov was granted discretion to vary the details, but if the Turks rejected the essential Russian proposals, he was to break off diplomatic relations. A settlement was to be achieved speedily: the mission 'must be of very short duration'.[7]

Although he agreed to the mission, the Tsar remained convinced that the collapse of the Ottoman Empire was at hand. Setting aside Nesselrode's advice that raising the issue would alarm the other powers, he engaged in conversations with the English ambassador, Sir Hamilton Seymour, between January and April, during which he proceeded from assurances of his commitment to preserve the Empire and to concert his policy with England, to canvass detailed suggestions for partitioning it among the powers. This did indeed alarm the ambassador and the then Foreign Secretary, Lord John Russell, but did not disturb Prime Minister Aberdeen nor Clarendon, who replaced Russell on 21 February.[8]

Nesselrode seriously misled the British and French ambassadors concerning the scope of the mission's objectives, assuring them of their moderation and even denying that there were demands over and above the settlement of the dispute over the Holy Places.[9] This deception may have stemmed from a decision of the ambassador in London, Brunnow, to inform the British government of Menshikov's instructions very selectively, withholding all mention of the proposed Convention. Brunnow also advised Nesselrode of the need to obtain Turkish agreement promptly, before the experienced British ambassador, Lord Stratford de Redcliffe, should return to Constantinople.[10] Nesselrode, however, was slow to communicate this.

Menshikov arrived in Constantinople on 28 February, after well-publicised reviews of the military and naval forces in southern Russia, aboard a warship, the *Thunderer*. His first act was to humiliate the Foreign Minister, Fuad Effendi, who had signed the agreements with France, by refusing to call on him. This, as intended, led him to resign. He violated convention by presenting his credentials in civilian dress, not full uniform, and sent emissaries to inquire into the needs of the

Orthodox Church throughout the Empire.[11] But he was slow to communicate Russia's demands to the Ottoman government, waiting until 22 March to place the proposed Convention before the new Foreign Minister, Rifaat Pasha. The Turks diverted negotiations into the intricacies of the Holy Places dispute and succeeded in prolonging them until the arrival of the British and French ambassadors, Stratford and de la Cour, on 5 April.

The British and French chargés d'affaires in Constantinople had reacted to Menshikov's initial moves by recommending the dispatch of their respective fleets to Constantinople. Napoleon, overruling most of his advisers, ordered the French fleet to Salamis in the expectation that the British would do likewise. The British Cabinet, however, believing at this stage that such a move would impede a diplomatic solution, rejected the recommendation.

A settlement of the Holy Places dispute was achieved on 5 May, Stratford having encouraged the Turks to detach it from the wider issues. Menshikov, impressed by Turkish resistance to the draft Convention, sought advice on 10 April whether he should indeed sever relations if it was rejected. The Tsar reaffirmed that he should, but also indicated that he need not insist that the agreement be concluded as a formal treaty.[12]

Within a few days of their arrival, the British and French ambassadors became aware of the full nature of the Russian demands, and accordingly informed their governments that they had been misled. The demands confirmed Stratford in his expectation that Russia was seeking an exclusive protectorate over the Ottoman Empire, and he strongly encouraged the Turks to resist them. 'If the Russians are in the wrong,' he wrote to his wife, 'my business is to make the wrong appear, and to stand by the Porte, or rather make the P. stand by me.'[13]

On 5 May Menshikov presented Turkey with an ultimatum demanding that it sign within five days a Convention modified by the removal of some of the most far-reaching of the original provisions, in particular that for Russian representations on behalf of Orthodox Christians throughout the Empire. Menshikov was persuaded to extend the deadline, and on 13 May, after he had had an audience with the Sultan, the Ottoman government was reconstituted in circumstances which have not been fully clarified but which were marked by a high level of political intrigue involving the Russian and British embassies. A Grand Council summoned to consider the Convention rejected it on 17 May by a vote of 42 to 3. The next day Menshikov, rejecting Turkey's limited counter-proposals, boarded his ship but was persuaded by an appeal from the representatives of the four powers to resume negotiation. He now offered a further concession, that the guarantees of the preservation of Russia's traditional rights could take the form of a diplomatic note – not even a declaration of the Sultan, still less a formal treaty. The representatives of the four powers advised Reshid Pasha, the new Foreign Minister, that the Porte alone could decide if this was acceptable – informal advice that it was safe to reject it. The Ottoman government proceeded to do so, and Menshikov at last carried out his threat to leave. In departing, he committed what has been termed 'une suprême maladresse'.[14] The Turks had let it be known that the Sultan was willing to proclaim a guarantee of the spiritual rights of the Orthodox clergy. Menshikov replied that such a guarantee would tend to invalidate the Church's other rights, seeming to confirm the suspicion that the Russian proposals would indeed threaten the Sultan's sovereignty and independence.[15]

Phase 2: Escalation and negotiation (May–October 1853)

After initial mixed reactions in London, feeling hardened against the Russian draft convention, especially when Turkey's objections became known.[16] On 31 May, learning of Menshikov's departure, Cabinet authorised Stratford to summon the fleet in an emergency, and on 2 June, after lengthy discussion, decided to send it to Besika Bay. While Aberdeen argued for delay, Palmerston urged that the fleet should be sent not just to the Dardanelles but to the Bosporus in order to forestall any attempted Russian coup. This deployment imposed a deadline on diplomacy: the ships could not remain in Besika Bay through the winter storms, thus by November there would be pressure to move the fleet up to Constantinople unless a settlement could be achieved which would justify its withdrawal.[17] Meanwhile Russia responded to the rebuff of Menshikov by increasing the pressure on Turkey. On 31 May it sent an ultimatum giving Turkey a week to accept Menshikov's final note, or the Principalities of Moldavia and Wallachia (subsequently Roumania) would be occupied and held as a 'material guarantee'. This was rejected by Turkey on 16 June, and Russian troops moved into the Principalities on 2 July.

Attempts to negotiate a settlement began in mid-June, the first phase culminating in the drafting of the Vienna Note at the end of July. During this period numerous proposals were considered in diplomatic circles, three of which reached the stage of formal drafts.[18] The first, the 'Turkish ultimatum' of 23 July, supported by Stratford, fell short of an outright pledge to preserve traditional Orthodox rights, but stated that it was the Sultan's 'sincere intention' to guarantee the spiritual privi-

74

leges confirmed in recent *firmans* and to grant to the Orthodox any privileges extended in future to other Christian subjects.[19] The conference of ambassadors at Vienna followed Buol, the Austrian Foreign Minister, in rejecting this as insufficient. Second, Clarendon proposed a draft convention, which would have granted Russia more with respect to form but little in substance. It confirmed the relevant treaty provisions and undertook that any new privileges for other Christians would be granted to the Orthodox.[20] The Russian government, resolving to 'wait calmly for the proposals which will be made to us and choose those which suit us best',[21] deliberated over possible amendments.

The conference, however, preferred a draft by the French Foreign Minister, Drouyn de Lhuys, which it revised with little awareness of Turkish sensitivities – the 'Vienna Note'. The Note would be from Turkey to Russia, acknowledging Russian solicitude for the Orthodox Church, stating that the Sultans had always confirmed its privileges, that the Turkish government would 'remain faithful to the letter and to the spirit' of the Treaties of Kainardji and Adrianople, and that the Sultan was bound in honour to preserve all the spiritual privileges of the Orthodox Church and would grant it any future advantages accorded other Christian rites.[22] The Note, agreed on 1 August, was accepted by the Tsar on 5 August.[23]

On 20 August, after discussion with the ambassadors, the Turkish government demanded amendments. These stated that the Orthodox privileges and immunities had been *spontaneously* granted by the Sultan, removed the reference to the *letter and spirit* of the former treaties, and specified that the reciprocal grant of new privileges referred only to those granted to Ottoman subjects.[24] Stratford was widely blamed for Turkey's refusal to sign the Note, acting allegedly out of pique that his preferred solution had been so brusquely set aside at Vienna. He himself claimed to have done his 'official best' in support of the Note, but it is doubtful that his mysterious *personal* influence could have been decisive. A joint representation by the powers might have prevailed on Turkey, but the atmosphere of war preparation in Constantinople, resentment at the occupation of the Principalities and the political weakness of the government, counted strongly against its accepting the Note. The British and French governments were not prepared to threaten the most potent sanction, the withdrawal of their support. Even Nesselrode recognised the strength of the war party in Constantinople and the limits to Stratford's influence, and the Austrian envoy, Bruck, concurred that the Turks could not be brought to accept the original Note.[25] Turkey's rejection came as a shock to those for whom Russia's acceptance had signalled the end of the crisis. Buol, Nesselrode and Clarendon were not surprised, but Aberdeen and his supporters, indignant and amazed, placed the blame on Stratford.

Nicholas hesitated and is reliably reported to have been willing to accept the amendments, never having been overconcerned with the form of words, fearing diplomatic isolation and perhaps still expecting the Ottoman Empire to disintegrate. However, he accepted Nesselrode's advice that it was contrary to his honour and dignity, having accepted the Note on condition that Turkey do likewise, to allow Turkey to make amendments.[26] The Tsar's rejection of the amendments (13 September) was not at all unexpected, and further efforts to persuade Turkey to accept the Note proved futile.

At the beginning of September Aberdeen was able to resist pressure from his colleagues to authorise the entry of the fleet into the Dardanelles, obtaining Admiralty advice that Besika Bay was safe until winter, and Britain rejected a French suggestion that Turkey be encouraged to declare war in order to legalise the fleets' entry into the Straits.[27] On Palmerston's suggestion Britain proposed that the four powers issue a statement interpreting the Vienna Note in the sense of the Turkish amendments, but this initiative was undermined by the publication in Germany in mid-September of Nesselrode's 'violent interpretation' of the Note, according to which Turkey was required to 'take account of Russia's active solicitude for her [twelve million] co-religionists in Turkey'.[28] In the face of denunciation of Russia in the British press, Clarendon abandoned Palmerston's proposal and in effect withdrew his support for the Vienna Note.

Was the violent interpretation the cause of Britain's change of position, or merely a pretext? It is true that it rendered the specific Palmerston proposal futile, but the decisiveness of Britain's rejection of the Vienna Note in any form from this point on reflects the internal political pressures on the government.[29] Given the government's slender majority, parliamentary support for Turkey and the attitudes of Palmerston and Russell ruled out any attempt to coerce Turkey. Yet strong support for Turkey was difficult when Russia had placed itself 'in the right' by accepting the Vienna Note. Clarendon welcomed a development which placed Russia 'in the wrong', enabling the government to move to the more popular ground of supporting Turkey and thus to stave off the threat of resignations which would endanger its survival. Clarendon indeed appears to have lost hope in a negotiated settlement at this time.[30]

On 23 September, for quite different reasons, Clarendon and Aberdeen ordered Stratford to summon the fleet to Constantinople. For

Clarendon, riots in Constantinople offered a good opportunity for a move for which there was pressure from the French, the press and his strongest colleagues. For Aberdeen, who had insisted earlier that so vital a decision must await a full Cabinet, the human emergency – possible danger to British lives, and to the Sultan – was sufficient to override the 1841 Treaty and he now played down the consequences of a move which others perceived as crossing the Rubicon.

At the end of September Russia made its greatest concessions as Turkey was about to declare war, but these were promptly rejected by Clarendon, whose policy was endorsed by the British Cabinet on 7–8 October. At a meeting at Olmütz between the Russian and Austrian leaders, Nicholas agreed to the terms of a declaration to be issued by the four powers in once again requesting Turkey to sign the Vienna Note. The powers would assure Turkey that the Tsar 'demands nothing contrary to the independence and the rights of the Sultan, nothing which implies an intention to interfere in the internal affairs of the Ottoman Empire', but only 'the strict maintenance of the religious *status quo*', and equality of rights between the Orthodox and other Christian subjects of the Porte.[31]

The French government at first proposed to accept the declaration but Clarendon raised the problem of Turkey's probable rejection of the Note, even thus reinterpreted. Stratford had been re-emphasising Turkish hostility to the Note, and indeed a meeting of the Grand Council was about to decide on war. To Clarendon, Turkey's rejection of their recommendation would render the position of Britain and France 'false and embarrassing'. Schroeder's examination of his correspondence suggests that it was this calculation, reflecting his sensitivity to public opinion and the parliamentary balance, not suspicion of Russia, which lay behind Clarendon's prompt rejection of the Olmütz proposals.[32] Only Aberdeen wanted to respond favourably to Olmütz, but did not press the point. Palmerston and Russell, claiming that Turkey was justified in declaring war against the Russian invader, advocated operations in the Black Sea. Aberdeen resisted this, but the Cabinet authorised the fleets to enter the Black Sea if Russia should attack Turkey.[33]

Turkey's declaration of war on 4 October did not lead to immediate hostilities: initially the Grand Council authorised the Sultan to send Russia an ultimatum to leave the Principalities. Stratford and the other ambassadors sought to postpone actual fighting, but on receiving a negative Russian reply the Turkish commander, Omer Pasha, began operations on 23 October. Pressure for war had been mounting: there were riots demanding war in September and the presence of English and French ships created an impression of allied support, undermining attempts to exercise restraint.

The options in this phase were narrower than in the first, and much narrower by October than in July–August. It was easier for Menshikov and the Turks to make concessions before June than for either government to do so after public commitments had been made, and above all after the occupation of the Principalities. Intended to coerce Turkey, this had the effect of strengthening its resistance, as did the sending of the fleets to Besika Bay. It is not clear whether even the threat to withdraw British and French support would have induced Turkey to sign the Vienna Note. Russia was close to accepting the Turkish amendments and the Tsar's subsequent policy at Olmütz shows that he was prepared to go very far in concessions to avert war. Nesselrode's advice, ironically, prevented the former concession, and his insistence at Olmütz on retaining the Vienna Note was a further misfortune. With Turkey now resolved on war, a greater symbolic concession was needed to reverse the situation. However, it is unlikely that any Russian concession could have been effective at this point, given Clarendon's attitude and the state of British opinion after the 'violent interpretation'. As the conflict intensified, Turkey's popularity in Britain limited its diplomatic flexibility, much more so in October than earlier.

Phase 3: Limited war (October 1853–March 1854)

The third phase was divided into two distinct sub-phases. Before the battle of Sinope introduced new pressures for war, relations were dominated by diplomatic initiatives; after Sinope, although these continued, they were overshadowed by the Anglo-French decision on 24 December to prevent Russian naval movement in the Black Sea, and its repercussions. From this point on, given the attitudes of the British government and public, war became unavoidable.

The new diplomatic initiatives were less promising than earlier. This was partly because they were more partisan, but more importantly because the situation was now much less favourable to a negotiated agreement. In October Clarendon and Stratford each put forward drafts of a new document, based on the Vienna Note and substantially including Turkey's modifications; its nuances were in accord with Turkish rather than Russian susceptibilities.[34] Buol set these aside, arguing that the outbreak of war created a new situation: there would now have to be some reference to an armistice or peace settlement. Modifying an earlier Russian suggestion, he proposed that Turkey send a plenipotentiary to negotiate with Russia in a neutral place.[35] This initiative, which obviously favoured Russia, was rejected by Britain, France and Turkey.

A new procedure was now attempted. The four-power proposal of 5 December (the first agreed document since the Vienna Note) consisted of two notes to Turkey, one inviting it to set out its proposals, the second setting out the basic conditions for a settlement, in the form of a list of assurances that would be given by both sides, and *inter alia* ruling out territorial changes.[36] This was 'held up' by Stratford, who had just submitted to the Porte a proposal drafted by the four ambassadors in Constantinople, which Turkey accepted on 21 December. This set out certain 'bases for peace': the evacuation of the Principalities, the renewal of ancient treaties, the reaffirmation of the relevant *firmans* and the agreement on the Holy Places.[37] The Vienna conference agreed that Turkey's reply was in accord with the wishes of the governments, but Russia's response was delayed pending a special mission by Orlov to Vienna, and in any case was overtaken by the events leading to the rupture of relations with Britain and France.

The destruction of part of the Turkish fleet at Sinope took place on 30 November and was known in England about twelve days later. The press united in denouncing Russia and condemning England's weakness in failing to protect the Turkish fleet. A feeling of dishonour was widely voiced. Political excitement was increased by Palmerston's resignation; with Russell, he had for some time been pressing for confining the Russian fleet to Sebastopol if Russia crossed the Danube, and Clarendon had privately conveyed this threat to St Petersburg.

In a series of Cabinet meetings from 17–22 December, it was first decided that the fleets should be ordered into the Black Sea for defensive purposes. Under pressure from Russell, the Cabinet finally accepted a French proposal similar to Palmerston's, demanding that the Russian fleet return to Sebastopol. Aberdeen was persuaded to agree to this by a French threat to do so unilaterally. This was essentially a bluff, and Schroeder argues plausibly that Clarendon at least was more worried by the possibility of France's disengagement from the conflict. Most of those involved perceived this as a crucial decision almost certain to provoke war, but Aberdeen and Gladstone for different reasons still saw possibilities for peace.[38] From this point the climate in England was one of expectation of war.

Russia's response to the demand was not to treat it as a *casus belli*, but to inquire from the British and French governments whether the Turkish fleet was similarly to be confined to port. France wished to delay the reply until Russia responded to a letter from Napoleon to the

Tsar (29 January), but England refused to wait. Napoleon proposed that the sea powers withdraw from the Black Sea in return for a Russian withdrawal from the Principalities – an initiative that held some promise in that it involved reciprocity. Without Cabinet discussion, however, Clarendon replied to the Russian inquiry rejecting reciprocal treatment for the Russian and Turkish fleets.[39] France acquiesced; the Russian ambassadors left London and Paris on 4–5 February, and the British and French ambassadors were withdrawn from St Petersburg a few days later. Nicholas now rejected Napoleon's proposal. He still did not declare war, leaving the onus on the sea powers which had been responsible for escalating the conflict. At the end of February Britain and France demanded the evacuation of the Principalities, and when Russia refused to reply, declared war on 27–28 March.

Values, interests and objectives

With one important exception, the basic values of the powers were as in the previous Eastern crisis (1839–41). The four imperial powers – Russia, Britain, France and Austria – were acutely aware of the extent to which the maintenance of their positions in the Levant depended on their prestige, manifest in their actions and relationships in the region. All four preferred to preserve the Ottoman Empire, and there was a general perception that it might be extremely difficult to accommodate their vital interests with respect to Constantinople if it should collapse.

It was no longer the case, however, that all were committed to the stability of the European social order, the territorial system and the rules of the European Concert. France under a second Emperor Napoleon could not but aspire to revising the territorial settlement, no longer by direct assault but by supporting the forces of movement and change, and by diplomatic initiatives calculated to enhance French prestige with little regard for the system as a whole or for the Concert mechanisms which sustained it. The defection of one of the five powers placed those mechanisms under a strain which was to prove too great.

If it was Napoleon who unsettled the delicate balance of prestige in the East, however, the two powers which played the most crucial roles in the crisis were Russia and Britain. The ambiguity in Russian objectives contributed to a heightening of the crisis, while major differences over the nature of Britain's interests and the course of action most likely to promote them left British objectives subject to conflicting pressures and led to policies which rendered a peaceful outcome of the crisis unattainable.

Russia

The differences over Russian interests which divided the 'nationalists' from the 'Europeans', so prominent at the outset of the Eastern crisis, do not emerge clearly in the available evidence in the present case. Some few indications are noted below, but it is not possible to identify opposed schools of thought, perhaps because there was initial agreement on the need to obtain redress for the Ottoman concessions to France and the Latin Christians.

Three major Russian interests can be readily identified: protecting the Orthodox Church, exercising influence at Constantinople, and achieving a favourable partition of the Ottoman Empire if it should collapse. The first of these required that public respect be paid to Russia's role and that there be no retraction of Orthodox rights, above all in response to pressure from other powers. The second amounted to an interest in reducing the ascendancy which Stratford had achieved for Britain and, ideally, replacing Britain as the leading external power in Constantinople, but not, in reality, to a protectorate. The third interest was articulated by Nicholas in his conversations with Seymour and other diplomats. The main features of his thinking were that neither Britain nor France should have Constantinople, that Russia would control the Principalities and exercise a loose protectorate over Serbia, Britain could annex Egypt and Cyprus, Austria the Adriatic coast and France might have Crete. He had always been more insistent on what should be ruled out for Constantinople than what should be done, but now – though not to the British – he hinted at a temporary Russian occupation, after which it might be a free city with Russian and Austrian garrisons at the Straits.[40] Such a partition would have served Russia's economic interests, but it is not clear how salient this was for the Tsar.

However, it would go too far to say that it was Nicholas's *objective* to partition the Ottoman Empire. His immediate objective was to achieve understandings with Britain and Austria on consultation, and the general outline of a partition, in a contingency which he alone thought imminent. These understandings would probably have broken down in the event, as Britain would have reacted strongly against his plans for Constantinople. Beyond this, Russian objectives remained unclear.

> Canvassing the various possibilities for action before the Menshikov mission, he ended up determined to settle issues with Turkey,

though not sure what the issues were; insistent on getting repar-
ations and guarantees, though unable to define them or assess their
worth; ready for strong measures and confident Turkey would
collapse under pressure, though convinced the status quo was still
desirable and anxious about the final outcome. In short, Nicholas was
ready to open up and solve the Eastern question without believing
that a really good solution was available.[41]

Schroeder's analysis captures the mood of confusion and also suggests
that Nicholas's belief in the imminence of ultimate solutions made it
difficult for the Russian government to formulate well-defined, limited
objectives.

The minimum Russian objectives were to obtain redress for the
Orthodox grievances over the Holy Places and to obtain guarantees for
the future. The first proved feasible, the latter provoked a crisis. One
reason for this, as we have seen, was confusion between ill-defined
'traditional rights' and formal treaty provisions. Nesselrode sought to
make clear to Menshikov that Russia was not in fact seeking a 'protectorate', and the readiness to remove these connotations from its proposals showed a lack of commitment to this larger objective.

But some qualification is in order. The minimum Russian objective
was complicated by a vaguely defined maximum objective which
reflected Russia's interest in primacy in Constantinople. Although this
did not reverse the 1829 policy of preserving the Ottoman Empire, it
did amount to a reversal of 1840–41 in favour of 1833. The proposed
treaties would have granted Russia special rights in Constantinople,
which must have provoked a hostile British reaction. It is surprising
that the Tsar and Nesselrode seemed unaware that this would be the
consequence of a successful Menshikov mission. This wider objective,
and the discussion of even more alarming contingencies, made it
difficult for Russia to give convincing assurances of moderation and
imposed a heavy burden of crisis diplomacy on the other actors.
Moreover, it is arguable that the ambiguity was inherent in the delicate
'balance of prestige' in Constantinople: once this had been disturbed
by Napoleon, the emphatic restoration of Russia's 'traditional rights'
was likely to tilt the balance 'too far' in the eyes of British representatives and their Ottoman supporters.

Britain

Britain's strategic interest in the route to India was not threatened as in
the 1839–41 crisis, though it remained an important underlying consideration. Britain's trade interests in the Ottoman Empire had

increased substantially since the earlier crisis – the Empire was a rapidly growing market for British exports – and this would be threatened by its partition. The British government was well aware of the value of this commercial relationship, but there is little evidence of its importance in British decisions in the crisis.[42] The Peelites with their free-trade principles would have been sensitive to the threat of further annexations by protectionist Russia, but this does not appear to have been a primary concern of decision makers.

Even Aberdeen perceived the prevention of Constantinople's falling under Russian control as a vital interest.[43] Beyond this there was no consensus. Three views of Britain's interests in relation to Russia had crystallised in the 1840s. To liberal and radical opinion, Russia's role in 1848–49 had reinforced its image as the bulwark of reaction; this vocal sector of British opinion welcomed any policy directed against Russia on ideological grounds. Second, politicians such as Palmerston and Russell were ready to exploit this climate of opinion even though their own view of Russia was based on geopolitical considerations: the long-standing conflict over the approaches to India, and the fear that further expansion of Russia in Europe would threaten the balance of power. 'If we do not stop the Russians on the Danube, we shall have to stop them on the Indus.'[44] The third view, that of Aberdeen and his supporters, was that Russia's aims were moderate and the Tsar was willing to abide by the restraints of the European Concert. Despising the popular enthusiasm for Turkey, which he perceived as a backward barbarian state incapable of reform, Aberdeen saw Britain's interest as maintaining good relations with Russia, avoiding overreaction in minor conflicts.

The British government was unable to formulate a coherent objective based on such incompatible analyses. There was agreement that Russia should not be granted a 'protectorate' over Turkey, but disagreement over whether Russia was bent on achieving this and whether it was worth a war to prevent it. Aberdeen's inclination throughout was towards appeasement: to meet reasonable Russian demands and to urge (if necessary coerce) Turkey to comply with them. Palmerston (and Russell for the most part) moved from an initial aim of deterrence to one of military support for Turkey carrying a high risk of war. The public became increasingly convinced that the British objective was to protect Turkey against Russian aggression, even through war. As Palmerston's hope in deterrence faded, he appears to have sought either a diplomatic triumph over Russia or else a variety of war aims directed at weakening Russian power.[45] Russell occasionally formulated a crisis objective, coinciding with Napoleon's, of imposing a settlement on both sides, but never held to this position for long enough to impress it on the Cabinet or to persuade Aberdeen that this was the logic of his own policy.[46]

The British government, then, improvised from stage to stage, compromising between the increasingly powerful demand for firmness against Russia and Aberdeen's dogged resistance to moves closer to the brink. Policy was not guided by clear objectives, but at best by *ad hoc* goals which emerged at each stage. There is much to be said for Schroeder's view that the effective aim, or at least the rule governing policy after the first phase, was to avoid a breach with Turkey and as far as possible to put Russia in the wrong.[47] On this view, the avoidance of war had become by October a residual objective for Clarendon, whose role became increasingly more important than Aberdeen's.

France

France did not have England's strategic and economic stake in the Eastern question, and with the decline of Mehemet Ali French interests were less than in 1839–41. Although France supported the 'European' policy of preserving the Ottoman Empire, the prospect of a Russian fleet in the Eastern Mediterranean did not really alarm French public opinion. The hostility of the left towards Nicholas was not reinforced by imperial rivalry as in the case of England; conflict with Russia was not popular.

The key to French policy lies in Napoleon's wider objectives. His ambition was to remake the map of Europe, but not by the old method of conquest. His appeal, 'I tell you, the Empire means peace', was to the pacific French electorate more than to foreign diplomats. It may have been sincere, but this was against a background of high expectations: France shared a general resentment against the restrictions of 1815, and Louis-Philippe had been condemned for his passive foreign policy. Napoleon must offer something more – *la gloire*. He sought to promote movement and change in Europe and espoused the cause of nationalism, especially in Italy and Poland. France was to regain its place at the centre of European affairs, obtain its sphere of influence, and recover frontiers not clearly specified. Seeing himself aligned with the forces of progress, Napoleon seems to have envisaged the role of military force as legitimate but secondary in bringing about these changes. In the first place, France must avoid diplomatic isolation and must take advantage of opportunities to split the Holy Alliance. A dramatic diplomatic coup would serve his interests better than a war, but he could not rule out all risk of war.[48]

The French interest in the Holy Places was relatively recent and much less explosive than the Russian. Napoleon's energetic diplomacy won France a strong position in 1852, but by 1853 he was willing to compromise so long as he did not suffer a blow to his prestige. It was this, much more than Stratford's diplomacy, which made it possible to resolve the dispute by May 1853.[49]

The events of 1853–54 showed that Napoleon placed a high value on his alliance with England: once committed to a course of action with England, he was trapped into going further than he might have originally envisaged. Of the two allies, it was Napoleon who favoured the flamboyant gesture and who initiated most of the movements of the fleets. As the crisis intensified, however, a basic difference in objectives became clear: as Britain became increasingly committed to unconditional support for Turkey, France more clearly sought to use the sea-powers' military position to impose a settlement on both sides.

The interaction of these objectives can be seen in certain key decisions. Napoleon decided to send the fleet to the East in March without consulting England, accepting the argument that England would have to support a French *fait accompli* because of its stake in Constantinople.[50] The French government urged moving the fleets up to Constantinople in September on the news of rioting there, but unlike Britain, France was willing to recommend the Olmütz proposal to Turkey. By November it was clear that Napoleon differed from Britain in seeking an imposed settlement, uninhibited either by personal or national sympathy for Turkey.[51] Yet he did not break with England over the Olmütz proposals, or even threaten to: a reversal of policy, a break with his only potential ally, risked humiliation or isolation.

French policy in December–January shows the same objectives and the same inability to check the process of escalation. France was first to propose that the fleets not only enter the Black Sea but also demand the withdrawal of the Russian fleet to Sebastopol, on the principle that the dishonour of Sinope required such a step. As the unpopularity of the impending war became clearer, France reverted to the policy of seeking to exploit the strengthened military position diplomatically, clashing with Britain in January. Napoleon broke the deadlock by sending his letter to Nicholas advocating mutual withdrawals, but given Britain's rebuff to Russia over reciprocity in the Black Sea, Napoleon's letter was several days too late, and he still declined to threaten Britain with the possibility of withdrawing French support.[52] His actions were also such as to persuade reluctant French opinion that he had sought to avert the war, but there is no reason to suppose they were for appearances only: a dramatic success would have avoided the risks of an unpopular war.[53]

Austria

Austria's interests were more vitally affected than those of any other power, but they did not point to a clear course of policy. If Russia remained in the Principalities or established client states there, Austria's trading interests would be damaged. If it advanced beyond the Principalities and appealed to Christians to revolt, Austria saw itself with hostile revolutionary neighbours and feared that its own subjects might rebel. On the other hand, the value of the Russian alliance had been proved as recently as 1848–49: some Austrian aristocrats were moved by feelings of sympathy or solidarity, others by insecurity. Austrians were also aware that the vulnerability of their Italian possessions was a source of leverage for Britain and France. Italy was not the only part of the Empire which the Austrians feared losing if they became involved in a revolutionary war, but it was the most vulnerable. It followed that Austria had an overriding interest in seeking to prevent such a war, but there was no consensus on how this was to be done.

Most of the military leaders and Bruck favoured siding with Russia, partitioning European Turkey: Austria would annex or establish a protectorate over Serbia and Bosnia-Herzegovina. Francis Joseph frequently seemed attracted to this solution. Against it Buol raised two fundamental objections: the danger of the loss of Italy, because Britain and France would not accept it; and the need for Russia to moderate its demands in the Balkans to prevent the whole area from becoming a source of revolution. The second argument seems to have counted more heavily. Moreover, Austria as a great power could not become dependent on Russia, which must not be allowed to assume that 1848–49 entitled it to settle the future of the Balkans solely on its own terms.[54] A 'radical' option, alliance with the Western powers, was urged by Hubner and, as war approached, by Buol, but was repugnant to most of the Austrian leaders and was militarily risky: in March 1854 the government made it conditional on an alliance with Prussia, which could not be achieved on these terms.[55]

It is not surprising that a compromise policy was followed. Austria sought indefatigably to promote negotiations in order to avoid war. In the course of these its position shifted from leaning towards Russia to leaning towards the Western powers. In the period of the Vienna Note the main thrust of Austrian diplomacy was to seek to persuade Turkey to make the necessary concessions, and at Olmütz the aim was to patch up a more acceptable version of the Note. Buol then sought to start up fresh negotiations, first in a manner favouring Russia, but when this failed to win support, in a form more attractive to Turkey. In the final phase he continued his efforts to save the peace, taking advantage of whatever circumstances came to hand. In its role as mediator Austria, resisting the more extreme demands from both sides, found itself regarded by all as unreliable and weak, a diplomatic cost which even Metternich had been unable to avoid in a similar situation.

Buol's proposal for an alliance with the Western powers was based on the argument that the immediate threat came from Russia. He calculated that a short war was less dangerous than a protracted one, and saw some hope of avoiding war if the allied demand could be limited to a Russian withdrawal from the Principalities. This adaptation of objectives was initially too radical for his colleagues, but foreshadowed Austrian policy in the war, when precisely such a withdrawal was achieved without Russia's declaring war and thus causing Austria to become a belligerent.

Perception

With the major exception of Britain, the significance of differences of perception within governments was less than in the 1839–41 crisis. Misperception on the other hand was of greater consequence. Russia's failure to perceive the effects of the Menshikov mission on the attitudes of the other powers was responsible for generating an acute crisis, and the strength of a misleading stereotype of Russian aggressiveness among those who shaped British public opinion was a major reason for the repeated failure of attempts at accommodation. Another major failure of perception was the obtuseness of the governments of the powers with regard to the sensitivity of the Ottoman leaders towards the diplomatic formulae which were subject to such frequent variation.

The sources on Britain's role in the crisis provide exceptionally rich documentation on changing perceptions. In view of the crucial nature of that role, British perceptions are traced in greater detail than those of the other actors.

Britain

British decision makers, it has already been noted, differed widely in their perception of the issues, but an even more basic divergence in perception was between the popular image of aggression by the wicked Russian autocrat against the virtuous and chivalrous Turks, and the governmental perception of Turkish independence and integrity as a necessary fiction, and of Nicholas's intentions as uncertain and open to influence. For the most part, however, people and government shared an image of the Russian colossus as a potential threat to Europe and to the Empire. Aberdeen stood apart from this consensus, perceiving Nicholas as fundamentally pacific but capable of being goaded into aggressive reactions. Palmerston's perception of Russia as opportunistically expansionist, encroaching on its neighbours unless it met with strong resistance, lent itself to rhetorical simplification in line with the popular stereotype.

A hostile public image of Russia dated from the 1830s but was intensified by the memory of recent events, especially the oppression of liberalism by Austria and Russia in 1848–49, Turkey's role as sanctuary for the Hungarian and Polish refugees, and Britain's successful use of the fleet to support Turkey on that occasion. The English press, with *The Times* the main exception, achieved a fusion of liberal and patriotic values in interpreting the crisis in this sense. Russia was again the aggressor, Turkey this time the victim, but Britain was laggard in playing its expected role.[56] The press followed the successive acts of the drama, calling for stronger action when Russia occupied the Principalities, expressing relief, tempered by suspicion that Turkey was being sold out, when Russia accepted the Vienna Note, seeing the 'violent interpretation' as proof of Russian duplicity and the Cabinet's gullibility, suspecting the subsequent negotiations and finally erupting in outrage at the news of Sinope. At this point *The Times* finally abandoned its unpopular role of presenting the complex, governmental image of the crisis and joined in the hue and cry, and the *Manchester Guardian* declared that war was inevitable. There followed the campaign in January against Prince Albert, the pillorying of Cobden, Bright and the Peace Society, and the fomenting of a climate of opinion in which a number of prominent dissenters expressed their views in the privacy of their diaries but went along with the popular clamour in public. The assumption behind the public mood is captured in a *Punch* cartoon which sums up the fusion of liberalism and patriotism in depicting Britannia and the lion over the motto, 'Right against Wrong'.[57] The ways in which this stereotype constrained British diplomacy in the later phases of the crisis are discussed below.

The process by which the British government came to perceive Menshikov's proposals as a demand for a 'protectorate' over the Orthodox Christians in the Ottoman Empire provides an extended illustration of the interaction between expectations and perception. As early as December 1852 Colonel Rose, the chargé d'affaires in Constantinople, reported that his Russian counterpart was asserting a protectorate over the Orthodox religion in Turkey under the Treaty of Kainardji, and in March 1853 he reported that the Turkish Foreign Minister shared the same fears.[58] On 9 April Stratford reported that the Russian proposals amounted to 'the exclusive right of intervening for the effectual protection of...the Greek Church'.[59] The threatening tone of the text was heightened by a mistranslation: the right to 'make representations' became a right to 'give orders' to the Churches.[60] On 20 April Stratford reported that Menshikov was still demanding rights of protection over the 'Greek' (Orthodox) Church and thus a vast exercise of influence over the Orthodox population;[61] and he found all the old Russian demands in Menshikov's draft of 5 May, which he read as giving Russia a general right of interference in the Ottoman Empire.[62]

First impressions in London were quite different. The Cabinet had accepted Russian assurances that the demands did not go beyond settling the dispute on the Holy Places, and regarded Rose as alarmist. Aberdeen, who was shown the first draft by Brunnow in mid-April, found 'nothing absolutely new or humiliating to the Porte'. Clarendon found the 5 May draft greatly amended: it did not go beyond existing treaties – 'at least, if it does, the excess will hardly justify an *European war*'. Russell, on the other hand, found the draft hard to swallow and did not blame the Turks for rejecting it.[63] On 16 May Clarendon, now perceiving those same demands as threatening, wrote to Seymour that in view of the many Russian assurances, Menshikov must be exceeding his instructions. On 26 May, he wrote to Stratford that the proposals were incompatible with the honour and independence of the Sultan.[64] It seems clear that the draft Convention confirmed the expectations of those who believed that Russia was seeking a protectorate, but to those not already suspicious of Russian intentions it did not suggest a claim to a general right of interference.

The British government was highly insensitive to the symbolic meaning of changes in the formulation of potential Russo-Turkish agreements. This is shown most clearly in the reaction to reports of the Turkish amendments to the Vienna Note. To Clarendon the amendments 'seem to be made simply for the purpose of *a change*, and of losing time, because on comparing them with the Note, I cannot discover that they alter its sense'. Even Russell found the Turkish response 'wrong-headed', and Aberdeen argued that the Turks could not be sincere. 'Had they rejected the Note altogether, it would have been intelligible.'[65] The whole episode of the Vienna Note demonstrates insensitivity: there was no awareness on the part of the European diplomats of the symbolic import of the changes from the formulations in the 'Turkish ultimatum', nor of the political atmosphere in Constantinople.

The variations in the perception of the risk of war among the leading Cabinet members underline the absence of any shared view of the crisis. They appear to reflect not only different images of the situation and momentary impressions, but also political concerns and perhaps responses to stress.

Aberdeen's expectations are most fully documented. Early in June he thought that the Cabinet did not sufficiently realise the danger of the position, especially in Stratford's authorisation to call up the fleet, and felt that 'we are drifting fast towards war'.[66] By late June Cabinet seemed to have regained control over events: Turkey had been advised not to treat the expected occupation of the Principalities as a *casus belli*, and restrictions had been placed on Stratford's discretion over the fleet; the desire for peace in the Cabinet was increasing 'in proportion as the war mania has increased in the country'. By mid-July he saw 'every probability of success' in the effort to secure a peaceful settlement.[67] The public would soon come to reject the war for which there was now a clamour, and he assured Queen Victoria that peace would not be seriously endangered. But following the 'violent interpretation', he found the prospect almost hopeless, in view of the Emperor's pride, the Turks' fanaticism and Stratford's dishonesty.[68] By early October he felt that the war frenzy in England would soon be beyond his control, but in mid-November, though the state of tension was 'scarcely to be endured', he persisted in thinking it would not lead to the disgraceful insanity of war.[69] His perception of the offensive occupation of the Black Sea was unique: he doubted whether the step was any more dangerous than the existing risk of accidental 'collisions', and in January he was still expressing hope in the latest diplomatic initiatives.[70] Arguably, he overreacted to immediate impressions, was overoptimistic about the prospect of negotiation, and failed to perceive the seriousness of Britain's escalatory moves.

Palmerston moved from a perception that war could be deterred to accepting its probability. Stronger action at the time of the Menshikov mission would have deterred Russia, whose policy was 'always to stop and retire when it was met with decided resistance'.[71] His argument for moving the fleet to the Bosporus at the beginning of July was also in terms of deterrence: it would encourage Turkey, stimulate Austria and Prussia to restrain Russia, and impose a 'wholesome check' on the

Emperor and his advisers. A little later he inferred from a strong Russian statement that the Emperor was bent on a 'stand-up fight', but in September was uncertain about Russian objectives.[72] His October proposals to 'detain' Russian ships in the Black Sea appeared to accept war, and in November he argued that Britain and France should direct the war and the subsequent negotiation. Even so, he still argued that it was right to try for a settlement, though it might be too late.[73] Surprisingly, he did not see the occupation of the Black Sea as necessarily provoking war: Nicholas might feel that he had more to lose than to gain by continuing the war with Turkey.[74] It should be noted, however, that whereas Aberdeen's perceptions were mainly expressed in private communications, Palmerston's were often in political debate, and thus are less reliable.

Clarendon's initial perception of the risk of war resembled Aberdeen's: he expressed alarm over likely Russian reactions to the failure of the Menshikov mission but agreed that the issue in no way justified war.[75] He was optimistic about the July diplomatic initiatives, though not confident that the Turks would accept the Vienna Note. Soon after this he came to see war with Russia as likely, and by early October as close to inevitable. Whereas in mid-September it was impossible 'even to guess how we shall get out of the most curious, and at the same time embarrassing, entanglement that six great nations ever found themselves in', on 9 October, writing to the same correspondent, he saw 'little chance of averting war'.[76] He resented Britain's being tied to Turkey but saw no alternative, and had come round to approving of Palmerston's view in retrospect. 'Russia would then, as she is now, have been ready to come to terms, and we should have exercised a control over the Turks that is not now to be obtained.'[77] Clarendon's perceptions appear to have been dominated by two considerations: that it was too late to follow the most promising policy for avoiding war (Palmerston's), and that the state of public opinion and the precariousness of the government's position ruled out any diplomatic pressure on Turkey. From this perspective it became impossible to perceive any real chance of averting war, even though his role as Foreign Secretary required him to seek diplomatic solutions.

It is likely that British perceptions were affected by stress, but not in the same way as in cases of severe time pressure. Clarendon and Stratford complained of the pressure of attending to dispatches, but there was never the need for rapid decisions characteristic of the 'short' crisis. Reasons for stress included: continuing differences within the Cabinet and threats of resignation; lack of control over the 'ally' Turkey, accentuated by time lags, Stratford's independence and the Turks' increasing 'fanaticism'; and dissonance between the public image of Russia and that of most of the decision makers. Clarendon, in particular, became increasingly unable to tolerate the degree of uncertainty imposed by a serious effort to negotiate in a hostile climate of domestic opinion. In contrast to Buol, Aberdeen and Napoleon, he did not strive for new options.[78]

The most characteristic form of Aberdeen's reaction to stress was to indulge in rationalisation. He denied that his hasty decision to order the fleets to Constantinople or the ultimatum to Russian ships to remain at Sebastopol would have the major escalatory consequences which almost all contemporaries and historians attributed to them.[79] His tendency to blame Stratford for the failure of the government's initiatives illustrates another kind of rationalisation, to place the blame on an individual rather than acknowledge the fundamental weakness of the policy.

France

During the Menshikov mission the French in Constantinople had much the same expectations as the British, perceiving a bid for a protectorate and a claim to a general right of intervention in Turkish affairs.[80] The French government was more apprehensive than the British during this phase: a senior diplomat, Thouvenel, referred to perplexities and fears, and the British ambassador, Cowley, reported in April that 'in Paris the fear that complications would lead to war was universal'.[81] The perception of acute crisis came earlier in France because Nicholas had succeeded in winning the confidence of the British government. Napoleon's early decision to advance the fleet, however, was not so much an attempt to ward off the perceived Russian threat as a bid to secure larger objectives, noted earlier.

The French government was never, like the English, constrained by a public image of the Russo-Turkish conflict, and thus could retain diplomatic flexibility. A question which remains unresolved is how Napoleon and Drouyn perceived the consequences of naval escalation. Only for a brief period, at the time of the Olmütz initiative, was France more hesitant than Britain. For most of the time the French government, like Palmerston, was pressing the British Cabinet to escalate. The available sources do not indicate how the French perceived the risks inherent in their policy.

This may be due to the complexity of French objectives in this phase. If Schroeder is correct, Drouyn, though following the same tactics as Palmerston, consistently sought to achieve a quite different objective:

to divide Austria from Russia, by raising the risk of war and involving Austria in mediation with a view to imposing a settlement. He expressed exasperation with Britain in September for failing to choose between a settlement and stronger support for Turkey, and seems to have continued to think a settlement possible. In November–December French collaboration with Austria was sufficient to alarm Clarendon. Drouyn wished to occupy the Black Sea to gain a counterweight to the occupation of the Principalities, but unfortunately there is no evidence of his expectations concerning the 'ultimatum' confining the Russian fleet to Sebastopol, the most provocative of the French initiatives. France recognised and accepted some risk of war in its escalatory policies, preferring a settlement but tied to the alliance with Britain.[82]

Russia

There can be no doubt that Nicholas's faulty perceptions and expectations played a large part in drawing Russia into a situation far more dangerous than he would knowingly have entered into. He was just as confused as the British government over the implications of the formulae in the Russian proposals to Turkey, wrongly believing that the rights demanded were already granted in the Treaty of Kainardji. Even so, it is difficult to see how he failed to realise that Menshikov's proposals would be perceived as a reversal of the 1841 policy of working with the European powers, and a return to the 1833 policy of unilateralism, and the effect that this must have in the other European capitals.

Three factors go some way towards explaining this, without entirely resolving the puzzle. First was Nicholas's expectation that Turkey was about to collapse, and his consequent preoccupation with understandings relating to that contingency. Second was his overconfidence in solidarity with Austria, based on Russia's role in 1848–49 and reinforced by cooperation with the Leiningen mission: 'but as for Austria I am sure of her, our treaties define our mutual relations'.[83] He was not so sure of Britain, and here the third factor, the absence of warning signals – in contrast to Palmerston's vigorous signalling in 1838 – was important. Nicholas was reassured by Russell's dispatch of 9 February, with its 'eulogies' and 'precious assurances', and continued to be encouraged by Brunnow's dispatches. It is often suggested that he perceived the situation too much in personal terms and was led astray by confidence in his relationship with Aberdeen.

But why did Nesselrode not warn Nicholas of the provocative

character of Menshikov's demands? The Tsar's confusion was far more understandable than the obtuseness of the experienced Chancellor. Part of the reason appears to be that Nesselrode saw the mission as the lesser evil: his principal effort was to dissuade the Tsar from an immediate recourse to force or from raising the issue of the partition of the Ottoman Empire. Nesselrode's apparent confusion over the terms of the Treaty of Kutchuk Kainardji remains surprising, but was in a long-standing tradition of reinterpreting the Treaty as an endorsement of the Tsar's traditional claim to protect the Orthodox Church.[84]

A crucial difference of perception arose between Nicholas and Nesselrode over Turkey's amendments to the Vienna Note. Nicholas, not concerned over formulae and worried by Russia's isolation, considered accepting the amendments. Unfortunately, however, he followed Nesselrode's advice that it would be incompatible with his honour and dignity to do so. Nesselrode failed to perceive this as a crucial turning point, the last occasion on which a diplomatic settlement could have been achieved through a single decision, but his expectation was not unreasonable. He believed that time was on Russia's side: the weather would soon prevent naval operations in the Black Sea, and he assumed that Turkey would not attack the Russian forces in the Principalities.[85] Later, though noting the 'surexcitation des esprits' in London and Paris, gloomy reports and Palmerston-like chicaneries which led him to conclude that Clarendon was building up a case for war against Russia, he still thought that there would be a standstill during the winter.[86] Later still, the tone of Brunnow's denunciations of the British reaction to Sinope suggests that in lamenting its irrationality he failed to perceive its political significance and to send the appropriate advice.[87] The Russian government appears to have been just as surprised as the Austrian by the Anglo-French ultimatum; a mood of gloom set in, which nonetheless did not prevent Russia from taking initiatives in London and Paris seeking to avert the war without dishonour, and in Vienna in the hope of a last-minute understanding with Austria.

Austria

Divergences in the perception of Austria's interests have been discussed in the preceding section. It is not surprising, given his intense concern to prevent the outbreak of a European war, that Buol perceived more possibilities for achieving this, and for longer, than most other decision makers. Aberdeen shared his concern but, subject to the constraints noted above, was much less perceptive. In the light of

Austria's non-partisanship, its perceptions serve as something of an independent check on those of the other powers. Despite his initial support for the Menshikov mission, Buol perceived Menshikov's actions and demands as increasingly threatening and incompatible with Russian promises of moderation, and feared that Russia was claiming a protectorate. The chargé d'affaires, Klezl, had a similar change of perception.[88] One reason, it appears, was the absence of communication with Menshikov or the Russian government, suggesting a unilateral rather than a European policy. Subsequently, Bruck's judgment that Turkey could not be persuaded to sign the Vienna Note provides confirmation that Stratford's role was probably not decisive.[89]

A lively perception of the danger to Austria of any involvement in war motivated Buol's efforts at mediation: he never (at least until February 1854) abandoned all hope that negotiation might yet succeed. He did not have Metternich's awareness of the implications of domestic political pressures, in this case in Britain, and thus did not perceive the effects of Sinope on the prospects for negotiation, and the Austrian leaders were shocked and surprised by the December ultimatum to Russia, which they perceived as extremely provocative; the Emperor is reported to have exclaimed, 'C'est la guerre!'[90]

Strategy and bargaining

To what extent were the parties pursuing coherent bargaining strategies, and what was the overall significance of bargaining in the crisis? For this case, the questions can best be approached by reviewing each phase of the crisis in turn. It will be argued that, while there were numerous actions which appeared to be typical bargaining moves, many of these did not form part of a bargaining strategy, and that even where strategies can be discerned, their implementation was often ineffectual. Thus despite the appearance of intensive bargaining activity, there were important limits to the role of bargaining in the crisis.

During the first phase the initiative was with Russia. If there was confusion over Russian objectives, the immediate strategy was relatively clear, even though its repercussions were underestimated. Menshikov was to achieve a *fait accompli* through intimidating the Turks, and intervention by the powers was to be averted through a policy of reassurance to Britain in order to forestall a hostile Anglo-French coalition. Austrian acquiescence was taken for granted, not bargained for.

Menshikov has frequently been criticised for his delay in executing the strategy. Instead of pressing the Turks while the effects of his military demonstrations and initial humiliation of the Porte were fresh, he indulged in empty threats to leave if his proposals were revealed to the other powers, losing the opportunity to achieve a settlement before de la Cour and Stratford arrived on the scene. Nesselrode wrote expressing concern at the delay, but it seems that the urgency was not sufficiently emphasised.[91] Timing was also important in the final stages of the mission. Menshikov showed flexibility in dropping the more contentious of the provisions, but this was offset by his recourse to ultimata, which was out of harmony with the preceding lengthy delay. Turkey's failure to compromise until the final moment (when the move was 'too little and too late') made a further negative contribution to the course of events: timely counter-proposals would have required Menshikov to reciprocate or else risk putting Russia in the wrong with the other powers.

Menshikov's failure was also due to the nature of the objective he was required to achieve. In February 1853 an Austrian envoy, Marshal Leiningen, had prevailed over a specific demand, that Turkey withdraw from Montenegro and sign an armistice, by means of a credible threat that Austria would go to war. Menshikov was seeking something much less clear-cut: both the form and the wording of the necessary document were open to modification, and the threat was less immediate or compelling. A sudden ultimatum that a particular form of words be accepted lacked credibility.

With France an adversary and Austria assumed to be a supporter, Russian efforts were directed to winning British support or acquiescence. This was done through reassurances, some honest, some misleading or amounting to outright deception. The most straightforward was the pledge that Russia was not seeking to break up the Ottoman Empire and that it would consult Britain in the event of its impending collapse. Even so, Nicholas, in failing to inform Britain of his plans for Russian and Austrian garrisons at the Straits, was misleading, and Brunnow and Nesselrode were even more so in their selective versions of Menshikov's aims. Outright deception took place when Nesselrode assured Seymour that there were no further demands beyond the settlement of the Holy Places dispute.[92]

In view of this deception, Henderson's criticism of the British government is overstated. 'If Nicholas was singularly willing to deceive himself, the British Ministers were singularly unwilling to undeceive him...(the Tsar's) blunders were equalled by those of the British Ministers'.[93] In the light of the many Russian reassurances and the feeling that the Russians had a good case on the Holy Places, the

British ministers' trust was a blunder only if it is held that they should have been suspicious of Russian intentions – but initially there was no strong reason for suspicion.

On Palmerston's view of Russia there was such a reason, based on his view of Russian expansionism.

> The policy and practice of the Russian Government has always been to push forward its encroachments as fast and as far as the apathy or want of firmness of other Governments would allow it to go, but always to stop and retire when it was met with decided resistance, and then to wait for the next favourable opportunity to make another spring on its intended victim.[94]

In November Clarendon told Aberdeen that he now thought that Palmerston had been right, and this 'missed opportunity' has remained a focus of controversy. Conacher sees the Palmerston policy as 'always a risky one, a gamble that might or might not have paid off', but any evaluation must take account of timing.[95] To have sent the fleet to the Dardanelles in March would have been a clear warning signal. By the time it was sent, it was too late to deter the occupation of the Principalities, and a forward policy seemed more and more likely to lead to war rather than deterrence. Schroeder doubts that Palmerston's policy could have succeeded, given the strength of Nicholas's commitment *by late May* – that is to say, after the first phase.[96] But Schroeder's central argument is that, whatever its effect in this particular case, Palmerston's policy of confrontation would have destroyed the understandings on which the Concert of Europe rested, thus weakening the long-term bases of peace. While this is plausible in the later phases, it overlooks the fact that the warning signal had been used successfully in earlier crises and that force demonstrations were a recurring feature of diplomacy in the Eastern question. France and Austria had provided the most recent examples.

The second phase opened with independent Russian and British moves. The occupation of the Principalities was a bargaining move, described by the Russians as a material pledge, intended to induce Turkey to concede Menshikov's demands. Its effect, on the contrary, was to bring about the political climate which eventually led to the declaration of war. The movement of the fleets to Besika Bay was not a clear signal. It expressed an interest and a tacit threat to intervene if Russia encroached too far, but since Turkish territory was already occupied, it was not clear under what circumstances the two powers would advance further. The presence of the fleets, however, inevitably encouraged the Turks, heightening their readiness for war.

We have seen that the Vienna Note emerged as the least partisan of the various suggestions for a settlement. By accepting it, Russia improved its diplomatic credit, but the acceptance also expressed its genuine willingness to settle the conflict. Turkey's demand for amendments was more complex. Buol had first encouraged Turkey to prepare a 'fusion' of the Russian and Turkish notes, and had taken the lead only after this had been delayed.[97] The Ottoman reaction may have reflected resentment at the powers' setting aside of Turkey's own note as much as objections to the provisions themselves. But it was also crucial that there were no sanctions. The British government was unwilling to threaten to withdraw its support if Turkey failed to accept the Note. Aberdeen was willing to do so, but the issue was not confronted squarely by the Cabinet. Clarendon's instructions to Stratford made no reference to sanctions.[98] Only when Turkey rejected the Note was there discussion of withdrawing the fleet, but Aberdeen was alone among the senior ministers in advocating it. Cabinet endorsed Clarendon's view that it was not in Britain's interests to abandon Turkey to Russia and Austria.[99] The possibility of a concerted representation by the four powers does not appear to have been considered. The strength of Turkey's objections to the Note was not put to the test.

The Olmütz declaration made Russian moderation clear, but was not sufficiently responsive to Turkish concerns to bring the parties close to agreement. First, it was another version of the Vienna Note, and the Turkish government had become even more committed to rejecting the Note, although this was not clear to the powers. Second, it was put forward precisely at the time that the Grand Council was meeting to declare war. Stratford saw the diplomatic possibilities of exploiting the delay between this decision and the start of actual hostilities, but something more than the Olmütz declaration was required to put this to good use. There was a need for a 'new' formula, such as Buol had indeed proposed at Olmütz, which would have had to include a pledge to evacuate the Principalities.[100] As it was, hostilities began when the Russian commander rejected a Turkish demand for their evacuation.

Thus, although some of Clarendon's arguments against the Olmütz declaration were very weak, it was not a true 'missed opportunity'. It resolved the conflict satisfactorily from the standpoint of the European powers, but only by ignoring the attitudes which had developed in Turkey as a consequence of the occupation of part of the Ottoman Empire. As in the case of the deterrence of Russia, measures which might have been successful at an earlier stage were insufficient by the time they were attempted.

In the pre-Sinope part of the third phase the powers manoeuvred to find a new basis for a settlement. Buol was able to reject British proposals as pro-Turkish, but Britain and France could equally frustrate a joint Austro-Russian approach. Buol, the decision maker most anxious for a settlement, then gave ground and thus the 5 December proposal appeared relatively favourable to Turkey. After Sinope the search for a settlement was overwhelmed by the moves which escalated the conflict until the declaration of war, above all the Anglo-French decision to 'occupy' the Black Sea and demand the return of the Russian fleet to Sebastopol. Since this fell just short of provoking a declaration of war, it must be regarded as a very risky raising of the stakes. As noted, Napoleon sought to use it to bring about a last-minute bargained settlement, but although Russell for a brief period as well as Aberdeen supported this, Clarendon returned a brusque negative to the Russian request for reciprocity, which in turn led to the breaking of diplomatic relations and the Tsar's scornful rejection of Napoleon's initiative. From then on it was merely a matter of manoeuvring over the grounds for a declaration of war. The frustration of bargaining, despite the French and Austrian efforts, was due to the tacit preference for war on the part of some of the British Cabinet by this time, and an acquiescence in war as inevitable in the case of others, such that there was no effective support in London for reciprocity or even for a delay to consider Napoleon's offer.

Some conclusions may be drawn concerning the limits of bargaining in the crisis as a whole. In contrast to the 1839–41 crisis, none of the powers was able to devise or implement a coherent strategy. Russia's failure was mainly in 'fine tuning' and implementation, both of its earlier coercive strategy and its later accommodative strategy. France did not have sufficient leverage over Britain to prevail with its ambitious strategy of escalating the level of conflict in order to impose a settlement. Britain's alternating moves did not amount to a strategy. In this unfavourable climate Austria, which even in 1839–41 experienced great difficulty in its role as mediator, could not find sufficient common ground to revive the European Concert. The case illustrates the complexity of multilateral bargaining in relation to a significant actor which was not itself one of the acknowledged powers. The powers themselves showed a very weak awareness of Turkey's payoffs, and failed to devise effective sanctions or incentives in their efforts to influence its decisions. Proposals tended to lag behind events: initiatives which might earlier have offered promise were 'too little and too late'.

Arguably, the major limitation on bargaining in the crisis stemmed from the divisions within one of the principal actors, Britain, which found expression in a deeply divided Cabinet. Britain could not adopt a coherent strategy, either of deterrence or accommodation, and its moves were not designed as part of a strategy. Each move of the fleet, for example, was made under pressure from an aroused public, but was not directed towards any well-defined diplomatic objective. The naval moves were what Britain could do and what was expected, but in the absence of a diplomatic strategy, their main effect was to escalate the conflict. They were irrelevant to deterring Russia, since it had moved as far as it intended and was seeking an acceptable settlement. They were not used to enhance Britain's leverage over Turkey, but encouraged it to harden its stand. The reasons for this weakness of British decision making must be sought in the state of Britain's internal politics.

Internal political pressures and constraints

While it was only the British government which was subject to major constraint by public opinion, the political situation in the other states set certain parameters for policy.

In France the Second Empire had been ratified by plebiscite by an overwhelming majority. Napoleon was not under immediate pressure, but was under two conflicting impulses from public opinion. On the one hand, he recognised the deep-seated desire for peace; on the other, Louis-Philippe had been discredited for his 'weak' foreign policy, and his regime had lost prestige accordingly. Thus Napoleon was under some pressure to achieve *la gloire*, but preferably without pressing conflicts to the point of war. As Thouvenel observed in August: the whole of France desires peace, but except for the *bourse*, France wants a policy that is strong and worthy (*digne*); a bad outcome would be very damaging to the Emperor's prestige.[101]

Many observers point to French aversion to war in early 1854.[102] When sympathies had been engaged in the cause of Mehemet Ali in 1840, French attitudes had resembled those in England in 1853. But France had no such sympathy for the Turks, and even Sinope did not greatly arouse French opinion; only Napoleon spoke (privately) of *le sentier d'honneur*.

> To devout Bonapartists it seemed shocking that the new Napoleon should at once seek the alliance of the victor of Waterloo. Napoleon's Russian campaign moreover had inspired France with a profound conviction of the invulnerability of Russia: surely it was foolish, as M. Hugo suggested, to begin one's empire with 1812?... Napoleon ... was engaged in forcing France, in alliance with the nation whom at

100

the time she most disliked, into an attack upon the nation whom she held least capable of being attacked successfully.[103]

In the case of Russia, the issue of the Orthodox Church in Turkey was one of the very few on which there was an effective public opinion. The 'Orthodox Party' not only created pressure to obtain public redress for Russian grievances over the Holy Places, but may also have influenced decisions such as the choice of Menshikov as special emissary, and conceivably the 'violent interpretation' of the Vienna Note. Some contemporaries were mistaken in supposing that Nesselrode was excluded from key decisions: the 'Orthodox' or 'Russian nationalists' did not take over the making of foreign policy. But there is some evidence that Nesselrode was under pressure from certain subordinates and from 'St Petersburg society' to take a hard line at certain crucial points, and that he may have yielded to this pressure.[104] The depth of the animosity towards him in some circles can be seen in vituperative lines composed by the nationalist poet, F.I. Tyutchev, in 1850:

> No! my dwarf, coward without equal...
> You, with your soul of little faith
> Will not lead Holy Russia astray...
> The universal destiny of Russia –
> No! This you cannot change![105]

The most striking feature of the Russian situation, nonetheless, is the extent to which the Tsar was willing and able to make concessions. Not even the exclusion of Russian ships from the Black Sea was a *casus belli* in itself, and the denial of reciprocity was the occasion for breaking relations, not declaring war.

In the case of Austria the position was very different from 1839–41, when Metternich was constrained by Kolowrat's internal priorities. The Emperor now played a larger part in government, the ministerial council serving as an advisory body, though the Emperor's decisions appear to have followed the 'sense of the meeting'. Buol's policies did not enjoy general support: he was too much a 'Westerner' for the conservative military (though not Western enough for a few of his diplomats), but his policies had logic and coherence, given his view of Austria's interests, essentially that of Metternich. Francis Joseph supported him until his recommendation of a Western alliance in March 1854. Nonetheless, Buol was somewhat out of line with the prevailing pro-Russian sentiment in the Austrian aristocracy; thus Austria's role as mediator ultimately leaning towards the Western powers depended in some degree on the accident of personality. It was open to argument

101

where Austria's best interests lay, and others in Buol's position might well have chosen differently.[106]

Britain's entry into the Crimean war has usually been seen as a classic case of the influence of public opinion on foreign policy. Schroeder argues that this has been overstated. Public opinion, he contends, did not dictate the government's course, but only established certain limits. Britain could not openly support Russia against Turkey or accept defeat at Russia's hands. But it was not public opinion which prevented Britain from 'participating in Concert diplomacy': the government could have stopped raising the price of peace or 'exercised enough pressure on her client Turkey to get her to accept a European solution'.[107]

It is clear, however, that public opinion was far more important in this case than in most instances of crisis diplomacy. Schroeder does not sufficiently allow for the extent to which the British government was under pressure from public opinion to make choices which it might prefer not to, given its values and its calculation of interests and consequences. The public image of the issues was, from the governmental point of view, oversimplified and dangerously charged with emotion. Moreover, timing is relevant to some of Schroeder's contentions: Britain's influence over Turkey, as we have seen, diminished as the crisis intensified.

One major effect of the public climate was to strengthen the hand of Palmerston and Russell in pressing for stronger measures. Their threats to resign spelled danger not only to the government's slender majority but to its policies: any successor to Aberdeen would have been far less pacific. A divided coalition government uncertain of its parliamentary majority was far more vulnerable to the pressure of public opinion than a government with a clear majority, or even a united government with a narrow majority, would have been.

Apart from inhibiting the government from putting pressure on Turkey, and establishing a presumption that war for Turkey was the courageous, *right* course of action – the alternative being weak, cowardly and immoral – the desire to placate public opinion played some part in the three main decisions on the fleet. Clarendon saw the first as the least that would satisfy public opinion.[108] Although the second, the decision by Clarendon and Aberdeen to order the fleet to Constantinople, was not overtly a response to public pressure, it was taken in an irregular manner shortly after the storm over the 'violent interpretation'; Aberdeen's recourse to unconvincing justifications suggests that he was tacitly responding to the public mood. The final decision to deny the Black Sea to the Russian navy was taken in the aftermath of the outburst over Sinope and Palmerston's resignation. Public attitudes ensured that a further escalatory move would be made, and the sense of the inevitability of war – unique to Britain – reduced the incentive for caution.

Determinants of the outcome

Historians, seeing this as a case of an 'unnecessary' war, have speculated on the contingencies of circumstance and personality which might have led to a different outcome. 'Had Nicholas been weak, Aberdeen strong, or Menshikov tactful, there might have been no war.'[109] Thus Temperley. More elaborately, in Schroeder's words:

> Had a better negotiator than Menshikov been sent, or had he presented his compromise proposals before Redcliffe arrived, or had the Grand Vizier Mehemet Ali not been overthrown in favour of Redcliffe's protégé Reshid Pasha, or had Russia simply been clearer from the outset what guarantees she wanted, the outcome could have been different.[110]

Richard Smoke sees the case as 'a classic example of an escalation sequence that got out of control'.[111] The present account endorses this widely shared judgment. The war did not come about because of basic incompatibilities between the values and interests of the powers. Although there were stakes in the Eastern question for which they were prepared to go to war, they preferred to maintain the uneasy equilibrium which had been reaffirmed in 1841.

There was a progressive narrowing of options through the successive phases of the crisis. The main 'lost opportunities', it has been suggested, occurred during the Menshikov mission, when Russian policy was still relatively flexible and diplomatic formulae had not yet acquired the symbolic significance which was to render agreement so elusive. Once Russian relations with Turkey were broken off, the conflict became much more difficult to unravel. The Vienna Note was the only diplomatic initiative which came at all close to success: more skilful drafting, concerted pressure on Turkey or less rigid advice by Nesselrode could have led to a compromise. By the time of the Olmütz initiative, with Turkey already at war with Russia, the chances of a diplomatic settlement had greatly receded and the proximity of the English and French fleets to the fighting created a likelihood of escalation among the three powers. Sinope provided the catalyst: given the internal political context, Britain had to respond. For somewhat contingent political reasons, the harshest of the range of possible

103

responses, the offensive occupation of the Black Sea, was chosen. The same political constraints led Britain to reject out of hand the Russian request for reciprocity, preventing the last-minute bargaining preferred by the other powers. From the standpoint of those powers, Britain was something less than a 'rational actor' in the later phases of the crisis. To understand British policy one needed a comprehensive grasp of the working of Cabinet and parliamentary politics on an issue which roused exceptional public emotion – a setting quite alien to the experience of continental aristocrats.

What, then, are the primary elements of a satisfactory explanation for the outcome? We have rejected one of the traditional British explanations, that there was a deliberate Russian challenge to the status quo. This is reaffirmed by F.H. Hinsley, who argues that Russia's policy of unilateral aggrandisement amounted to abandoning the ground rules of the Concert of Europe. Like Gladstone, Hinsley sees Britain and France as going to war in order to preserve that system.[112] Schroeder's interpretation stands this traditional British view on its head. Though Russia was mainly responsible for starting the crisis, it was Britain which was mainly responsible for preventing its resolution, by abandoning the norms and constraints of the Concert system. In particular, Britain obstructed the diplomatic efforts centred on the Vienna conference, turned the crisis into a head-to-head confrontation and broke the first law of the Concert, 'Thou shalt not challenge or seek to humiliate another great power.' Historians have failed to see this because they have accepted a crude balance of power model, and have not realised the incompatibility between the diplomacy of confrontation favoured by Palmerston and the Concert rule of 'grouping' the offending power and achieving a solution collectively in terms of agreed norms.[113]

Schroeder's penetrating analysis is far superior to the traditional view, but requires some qualification. It is true that Britain's policy, at least from October, was not in accordance with the norms of Concert diplomacy, and that its unconditional support for Turkey was the main reason for the frustration of the diplomatic initiatives in the later phases of the crisis. Britain was indeed the crucial actor in those phases: it was Britain's inflexibility, due to internal political instability and the strength of anti-Russian sentiment, which negated any prospect of a settlement. But this was after the best opportunities had already been fumbled.

Moreover, the ineffectiveness of the Concert in 1853 was not solely due to Britain's defection. As the 1839–41 crisis shows, the norms of the Concert had often been stretched or observed only grudgingly. Direct confrontations had taken place before, especially in relation to the Eastern question. In the early 1830s the other powers had acquiesced in unilateral Russian action *vis-à-vis* Turkey. The 1839–41 crisis established the principle of European regulation of major questions concerning the Ottoman Empire. France was the first power to violate this understanding, in 1852; Russia's unilateral response further weakened it.

More fundamentally, the advent of Napoleon III brought to power a government in France which not only lacked any commitment to the Concert, but sought in the long run to undermine the 1815 settlement and the Concert norms and mechanisms. France's defection was more thoroughgoing than Britain's: arguably, the eclipse of the Concert after the Crimean war was not only due to its failure to prevent that war, but also due to the strengthening of the position of France – the adversary of the system – and the weakening of Austria, its most consistent protagonist. This speculation aside, so far as the crisis itself was concerned, the Concert was weakened from several quarters, not only from one. The most bellicose of the powers was not isolated, like France in 1840, but allied to an exponent of brinkmanship. It is instructive to compare the roles of two of the architects of the 1841 settlement, Nesselrode and Palmerston, in the two crises. Nesselrode did not enjoy the degree of control which the Tsar had accorded him in 1839–41, while Palmerston's relative restraint and Concert-mindedness in the earlier case gave way to his confrontationist propensities, not disciplined by the responsibilities of office. The reasons for the failure of diplomacy in 1853–54 were many, and multidimensional.

6 THE RUSSO-JAPANESE CRISIS, 1903–1904

The crisis between Russia and Japan offers an instructive example of an unfamiliar path to war, but one which may have parallels when established powers are challenged by adversaries not yet accepted as major actors. For the greater part of the crisis the Japanese leadership was preoccupied with the potential *casus belli* and the other European powers had no doubt that there was a serious risk of war, but until the final weeks the Russians found the idea of a Japanese attack almost unthinkable – a state of mind not unlike the American in 1941 and to a lesser extent in 1950 preceding China's intervention in the Korean war. When the Russian leadership became aware of the danger it began to seek to avert it, but never reached the point of squarely confronting its choices. The war is seen here as stemming from this deep-seated Russian misperception of the seriousness of the Japanese challenge, not from any 'inevitable' clash of the two empires. Thus it was an 'unnecessary' war, though for quite different reasons than the Crimean.

This interpretation runs counter to the view of the leading UK authority, Ian Nish, that the differences between the two sides over Korea and Manchuria were too great to permit compromise:[1] in effect, Russia would concede a sphere of influence to Japan only if defeated in war. While neither view can be demonstrated conclusively, reasons will be offered for the present interpretation.[2] The issue brings out the significance of the setting, a contest for local influence between a newly emerging modern power for which the region was of vital concern and an overextended empire for which, in the last analysis, it ranked low in its priorities. There were no accepted ground rules for such a contest.

The adversaries present a striking contrast. Japan's goals and strategies were carefully formulated whereas Russia's remained undefined; Japanese perceptions were sharp but Russia suffered from 'blurred vision'.[3] Japan's decision making processes fully satisfied the criteria for procedural rationality, whereas for most of the crisis Russia's

106

suffered from a high degree of fragmentation. In these circumstances, while there was the appearance of bargaining, a true bargaining process which might have clarified the issues never developed: the Japanese government's decision for war, entirely reasonable in the light of the evidence available to it, was based on a misreading of Russian attitudes.

The setting[4]

The mid-1890s saw intense imperialist rivalry in Northeast Asia: the powers most vitally concerned were Russia and Japan, but they were constrained by the policies and alignments of the other powers. The two appeared unevenly matched: the giant Russian Empire extended its territorial control as far as Port Arthur and established a predominant economic position in Manchuria, while Japan was constantly frustrated – compelled to relinquish the gains resulting from its victories over China in 1894–95 and denied a free hand in Korea as a counterweight to Russia's gains in Manchuria.

The strategic significance of Russia's frontier with the decaying Chinese Empire was greatly enhanced by the construction of the Trans-Siberian Railway, which began in 1891, and Sergei Witte's appointment as Finance Minister the following year ensured that the project would be pursued with vigour. Russia's opportunity to establish a presence in Manchuria arose after the Sino-Japanese war of 1894–95. Despite Japan's victories over China, it was compelled to return the Liaotung Peninsula, including Port Arthur, to China by a joint demand from Russia, France and Germany. Russia adopted this policy after considering supporting Japan against China and the powers, in return for an ice-free port in Korea, but the danger to Russia's ambitions in Japan's establishing itself in southern Manchuria counted against this latter option.

Although Russia made no immediate demands on China, it rightly anticipated being able to do so in the guise of the latter's friend and protector. In 1895–96 it joined France in a loan to enable China to pay its war indemnity, established the Russo-Chinese Bank to promote Russian projects in Manchuria, and obtained an eighty-year lease of a zone to construct the Chinese Eastern Railway across northern Manchuria, thus shortening the Trans-Siberian Railway and establishing an important interest on the periphery of China. At the same time, Russia denied Japan compensation to balance its own advances. It rejected Japan's proposal for separate spheres of influence in Korea: the Lobanov–Yamagata Agreement of June 1896 required the agreement of both powers for any intervention in Korea, but was followed by unilateral Russian attempts to gain influence.

The precarious equilibrium was upset in 1897 by Germany's seizure of Kiaochow, in response to the murder of German missionaries. Russia obtained as compensation a twenty-five-year lease of Port Arthur (March 1898), and sought to consolidate its new position by the construction of a railway link, the South Manchurian Railway, joining the Chinese Eastern Railway at Harbin. Russia had now acquired an ice-free port and a railway network generally seen as guaranteeing its commercial and strategic dominance in Manchuria. Witte had questioned the timing and tactics of expansion, but not the goal itself. Angered by this turn of events, Japan sought greater compensation – a free hand in Korea in return for renouncing any interest in Manchuria (the 'exchange policy') – but was again rebuffed. Under the Rosen–Nishi Convention of April 1898, Russia acknowledged Japan's predominant commercial interest in Korea, but both powers were accorded equal rights with respect to military or financial intervention, and continued to compete vigorously for influence.

When the Boxer Rebellion of 1900 threatened the interests of the European powers in China, Russia sought to take advantage of its geographical position to further consolidate its hold over Manchuria. Its troops occupied not only the railway zone, where they were needed to maintain order, but the whole of Manchuria. However, Russia was unable to derive political benefit from the occupation. In February 1901 it attached conditions to its withdrawal, in particular that China would grant no railway or economic concessions to others in any of the regions bordering on Russia. The Chinese government, however, conscious of British, American and Japanese support, rejected these proposals. Russia in turn rejected Japan's protest against the terms of the proposed agreement, provoking renewed anger in Japan. In the second half of 1901 Russia remained unable to negotiate acceptable conditions for its military withdrawal, and the leading Japanese proponent of cooperation with Russia, the elder statesman Ito, was again unsuccessful in persuading Russia to agree to grant Japan a free hand in Korea.

To the Russians' surprise, Britain agreed to this key Japanese demand as one of the provisions of the Anglo-Japanese alliance of February 1902. The alliance protected the two partners by the reciprocal undertakings that each would remain neutral if the other became involved in war with one other power in defence of its interests in China or Korea, but would provide armed support if it became involved in war with a second power. This unexpected development

108

led Russia to reduce its terms for withdrawing from Manchuria. The convention signed with China in April 1902 provided for a withdrawal in three six-month phases, subject only to the general proviso that there must be no disturbance nor action by other powers which might prevent it. The first phase of the withdrawal was completed on schedule by October 1902.

The Russian government reviewed its Far Eastern policies in the later part of that year. Order had not been fully restored in Manchuria and economic competition from Britain, the United States and Japan threatened its investment there, at a time when the extraordinary cost of that investment was becoming more widely understood. In August, when Japan once again proposed a spheres of influence understanding with respect to Manchuria and Korea, Russia deferred its answer. Witte recommended that the military withdrawal be completed and that Japan be accorded a free hand in Korea. His long-term goal remained imperialistic: to delay the expected partition of China until Russia could consolidate its position in Manchuria, eventually oust Japan from Korea and gain a larger share of China than it could expect at present. In the meantime, his Finance Ministry would retain the full responsibility for Russian interests in Manchuria.

However, he could no longer dominate Russia's Far Eastern policy. In a series of meetings between November 1902 and July 1903 the principal ministers, the ambassadors in China, Japan and Korea, and certain other advisers formulated the policy termed the 'New Course', essentially a compromise between the views of Witte, Defence Minister Kuropatkin and Aleksander Bezobrazov,[5] discussed below, but lacking the clear strategic rationale of any one of them. It was agreed that the second phase of the military withdrawal, due in April 1903, should be delayed. The reasons included immediate difficulties relating to logistics and weather, the desire to seek further concessions from China and a perceived need to reinforce the Russian troops in the region, which had been reduced after the defeat of the Boxer Rebellion. They now appeared insufficient to secure Russia's exposed interests when Japan's military strength was increasing and China was being encouraged to resist Russian demands.

The guarantees now sought from China were intended to exclude foreign competition in Manchuria by prohibiting the lease of any of the evacuated territory to a foreign power or the opening of any further treaty ports, and requiring that if any further Chinese administrative responsibilities were transferred to foreigners, a separate Russian administration would be provided for Manchuria. While the Russians may have regarded these as clarifications, as Malozemoff claims, they appeared to China and the powers to be new conditions for withdrawing.[6] China's prompt rejection of the conditions in April precluded a quick resumption of the withdrawal.

With regard to Korea, approval was finally given in April to a long-standing proposal to develop a Russian concession on the Korean side of the Yalu river. It was to be on a purely commercial basis, but was to be defended militarily. Policy towards Korea as a whole was formulated at a ministerial conference in Port Arthur in July. Although Bezobrazov suppressed Tsar Nicholas II's directive that Japan should be permitted to occupy most of Korea after the military reinforcement in Manchuria had been completed, the conference nonetheless reached a similar decision: Russia should not occupy northern Korea, and should limit itself to a protest if Japan occupied southern Korea.

The final aspect of the New Course was administrative. Russian interests in Manchuria would no longer be controlled by the Minister of Finance, with military and diplomatic representatives reporting separately to St Petersburg. The administration of the whole of the Russian Far East, including diplomatic relations as well as the armed forces and economic interests, was to be unified in the hands of a single official, Admiral Alekseiev, the governor of Port Arthur and commander of the Pacific Fleet. In a telegram to Alekseiev confirming these new powers, the Tsar summed up the central thrust of the New Course:

> In minimal time and without balking at the necessary expenditure, our fighting power in the Far East is to be placed in complete equipoise with our politico-economic tasks, giving a demonstration palpable to all of our determination to defend our right to exclusive influence in Manchuria.[7]

The phases of the crisis

Phase 1: The onset of crisis (April–June 1903)

The initial phase of the crisis may be taken as the period from Russia's postponement of its withdrawal from Manchuria in April to the decision of the Imperial Conference in Tokyo in late June to seek a general settlement of Japan's differences with Russia. Russia's actions precipitated a crisis in the eyes of the Japanese decision makers. Opinion in Japan ranged from the view of the *genro* ('elder statesmen', the former prime ministers) – that Japan should seek to improve its position in Korea but not raise the issue of Manchuria – to the view of the Anti-Russian League and the division chiefs of the General Staff, that it should demand Russia's withdrawal from Manchuria even at the risk of war.[8]

110

The first indication of the government's policy was the decision of a meeting of the Prime Minister and Foreign Minister (Katsura and Komura) with two of the *genro*, Ito and Yamagata, on 21 April. The meeting agreed on four principles, amounting to the Korea–Manchuria 'exchange' policy: Japan should protest if Russia failed to withdraw its troops from Manchuria; taking advantage of the Manchurian issue, it should open negotiations to solve the Korean question; it should insist that Russia recognise its predominant rights there, and should be prepared to recognise Russia's predominant rights in Manchuria. The Korean question was to be resolved once and for all.[9]

The Imperial Conference of 23 June, attended by all five *genro*, Katsura, Komura and the Ministers for the Army and Navy, agreed to open negotiations with Russia on the basis of a memorandum by Komura. Although he stated that the principal aim was the security of Korea, Komura's suggestion that this required the restriction of Russian conduct in Manchuria within the limits of existing treaties appeared to go beyond the 'exchange' or spheres of influence concept, an issue on which the Japanese were to remain ambivalent. His specific proposals included, in addition to the mutual recognition of predominant rights in Korea and Manchuria (the 'exchange'), acknowledgment of the independence and territorial integrity of China and Korea, and the principle of equal opportunity, presumably intended to preclude the annexation of Manchuria and also challenging Russia's economic monopoly there. Okamoto notes a difference in perspective between the *genro* and the government leaders, the former anticipating a peaceful solution, the latter being more ready to press Japan's demands and more inclined to expect war. Komura's concluding words acknowledged the risks in the course on which Japan was embarking: 'Consequently, I believe it to be essential that, in commencing negotiations, Japan be fully resolved to achieve its objectives, whatever the costs.'[10] This left open, however, the question for precisely which objectives Japan was to be prepared to risk war. What was clear was that Japan would not accept another rebuff to its basic demands concerning Korea. This was a new Japanese attitude, reflecting an improvement in Japan's military position: without this new resolve, there would have been no crisis.[11]

Phase 2: The opening bids (July–early October)

Komura sought to make clear that this was a new departure by instructing the ambassador, Kurino, to inform the Russian government of Japan's desire for a general understanding with respect to 'the regions of the extreme East, where their interests meet, with a view to defining their respective special interests in those regions'. The Russian Foreign Minister, Lamsdorf, accepted the desirability of a 'full understanding'. Komura advised Kurino that the Japanese government believed that the moment was opportune, 'and it is believed that, failing this opportunity, there would be no room for another understanding'.[12]

Japan's opening proposal, submitted on 12 August, followed the lines set out at the Imperial Conference, and was formulated in the one-sided manner to be expected in an opening bid, but suggested that the government sought something more than a symmetrical 'exchange'.

1 Respect for the independence and territorial integrity of China and Korea, and equality of commercial rights (the 'Open Door');

2 Recognition of Japan's *dominant* interests in Korea and Russia's *special interest in railway enterprises* in Manchuria (emphasis added);

3 Russia to accept the possible extension of the Korean railway into South Manchuria;

4 The right to send troops to Korea or Manchuria, respectively, for limited purposes and for a limited duration;

5 Japan's exclusive right to advise the Korean government on reforms or military matters.[13]

The proposals went far beyond those submitted by Ito in 1901, which had been limited to Korea and even there had excluded the use of Korean territory for strategic purposes. They represented a further stiffening of the proposals submitted in 1902, to which Russia had not responded.[14]

A number of developments before the Russian counter-proposal of 3 October worsened the atmosphere from the Japanese standpoint. There was greater activity in Russia's Yalu concession, even though reports may have exaggerated its significance. New conditions submitted to China on 6 September were more limited than those rejected in April, but heightened the suspicion that Russia was seeking a pretext to remain. Most importantly, on 23 August Russia demanded that the negotiations be transferred from St Petersburg to Tokyo, where they would be under the authority of the Viceroy of the Far East, a new office created on 12 August, to which Alekseiev had been appointed. Komura resisted this apparent downgrading of the significance of the negotiations, but on 9 September consented to a procedure which was to introduce further delays into the already cumbersome Russian decision making process.[15]

Protracted communications among the Russian leaders delayed their reply until 3 October. Whereas the Tsar's initial draft fore-shadowed an acceptance of the 'exchange' concept, the final proposal was as one-sided an opening bid as its Japanese counterpart.[16] The sole reference to Manchuria was Japan's acceptance that it was 'in all respects outside her sphere of influence'. Whereas this left Russia entirely unrestricted, Japan would accept a number of restrictions in Korea which would qualify Russia's recognition of its 'preponderating interests' and right to give advice and assistance: the requirement that troops be recalled after completing a specified mission, the non-use of Korean territory for strategic purposes, and – an entirely new pro-vision – the establishment of a neutral zone in Korea north of the 39th parallel, that is, in more than one-third of the country. Thus both sides had now made proposals more extreme than those in the earlier negotiations.

Phase 3: The second round (mid-October–mid-December)

This can be seen as the crucial phase in the negotiations, the turning point in the crisis. Japan offered significant concessions, but the Russians failed to reciprocate. In consequence, the Japanese attitude hardened; the position of the *genro* favouring a conciliatory line was weakened. By the end of this phase the Japanese leaders could agree on the initiation of war, unless Russia were to make concessions which now appeared unlikely. The significance of this phase was clear to the Japanese leadership, but not at all to the Russians.

The opening moves were not conciliatory. On 8 October, the origi-nal date for the completion of the Russian military withdrawal from Manchuria, Alekseiev conducted a military review which an observer described as 'a review of defiance: defiance of China, defiance of Japan, defiance of the world's public opinion'.[17] On the same day the United States and Japan signed treaties with China, opening three cities in Manchuria – Mukden, Tatungko and Antung – to foreign commerce. In late October the Russians reoccupied Mukden after friction with Chinese officials.

Nonetheless, some possibility of a compromise appeared to emerge in the negotiations. The second Japanese proposal, on 30 October, was formulated after four meetings between Komura and Rosen, the Russian ambassador, and after the *genro* had pressed for a more conciliatory stance.[18] The proposed 'exchange' was now much more symmetrical: each side would acknowledge the other's special interests and accept that Korea/Manchuria respectively were outside its sphere of special interest, though the respective commercial rights were to be acknowledged. The extension of the Korean railway was now subject to Russian agreement, Japan would refrain from establishing military installations on the Korean coast, and a neutral zone extending fifty kilometres on each side of the Korean–Manchurian frontier was proposed. There was no longer a restriction on Russian military intervention in Manchuria (nor the parallel restriction on Japan in Korea), and no insistence on equal economic opportunity.

Russian decision making was delayed by the absence of the Tsar, on vacation in Darmstadt and later on his Polish estate. The main responsibility rested on Alekseiev, whose preference appears to have been to prolong the negotiations pending Russia's military reinforcement.[19] There was little or no awareness of the seriousness with which the Japanese might view the Russian response. The second proposal, finally communicated on 11 December, failed to reciprocate Japan's concessions, except on two minor points. There was now agreement on the extension of the Korean railway and on a broad definition of Japan's rights of military intervention in Korea. On the major points, however, the gap remained, or was even wider. There was no mention of Manchuria, and Russia maintained its insistence on the complete prohibition of any strategic use of Korean territory and on its original proposal for a neutral zone north of the 39th parallel. In effect, while Japan was now prepared to accept marginally greater restrictions in Korea than it was demanding in Manchuria, Russia was still demanding major restrictions in Korea but offering nothing at all in Manchuria.

The French Diplomatic Documents confirm that Rosen had provisionally accepted Japan's proposals on Korea ('agreed to *ad referendum*') but that the Tsar had subsequently upheld Alekseiev's objection to them.[20] This would explain why there was optimism in Tokyo in October–November, and would suggest that the Japanese were disappointed not only by the uncompromising content of the second Russian proposal, but also because it withdrew a concession which they had expected to receive as part of a quid pro quo for their own concessions, and which must have been taken into account in their formulation of their own second proposal.

Phase 4: The late negotiations (mid-December 1903–February 1904)

The Japanese responded promptly to the Russian note. A *genro*

114

conference accepted Komura's proposal that Russia be asked to reconsider its exclusion of Manchuria from the negotiations. On 21 December, the date of the third Japanese proposal, Katsura assured Yamagata that Japan would not resort to war for the sake of Manchuria, but the *genro* now seemed to be reconciled to war over Korea unless Russia unexpectedly accepted Japan's conditions.[21] These were formulated as amendments to the second Russian proposal, and amounted to a return to Japan's more limited restriction on military installations on the Korean coast and the complete suppression of the clause proposing a neutral zone. These, the Japanese now claimed officially, had been previously agreed to *ad referendum*. At the same time, in support of the inclusion of Manchuria, Japan referred to the initial agreement that the negotiations were to cover every region of the Far East. On 24 December the senior *genro* gave their consent to war preparations, which were approved by a special Cabinet on 28 December.[22]

The Russian leaders, meeting on that date for the first time since the beginning of the negotiations, now at last realised the gravity of the situation.[23] The meeting rejected Alekseiev's advice that the negotiations be discontinued, and that Japan be permitted to occupy Korea without formal Russian approval. It resolved to continue the negotiations in an attempt to avoid war, and agreed on the significant concession of reintroducing Manchuria, accepting Japan's rights there under existing treaties 'exclusive of the establishment of settlements'. At Kuropatkin's insistence, however, the neutral zone in Korea and the broader renunciation of all strategic uses of Korean territory remained in the third Russian counter-proposals of 6 January.

The deadlock over Korea determined the Japanese reaction. An Imperial Conference on 12 January resolved that the negotiations had become futile, but that since military preparations were not yet complete, a fourth proposal should be formulated.[24] It reaffirmed Japan's previous stand on all the contested issues, in particular demanding the suppression of both Russian amendments on Korea. The only concession was with respect to settlements in Manchuria: Japan would be satisfied provided it received equal treatment with any other power with settlements. The tone of the fourth proposal was close to peremptory: the note concluded with the phrase 'further delay in the solution of the question will be extremely dangerous to the two countries'.

Far from expressing outrage or construing this as an ultimatum, the Russian government began to explore the possibility of a compromise far more seriously, taking advantage of France's interest in averting the impending war. The French Foreign Minister, Delcassé, had two concerns. A war in the Far East would divert Russia from maintaining the European balance against Germany – and the Kaiser was encouraging Russian ambitions in East Asia for precisely that reason. And it would obstruct Delcassé's goal of bringing about a *rapprochement* with Britain, since they would be supporting opposite sides.

Although the Japanese ambassador in Paris, Motono, was not empowered to negotiate, Delcasséé sought his 'personal' views on the potential for compromise, and drew him sufficiently far into an informal negotiation to earn him a rebuke from Komura for his failure to insist that the last Japanese proposal was an irreducible minimum.[25] The French diplomatic documents show that Lamsdorf, while not authorised to concede the whole of the Japanese demands, was seeking to ascertain the Japanese minimum and was ready to recommend substantial concessions.[26] The final Russian proposal, on 3 February, abandoned the reference to settlements in Manchuria and abandoned entirely the proposed neutral zone in Korea, the principal issue in the deadlock in the second round.

The sources differ over the reason for the delay in communicating the final Russian proposal to Tokyo until after Japan had initiated hostilities. While there is some support for Russian allegations that the Japanese delayed the transmission of the coded telegram from Port Arthur to Rosen in Tokyo from 4 or 5 February until 7 February, the French documents provide an explanation which is more credible in view of the relevant dates and the lack of motive for deception. On 4 February Lamsdorf requested that Delcassé explain to Motono that it was necessary to seek Alekseiev's agreement before the proposals could be sent to Tokyo, which would delay them until 5 February or even 8 February.[27]

Meanwhile, by the end of January the Japanese leaders had concluded that the Russians would not respond favourably. Kurino could obtain no response to his increasingly urgent requests for Russia's reply, but his impressions led him to the incorrect assessment that Russia would not abandon the proposed neutral zone in Korea. The French mediation was suspected because France was also tacitly supporting a Russian attempt to encourage the Korean government to issue a declaration of neutrality, a step which would have greatly embarrassed Japan, and moreover, any mediation at this point was perceived as assisting Russia's delaying tactics.[28]

On 30 January the *genro* agreed with the governmental leaders that the time for a resolute decision had arrived, since nothing was to be expected from the negotiations. An Imperial Conference on 4 February decided unanimously for war, despite the risks which were fully recognised: delay was seen as even more disadvantageous.[29] On 5 February diplomatic relations with Russia were broken off; the next day Japanese troops embarked for Korea; and on 8–9 February Japan launched its surprise attack on the Russian squadron at Port Arthur.

Both White and Nish argue that the two sides remained so far apart that, even if the final Russian proposal had arrived in time, Japan's decision of 4 February was unlikely to have been changed.[30] This may be a correct reading of the attitudes of the Japanese leaders by then, given all that had gone before. Even as late as 24 January, however, Katsura had advised the Emperor that, whereas Japan's decision for peace or war was clear if Russia were to accept fully or reject the final Japanese proposal, the decision would have to be considered further if Russia were to accept only in part.[31]

Reviewing the negotiations as a whole, their most remarkable feature is that it was only in the final phase, when the Japanese perceived the negotiations to have failed, that Russia's proposals came close to reflecting its willingness to accept the essentials of a Korea–Manchuria 'exchange' in order to avoid war. If the Tsar had not supported Alekseiev against Rosen in the second round, a compromise would have been within reach at that stage. Concerns for prestige and a divergence in long-term perspectives and expectations would still have represented obstacles to agreement, but a convergence of short-term interests would have worked in its favour. The war came as and when it did because bargaining did not take place soon enough to modify the parties' misperceptions.

The role of the powers

The crisis was essentially between two parties, the other powers remaining on the sidelines. This was in marked contrast with the situation in 1895, when France and Germany had joined Russia in compelling Japan to surrender part of its gains from the Sino-Japanese war. The pattern of alignment was changed fundamentally by the Anglo-Japanese alliance, in particular its provision that Britain would support Japan if it were at war with two powers in defence of its interests in China and Korea.

This would probably have deterred France from intervening in support of Russia, but as we have seen, Delcassé was seeking an entente with Britain for other reasons: for support against Germany, and more immediately in order to win British agreement to France's gaining control of Morocco.[32] France also feared that Russia might be weakened by the war and of less value as an ally against Germany.

117

It was precisely this prospect which attracted the German government, and Kaiser Wilhelm II's correspondence with the Tsar sought to stimulate his ambitions in the Far East. Germany had, however, made it clear to Russia before the crisis that its own interests there were purely commercial. It had previously disappointed Britain and Japan by declining to support them against Russian expansion in Manchuria, Chancellor von Bülow having gone so far as to state that Manchuria's fate was 'a matter of absolute indifference to Germany'.[33]

Britain, having ended its policy of isolation in order to promote a balance against Russia in the Far East and to reduce the potential overcommitment of its navy, was nonetheless aware of the alliance's potential risks. A number of competing views of Britain's interests were formulated, ranging from Foreign Secretary Lansdowne's proposal to seek to avert war through mediation to military advice that Britain should enter the war at the outset in order to prevent a Japanese defeat. The Cabinet recognised that this would be adverse to British interests, but the Prime Minister (Balfour's) view prevailed: that Britain should avoid being drawn into war with Russia through too close involvement with Japan, the assumption being that Japan would suffer at most a limited defeat and that Russia would be weakened and overextended.[34] The ensuing policy of strict neutrality reflected a reluctance to assume responsibilities or to create expectations by seeking to advise or influence Japan's decisions: thus Britain declined to join France in mediation. Japan's readiness to risk war to 'contain' Russia served British interests, but the evidence does not support the charge that Britain 'egged Japan on'.[35]

The remaining power with interests in Northeast Asia, the United States, which had recently proclaimed the Open Door policy towards China, was hostile to Russia's monopolistic designs in Manchuria and ready to cooperate with Japan and Britain in asserting its commercial rights, but entirely unwilling to use force to support its claims. Thus, cooperation with Japan on commercial issues did not extend to wider political cooperation and certainly did not amount to *de facto* alliance.[36]

The diplomatic constellation thus tended to isolate the crisis: except for the late French involvement, the powers found it in their interest to stand aside, even while recognising that the conflict would have important consequences for the balance of power. The constellation offered Russia and Japan opposite incentives with respect to timing. Japan, enjoying the support of two of the powers, could not hope for a more favourable configuration than that which White terms 'the isolation of Russia'. Russia, on the other hand, could reasonably expect that at some stage the ever-changing pattern of European power politics would strengthen its position. Thus the Japanese had every incentive to seek a prompt settlement, the Russians to delay. This reinforced the military incentives: the longer the delay, the more Russia could reinforce its armed forces in the region.

Values, interests and objectives

Japan

Imperialist self-assertion, security and a tacit demand for great-power status were the most prominent of Japan's foreign policy values. The demand to be accepted as an equal among the powers implied, if historical precedent was relevant, a readiness to prove the point in war. These were the values of the new generation of political leaders who had just come to power: they were especially prominent among military and civilian officials and in newly formed nationalist associations which expressed resentment over past humiliations and articulated new imperial ambitions. These sentiments were widely shared: radical, pacifist intellectuals found little support; on the other hand, the *genro*, reluctant to place the achievements of their generation at risk against a power of vast military potential, were highly influential.[37] Korea was the primary focus of the government's concerns and ambitions – on the one hand, Komura's 'dagger pointing to the heart of Japan', on the other, a weak, unreformed polity ripe for Japan's imperial guidance.

Japan's new political leaders, in particular Katsura and Komura, formulated a coherent conception of Japan's interests in the new circumstances of 1903, which the *genro* were gradually persuaded to accept. Japan's political and military predominance in Korea, hitherto pursued solely by diplomatic means, now came to be defined as a vital interest justifying war. Japan's interests in Manchuria were to be pressed vigorously but not to the point of war. Any Korea–Manchuria 'exchange' must be symmetrical, that is to say, Japan would not accept greater restrictions on its freedom of action in Korea than Russia would accept in Manchuria – a point which Delcassé was to perceive clearly.[38]

The explanation for the new resolve on Korea appears to be found in the convergence of four developments:

1 The change in political generations in 1902–3 brought to power leaders with new values;

2 Japan's military build-up since 1895 had reached the point that its army and navy could be seen as equal to their Russian counterparts in

119

the Far East; but Russia's naval programme and the completion of the Trans-Siberian Railway – which still depended on a ferry crossing of Lake Baikal – would soon strengthen Russia's position;

3 As noted above, alliance with Britain protected Japan against French or German intervention, and the common front on commercial issues with Britain and the United States placed Russia on the defensive;

4 Russia's decision to continue its occupation of Manchuria foreshadowed an increased threat to Japan's ambitions in Korea.

The precise character of Japan's interests in Manchuria is more difficult to determine. They did not justify war, yet they amounted to more than merely bargaining counters. The new generation would not accord Russia a free hand in Manchuria because of a potential security dilemma: an unrestricted Russian military presence could always threaten Korea, just as an unrestricted Japanese presence in Korea could threaten Manchuria. The shared commercial interests with the United States and Britain were not unimportant, but a more fundamental reason for Japan's insistence on equivalent treatment of Korea and Manchuria was that only thus could its great-power status be made clear. No specific interest in Manchuria was vital, but the overall balance in the agreement was of crucial symbolic concern.

Japan's immediate objective in the crisis was well devised in relation to its leaders' partially divergent perception of its interests: to clarify the options by pressing for a settlement without delay, while the favourable political and military circumstances held. The ministers could agree with the *genro* in preferring a diplomatic settlement to the hazards of war; the *genro* could reluctantly agree to accept war if Russia persisted in rejecting Japan's essential demands. The negotiations would put the differing perceptions of Russian intentions to the test.

The course of the negotiations was such that the Japanese leaders did not have to determine *precisely* what were their basic demands, what was their vital 'minimum'. Komura's insistence to the diplomats that the final proposal was not negotiable cannot be taken at face value in view of Katsura's assurance to the Emperor that further discussion would be needed if Russia were to propose a compromise. A timely Russian compromise might have shaken the Japanese consensus. By the close of the negotiations, disillusionment with the Russians ensured a consensus that war was unavoidable, and in this climate it became difficult for the Russians to make a credible offer.

Russia

Russian values may be summed up as 'imperial': the maintenance, security and prestige of the vast Russian Empire. The lack of public interest in the Far Eastern empire was of no concern to the decision makers: all were imperialists, agreed on the need to consolidate Russia's gains in Manchuria. Russia expected to absorb much of China, but would forego immediate expansion in the face of resistance. Prestige was at once a value and a means – the maintenance of an image which would deter challenges.

Despite the vast sums expended on the railways and on city development, Russia's economic stake in Manchuria was not especially prominent in the values of the leadership.[39] The immediate economic return was slight; apart from Witte's economic vision, the significance of the railways was primarily strategic, a link between the exposed periphery and the imperial centre.

Russia's interests were not clearly defined, in part because of the region's low priority. For Kuropatkin, Russia's interests in Manchuria ranked above only those in Korea, below the defence of the Maritime region toward Japan and China, the southern frontier towards Afghanistan, Persia and the Ottoman Empire, and far below the defence of the Western frontier.[40] These priorities were not controversial, but the other decision makers rejected Kuropatkin's conclusion that Russia should establish a protectorate in northern Manchuria but withdraw entirely from southern Manchuria in order to shorten the defence perimeter and allay Chinese and Japanese hostility. This ran counter to the interests of the Navy and Alekseiev was in a position to veto it.

The government did not accept that Russia was overextended but resolved on the 'New Course'. An increased military presence would be needed in the region in order to deter any threat to Russia's sphere of influence in Manchuria, but precisely what this entailed in terms of the commercial rights of other powers remained to be determined. The French ambassador, Bompard, correctly perceived Russia's intention in commenting that Kuropatkin was going to Manchuria in June 'to organise Russian dominion there, or, if one prefers the official terminology, to prepare the evacuation'.[41]

With respect to Korea, while there was an element of brinkmanship in the May decision to develop the Yalu concession, this proved to be short-lived: because of the unsatisfactory condition of the timber and to accumulating debts, the company's operations were wound up before the end of 1903.[42] The weight of evidence supports the view that the Russian decision makers did not see the Korean issue as a *casus belli* in 1903, and were prepared to accept a Japanese occupation of most of the country. This was indicated in the Tsar's directive in July, the decisions of the Port Arthur conference, and the initial reaction to the Japanese proposals; it was reaffirmed in January that Japan might occupy Korea as far as the watershed of the Yalu and Tumen rivers.[43] The Russians believed, however, that the decision on war or peace was in their hands. The Tsar's otherwise bizarre order to Alekseiev in October – 'I do not want a war between Russia and Japan and will not allow it. Take all measures so that war will not occur'[44] – reflects this assumption, as does his decision at the same time to withdraw the Viceroy's power to order mobilisation. The same desire to avoid war, and confidence that it could be avoided, were evident in the meeting of the Russian leaders on 28 December.

In holding out for major restrictions on Japan's military role in Korea, the Russian leaders did not see themselves as risking war. That Kuropatkin and Alekseiev should favour a neutral zone in northern Korea and a prohibition on strategic uses of Korean territory was to be expected, but their lack of awareness of the risks in taking this stand calls for explanation, which must be sought in the first instance in an examination of Russian perceptions, below. The inconsistency between the Russian leaders' eventual willingness to yield on Korea and their rigid negotiating stance indicates the absence of a realistic formulation of their interests. Crucial issues were not discussed. Until the December meeting they proceeded unilaterally, never explicitly addressing their interests in relation to Japan.

Given that the definition of Russian interests remained hazy, it is not surprising that Russia lacked a clear objective in the negotiations. Having accepted Japan's invitation to discuss a general settlement, Russia proceeded to act as if it were seeking to evade the undertaking, perhaps in order to buy time, or even to humiliate the Japanese. The question whether there was any such negotiating strategy is discussed below.

Perception

Russia

Differences of perception among the Russian decision makers were of limited significance, though their differing awareness of the risk of war is of interest. Their shared misperception of Japan's capabilities and intentions, however, was a fundamental determinant of the outcome of the crisis.

Kuropatkin's *apologia* must be read with caution, but other sources confirm his claim that, despite a few sound analyses, Russian intelligence reports greatly underestimated Japan's military capabilities.[45] Their principal shortcoming was their underestimate of the quality of Japan's armed forces.

> Though our information as to the material points of the enemy's strength can hardly be described as good, we very much underestimated – if we did not entirely overlook – its moral side... The nation's belief in and deep respect for the army, the individual's willingness and pride in serving, the iron discipline maintained among all ranks, and the influence of the *samurai* spirit, escaped our notice... One of the so-called 'Japanese experts' declared in Vladivostok before the war that we might count one Russian soldier as being as good as three Japanese.[46]

Such judgments merely confirmed the unquestioned assumption of superiority, deeply rooted in European racial and cultural attitudes, with which the Russians contemplated the Japanese. The military attaché in Tokyo, 'seems to have taken the view that the Japanese would need about a century to develop a modern army comparable to that of the weakest army in Europe'.[47] That Japan – 'a power which we regarded as belonging to the second class' – could defeat one of the European great powers was unthinkable. In January 1904 Kurino commented that the Russian government did not want war, but 'seems to be labouring under a tremendous conceit which leads to the opinion that an agreement regarding Manchuria would be looked upon as a great humiliation'.[48]

Kuropatkin noted the crucial consequence of this misperception: the assumption that the initiative with respect to war or peace rested with Russia.

> We ourselves were not ready to fight, and resolved that it should not come to fighting. We made demands, but we had no intention of using weapons to enforce them... We always thought that the question whether there should be war or peace depended upon us, and we wholly overlooked Japan's stubborn determination to enforce demands that had for her such vital importance, and also her reliance upon our military unreadiness.[49]

He left Port Arthur in July convinced that the avoidance of a rupture, with Japan 'was a matter entirely within our control'.[50] As noted above, the Tsar shared this assumption, and it explains Russia's lack of urgency over the negotiations.

But did the Japanese signal the seriousness of their intent? Were their signals insufficiently clear, or were the Russians unreceptive to any signals, however clear? In opening the negotiations, Kurino was instructed to emphasise that 'we attach great importance to the subject'.[51] The history of Russia's response to earlier Japanese proposals suggested that there was little chance of a more favourable reaction unless the Russians themselves had decided that a general settlement was desirable. Japan posed precisely this question and received an affirmative response.[52] It should be noted, however, that whatever Lamsdorf's intentions may have been, his influence was about to decline due to Witte's dismissal and Alekseiev's appointment as Viceroy.

Between August and December Japan's signals were mainly conciliatory. It accepted the transfer of the responsibility for the negotiations to the Viceroy; its second proposal offered substantial concessions; and it refrained from military signals in response to a number from the Russian side. Japan's only strong signal was the October treaty with China opening additional Manchurian cities to foreign commerce. It was only in the later stages of the negotiations that Japan began to send strong diplomatic signals. In handing over the third proposal, Kurino stated that 'it might cause serious difficulties, even complications, if we failed to come to an *entente*',[53] and the proposal itself was couched in very firm language. The message succeeded in alarming the Russians for the first time. Japan's fourth and final proposal concluded with the explicit warning that 'further delay will be extremely disadvantageous to the two countries',[54] and in a meeting with Rosen Komura let slip the phrase, 'but we might compel you', Kurino warned Witte that Japan was losing patience, and the ambassador in London, Hayashi, referred to the possibility of 'energetic measures'.[55] By now, the message had got through. But there was still little sense of urgency: the Russians still could not bring themselves to believe that the Japanese might be about to seize the initiative.

If the leadership as a whole did not perceive a risk of war until the end of December, some individual decision makers perceived it earlier, but the autobiographical nature of the evidence requires care in its interpretation. There are hints that Alekseiev may have had an apprehension of armed conflict sooner than the leaders in Moscow, but he appears to have regarded forward deployments and military demonstrations as best calculated to deter adversaries.[56] Kuropatkin and Rosen both claim to have recognised Japan's determination by the time of Kuropatkin's visit to Japan, in June, and each was convinced that the risk of war could be averted if his preferred policy was followed.[57] Since their policies were rejected, both expressed their alarm, but were not in a position to sway the Tsar and his other advisers.[58] Moreover, Kuropatkin's insistence on a neutral zone in Korea was detrimental to his aim of avoiding war. The Tsar, who had the final say, wanted to avoid war but also to avoid concessions: his confidence that the decision was in Russia's hands enabled him to avoid any sense of a 'trade-off' until too late.

The explanation of the shared Russian misperception is not to be found in the psychology of stress: the time pressure associated with stress was entirely absent. Nor can it be traced to political compulsions. The case illustrates some cognitive effects of the general acceptance of an erroneous image of an adversary: so pervasive an image is not readily modified by sound military intelligence, had this indeed been available. The sources of the misperception were to be found in nineteenth-century European historical experience and racial and cultural attitudes: perhaps nothing less than war itself could have fully corrected it. It should be noted, however, that few European observers in Japan fully shared the Russian complacency, and by the later phase of the crisis most European governments were expecting war. Only the Russian government, its self-esteem threatened by the Japanese, was unable to adjust its pre-existing image. This is not to argue that the outcome of the crisis was predetermined. The Tsar, whose initial response to Japan's proposals had been accommodative, could have accepted Rosen's advice in the second round of the negotiations. But the consequence of the prevailing misperception was a disinclination to offer concessions: the Tsar, perceiving no risk, preferred to support the Viceroy against the ambassador.

If the case suggests a general hypothesis, it is that established powers tend to underestimate the capacities of emerging new powers, or of lesser powers with intense local interests; that they underestimate, in particular, the capacity of such adversaries to take unwelcome initiatives; and that these tendencies are all the greater when the historical experience of superiority is reinforced by racial or cultural attitudes.

Japan

The Japanese, with their ancient and refined culture, were the last comers to join the community of the civilized Western nations. Their advent on the stage of terrestrial world politics was like the arrival of inhabitants of another planet gifted with acute powers of observation, unhampered by hereditary prejudices or preconceived ideas, unmoved by sentiments of traditional rivalry or hatred born of centuries of strife and struggle for supremacy, with no inherited friend-

125

ships or enmities to indulge or cultivate – in short, with nothing to obscure the clearness of their vision or affect the soundness of their judgment.[59]

Thus Rosen summed up his impressions. The Japanese decision makers were indeed exceptionally free from cognitive rigidities. There were significant differences of perception and expectation, but these were put to the test of experience. The Japanese reading of the signals available to them cannot reasonably be faulted, despite the irony that this led them to misread Russian intentions.

At the outset, the *genro* and the second-generation leaders held different expectations concerning the possibility of a settlement, based on different readings of Russian attitudes and intentions, and coinciding with a lesser or greater willingness to accept the risks of war. On the one view, Russia had gone some way towards acknowledging Japan's special position in Korea, had no interest in war and thus could be expected to compromise if it could be convinced of Japan's determination. On the other view, which was closer to popular sentiment, Russian arrogance and expansionism were such that its leaders could be brought to take Japan's interests seriously only through war.

The Japanese decision makers were responsive to the new information obtained through the negotiations. Thus Komura, initially one of those most sceptical of a settlement, was sufficiently impressed by Rosen's provisional acceptance of Japan's conditions on Korea in October to inform the British and Belgian ambassadors that he was confident of success in the negotiations.[60]

This, however, was the only signal which encouraged such optimism. Russian military moves between April and the end of the year pointed consistently in the opposite direction: the deploying of troops in the Yalu region in May, the developments relating to the Yalu timber concession, a naval visit to Chemulpo, the port of Seoul, in June, the military review in Port Arthur and the reoccupation of Mukden in October, and the transfer of 40,000 troops to the region during the crisis. The Japanese press constantly reported indications of Russian hostility, such as the aggressive promotion of Russian interests in Korea by the ambassador, Pavlov, and his alleged boasts of Russian military superiority.[61] Perhaps the most alarming signal of all was Alekseiev's appointment as Viceroy and the transfer to him of responsibility for the negotiations. Bompard perceived this as a setback for the partisans of peace,[62] and the experienced Belgian Minister to Japan, d'Anethan, reporting on the adverse reaction in Tokyo, commented that:

126

The nomination of Admiral Alexeiev, with the widest possible powers, to the position of Viceroy and the new demands made by Russia on China have not only rekindled but also poked the fire which has been smouldering for over two years and which threatens increasingly to bring about a terrible conflagration.[63]

Nonetheless, the Japanese leaders appear to have kept their attention focused on the negotiations. Rosen's claim that the Yalu timber concession – often regarded as a major cause of the breakdown – was not so regarded by the Japanese government, is probably correct.[64] It was the second Russian proposal, falling so far short of the expectations created by the Rosen–Komura talks, which shook the confidence of the *genro* that a settlement was attainable, and the third proposal which convinced them that it was not. As regards the final negotiations, Komura had reason for suspicion of French intentions, and at the same time that he was hearing from Motono that Russia might be prepared to return to Rosen's offer of October, he was hearing from Kurino in St Petersburg that this was unlikely. In view of all that had preceded it, the reading of the new information as yet another delaying tactic was not unreasonable. The more important point is that the Japanese leaders, in reaching the conclusion that they did at the time of the third Russian response, drew the conclusion which seemed inevitable in the light of the very considerable body of evidence before them.

The Japanese leaders did not consider the hypothesis that Russia's signals were inadvertently misleading, and that even more emphatic representations might break through the misperception which had sustained a diplomatic stance so greatly at odds with the Russian leaders' reluctance to go to war. They had no evidence that this was in fact the situation. Such a case may be termed a 'secondary misperception', on the part of the Japanese – a misperception which was a natural and almost unavoidable consequence of the 'primary' Russian misperception.

The Japanese perception of the military balance was highly realistic, and provides an exception to the generalisation that governments do not embark on war unless they are confident of a favourable outcome. At the outset of the crisis the prevailing view of the staff officers was that Japan could expel Russia from Manchuria provided war was not delayed, but they failed to persuade the Cabinet or the *genro*.[65] At the time of the decision for war, the official Army advice was that Japan had only a fifty-fifty chance of victory and the Navy showed itself fully aware of the danger of war with evenly matched fleets.[66] The hope was that if Japan could win early successes, it would be in a position to take advantage of international mediation to achieve a peace settlement before Russia's superior mobilisation potential could be made effective.[67] The Japanese took high risks, believing the opportunity to be the most favourable likely to be available, and believing that Russia had conclusively demonstrated its unwillingness to reach a settlement even when in a position of relative military weakness.

The other powers

The perceptions of the decision makers of the other powers are of interest in demonstrating the extent of their uncertainty and the divergences among their expectations, based on differing perceptions of the military balance and the intentions of the protagonists. There was no informed consensus.

The British were divided over the military prospects: while some advisers saw Japan's navy as superior to Russia's, the predominant military advice was pessimistic, reflecting reports from representatives in the Far East during the preceding months.[68] As regards the prospects for the negotiations, the British ambassador in Tokyo, Sir Claude MacDonald, was pessimistic but also reported contrary evidence.[69] Reports from Paris and St Petersburg reflected the optimism in those capitals in January 1904, but it appears that the government was more influenced by its contacts with Hayashi, who reflected his government's disillusionment.[70]

French representatives were not convinced of Russian superiority: the Russian military were said to expect that a war would be long and difficult, and Japan was seen as having the superior navy.[71] Given their lack of detailed information on the earlier phases of the negotiations, the reporting was perceptive. Delcassé's involvement in the final phase generated a surge of optimism based on knowledge of Russian attitudes, but the reports from Tokyo introduced a cautionary note.[72] The German General Staff expressed the most confident of the judgments on the military balance: Russia was not at present equal to the Japanese in East Asia, and thus would not be drawn into war. In late December the ambassador in St Petersburg, von Alvensleben, judged that both sides were bluffing. German reports in January reflected Franco-Russian optimism for the negotiations, but the Kaiser was not convinced: he recorded his mounting sense of disbelief and astonishment.[73]

The US documents record no analysis of the military prospects but show that Ambassador Griscom had a sound perception of Japanese politics and the decision making process.[74]

Bargaining

Japan

In making an offer backed by a threat, the Japanese were bargaining. They held out the prospect of the alleviation of tension through a settlement based essentially on spheres of influence. The tacit threat of war was kept firmly in the background in the early phases but was alluded to with increasing emphasis near the end. They saw little scope for bargaining over the essential elements of the proposed settlement, but were flexible over its detailed provisions and were prepared to move considerably from their one-sided opening bid. One unusual feature of their negotiating strategy was the move from the opening bid directly to the essentials of the final position, in advance of any formal Russian concession, thus leaving little further room for manoeuvre. Japan's move, however, was premised on Rosen's informal acceptance of the second Japanese proposals: when this expectation was disappointed, the worst reading of Russian intentions seemed beyond doubt.

The Japanese appear to have envisaged the negotiations as revealing Russian intentions, rather than seeking to influence them by means of coercive bargaining tactics. But it is arguable that the overall diplomatic context required Japan to adopt a low-key bargaining style, ruling out stronger threats and signals. The use of strong language, open pressure or a direct challenge to Russian prestige would not have been conducive to negotiating a settlement with so arrogant an imperial power. Moreover, Japan gained the approval of the diplomats of friendly powers by appearing moderate and reasonable, not carried away by the clamour of anti-Russian nationalism – which might, however, have been construed as a warning by a more perceptive adversary – nor responding in kind to the more provocative Russian signals.[75] Thus the military means of signalling resolve would not have served Japan's interest, and there were indications that Russia may even have hoped to provoke such a response. These considerations may explain the paucity of bargaining moves on Japan's part and the difficulty of identifying a bargaining strategy for the attainment of Japan's clearly defined goals.

Russia

Prima facie, the Russians were not bargaining: their signals did not communicate their intent – their aversion to war and their willingness, in the last analysis, to make concessions on Korea.[76] But the question is whether they were indeed bargaining more subtly, but on different assumptions and in a different time frame from the Japanese. Was there a shrewd purpose behind their apparent incoherence? Was there a *strategy* of delaying a settlement until their military position improved? The slowness of their decision making process, so exasperating to the Japanese, was convenient to the Russians. While it is true that they failed to perceive Japan's resolve, and misconstrued Japanese expressions of urgency as merely tiresome indications of weakness, a strategy can be based on a misperception. The strategy of delay would demonstrate that Russia could not be pressured to accept a quick settlement and would minimise the concessions which would eventually be necessary.

If this interpretation were correct, it would follow that an important part of the explanation of the outcome was that the opponents were bargaining on different assumptions and within different time frames. However, this interpretation is not supported by the evidence, which points toward quite a different account of Russian policy. It constructs a 'rational actor' which was not present: it is thus essentially a rationalisation, not a description of actual policies. It is true that it was convenient for the Russians to delay a settlement and that they preferred to minimise concessions. But the evidence does not support the view that the Russian decision makers, individually or collectively, formulated a negotiating strategy along the lines suggested.

There was no central policy making body: Tsarist Russia had no cabinet and no prime minister. The *ad hoc* conferences which formulated the New Course ceased after early July; there was no meeting to examine the Japanese proposals or to formulate a negotiating strategy. The Tsar, the final rather than the central decision maker, rejected a number of strategies proposed by individual advisers, or else they were abandoned for other reasons.

Thus, Witte's initial strategy of military withdrawal from Manchuria and acceptance of spheres of influence was rejected in favour of the New Course, which was clear with respect to Manchuria but not Korea, and was essentially a unilateral policy, not addressed to the possibility of agreement with Japan. Nonetheless, Lamsdorf accepted Japan's proposal to negotiate a general settlement, and this was eventually confirmed as Russia's policy, but not until the meeting on 28 December. In between, the Tsar endorsed Alekseiev's rejection of Rosen's spheres of influence strategy. The Viceroy's own strategy became clear during the middle phase of the crisis when he carried the principal responsibility for the negotiations. It included an element of buying time to await the arrival of reinforcements, but he recommended that the negotiations be broken off, rejecting the Japanese concept of a general settlement, and preferring what he probably expected to be a 'cold war' type of conflict with Japan.[77] His signals were consistent with this strategy, but not with a policy of negotiating a settlement. The Tsar and his ministers, however, rejected Alekseiev's strategy, and also Kuropatkin's strategy of withdrawing from southern Manchuria but establishing a protectorate in the north.[78]

Thus several decision makers had their preferred strategies, but the Russian government had none. Only Alekseiev was for a time in a position to implement his own strategy, and this conflicted with the policy of seeking a settlement. There is no evidence to suggest that the other two key decision makers, the Tsar and the Foreign Minister, had worked out a strategy. Lamsdorf was characteristically passive, accepting the transfer of responsibility to the Viceroy, defending the exclusion of Manchuria from the negotiations, accepting its re-inclusion, and responding to Delcassé's initiatives in January when a direct approach to Kurino might conceivably have revived the negotiations. The Tsar did not give the issue his sustained attention until late December: he was concerned to uphold Russian prestige but he also wanted to avoid war and was prepared to consider a sphere of influence agreement in October, but did not insist on it. He did not consider the negotiations urgent, and remained confident that there would be no war, because 'he did not wish it'.[79]

The evidence does not sustain a 'rational bargaining' interpretation of Russian policy, but reveals the divergent views of those involved in the decision making and the *ad hoc* nature of their inputs. The negative signals between July and December were actions of a bargaining type, but they were not bargaining moves by the Russian *government*, designed to achieve its specific ends. It was only in the final phase that the crisis began to take on some of the characteristics of a bargaining process.

Despite this, the case study nonetheless illustrates an important hypothesis on bargaining advanced by Snyder and Diesing – that a crisis is not ready for settlement until there has been a confrontation.[80] A premature accommodative move may encourage the adversary to become more intransigent, and even a government willing to make major concessions is unlikely to do so early in a serious contest. On the information before them, the Japanese leaders did not regard their second-round concessions as premature; yet it is evident that the Russian government did not take the crisis seriously before the confrontation brought about by Japan's third proposal. It was only then,

131

too late to influence Japanese perceptions, that it began its leisurely search for accommodation. Thus bargaining theory can offer insights even where the bargaining process does not come into operation.

Internal politics

Both governments were unusually free from political pressures sufficient to constrain their freedom to pursue the foreign policy of their choice. Criticism in financial circles of the cost of Russia's Far Eastern empire was only of marginal concern to the government; and if Interior Minister Plehve did in fact make the notorious remark that 'what this country needs is a short victorious war to stem the tide of revolution',[81] those involved in the decision making did not expect any kind of war, thus could not adopt this means of averting revolution. There was some awareness that war would expose the fragility of Russia's financial system, but 'there are no firm indications in the source materials that discussions during the winter of 1903–04 gave serious consideration either to the domestic political situation or to hopes that conflict with Japan could be used to squash rebellion'.[82]

Public pressure was potentially of greater significance in Tokyo, and dissatisfaction with the eventual peace treaty was to cause three days of rioting. The governmental oligarchy, however, accorded no legitimacy to public opinion. Its influence could only be indirect. Nationalist sentiment in the Diet caused the government some embarrassment, but more important, and foreshadowing developments later in the century, were attempts by military staff officers to press the government to initiate war at the outset. Though unsuccessful, they found some sympathy among members of the Cabinet, and foreign diplomats were impressed by the extent of bellicose sentiment.[83] The position of the *genro* depended on the Emperor, who was not, like the Tsar, actively involved in decisions, but whose final assent was something more than a formality.[84]

In Russia, the decision making process as such can be seen as a major impediment to the effective formulation of policy. In Japan, on the other hand, the process was thoroughly effective. Each step in the negotiations and in the preparation for war was preceded by one or more meetings of the Cabinet, a *genro* conference or an Imperial Conference at which the issues were squarely confronted and purposeful decisions taken.[85] Russian decision making between November 1902 and July 1903 also took the form of high-level conferences, and White justifiably sees the ensuing policy as 'well-considered and not a product of hasty improvisation devised under pressure from a group of adventurers; it must be viewed, therefore, as a national policy'.[86] But the same cannot be said of decision making in the second half of 1903. In the absence of high-level meetings, decisions were taken on the basis of communications between Rosen, Alekseiev, Lamsdorf and the Tsar, other ministers making *ad hoc* representations. Since they were not brought together to confront the issues, their differences remained unresolved. The reasons owed something to the Tsar's propensity to take long vacations at that time of year, but also to the vicissitudes of court politics in 1903.[87] The influence of the 'triumvirate' of Witte, Kuropatkin and Lamsdorf, a source of policy continuity in the preceding years, was weakened by the faltering of Witte's policies and the activities of Bezabrazov and his circle, leading to Witte's dismissal as Finance Minister and Alekseiev's appointment as Viceroy.

Since Russian policy during these months was the product of a fragmented decision making process as well as a shared misperception of Japan, it is impossible to establish conclusively which was the more important reason for its weaknesses. Ministerial discussions might have led much earlier to the stance of January 1904, but in view of the pervasiveness of the shared misperception, this seems unlikely. Had the perception of Japan been sounder, the decision making process would not have led to so uncompromising a second proposal. In this sense the misperception may be regarded as the more fundamental determinant of the policy.

Determinants of the outcome

The scope of the differences over the interpretation of the crisis is relatively narrow. All recent accounts emphasise the disorganisation and confusion of the Russian decision making process and its leaders' misreading of the Japanese challenge.[88] Nish writes that:

> Our broad view in this study has been that Russia did not want war but by sheer dilatoriness over the negotiations let war occur... It does not seem to have occurred to the cautious and inefficient ministers that their dilatoriness would push even the peace party in Japan to a determination to teach Russia a lesson.[89]

Nonetheless, after reviewing the divisions within both governments, Nish concludes that it was unlikely that the two sides could have found a basis for compromise, and thus rejects the comment of a contemporary, Cecil Spring-Rice, that the war was 'wholly preventable'.[90] While some of the Russians were prepared to concede Korea as a

Japanese sphere of influence, others wanted to insist on Russian strategic interests there; and while some of the Japanese were prepared to limit themselves to Korea, others were not, and the army planned to campaign in Manchuria.

These conflicting preferences point to the difficulty of achieving a stable demarcation between the interests of the two restless empires, but do not show that they could not have reached a settlement in 1903–04, given that this was preferred by important elements in both governments. The conclusion of the present analysis is that, in terms of the preferences of the decision makers as revealed during the crisis, either outcome was possible. This conclusion, although indeterminate, is nonetheless highly significant: it implies that the outcome depended on the actors' decisions during the crisis – on crisis diplomacy. It could not be seen as predetermined by their basic values and capabilities. The case provides an important exception to the generalisation that the bargaining process could be expected to correct initial mispercep- tions of relative interests and capabilities. Pervasive misperception, a lack of clear goals and a chaotic decision making process made for a pattern of signals which misrepresented Russian preferences as a whole and, despite the painstaking rationality of Japan's decision making, precluded effective bargaining. The war was the outcome of contingent circumstances, not of larger necessities.

The rivals conducted their diplomacy in accordance with the norms of the time, which legitimised great-power imperialism but provided no rules for regulating imperial conflicts. Nor was there any presumption, as in the Concert of Europe system, that the powers should confer together in order to resolve such conflicts peacefully, nor recent precedents for such consultations. The French diplomatic involvement in the later phase of the crisis was thus opportunistic, and was perceived as such – but no more so than the non-involvement of the other powers. War, always a potentiality, was avoided in other imperial clashes at the time, over Fashoda and over Morocco, for example; its occurrence in this case was the product of unusual circumstances.

7 THE SUDETEN CRISIS, 1938

Even after half a century 'Munich' remains one of the most powerful images influencing the contemporary understanding of international relations – a symbol for the failure of appeasement, for the surrender of vital principles to a totalitarian aggressor, for a self-defeating policy of unilateral concessions which, in seeking to avert war, rendered it all the more certain. Historical scholarship has now moved beyond this traditional image, offering a far more complex account of the Sudeten crisis, the term preferred here to 'Munich crisis', since it refers to the six months during which the future of the Sudeten German minority in Czechoslovakia was the issue that raised the question of war.[1] As in the previous case studies, the focus is on the views and debates within the decision making groups and not, for example, on the wide range of issues addressed in the public debate, especially in Britain, nor the question whether the radically different policy recommended by Churchill offered a better prospect for success – issues on which the decision makers' minds were closed.

The setting was exceptionally unstable. There was no accepted structure of international order but the 1930s saw rapid changes in military technology and in the relative strength of the great powers. Nonetheless, the crisis was in some ways conducive to 'management': Germany was not yet prepared for major war and Britain, having undertaken a systematic assessment of its interests and options, made a sustained effort to *avoid* a confrontation. For the British and French decision makers, the most fundamental issue was to define precisely what would constitute the *casus belli*, on which their views were clarified only under the pressures of the crisis, after the collapse of their initial strategy of averting confrontation. Hitler, like the British, had a well-defined strategy – to achieve his goals by manipulating the situation in Czechoslovakia, not through bargaining with Britain and France. In the final phase there was some improvised bargaining, but essentially both sides lost control over events. The case study illustrates some reasons why crises are so difficult to manage or to avoid.

The crisis does not offer the classic case of misperception which it is so often assumed to have done. The British decision makers did not *misperceive* Hitler's larger intentions: rather, their policy was premised on uncertainty. So long as this remained, they would refrain from any step which they believed would heighten the risk of an otherwise avoidable war. On the other hand, neither side correctly perceived the other's specific intentions, and many of the actors' perceptions were highly selective, screening out an awareness of value trade-offs. Domestic political constraints were important in Britain and France, but their governments were able to insulate themselves from immediate political pressures in devising policies of their choice. Hitler's intentions in the final phase remain elusive: it cannot be determined with any confidence how close the powers were to war.

The setting

The balance of power was discredited, but the norms of the League of Nations did not win sufficient acceptance to provide new foundations for international order. The United States had withdrawn into strategic and diplomatic isolationism and the Soviet Union, deeply distrusted by most European governments, was shunned as a potential coalition partner. Germany, Italy and Japan emerged as revisionist powers dissatisfied with the international status quo. Britain and France were divided over how to maintain that status quo, France favouring insistence on the full terms of the Versailles treaty, Britain – keenly aware of its declining relative power – the accommodation of legitimate demands for change.

By 1938 the Versailles system and the League of Nations were disintegrating. The League's failure to check Italy in Abyssinia in 1935–36 demonstrated its ineffectiveness, but the attempt to activate it alienated Italy from Britain and France, while the latter's failure to intervene to maintain the demilitarisation of the Rhineland in March 1936 signalled the breakdown of its attempt to maintain the Versailles system; and French reservations had prevented any serious attempt to activate the abortive Franco-Soviet alliance. While British rearmament advanced only slowly and France based its security on the Maginot Line and allowed its air force to decline, German rearmament forged ahead remorselessly. The Spanish Civil War exacerbated ideological cleavages in Western Europe, above all in France, already subject to demoralising conflict between Right and Left. Thus on the one side were the fascist powers, aligned and displaying the appearance of ideological unity; on the other were powers weakened by internal cleavages and divided by a legacy of mutual suspicion and two decades of non-cooperation.

The immediate background

The Chamberlain government, which came into office in May 1937, reviewed Britain's military policy in the light of its financial constraints. Concluding that the requirements of the peacetime economy necessitated drastic decisions on priorities, it opted for accelerated air defences and, in the case of the army, priority for the Empire over Europe.[2] Britain's inability to confront its three potential enemies simultaneously was uppermost in the government's thinking. Given its reservations about the Soviet Union and lack of confidence in France, its response was not the classic one, the search for allies. Foreign Secretary Eden favoured a policy of buying time, demanding German and Italian restraint, rearming and 'keeping the dictators guessing' until Britain reached a position of greater strength from which to negotiate.[3] Chamberlain found this inadequate, since it left legitimate grievances to rankle: in order to avert the risk of war, it was essential to take the initiative to improve relations with Germany and Italy, and only thus could Britain's potential commitments be brought into balance with its military means.[4] These differences over the basis for negotiation with 'the dictators' and over the general conduct of diplomacy led Eden to resign as Foreign Secretary in February 1938; he was succeeded by Halifax.

Germany did not reciprocate Chamberlain's attempts to improve the relationship, cancelling a projected visit by Foreign Minister von Neurath to London in mid-1937 because of an incident in Spain. In November, when Chamberlain took advantage of a private visit by Halifax to Berlin to press for him to see Hitler, the latter remained at Berchtesgaden and gave the visit no encouragement. Nor was the meeting itself encouraging. Hitler resisted the suggestion that Germany return to the League of Nations and expressed little interest in negotiations on colonial questions. Halifax accepted the case for political change where Germans had been denied self-determination – in Austria, Czechoslovakia and Danzig; it is not clear to what extent Hitler noted his rejection of the use of force.[5] Hitler rejected Britain's proposal on colonial transfers in central Africa in a bad-tempered meeting with the British ambassador, Nevile Henderson, on 3 March 1938; he denounced the British press and sought to discourage any British interest in developments in central Europe.[6] Thus he rebuffed Chamberlain's interest in resolving differences between the two powers, barely leaving the door open for further negotiation.

137

Hitler's policy in this period is best explained in terms of the formula 'ohne England'. He had given up his earlier hope of achieving a partnership whereby Britain would assist him to achieve his continental goals in return for security for the Empire. Hitler's goal was now British non-intervention in central and eastern Europe.[7] Germany gave little publicity to the Halifax visit and the Henderson interview: British interference was not welcome. However, it was prepared to keep up the appearance of negotiation with the British if they insisted on expressing interest in what was properly Germany's sphere of interest, so long as their 'meddling' remained verbal, since an open breach might be damaging.

In November 1937 Hitler explained his objectives at a meeting with the War and Foreign Ministers and the Commanders-in-Chief of the three services (Blomberg, Neurath, Fritsch, Raeder and Goering). He signalled the end of a phase of consolidation and a willingness to embark on a course of action to achieve *Lebensraum* for the next two generations, at the latest by 1943–45. If an opportunity presented itself for overthrowing Austria and Czechoslovakia before then, even as early as 1938, he would move.[8] By the beginning of February 1938 Hitler had removed from office the three participants who had expressed reservations – Neurath, Fritsch and Blomberg.

The *Anschluss* with Austria in March 1938 provides a classic example of Hitler's decision making style. He acted suddenly and unilaterally, surprising the world not by the initiative as such, but by its manner and timing.[9] In February he sought to accelerate the process by which Germany had been gaining influence in Austria since 1936, summoning Austrian Chancellor Schuschnigg to Berchtesgaden and presenting him with demands which would make the Austrian government dependent on external German and internal Nazi support. On 8 March, however, Schuschnigg attempted to reverse the process by announcing a plebiscite, which he hoped would demonstrate support for independence. Hitler now improvised plans for an invasion and used this threat to bring pressure on Vienna for the abandonment of the plebiscite, Schuschnigg's resignation, his replacement by a Nazi sympathiser, Seyss-Inquart, the latter's 'invitation' for German military intervention, and finally the formation of a government dictated by Berlin (11–12 March). Hitler's decision for *Anschluss*, reducing Austria to the status of a German *Land*, appears to have been taken only during the night 12–13 March, after the triumphal entry of the German armies and when the acquiescence of the powers had become clear.

This created an expectation throughout Europe that Czechoslovakia was Hitler's next objective. He had spoken of ten million Germans in subjection outside the Reich.[10] Seven million had now been incorporated: the other three million were the Sudeten Germans. This created a novel situation for his diplomacy, depriving him of the element of surprise which had facilitated his previous unilateral decisions. Each of these had precipitated a momentary sense of crisis, but no confrontation. However, Czechoslovakia's alliance with France ensured that a move against it would cause a genuine crisis.

The phases of the crisis

Phase 1: Taking up positions (March–April)

On 28–29 March Hitler met Konrad Henlein, the leader of the *Sudetendeutsche Partei*. Rejecting his request for German intervention, Hitler insisted that he restrain his activists. The Sudeten Germans were to maintain the appearance of negotiation with the Czech government: to make unacceptable demands but not to press for its violent overthrow.[11] The strategy would remain under Hitler's control. He envisaged two contingencies: diplomatic controversy or an incident which could furnish a pretext for invading Czechoslovakia; his interest in the Sudeten grievances was to use them to open the way to the destruction of the Czechoslovakian state.[12] Henlein's Karlsbad Programme, announced at the party conference on 24 April, implemented Hitler's strategy by formulating eight demands for autonomy in a manner which appeared reasonable to foreign opinion yet opened the way to unlimited haggling with the Czechoslovakian government.[13]

Britain formulated its policy within ten days of the *Anschluss*. The principal concern was that if Germany attacked Czechoslovakia and France acted in fulfilment of its treaty commitments, Britain might have no alternative but to fight in support of France. The Cabinet's Foreign Policy Committee considered three options: the formation of a 'grand alliance' against Germany, advocated by Churchill with some Foreign Office support; a new commitment to Czechoslovakia or to France; or an attempt to persuade France to press Czechoslovakia to resolve the Sudeten question through concessions to meet the German grievances. In line with preponderant Foreign Office and military advice, the Committee favoured the third course, which was endorsed by the Cabinet.[14] Speaking in Parliament on 24 March, after making it clear that Britain had no specific treaty obligations to Czechoslovakia, Chamberlain warned that, nonetheless, 'the inexorable pressure of facts' might well mean that Britain would 'become involved'.[15]

On 28–29 April Daladier and Bonnet, the French premier and

Foreign Minister, conferred with Chamberlain and Halifax in London and agreed to press Czechoslovakia to make major concessions to the German minority, while Britain would seek to clarify the German demands and would warn Germany of the risk in using force.[16] The French leaders were as alarmed as the British by the possibility that a German attack might confront France with the choice of whether or not to act in fulfilment of its treaty obligations. During the following days German diplomats received many indications of French and British reluctance to be drawn into war, and Chamberlain, in providing 'background information' to American journalists, went so far as to suggest the eventual possibility of a transfer of territory.[17] In Prague, British and French diplomacy was poorly coordinated, and was initially limited to seeking to persuade the Czechs of the desirability of making concessions.[18]

Phase 2: The May crisis

Against a background of violence in the Sudetenland preceding local elections scheduled for 22 May, a hostile German press campaign and reports of unusual German troop movements close to Czechoslovakia, the government in Prague, claiming to have reliable information that German forces were concentrating in a position to attack Czechoslovakia, ordered a limited mobilisation and occupation of the frontier region on 20 May.[19] The British and French embassies in Berlin, after initially reporting unusual troop movements, subsequently concluded that these had not been on a major scale. Later research has endorsed this: German documents reveal no orders for such movements.[20] It remains unclear whether the Czech government exaggerated the military threat, or whether it believed that inaction would be dangerous, permitting a level of violence which would provide a pretext for German intervention. It is also unclear whether, as some suspected, President Benes provoked a crisis in order to deter a German attack by demonstrating the commitment of France and Britain to Czechoslovakia's independence. In the event, order was restored, and the larger diplomatic objective also appeared for a time to have been achieved.

On 21 May Bonnet strongly reaffirmed France's treaty obligations, and Henderson warned the German government that circumstances might compel Britain to become involved.[21] Britain's warning, but not its precise terms, rapidly became public knowledge. Hitler was infuriated by the depiction of the crisis in the foreign press as the successful deterrence of a German military attack, and proceeded to revise the directive for war against Czechoslovakia. Whereas it had ruled out attack in the near future unless internal conditions forced the issue or there was an especially favourable opportunity, on 30 May Hitler stated his intention to 'smash Czechoslovakia' in the near future, and military preparations were to be completed by 1 October.[22]

Chamberlain believed that the British warning had deterred a German move, as did some of his intelligence advisers. For Henderson, however, the principal lesson was the necessity of avoiding another such crisis. Hitler was close to becoming uncontrollable, and a second 21 May would push him 'over the edge'.[23] The British government sought to intensify the pressure on Czechoslovakia to come to terms with the Sudeten Germans. However, although Bonnet rebuked Czechoslovakia for involving France in the risk of war, there was little pressure and no hint of withdrawing French support.[24] He went much further in his reassurances to Germany, indicating that France would revise its alliance arrangements unless Czechoslovakia became more yielding.[25] These 'signals' must have reinforced the earlier indications of the French government's reluctance to stand by its treaty with Czechoslovakia. The Czechoslovakian government, however, rendered more confident by the success of the mobilisation, was even less willing than previously to yield to Anglo-French pressure.

Phase 3: Stalemate (June–August)

The following three-month stalemate saw the erosion of the British hope of avoiding a confrontation, and perpetuated the image of Czech intransigence in Paris and London. British and French pressure in Prague was poorly coordinated, nor were there reassurances of support if the proposed approach was indeed adopted. Despite undertakings given to Halifax in early June, Bonnet did not strengthen the pressure by threatening to reconsider the alliance. It was not until 20 July that he delivered an explicit warning, and then only orally. France would publicly affirm its solidarity in order to enable the Czechs to obtain an honourable solution, but would not go to war over the Sudeten issue. Benes was shocked: the report illuminated French intentions 'like a flash of lightning'.[26]

On the same day the British minister pressed Benes to 'invite' Britain to appoint an independent mediator, Lord Runciman – threatening to make the proposal public.[27] Runciman's arrival in Prague led to further delay as each side sought to impress him. After several abortive Czech proposals, the British warned Benes that he should be in no doubt as to Britain's choice if it had to decide between the Karlsbad

141

proposals – Sudeten German autonomy – and war.[28] Benes' Fourth Plan, on 6 September, conceded virtually the whole of those proposals. Unfortunately the Plan was too late to affect the outcome. The Sudeten leaders were temporarily disconcerted, but a timely incident at Mährisch-Ostrau came to their rescue, enabling them to have further negotiations postponed until after Hitler's speech at the Nuremberg Rally on 12 September.[29] The decision makers in London were pre-occupied with other issues, and public attention was captured by an editorial in *The Times* proposing far more than the Fourth Plan – a transfer of the territory occupied by the Sudeten Germans.[30]

Phase 4: Nuremberg and Berchtesgaden

The British became increasingly concerned that Hitler's speech at the Nuremberg Rally represented a danger point, when he might commit himself to a fatal course of action. There had been reports from supposedly reliable sources that Hitler planned to attack Czecho-slovakia in late September or early October.[31] The Cabinet briefly considered several options for restraining Hitler – that Runciman make a recommendation for a settlement, that Britain express con-fidence in the success of his mission, or that it support a French suggestion for a four-power conference – but found reasons to reject each of them. A fourth possibility, a further warning to Hitler, became the focus of British policy deliberations.[32] Some officials feared that Hitler had become convinced that Britain and France had been bluf-fing in May and would not fight in September. Bonnet, having reaf-firmed France's obligation to support Czechoslovakia, appealed strongly for a parallel British statement. On 30 August, however, the Cabinet decided against a further warning: it was thought likely to encourage the Czechs to stand firm, and at best would merely delay Hitler's move.

The question was reopened after further representations by Bonnet and after the Fourth Plan had reduced the risk of excessive Czech firmness. The 'inner group' of the Cabinet decided on 9 September that Henderson should deliver a formal warning to German Foreign Minis-ter Ribbentrop, stating that if France were to go to war under the 1925 Treaty, 'a general conflict, from which Great Britain could not stand aside', seemed inevitable.[33] The same group, however, acceded to Henderson's vehement request that he not be required to deliver the warning: it would be a provocation which might drive Hitler 'over the edge'.[34] Thus the principal move contemplated by the British to influ-ence Hitler proved abortive.

In the event, Hitler left his options open, limiting himself to denunciation of the Czechs and the demand for self-determination. The speech, however, created a mood of heightened tension, and a series of incidents in the Sudetenland on the night of 12–13 September led to the imposition of martial law. On 13 September the Sudeten leaders demanded the repeal of martial law and the transfer of police functions to the Sudeten Germans. When this was rejected, Henlein dissolved the negotiating team and broke off negotiations with the government.[35] By the afternoon of 13 September there was extreme alarm in Paris and London. Bonnet sought the immediate publication of Runciman's proposals, and Daladier proposed a three-power conference; the British ministers concluded that French nerve had collapsed. Setting aside Daladier's proposal, they approved the principle of a plebiscite to decide the future of the Sudeten territories and authorised Chamberlain to approach Hitler with a view to meeting him in Germany.[36] The full Cabinet welcomed the initiative but questioned the plebiscite, insisted on avoiding the use of force, and proposed that Runciman be asked to arbitrate the dispute and that an international commission supervise the agreement.[37]

The meeting at Berchtesgaden, expected to last two days, was limited to the evening of 15 September. A few hours before Chamberlain's arrival Henlein had appealed for the Sudeten Germans to 'come home to the Reich'. Hitler could present Chamberlain with a *fait accompli*, the collapse of the ostensible aim of the Sudeten–Czech negotiations, Sudeten autonomy.[38] This met with no objection. Speaking violently and grossly exaggerating the number of Sudeten German deaths, Hitler narrowed the issue down to the demand for immediate self-determination. There was no discussion of the Runciman mission, and no countering of Hitler's charges against the Czechs. Chamberlain expressed his personal acceptance of self-determination, but would need to obtain Cabinet approval; he did not specify the conditions on which he would insist. Hitler had reason to boast that he had 'cornered' Chamberlain.[39]

The Cabinet readily accepted self-determination, and the conditions governing the transfer of territory were discussed with the French leaders on 18 September. There was agreement on the cession of territory and on safeguards through international supervision, and Britain was to be a guarantor of the new Czechoslovakia.[40] Details of the agreement became known the next day through leaks to the French press. Bonnet now threatened Czechoslovakia with the loss of French support if Prague rejected the proposals, while Churchill and the French ministers opposed to appeasement encouraged it to resist.

On 20 September the ambassadors in Prague reported that the Czech government had rejected the proposals, but would accept them if presented with an ultimatum.[41] Benes' acceptance was obtained through this means at 2 a.m. on 21 September. It is likely that the Germans intercepted Bonnet's telephone communications with Prague, obtaining further compelling evidence of France's unwillingness to fight.[42]

Meanwhile Hitler had stepped up the pressure on Czechoslovakia through press attacks, a gradual military build-up and inciting Hungary and Poland to make territorial demands.[43] On 18 September Henderson advised that the military preparations would be completed in about a week, and the German motorised force was soon concentrated around Bohemia. On 16 September Hitler had ordered the establishment of the Sudeten German Free Corps, units of which occupied the towns of Asch and Eger on the night of 21–22 September. The French ambassador, André François-Poncet, drew attention to a change in mood and atmosphere in Berlin, a new confidence that Britain and France would not fight over Czechoslovakia.[44]

Phase 5: Confrontation and resolution

On 21 September the Cabinet discussed Britain's stance at Chamberlain's next meeting with Hitler the following day at Bad Godesberg. Chamberlain was granted some discretion, but would reject the inclusion of Poland's and Hungary's claims in an agreement or the exclusion of the Soviet Union from the proposed guarantee of Czechoslovakia. Some objected to the admission of the German Army into the Sudetenland, but as on a number of other points, the discussion remained inconclusive. The details were not drawn together into a formal proposal, nor discussed with the French.[45]

Chamberlain began the discussions at Bad Godesberg by reporting on Czechoslovakia's acceptance of the Anglo-French proposals, and recommended that they be implemented by an international commission. There was a sense of shock as Hitler rejected the proposals as no longer adequate: the situation in Czechoslovakia was now intolerable. He did not press the claims of Poland and Hungary but demanded the immediate German military occupation of the predominantly German parts of Czechoslovakia, to be followed by plebiscites in areas of mixed population. Chamberlain, having withdrawn to consult his advisers, urged Hitler to compromise; he could not recommend the German proposals to Czechoslovakia. At a further meeting on 23 September, however, Hitler offered only minor concessions. Both leaders were surprised to learn that the Czechs had ordered mobilisation. The governments in London and Paris, antagonised by the occupation of Eger and Asch, and feeling that they had gone to the limit of concession, had withdrawn their veto on mobilisation. The meeting ended without agreement.[46]

While the German Foreign Ministry sought to present the Godesberg meeting as a new accord, and Hitler continued searching for a way to divide Czechoslovakia from its great-power supporters, serious divisions opened up in the British and French Cabinets. Chamberlain recommended the acceptance of Hitler's proposals. The normally reticent head of the Foreign Office, Sir Alexander Cadogan, was horrified. 'We must go on being cowards up to our limit, *but not beyond.*' Shocked that Halifax was 'quite happily *défaitiste-pacifiste*', Cadogan 'gave him a bit of my mind', persuading him that the distinction between orderly and disorderly transfer was crucial.[47] With Halifax opposing the acceptance of the Godesberg terms, the Cabinet was now divided. Similar differences emerged in Paris, but on 25 September the Cabinet followed Daladier's lead in rejecting the Godesberg memorandum, reaffirming that France would stand by its treaty with Czechoslovakia; at the same time there was interest in seeking a compromise.[48]

Tension was high in the Anglo-French talks held the same evening. The British, suspecting that France did not plan a major offensive to take advantage of German weakness in the west, interrogated the French on their military plans. Chamberlain, still favouring substantial acceptance, rejected a suggestion by Daladier that an international commission should determine the areas for cession. Daladier was provoked into putting sharp questions to the British.[49] Later that night Chamberlain reversed his position. The British Cabinet approved the sending of a new emissary to Hitler – Chamberlain's close adviser, Sir Horace Wilson – to propose the formation of a joint commission, with representatives from Germany, Czechoslovakia and Britain, to implement speedily the proposals already accepted. Wilson was also to warn Hitler that if Germany attacked Czechoslovakia, Britain would feel obliged to support France in defending it.[50] Not surprisingly, the French leaders approved the mission.

Chamberlain's new initiative, however, was rebuffed. Repeatedly interrupting the reading of Chamberlain's letter, Hitler rejected the proposed three-party commission, and advanced the deadline for Czech acceptance of the memorandum to 28 September – or Germany would march.[51] When Wilson delivered the British warning, Hitler accused Britain and France of threatening to attack Germany.

Speaking in the Berlin *Sportspalast*, he reached new extremes in his denunciation of Benes and made public his determination that the issue be resolved by 1 October; nonetheless, keeping the diplomatic option open, he expressed appreciation for Chamberlain's efforts. Hitler proceeded to order the first assault units to be ready for action on 30 September. During the afternoon, however, he witnessed the marked lack of enthusiasm for war when a mechanised division passed through Berlin.[52] In the evening he wrote again to Chamberlain, offering no concession but inviting him to continue his effort 'to bring the Government in Prague to reason at the very last hour'.[53]

Alarm over the prospect of war intensified in Britain and France on 27 September. There were queues for gas masks and trenches were dug in the London parks. Bonnet's associates lobbied among parliamentarians to overcome the mood of resistance, but the French Cabinet could not resolve on a course of action.[54] The British Cabinet heard that Czech morale was poor and resistance likely to be brief, and the Chiefs of Staff, reaffirming that Britain and France could not save Czechoslovakia, argued for postponing war against Germany.[55] Nonetheless, the Cabinet rejected the Godesberg proposals and decided to mobilise the Navy; in effect, it accepted the likelihood of war.[56] It authorised the submission to Germany of a timetable for the orderly transfer of territory, with the transfer of predominantly German zones by 10 October, and decisions on all other areas by 31 October, but this amounted to no more than what Hitler had refused to discuss with Wilson. On learning of the British timetable, Bonnet drafted a proposal for accelerating the transfer.[57]

Chamberlain broadcast to the nation that evening, referring to 'a quarrel in a far-away country between people of whom we know nothing', expressing doubt whether 'it is really the great issues that are at stake'.[58] In response to Hitler's letter he declared his willingness to come to Germany again and to ensure that Prague's promises were kept, and appealed to Hitler not to take the responsibility for starting a world war over a few days' delay. He also sought Mussolini's intervention to forestall the outbreak of war and his participation in a conference to that end.[59]

During a morning of frantic diplomatic activity in Berlin on 28 September, Hitler was brought to accept a conference. While showing interest in the new French proposal, he did not commit himself, but promptly accepted Mussolini's proposal to defer the mobilisation for twenty-four hours. He was unresponsive to Chamberlain's letter until he had ascertained that Mussolini would accept an invitation to a conference.[60] The relative significance of the factors inclining Hitler to accept a conference – the attitude of the German public, the mobilisation of the British fleet, the new French concessions, the balance among his advisers, Mussolini's intervention, the lack of a plausible justification for war – remains open to debate.

The Munich conference itself is generally regarded as anti-climactic.[61] The draft which served as the basis for the discussion was put forward by Mussolini, but had been suggested to him by Goering and others who favoured a negotiated solution, drawing on the British and French proposals of the preceding days. It was agreed that all territory of 'predominantly German character' would be occupied by 10 October, with plebiscites in doubtful areas. The conference was poorly organised, reflecting Hitler's disdain for diplomacy in general, and this conference in particular. Few issues were pursued: Hitler angrily rejected Chamberlain's plea that the Czechs participate, and the British refused to discuss Polish and Hungarian claims. Other potentially contentious issues were referred to the International Commission, to consist of representatives of the four powers and Czechoslovakia.

Chamberlain's expression on returning to London, 'peace for our time', reflected the euphoria of the moment and the release of intolerable tension. More characteristic of his political shrewdness was his comment to his parliamentary secretary on the Anglo-German declaration signed on 30 September:

> if Hitler kept the bargain, well and good; alternatively ... if he broke it, he would demonstrate to all the world that he was totally cynical and untrustworthy, and ... this would have its value in mobilising public opinion against him, particularly in America.[62]

This demonstration came with the occupation of Prague, six months after the meeting at Berchtesgaden.

Values, interests and objectives

Germany

The values of National Socialist Germany have no parallel in the other case studies: nowhere else was nationalism so extreme – a cult of violence justified by an ideology of racial superiority – giving rise to the long-term goal of *Lebensraum* for the German *Volk*.[63] Hitler embodied these values, and his dominance of foreign policy decision making gave importance to certain of his personal values such as his determination to play for the highest stakes and his willingness to incur high risks in doing so. His conception of Germany's interests was

147

spelled out at the meeting with the key ministers and military commanders on 5 November 1937. It was imperative that the German racial community gain control of additional living space in the east. Neither autarchy nor participation in the world economy offered acceptable alternatives. The goal could be achieved only through war, at the latest by 1943–45, when Germany's relative power would be at its greatest. Germany's southern flank must be secured much sooner, taking advantage of any favourable opportunity – possibly even in 1938. Britain and France – 'hate-inspired antagonists' – would probably resist in the long run, but not over Czechoslovakia.

His statement provoked sharp questioning, foreshadowing the emergence during 1938 of a quite different view of Germany's interests, formulated by the Chief of the Army General Staff, General Beck, and shared by many of the senior officers. In this view, a war over Czechoslovakia would not be localised, and Germany was not yet prepared for war with Britain and France. The more Hitler argued that they would not intervene, the more the opposition felt it imperative to avoid the unacceptable risk that they might.[64] Although most of the opposition favoured expansion to the east, they dreaded a war on two fronts, especially in Germany's state of unpreparedness.

Following the success of the *Anschluss*, Hitler formulated the objectives which were to guide German policy until the last days of the crisis. While the ostensible objective was to support Sudeten German claims for a settlement of their grievances, the real objective was to promote conditions in Czechoslovakia which could furnish a pretext for a German invasion, sufficiently convincing that France and Britain would not intervene, despite France's treaty obligation to Czechoslovakia. Circumstances favouring an invasion might include diplomatic tension, a serious incident or an 'unbearable provocation'; there should be 'as much of the surprise element as possible'.[65]

It was suggested above that after the May crisis his contingency plan hardened into a firm commitment to attack Czechoslovakia 'in the near future'. This is sometimes contested. It is true that the next strategic directive, on 18 June, reaffirmed the political conditions for an invasion and responded to the concerns of senior officers by stating the further condition that he must be convinced that France and Britain would not intervene. But Hitler's prestige was now engaged, and he became further committed when, on 15 August, he informed the senior generals that he was resolved to use force against Czechoslovakia that autumn.[66] The September mobilisation enhanced the commitment, in that withdrawal would have meant a major loss of prestige. In effect, Hitler's hands were tied by his self-imposed deadline.

The Nuremberg speech provided a setting in which a violent incident or some other pretext for attack was widely expected -- the element of surprise had been lost. Chamberlain's visit to Berchtesgaden and Czechoslovakia's acceptance of the Anglo-French proposals then threatened, by achieving Hitler's ostensible objective, a Sudeten settlement, to deny him his true objective, the destruction of Czechoslovakia. He now reformulated his objectives. His Godesberg demand, the immediate occupation of the Sudetenland, left open his preferred objective, invasion, in the event of a last-minute breach between Czechoslovakia and the western powers. Alternatively, the acceptance of his Godesberg terms could be presented as a military solution. When neither hope was realised, he reluctantly reduced his objectives yet further, to the diplomatic solution at Munich.

Britain

Aversion to war was as prominent in British values as acceptance of war in National Socialist ideology. A repetition of the carnage of 1914-18 was unthinkable. The security of Britain and the Empire, the restoration of prosperity and the maintenance of Britain's global economic position were values taken for granted by the public; but for policy makers the obstacles to achieving and reconciling these goals were increasingly formidable.[67] They were guided by agreement on certain norms and values: national self-determination, peaceful change and the maintenance of a European balance of power.[68]

British interests with respect to Czechoslovakia were examined systematically by the Cabinet Foreign Policy Committee shortly after the Anschluss. This followed a series of earlier assessments which emphasised the constraints of Britain's limited military power. Even fully rearmed, Britain could not secure the Empire against three major powers, and until 1939 there was no adequate air defence. There was no confidence in any potential ally, but Britain would have to support France against attack by Germany. Britain had never supported the rigorous implementation of the Treaty of Versailles, but rather the accommodation of legitimate German grievances.

The Chiefs of Staff had previously advised that, once rearmed, Germany could easily overrun Czechoslovakia, and Britain had been urging the merits of accommodating the demands of the Sudeten Germans.[69] Taking the view that the retention of the Sudeten German minority in Czechoslovakia was not an issue that would justify general war, and that Hitler's long-term intentions were uncertain, his hegemonial ambitions unproven, the Foreign Policy Committee not surprisingly opted for pressing the Czech leaders to compromise. Given these perceptions, alternatives had little appeal. In particular, Churchill's 'grand alliance' proposal required working with a power which was deeply distrusted, the Soviet Union, and confronting Germany over an issue which was not seen as justifying war. The basis for alternative readings of British interests existed in the traditions of the 'idealist' Left and the 'realist' Right, but at the time of the Sudeten crisis these enjoyed only limited support.[70] The Left was still averse to national rearmament. Critics from the Right favoured resistance to Germany, but were divided over which of the powers should be sought as allies, and the logic of their policy pointed towards a great war. The Foreign Office was divided, Vansittart and his supporters advocating resistance to Germany, Henderson the acceptance of a German sphere of influence in eastern Europe, while Cadogan struck a balance close to Cabinet's preferred policy.[71]

A primary British objective was to avoid a situation in which the crucial decisions which would involve Britain in a general war would be taken by others. The specific aims which guided policy were, together with France, to press the Czech government to compromise with the Sudeten Germans, meanwhile warning Germany against armed attack. As Chamberlain and Halifax signalled in March, it was never a major British objective to preserve Czechoslovakia's territorial boundaries. Chamberlain's remark to Hitler at Berchtesgaden that he did not care 'two hoots' whether the Sudeten Germans were in Czechoslovakia or Germany, so long as there was a peaceful settlement, was not a concession under pressure, but an accurate, if undiplomatic, statement of British policy from the outset.[72] French objectives were essentially the same, but less openly expressed. France could not repudiate its treaty obligations to Czechoslovakia, even though it was determined not to be required to implement them. It thus preferred to appear to be yielding to British pressure, rather than itself initiating pressure on its ally.[73]

Hitler's demands at Bad Godesberg, going beyond what was regarded as legitimate, required a reformulation of these objectives. For Chamberlain and Bonnet, the objective of avoiding war remained primary, the procedure secondary. For Daladier, Halifax and Cadogan, the procedural issue signified the upholding of crucial norms and values, latent up to that point and not fully articulated even then. For some, it may have been Hitler's peremptory attitude and the fact that he made new demands, more than the content of those demands, which led them to insist on drawing a limit.

Perception

Germany

The differences between Hitler and those who opposed his policy in 1938 arose partly from his greater willingness to risk war, but also from different perceptions of British and French intentions. For those who expected them to fight for Czechoslovakia, the risk of general war was too great: for those who shared Hitler's confidence that they would not, there was little or no risk. Ostensible differences over capabilities, in particular the capacity of the modest German forces then available to defend the partially completed West Wall, were also fundamentally over Anglo-French intentions.[74] It was beyond dispute that France had the capability to overrun the German defences, but Hitler appears to have sensed that the French had no intention of mounting such an attack.

Hitler was circumspect regarding British and French intentions early in the crisis, when he spoke of the need to await the favourable political circumstances under which they would not intervene, but after the May crisis he expressed certainty that they would not. This served his interests in several ways – maintaining morale among his followers and reassuring doubters, but also, more subtly, enhancing the credibility of the threat to Czechoslovakia and, by tacitly projecting the strength of his own will to risk war, weakening the will of his adversaries. His statements in his debates with the military therefore cannot be equated with his perceptions. He never explicitly acknowledged uncertainty, but expressions recorded by his confidants of his willingness to risk a wider war may be taken as tacit acknowledgment of it.[75]

General Beck, the officers' spokesman, occasionally moved beyond his central argument, that there was too great a risk of provoking a general war for which Germany was not yet prepared, to claim that Britain would certainly intervene.[76] Hitler responded with his own certainty: 'As long as Chamberlain and Daladier were in power, there would be no European war as a result. He also drew the attention of the generals to his prophetic gifts.'[77]

On neither side was there gross misperception, but each misread some aspects of the situation. Beck and his supporters were aware of British and French reluctance to intervene, but they perceived correctly that this had its limit. Hitler was more fully aware of their reluctance to fight, but though he judged correctly that they would eventually resist German expansion, he underestimated the extent to which his demands and the manner of his presenting them at Godesberg would provoke immediate resistance. There was considerable realism, but also a measure of wishful thinking, in the long-term expectations both of Hitler and his critics. Hitler accepted the likelihood that his aims for Germany could be achieved only through war with the western powers, whereas his critics, despite their belief that Britain and France would fight if Germany invaded Czechoslovakia, hoped that they might not fight if it later sought greater gains in the east. But they judged much more clearly than Hitler the likelihood that the Axis powers would lose a general war.

In the final phase of the crisis, when Chamberlain's diplomacy had disrupted Hitler's schedule, he acted on the misperception that there was no limit to British acquiescence in his demands. This may have been true of Chamberlain and Bonnet, but not of the two governments as a whole. This misperception ensured that the final phase took the form of a confrontation rather than merely 'hard bargaining'. It should be noted, however, that many of the 'signals' received by the German government must have encouraged Hitler's expectation.[78]

Britain

While Britain in 1938 does not provide the classic instance of the misperception of an adversary's intentions, it illustrates the difficulty of achieving a sound assessment. Not even Churchill nor Vansittart discerned Hitler's immediate intentions of using the Sudeten issue as a pretext for the invasion of Czechoslovakia. In March the Foreign Office saw Germany's immediate aims as the incorporation of the Sudeten German minority within the Reich and the breaking of the Czech alliances with France and the Soviet Union, but left the question of larger German aims in the realm of uncertainty – and this uncertainty provided a basic premise for its policy recommendations.[79]

Until his meetings with Hitler, uncertainty was also the dominant theme in Chamberlain's perceptions: 'I do not take Hitler's peace professions at their face value ... once more we are given a little longer space in which to rearm.'[80] And later, 'Is it not positively horrible to think that the fate of hundreds of millions depends on one man, and he is half mad?'[81] Chamberlain's misperception that the British warning in the May crisis had deterred Germany provides further evidence of his reservations concerning Hitler's intentions. Intelligence reports during the summer did not resolve the uncertainty. Some stated that Hitler would attack Czechoslovakia as a first step towards greater expansion, others that his aims were limited to the Sudetenland.[82]

There was a widely shared misperception of Henlein and his role. He had made a positive impression in London in 1937, and in May 1938 he impressed even Vansittart and Churchill with his sincerity. Not even those most sceptical of German intentions suspected that Henlein was a full participant in Hitler's deception. During the Runciman mission the British continued to perceive Henlein as a moderate under pressure from extremists. François-Poncet, observing him more sceptically, noted the deft manoeuvre by which his proclamation of 15 September calling for the Sudeten Germans to return to the Reich succeeded in 'burying' the Karlsbad proposals and confronting Chamberlain with a *fait accompli*.[83]

Hitler's capacity to influence the perception of prominent visitors was widely recognised, and proved sufficient to overcome Chamberlain's earlier healthy scepticism. He was now 'satisfied that Herr Hitler would not go back on his word once he had given it', and confident that his object was 'racial unity, and not the domination of Europe'.[84] Cadogan thought that 'Hitler had evidently hypnotised him to a point'.[85] His scepticism was not, however, entirely overcome, as is shown by his comment, noted above, on the draft Anglo-German declaration signed at Munich.

Sustained contact with the Nazi leaders, however, was another matter. The long-serving French ambassador, François-Poncet, provided a uniquely perceptive commentary on the unfolding of the events of the crisis. He correctly identified the various manoeuvres which contributed to the build-up of tension preceding Berchtesgaden, and subsequently drew attention to changes in mood and to actions which foreshadowed the stepping up of Hitler's demands at Bad Godesberg. After that meeting he emphasised the way in which the German public was misled over its outcome.[86] He could not provide direct evidence of Hitler's larger intentions, but provided ample evidence that his immediate objective went beyond self-determination. However, there is no indication that his penetrating observations had the least influence on French policy.

The perception of military weakness, it was suggested above, was a central premise of the Chamberlain government's policy. 'We must not precipitate a conflict now – we shall be smashed', Cadogan noted in March, and Chamberlain commented on the Godesberg proposals that 'if we now possessed a superior force to Germany, we should probably be considering these proposals in a very different spirit'.[87] The most salient aspect was the absence of effective air defences. 'We cannot expose ourselves now to a German attack. We simply commit suicide if we do. At no time could we stand up against German air bombing.'[88]

When Colonel Ismay, Secretary to the Committee for Imperial Defence, was asked to report on the relative military advantage in fighting Germany in September 1938 or postponing the issue, he squarely supported the latter: Germany's gains in Czechoslovakia would be more than offset by the improvement in Britain's air defences.[89]

These perceptions were remarkably selective, and there was a striking reluctance to question key assumptions. Ismay's advice on the relative advantages of fighting now or later was sought very late and was little discussed. Positive appraisals of the Czech armed forces by the military attaché in Prague were not taken into account, whereas much was made of a pessimistic assessment by his counterpart in Berlin.[90] Above all, there was no serious questioning of the assumptions behind the expectation of a devastating air attack: whether the existing German bombers were capable of operating over the required range, and whether their training and logistic support were consistent with this view of their mission. It is now well established that the *Luftwaffe* did not have these capabilities.[91] On the other hand, the British did not overestimate the strength of the German army, but (quite rightly) did not expect France to exploit its temporary superiority.

It is often suggested that claims about the military balance served to justify a decision taken on other grounds – the decision makers' aversion to war and their view of the *casus belli*[92] – but it is likely that a sounder perception of the military balance would have rendered British decision makers more confident that they could afford to resist Hitler's demands. France, however, might not have been similarly emboldened, since its cities were vulnerable as soon as the *Luftwaffe* could be turned west after the expected victory over Czechoslovakia.

British perceptions illustrate a number of cognitive principles – the denial of trade-offs, the maintenance of cognitive consistency and balance, and the exaggerated perception of one's immediate concerns to the neglect of the wider context.[93] On the other hand, there was no denial of uncertainty with respect to the central issue of Hitler's intentions. A high level of stress was evident in September, but did not have the consequences often attributed to it: the foreclosing of options, panic, or the flight into unrealism. To the extent that misperception was important, it was firmly embedded in long-term policy assumptions, not a consequence of the pressures of crisis.

Bargaining

Although the leading protagonists, Britain and Germany, followed well-defined strategies, bargaining became central only in the final phase. Germany sought to define the issue as one solely between the local actors, Czechoslovakia and the Sudeten Germans; thus Hitler avoided bargaining with Britain and France until Chamberlain left him with no option. However, there were limited attempts to influence one another's intentions, and bargaining played an important part in Britain's relations with Czechoslovakia.

The British strategy

Before the crisis Britain had sought to interest Germany in a wide-ranging negotiation, relying on inducements insufficient to overcome Germany's preference for unilateral action. After Hitler's rebuff, Britain sought to negotiate on the Sudeten issue alone, but Hitler declined to take up suggestions that Germany make proposals (in May) or that it cooperate with the Runciman mission (in July). Germany was able to negate the British aim, but could not achieve its own aim, that Britain accord it a free hand in central Europe. By default, then, Britain and France concentrated their efforts on their second strategy: to press Czechoslovakia to make major concessions in order to achieve an internal settlement, meanwhile warning Germany that a military attack would lead to general war.

Their bargaining with Czechoslovakia moved through several stages. Initially, after concerting their policies on April 28–29, they sought to persuade the Czech government of the need for major reforms. After the May crisis Britain urged France to make the ultimate threat – to reconsider the alliance – but Bonnet delayed until after mid-July. Notably absent were inducements – new offers of support if Prague were to make the desired concessions. Nor was there any pressure on the Sudeten Germans to reduce their demands. Britain now invoked an option long held in reserve, mediation. The device of an 'independent' British mediator signalled Britain's increasing involvement, without any formal commitment to what might be proposed. Benes' eleventh-hour acceptance of the Karlsbad proposals came too late to win British and French support in early September. Britain was now ready to take up the last of the options held in reserve, the transfer of territory to Germany.

Britain's graduated coercive diplomacy was carefully and coldly designed, but worked too slowly to achieve its goal – or, alternatively, to expose the deception that the Sudeten Germans were negotiating in good faith. The main weakness in implementing the design was France's delay in making its crucial threat, but whether Benes would then have accepted the Karlsbad formula much earlier is uncertain.

The British overlooked, or chose not to see, how far-reaching a threat to Czechoslovakia's cohesion that formula represented.

If the British experienced little stress in coercing Czechoslovakia, they agonised over the problems of warning Germany against a military attack. They were well aware that threats can be counter-productive, but misperceived the actual effects of their May representation. Influenced by Henderson, they perceived the risk of provocation in excessively personal terms, not taking into account that the impact of the next warning would depend on the context: on its wording, on the means of communication, and its relationship to other signals. Those who argued in early September for a renewed warning to balance the other signals which Hitler was receiving were on strong ground. Britain and France had shown little awareness of their credibility problem. Their many signals of aversion to war were not offset by the seemingly pro forma French pledges, and until after the Godesberg meeting the British warnings were always subject to France's honouring those pledges.

The German strategy

As we have seen, Hitler could thwart one of Britain's aims by declining to enter into negotiation, but could not compel Britain to accord him a free hand. Within Czechoslovakia itself Hitler's strategy was even more successful in negating that of Britain. Henlein's demands were plausible enough to win outside sympathy, yet sufficiently open-ended to unsettle the Czechoslovakian government and make it appear obstructionist. Runciman's unsympathetic attitude to the Czechs, reinforcing similar views in London, indicated the success of this aspect of the strategy.

Germany adopted a number of standard bargaining devices to increase the likelihood that Britain and France would not intervene. Czech 'provocations' were presented as increasingly intolerable, justifying German military preparations. Parades and demonstrations deliberately exaggerated German strength.[94] British and French warnings of the risk of war were met with the standard response that this would be a war of aggression against Germany: the Franco-Czech Treaty applied only in the case of an unprovoked attack by Germany. If Chamberlain had not come to Berchtesgaden, the last fortnight of September could have been used to refurbish the pretext for attack.

The Berchtesgaden meeting marked the failure of both the British and German strategies. The British had failed to avert an acute crisis. One reason for Hitler's failure was his self-imposed deadline, Britain's perception of which was accurate enough to induce Chamberlain to make Hitler a procedural offer which he could not refuse.

The Bargaining Phase

Bargaining, however, was improvised and confusing. The British were ill prepared. Chamberlain's manifest readiness to accommodate 'legitimate' demands was not balanced by insistence on limits. Equally significant was the absence of specific proposals: Hitler was free to press the demands of his choice, thus to narrow down the discussion to the principle of self-determination, meaning the transfer of any area claimed to have 50 per cent German population. Nor were Britain's desiderata for the Godesberg meeting drawn together in a formal proposal.

The limits of accommodation now began to appear, but were not yet clear. Chamberlain could not accept Hitler's demands, but attempts to reach a compromise continued, now balanced by mobilisation. The Cabinet, after much soul-searching, confirmed that it would not accept the Godesberg demands nor press them on the Czechs. However reluctantly, it would resist Germany's use of force.

Hitler's strategy appears open to the interpretation that he was bargaining for the utmost gains short of war, maintaining the pressure until the last possible moment but intending to stop short of the brink. However, in view of his preferences throughout the crisis and his subsequent resentment over the Munich conference, the alternative interpretation is the more plausible. That is to say, he surrendered his preference for an invasion, and his conviction that Britain and France would not intervene, only with the greatest reluctance. Despising the norms and procedures of diplomacy, he resented being drawn into negotiation. Even though he found himself constrained by the logic of the bargaining process at the end, and played his role with some skill, he was not bargaining by choice or with conviction.

Internal politics

The British government, having a secure parliamentary majority and confident that its general approach enjoyed wide support, was relatively untroubled by short-term political constraints. The Daladier ministry, on the other hand, like any French Cabinet in that period, depended on shifting parliamentary coalitions, exposed to the tactical manoeuvres of parties and factions – though not, in practice, subject to immediate challenge. The political system, and in particular the

Cabinet, had developed certain defence mechanisms in this context, one of which was the paucity of the official record. Recorded expressions of views could be used against those taking controversial positions, and consequently were kept to a minimum.[95] The remarkably full record of the considerations which entered into British policy making will not become available for France. Other defence mechanisms included the studied ambiguity of much official language and the reluctance to accept responsibility for contentious recommendations or decisions. Both governments were able to restrict the flow of information and to influence the press.

The public's profound aversion to war was not perceived by the two governments as a constraint, since they fully shared it. But it was not a sentiment for peace at any price. There was concern over German expansion, and at the climax of the crisis there was a glimpse of the possibility that the governments might find themselves under pressure from outraged public opinion, not from fear of war but from revulsion against capitulation to Hitler. Such public pressure was to affect British policy after the occupation of Prague and in the last days preceding the outbreak of war. Normally, however, the Chamberlain government, like Daladier's, was able to remain comfortably within the ill-defined limits that these public attitudes prescribed.

The German political and decision making system imposed few constraints on Hitler's pursuit of the policies of his own devising. It is true that after the *Anschluss* there were expectations of further triumphs, and the political calendar provided occasions such as the Nazi party rallies where such expectations were heightened, but these pressures were not such as to require Hitler to make an early move against Czechoslovakia. The Sudeten German Nazis showed little independent initiative at any stage. The constraint of Hitler's October deadline was self-imposed. It was this which brought him up against the only important internal constraint which he experienced in the crisis, the reluctance of the military leaders to agree to so risky a programme, many months before Germany would have adequate defences against France. The outcome, if Hitler had persisted in his threat to attack Czechoslovakia, is one of the great uncertainties in the history of the time. There is no scholarly consensus, but as D.C. Watt has summed up the state of historians' opinions, a majority hold it unlikely that the military would have carried out a successful coup against Hitler, a minority withhold judgment, and none expresses confidence in the success of such an attempt.[96] But the attitude of the military must have been a major consideration counting in favour of Hitler's last-minute acceptance of a diplomatic outcome.

The risk of war: the outcome

The British and French leaders had a clear perception of how the crisis could lead to war. If Germany attacked Czechoslovakia, public pressure or the French government's own values might require it to go to war against Germany, and in that event Britain, for accepted reasons of national interest, would have to support France. The chance of avoiding war was seen as depending on their success in pressing the Czechoslovakian government to reach a compromise with its Sudeten German minority. This was essentially a misperception, but since they were sceptical of the chances of a compromise, they did not underestimate the seriousness of the crisis. Hitler's misperception of the risks was somewhat greater, in that he failed to perceive that there was a limit to Anglo-French acquiescence and had no understanding of the ways in which he might transgress this limit, nor of the consequences of his self-imposed deadline.

At the climax of the crisis, between Godesberg and Munich, the situation was out of control. Britain was now involved as a principal, not just as France's ally: its honour and reputation, as well as France's, were at stake. The mobilisations and the rejection of the Godesberg terms meant that the crucial decision on peace and war now rested with Hitler, however much Bonnet and Chamberlain sought to influence him. Arguably, this was due to crisis mismanagement. Chamberlain, having prevailed on Hitler to negotiate, was himself so unprepared and negotiated so passively that Hitler was inadvertently misled into assuming that he could safely increase his demands. His brinkmanship then left him dangerously exposed in the final hours before the acceptance of the conference. He may have still assumed that France would not exploit the weakness of Germany's western defences, but this was a risk which he had undertaken not to run.

How close, then, was war in September 1938? How finely balanced was Hitler's decision? As suggested above, the evidence is open to more than one interpretation. Hitler was a gambler. Hitherto his decisions had shown an acute judgment of risks: later there were to be momentous misjudgments. His impatience and scorn for military caution were already evident. If Bonnet and Chamberlain had been less resourceful in their last-minute initiatives for accommodation, or if Mussolini had declined to intervene, would Hitler have agreed to a further meeting? On the available evidence, he began to waver when François-Poncet displayed his map of the new French concessions, and his instant acceptance of Mussolini's proposal for a delay marks the turning-point. But was this the reality, or was he all along holding out for further last-minute offers, confident that they would be made? On any rational calculation he could not refuse a conference. The military and the public did not want war, and the British and French acceptance of the substance of his demands left the invasion without plausible justification. But the question remains, was Hitler the rational bargainer? Was he in control of the violent emotions which he expressed, or were they beginning to take control?

Could the outcome have been predicted in terms of the actors' initial preferences? In purely rational terms, the answer is affirmative. For Britain and France the issue did not constitute the *casus belli*, and Germany was not yet ready for a general war. However, this overlooks Hitler's preference for unilateral action and the difference between his real and his ostensible aim. It was only the latter which Britain defined as not constituting the *casus belli*. The British and French response to his real goal was not clear in advance. War in September 1938 would have been a surprising outcome, but could not be ruled out in advance on the basis of the actors' preferences. A peaceful outcome best reflected their confused preferences at this particular time. That it was achieved through great-power negotiation rather than unilateral action was an unintended consequence of Chamberlain's single-minded attempt to defuse the crisis. The larger conflicts of interest between the western powers and Germany were foreshadowed in the crisis; tensions were soon to increase and during the following months the likelihood of a general war was to become widely accepted.

8 THE FRANCO-PRUSSIAN AND AGADIR CRISES

Although the first of these crises led to war and the second did not, there were a number of similarities. The principal adversaries were the same, France and Prussia/Germany, the adversary relationship was of long standing and both parties were acutely sensitive to questions of prestige. Among the major differences were the systemic context, the significance of misperception and the willingness to risk war, but the last of these was related in complex ways not only to differing values among decision makers but also to the pressures of internal politics.

The Franco-Prussian crisis, July 1870

The Franco-Prussian is the only short crisis included in the study. It began when the candidacy of Prince Leopold of Hohenzollern for the Spanish throne became public knowledge in Paris on 3 July, and ended with France's declaration of war on Prussia on 15 July.

Compared with the other cases studied, the willingness to go to war was unusually high on both sides: each was highly sensitive to perceived threats to its prestige but quite prepared to engage in threatening behaviour. Bismarck was prepared to risk war in order to achieve his goals, provided the circumstances were favourable. France had resented Bismarck's brusque diplomacy after Prussia's victory over Austria in 1866, in particular his denial of French claims to compensation to balance Prussia's gains.[1] There was a general perception that French primacy among the continental powers was being challenged by Prussia. Moreover, there was a sense that great issues were soon to be resolved, that a serious attempt to achieve German unification was imminent. To many, this pointed to the inevitability of war between France and Prussia: the division of Germany had for centuries provided a foundation for French security, which a united Germany, superior in population, resources and industrial capacity would destroy. Must France not fight to preserve so basic an interest? So reasoned many, including, most crucially, Bismarck. French attitudes were in fact far more ambivalent, but Bismarck's perception was potentially a self-fulfilling prophecy.[2]

The crisis was precipitated by Bismarck's revival of the Hohenzollern candidacy in the spring of 1870. Both governments hoped to exploit it politically – Bismarck in order to generate a groundswell of support for national unification, Napoleon III to administer a rebuff to Prussia on a dynastic issue which would not, in the French view, arouse German national feeling. While looking towards a political or diplomatic breakthrough, respectively, each government appears to have assumed that it would be in a favourable position if it came to war: France, because Prussia would be isolated in Germany and would alienate the other powers; Prussia, because a confrontation would unite the whole of Germany and French aggressiveness would confirm the powers' reservations towards Napoleon. Each side was confident in its military superiority. The crisis would determine which set of expectations would be realised.

The setting

The overall setting was favourable to Bismarck's goal of ensuring that France would have no ally in the event of war. The conference diplomacy of the Concert of Europe had broken down after the Crimean war: the powers pursued their interests in relative isolation, with occasional opportunistic alliances such as that between Napoleon and Cavour. France had been shocked by the rapidity of Prussia's victory over Austria in 1866, but could not achieve an alliance with Austria, due to the reservations of Hungary – now an equal partner in the new Austro-Hungarian Empire – and the difficulty of winning the support of German Austrians for an alliance to prevent German national unification, especially since the moderation of Bismarck's peace terms had avoided the creation of a popular grievance against Prussia.[3] Russia, sharing a common interest with Prussia in suppressing Polish nationalism and resentful of French encouragement to it, preferred a strong Prussia to a strong France and was even prepared to station troops on the Austro-Hungarian frontier to deter Austria from supporting France.[4] In Britain the prevailing sentiment was in favour of German national unity, and a stronger Germany was perceived as a stabilising influence against the main potential troublemakers, Russia and France. Napoleon's recent diplomacy, in particular his attempt to gain control of Luxembourg in 1867 and proposals concerning Belgian railways in 1869, reinforced Britain's negative image of France.[5]

Pre-crisis manoeuvring

Leopold of Hohenzollern was not the first of the eligible princes whom Spain's provisional rulers, Serrano and Prim, approached after the overthrow of Queen Isabella in September 1868. After several had declined, the crown was offered to Leopold in September 1869, who in turn declined it. After a further failure Prim, observing extreme secrecy, again turned to Prussia in February 1870, this time approaching Bismarck and the King as well as Leopold and his father, Karl Anton. Bismarck, now directly involved for the first time, sought on 9 March to persuade the King of the strategic, political and dynastic advantages of having a Prussian prince on the Spanish throne.[6] Despite his arguments, and further pressure from a meeting of ministers, the King refused to order Leopold to accept the crown, and the latter refused to do so unless ordered to by the King, the head of the family. Bismarck sent two of his agents to Spain in April in order to obtain further information favourable to the candidacy: their reports aroused greater interest on the part of Leopold and his father, but despite Spanish pleas of urgency they were no closer to a positive decision until Bismarck pressed on Karl Anton the vital German interests which were being neglected. By 1 June Leopold and his father agreed that he should accept the offer, subject to negotiating the formal arrangements.[7]

On 11 June Prim, reporting to the Cortes on the unsuccessful negotiations, referred to an unnamed 'fourth candidate' who was widely understood to be Leopold. On 19 June Don Salazar, his representative, obtained Leopold's formal acceptance of the offer which the King authorised two days later 'with a heavy heart'. The intention was to keep the Cortes in session to approve the offer, provided Salazar could return with confirmation of Leopold's acceptance before 1 July. However, his telegram announcing his return on 26 June was jumbled in transmission, to read 9 July. This crucial 'accident' led to the adjournment of the Cortes, denying Prim the intended *fait accompli*: news of the candidacy became well known in Madrid political circles by 1 July.[8]

The debate over Bismarck's intentions in pressing the Hohenzollern candidacy on a reluctant candidate and an even more reluctant monarch was not resolved by the publication, as late as 1957, of extensive documentary evidence of his role, since the sources contain very few explicit references to his intentions, and these are inconclusive.[9] Lothar Gall's biography, taking account of the renewed debate, makes three important points which provide a sound basis for an interpretation. First, it is necessary to take account of 'the whole constellation of circumstances' affecting Prussia's prospects in the first half of 1870, in order to understand why Bismarck, 'in defiance of his tactics hitherto ... finally let himself in for something in which dangers and opportunities were ... precisely balanced and in which the risk of failure and defeat was exceptionally great'.[10] These circumstances included the increasing strength of particularism in southern Germany and of opposition to Bismarck in the Prussian parliament, in the context of the essentially impermanent constitution of the North German Confederation, a setting in which Bismarck was under increasing pressure to find a way of bringing about movement towards national unification, or risk losing control over the process.[11]

Second, Bismarck did not have the kind of single-minded objective which has been the focus of much of the debate: his policy, as always, was 'multi-track', allowing for the possibilities of armed conflict, peaceful settlement or a clear diplomatic defeat for either side. Gall notes that 'the idea of this kind of openness characterising the whole constellation of circumstances was downright intolerable to many contemporaries' and subsequent historians.[12] Third, however, he leans in the direction of those who argue that Bismarck was consciously provoking a confrontation with France in full awareness that it entailed a high risk of war. This reading is based on Bismarck's view of French hostility to German unity, on some of his comments in the relevant time period and, in particular, on his readiness to renew his pressure on the Hohenzollerns at the end of May, two weeks after the appointment of Gramont as French Foreign Minister, which he had perceived as a war-like indication of French intentions.[13]

The French government's silence in the face of the very considerable evidence of the Hohenzollern candidacy available to it in the spring of 1870 was an equally essential ingredient in the formation of the crisis, but has been much less commented on than Bismarck's intentions.[14] Once again, Gall offers a discerning interpretation. France could have prevented the candidacy by making its intentions clear to Madrid but, like Prussia, 'saw the Spanish succession question ... as offering a chance to impart some movement to international affairs' in the direction of its interests.

> The rumours from Spain signalled not only a danger but at the same time a substantial opportunity: that of inflicting a serious defeat on Prussia at no great risk and possibly obtaining after all that compensation for 1866 that was so desirable from the standpoint of domestic affairs.[15]

French policy towards Prussia after 1866 is usually seen as inconsistent and vacillating, in large measure due to the contradiction between the traditional French interest in the division of Germany and Napoleon's doctrine of supporting nationalism, not only as a way of undermining the 1815 settlement but also to place France on the side of the forces of change which were transforming the societies of central Europe.[16] One attempt at reconciling this conflict was Prime Minister Ollivier's formula that France could accept German unity 'if it was produced over time through a popular movement so strong that resistance would be childish and unjustified'.[17] On the other hand, French Liberal opinion had long been hostile to Bismarck's methods both in domestic and foreign policy. If German unity were to be perceived as the aggrandisement of Prussian power, or if French national honour were challenged, most of the conflicting strands in French politics could be readily mobilised against Prussia.[18] The Hohenzollern candidacy was an ideal symbol of such aggrandisement, arousing French hopes that it could be used to discredit Bismarck and to alienate southern Germany from Prussia.

The crisis may be divided into three phases. During the first (3–8 July), France and Prussia took up their initial positions in the confrontation and the other powers responded cautiously. The second phase (9–12 July) saw the negotiations at Ems between the Prussian king and the French ambassador, Benedetti, and initiatives which led Karl Anton to withdraw Leopold's candidacy. In the final phase (12–15 July) the French demand that the King guarantee that there would be no renewal of the candidacy led to the rapid escalation of the crisis: the breaking off of the Ems negotiations, Bismarck's editing of the 'Ems telegram' and, after last-minute vacillation, France's declaration of war.

Phase 1: The initial confrontation (3–8 July)

Ollivier's contention that the news of the Hohenzollern candidacy sparked off 'one of those sudden, volcanic and irresistible explosions' of emotion in Paris is borne out by most contemporary observers.[19] France's initial diplomatic reaction was limited to a 'brusque' enquiry in Berlin whether the Prussian government was involved in the affair, which Bismarck's deputy, Thile, rebuffed with the claim that the negotiation was a purely private affair between Spain and the Prince: 'for the Prussian government, the matter does not exist'.[20] 'In Berlin,' Ollivier wrote, 'they slammed the door in our face and laughed at us.'[21] In view of Bismarck's long-standing insistence on this official stance, there is little basis for the suggestion that a more subtle French response, a request for Prussian good offices to dissuade Leopold from accepting, would have been 'hard indeed for (Prussia) to refuse'.[22] Such an initiative might, however, have weakened Prussia diplomatically.

The French response took two forms: the formulation of an uncompromising public stand and a flurry of diplomatic initiatives aimed at terminating Leopold's candidacy. On 6 July Gramont, addressing a highly emotional Assembly, demanded the withdrawal of the candidacy as disturbing the balance of power and endangering French interests and honour. He relied on 'the wisdom of the German, and the friendship of the Spanish peoples' to prevent it. 'Should it turn out otherwise, strong in your support, gentlemen, and in the nation's, we shall know how to do our duty without wavering or weakness.'[23] Much criticised, the speech could however be likened to Kennedy's initial public statement of the US position in the Cuban missile crisis, a strong commitment signalling the seriousness of the interest threatened, supporting a clear-cut demand.

The accompanying diplomatic initiatives sought to maximise support for this demand. The German ambassador, Werther, was asked to appeal to the Prussian king to withhold his assent to the candidacy, Spain was warned of French concern and the other powers were warned that France could not tolerate the candidacy and were asked for their support to have it withdrawn: it would be sufficient if the Prince himself were to renounce it. By 7 July Spain indicated that it could accept such a renunciation but could not initiate it. France increased the diplomatic pressure on 8 July, sending Benedetti to Bad Ems to negotiate with the King, and warning the powers that further Prussian silence would compel it to begin mobilisation.[24]

These initial reactions reflected the assumption that France was in a strong position, militarily and diplomatically. The Cabinet meeting which approved Gramont's parliamentary statement heard from the Minister for War, Marshal Le Boeuf, that the army had superior weapons and was ready to take the offensive. Napoleon expressed the view that letters from the Emperor of Austria and the King of Italy constituted a 'moral alliance'.[25] The Austrian ambassador sought to discourage this line of thinking but shared the French view that the dynastic issue would divide Prussia from the rest of Germany. 'You have jumped at the chance of either scoring a diplomatic success or of fighting a war on a subject where no German feeling can oppose you.' Gramont replied: 'You put it exactly.'[26]

Bismarck's role in this phase consisted mainly in reaffirming

Prussia's official non-involvement. Werther should not have discussed the issue with Gramont and should have refused to place French concerns before the King. Prussia must avoid the acceptance of any discussion or giving the impression that it could be intimidated.[27] He found Gramont's speech 'insolent and bumptious beyond all expectations' but did not favour an official protest over a parliamentary address; however, 'the newspapers must become very rough, and ... as many of them as possible'.[28] The King, while adhering to Bismarck's diplomatic line, informed Karl Anton of the French reaction and privately reaffirmed his earlier misgivings and his resentment that Bismarck had involved the Hohenzollern name in such severe 'complications'.[29]

The responses of the other powers remained extremely cautious, amounting to little more than expressions of regret over the Hohenzollern candidacy and the vehemence of Gramont's speech. Britain indicated to the Spanish government the desirability of withdrawing the candidacy, and Italy expressed interest in joint action with Britain to resolve the crisis.[30]

Phase 2: Withdrawal of the candidacy (9–12 July)

Gramont's instructions to Benedetti in sending him to Bad Ems foreshadowed the ambivalence in French objectives which was to prove decisive in escalating the crisis. The official dispatch demanded only that the King advise Leopold to withdraw his candidacy. In a private letter, however, Gramont demanded that he refuse to approve it and order its renunciation. This must be achieved within two days: 'otherwise, it is war'.[31]

In his first meeting with Benedetti, on 7 July, William maintained the posture of official Prussian non-involvement, but admitted that in his private capacity, as head of the House of Hohenzollern, he had authorised the candidacy. He declined Benedetti's request that he advise Leopold to withdraw, but informed him that he was in communication with the Prince and his father and would approve a renunciation, if that was Leopold's decision. He would inform Benedetti of the outcome.

Karl Anton's reply, received the next day, expressed concern over the French reaction but saw it as a point of honour not to yield to French intimidation. If the King thought it advisable to withdraw, however, 'a hint from His Majesty will be sufficient'.[32] The King, alarmed by further reports of the war-like atmosphere in Paris, consulted Bismarck on the advisability of his sending an autographed letter to Napoleon or seeking the good offices of the other powers: Bismarck rejected both suggestions. Without informing the Chancellor, the King sent one of his officers, Colonel von Strantz, to Karl Anton at Sigmaringen, informing him of the alarming reports from Paris and containing the 'hint' which Karl Anton had sought and an assurance that he would approve a decision to withdraw.

In Paris, the salient points in Benedetti's report of his conversation with the King were that the latter had approved the candidacy and refused to advise its withdrawal. Gramont instructed Benedetti to obtain a quick decision and to send a dispatch which could be made public. Privately, he wrote that unless the King would advise a renunciation, 'it's immediate war and in a few days we'll be on the Rhine'.[33] Benedetti's second audience with the King, on 11 July, saw no advance: he resisted Benedetti's pressure to urge Leopold to withdraw, but again undertook to inform him of the Prince's answer. The French Cabinet, having authorised limited military moves, decided against 'observable preparations' in order to avoid provoking a Prussian response. Meanwhile, Napoleon sought to influence Leopold through an intermediary, the King of Belgium, and through assurances to the Roumanian envoy in Paris, J. Strat, who, in the interests of the Roumanian monarchy, left for Sigmaringen on 10 July in order to urge the withdrawal of Leopold's candidacy.[34]

While Leopold himself remained on an Alpine walking tour and out of communication, Karl Anton reached the decision to withdraw the candidacy on his behalf on the night of 11 July after a lengthy discussion with Strat, but awaited the arrival of Strantz early the next morning before announcing it. The decision was communicated to Prim and to the Spanish ambassador in Paris. The Prussian king, like most observers outside France, perceived the renunciation as the end of the crisis – 'a stone has been lifted from my heart'[35] – but the form of the renunciation permitted the formulation of new French demands which revived it more acutely. Several of the ambassadors in Paris sought to persuade the French government to make the most of its diplomatic triumph, but this attitude was shared by few in French public life.[36]

Phase 3: The demand for guarantees and the escalation of the crisis (12–15 July)

The expansion of French objectives was foreshadowed in several earlier developments. A parliamentary commotion on 11 July prevented Gramont from replying to a question on whether France had further objectives, but the incident was taken to indicate the strength of bellicose emotion.[37] Gramont's instructions to Benedetti pointed in the same direction: the King must forbid Leopold to persist in his candidacy (11 July), and just before learning of the withdrawal, he insisted that 'the participation of the King must, at all cost, be admitted by him or result from the facts in a striking way'.[38] Although Napoleon, speaking with the Austrian ambassador on the evening of 11 July, set aside the idea of 'complicating' the question, the British ambassador had anticipated as early as 10 July that 'if the excitement goes on, the French may choose to pick a quarrel on the form of the renunciation or some other pretext, even if the Prince retires'.[39]

The initial reaction of Napoleon and Ollivier was to accept the renunciation, but they were soon made aware that many deputies expected more, and the same emotion was evident on the boulevards. Gramont's first move was to ask Werther to convey a request to the King that he associate himself with the withdrawal in terms amounting to an apology. This *démarche* was soon overtaken by the formal demand, through Benedetti, that the King give an assurance that he would not approve the candidacy if it should be revived. Gramont persuaded Napoleon to endorse this demand in the late afternoon of 12 July, contrary to an undertaking to Ollivier that no decision would be taken before the Council of Ministers met the following morning. That meeting resolved to accept the renunciation, even without the guarantees, but the atmosphere in parliament that afternoon suggested that it might be unable to win support for this decision.[40]

On the morning of 13 July the King, firmly but without acrimony, rejected Benedetti's urgent pleas that he give the guarantee that the candidacy would not be renewed. It was the report of this incident, edited by Bismarck such that it appeared that offence had been given and that the King had broken off all communication with the ambassador – the 'Ems telegram' – whose publication brought the crisis to a rapid conclusion.[41] For two days Bismarck had been deeply disturbed, in Steefel's words, 'that the King, in spite of the menaces and insults of the French parliament and press, was continuing to negotiate with Benedetti instead of coolly maintaining his reserve and referring the ambassador to the responsible minister'.[42] He had spoken of resigning and, before learning of the final meeting at Ems, was contemplating a number of measures intended to stiffen Prussia's stance: that Prussia demand an explanation of Gramont's speeches or an assurance that there would be no further French demands, that Werther be recalled from Paris (he was indeed 'sent on vacation'), and the summoning of the Reichstag.[43]

169

News of the Ems telegram reached Gramont on the morning of 14 July. 'My friend,' he exclaimed to Ollivier, 'you are looking at a man who has just received a slap on the face.' On the previous evening, when it was learned that Spain had abandoned the candidacy and that William approved its withdrawal, the balance had appeared to be tilting away from war.[44] Even after the change of atmosphere the following morning the Council of Ministers initially did no more than approve the call-up of reserves, and it proceeded to draft a statement looking to a congress for an acceptable diplomatic solution.[45] During the afternoon, however, Napoleon and his ministers, sensing the extreme unpopularity of this course even before the Ems telegram became public knowledge, had second thoughts, and a reconvened Council abandoned the proposal for a congress. A brief meeting on the morning of 15 July approved a declaration of war, citing as the immediate grounds Prussia's communicating the King's breaking off relations with the ambassador 'to all the Cabinets of Europe', the recall of Werther and reports of Prussian mobilisation. The war credits were approved by the Chamber of Deputies by a vote of 245 to 10.[46]

Bismarck chose to exacerbate the crisis when he could have sought the opposite, but the Ems telegram was not really needed in order to ensure the outbreak of war. France's abandonment of the diplomatic option even before Bismarck's provocation was generally known shows that its weak and divided government saw no way to turn the situation to its advantage through diplomacy, in the face of a mood of public outrage and expectation of war which its own actions had done so much to foster.

The following aspects, of particular concern to the present study, are taken up in Part III: the setting and the initial conditions, seen as rendering war probable but not inevitable; the expansion of French objectives on 12 July, effectively ending the bargaining phase of the crisis; the thoroughgoing French misperception of the military balance, a crucial underlying premise of French policy; and pressures resulting from the particular character of the French regime and from its instability. If the focus is mainly on France, it is because its failings in crisis diplomacy point to important problems of a general kind.

The Agadir crisis, 1911

The Agadir (or second Moroccan) crisis was possibly the most serious of those which preceded World War One. There were numerous war scares, and moves were contemplated which could have provoked war, despite the governments' reluctance to treat the Moroccan issue as a *casus belli*. The protracted crisis played into the hands of nationalist forces, especially in France and Germany, increasing the expectation and acceptance of war and the pressures to accelerate the arms race.[47] The crisis itself offers an exceptionally clear example of coercive diplomacy – the attempt to achieve political gains through the threat of war – and its limitations. German State Secretary Kiderlen has often been criticised for his choice of tactics, seen as needlessly provocative and counter-productive, but the more plausible conclusion is that the particular circumstances placed Germany in a 'no-win' situation, offering little chance of diplomatic success, whatever its tactics.

Certain broad similarities and contrasts with 1870 are apparent. Germany's annexation of Alsace-Lorraine had ensured that France would remain its adversary. Its superiority to France in industrial and military capacity and its potential to achieve a hegemonial position in Europe had led to the formation of the Franco-Russian alliance and subsequently the Triple Entente, arrayed against the coalition of the central powers, the Triple Alliance.[48] French and German willingness to go to war was lower than in 1870 – no such issues as German unification or the rivalry for continental primacy were at stake – but the governments and publics were, as then, highly sensitive to perceived threats to national honour or prestige. The danger of war thus arose not from the direct stakes in Morocco but from the possibility that one or other party's handling of the issue might be sufficiently provocative to bring about an 'escalation' of the stakes and a sequence of reactions that would amount to a 'hostility spiral'. As July 1914 was to demonstrate, alliance commitments could then draw in the other powers, which had no greater direct interest in Serbia than in Morocco.

The setting

The alliance systems constituted part of the setting of the crisis, and tensions between and within them had been heightened by the preceding crises (Morocco 1905–06 and Bosnia 1908–09) and by the inability of Britain and Germany to achieve a naval agreement. The second dimension of the setting was European colonisation now in its final phase with few opportunities for further expansion. A potentially rich territory such as Morocco was thus of major interest. The Algeciras agreement of 1906 provided for Morocco to retain its nominal independence and for equal commercial rights for outside powers, but France and Spain shared control over the police in its open ports and France had the primary voice in controlling its state bank.

171

Franco-German frictions over commercial and financial issues in Morocco were not overcome by the Franco-German Accord of February 1909, whereby France undertook not to hinder German commercial and industrial interests and Germany to respect France's 'special political interests ... closely tied to the consolidation of internal peace and order'.[49] The Accord was open to misunderstanding: it could be perceived on the one hand as reaffirming the provisions of Algeciras, on the other as granting France a free hand.[50] While Germany looked towards economic collaboration, France moved cautiously towards securing full political control. By early 1911 disorder in the interior and around the capital, Fez, created conditions which France was tempted to exploit.[51]

The crisis may be divided into three phases. During the first, from April to June, France moved to occupy Fez, pleading the need to safeguard the Europeans there and disregarding repeated German warnings – in effect, seeking to achieve a protectorate over Morocco through a *fait accompli*. The second phase (July), which may be termed one of brinkmanship, was initiated by the arrival of the German gunboat *Panther* at Agadir and dominated by the German demand for the whole of the French Congo as compensation and by threats to go to 'extreme lengths'. The third phase, the 'diplomacy of attrition', lasted from August until the Franco-German agreements on Morocco and the Congo were signed on 4 November. Although Germany now moderated its demands and both governments were controlled by decision makers highly averse to war, there were further war scares, the negotiations were arduous and the outcome unpopular in both France and Germany.

Phase 1: Attempted fait accompli (April–June)

This is rightly treated as the first phase, not merely the prelude. Although the risks were not openly acknowledged, French officials were aware of challenging Germany and were apprehensive before the occupation of Fez. The British, also apprehensive, urged caution, and Germany gave explicit warnings and prepared a countermove. The French challenge, arousing fears of impending dangers, marked the opening of the crisis.

On 5 April Jean Cruppi, the Foreign Minister in the newly formed Monis ministry, advised the powers that France might find it necessary to occupy Fez. Kiderlen, already aggrieved by recent setbacks over economic issues in Morocco, warned that this would create a new situation contrary to the Algeciras agreement, in which Germany's interests would have to be taken into account.[52] Before the French Cabinet authorised the occupation of Fez (22 April) German Chancellor Bethmann-Hollweg had warned that this would open up the whole Moroccan question, and on 28 April Kiderlen informed the French ambassador that it would mean the dissolution of the Act of Algeciras and that Germany would resume its liberty of action. The warning was made public on 30 April.[53] The French ambassador and military attaché perceived that the warnings were serious, and Britain and Russia qualified their assurances of support with cautionary advice, but French policy, reflecting the views of the colonial lobby and a group of nationalistic officials in the Foreign Ministry, remained unaffected.[54]

On 3 May Kiderlen formulated a plan for Germany's response to the occupation of Fez. After an interval which was expected to establish that the French would not withdraw, Germany would declare that the Algeciras Act was no longer effective. Since French absorption of Morocco without compensation to Germany would be 'a moral defeat' and mere protest would be ineffective, Germany should seize 'an object' which would make France 'inclined to compensation'. Germany should send ships to the ports of Mogador and Agadir: this 'clenched pledge' could be exchanged for suitable colonial compensation elsewhere. In obtaining the Kaiser's approval, Kiderlen drew attention to the electoral implications of a favourable outcome.[55]

With minor revisions, this remained the basis for German policy. The director of the Hamburg-Morokko Gesellschaft, Dr Wilhelm Regendanz, who on the Foreign Ministry's request organised a petition from German interests in Morocco seeking protection, pressed the case for the annexation of southern Morocco and this option was included in a revised proposal on 12 June, but there is no indication that this was Kiderlen's objective. For tactical reasons he did not rule it out, but the Kaiser had consistently opposed German political involvement in Morocco, France would resist it bitterly, and the idea of compensation elsewhere in Africa was of long standing.[56] It was revived unofficially by the French Finance Minister, Joseph Caillaux, on 7 May.[57]

In accordance with the plan, Germany made no immediate response to the French occupation of Fez (21 May); Kiderlen had left Berlin for a six-week cure at Bad Kissingen, observing that by the time of his return 'a very serious situation would have developed'.[58] Spain, however, by occupying two centres in northern Morocco, further undermined the Algeciras settlement. Jules Cambon, the French ambassador in Berlin, persuaded his government to make an overture to Germany, but it withheld all concrete proposals, whether on contested issues in Morocco such as railway construction or on territorial compensation. In the absence of concrete proposals, Cambon and Kiderlen engaged in two days of diplomatic fencing at Bad Kissingen on 21–22 June. Cambon sought to rule out any territorial concession in Morocco, but 'one may seek elsewhere'. He could suggest nothing concrete, however, 'for these ideas are new'. Kiderlen concluded the talks with the faintly menacing 'bring us something back from Paris'.[59]

Nothing had been said to dispel Kiderlen's assumption that 'independent action' by Germany would be necessary to induce France to make a concrete offer, nor did the replacement of the Monis Cabinet by a new ministry under Caillaux on 28 June modify the German strategy. The only significant modification was the decision to send a ship to Agadir alone, not to Mogador. This has been plausibly explained as an attempt to avoid complications: at Mogador, an open port, there was a risk of an immediate clash with other Europeans. At Agadir the pretext of safeguarding German nationals was even less convincing but there was little risk that the symbolic challenge would have unwanted side-effects.[60]

Phase 2: Brinkmanship (July)

Except in Germany, where the nationalist press expressed 'jubilation' after the perceived 'humiliations' of recent years, reactions to the announcement of the *Panther's* arrival at Agadir on 1 July were muted: in France, shock rather than outrage, and appeals for calm; in Britain, expressions of support for France but reluctance to exaggerate the incident.[61] More importantly, both Caillaux and the British Cabinet decided independently not to send warships to Agadir or Mogador, a step which would have amounted to a dramatic escalation of the crisis, risking inflaming nationalist emotion as in 1870. French Foreign Minister de Selves sought unsuccessfully to circumvent the initial decision but was overruled; the Minister for the Navy, Delcassé, gave an explicit order that no ship be sent to southern Morocco.[62]

With Russia and Austria-Hungary offering no more than formal assurances of support to their respective allies, British support for France became of the greatest importance. While invoking the obligations of the entente in public, Britain saw no vital strategic interests at stake: it could even accept a German port in Morocco, but not a fortified port. Initially fearing that France might partition Morocco with Germany and Spain, it tacitly accepted that the main negotiation might be bilateral as French opposition to granting territorial compensation in Morocco became clear.[63]

The Congo was mentioned for the first time in Franco-German official conversations on 8 and 9 July, each side claiming that it was the other which had introduced this topic of years of speculation.[64] The meeting between Cambon and Kiderlen which raised the crisis to a new level of tension took place on 15 July when Kiderlen, once again pressed to state Germany's demands, unrolled a map of Africa and pointed to the whole of the French Congo – a demand perceived as so disproportionate as to revive the fear that his real aim was, after all, a share in Morocco. In response to Cambon's protest that the demand would cause the negotiations to fail, Kiderlen suggested that Germany might, in exchange, offer Togo or part of the northern Cameroon.[65]

The leaking of the German proposals in Paris and London, omitting mention of the offer of Togo, raised the temperature of public comment and brought about a much more serious view of the crisis in London. The Foreign Secretary, Sir Edward Grey, moved closer to the Foreign Office view that the entente was at risk, but Cabinet support for France remained strictly limited. France was informed that Morocco was not a *casus belli* and was advised to submit counter-proposals on the Congo; if the talks broke down, Britain would seek to act in concert with France and would propose a conference.[66]

A divergence between Kiderlen and the Kaiser became apparent when the latter, absent on his northern cruise, was informed of the meeting of 15 July and of Kiderlen's comment on the need to proceed forcefully (*sehr kräftig auftreten*). He reproached Kiderlen for missing the best opportunity for a settlement, in May, when Britain was reacting coolly to the march on Fez. While Bethmann-Hollweg sought to reassure the Kaiser that no threat of war was intended, Kiderlen submitted his resignation. When Bethmann declined to forward it to the Kaiser, he submitted a second letter: he would resign unless the Kaiser assured him of his continued confidence.[67] The response, sometimes interpreted as such an assurance, did no more than authorise the Chancellor to continue the negotiations in accordance with previous instructions.[68]

Kiderlen's letters set out his case for a credible threat in order to overcome French resistance to yielding worthwhile territorial compensation. They would do so only if convinced that 'we are prepared for the ultimate step ... i.e. if the others feel and know that we are. Anyone who announces in advance that he will not fight never achieves anything in politics.'[69] He had not threatened France, but the negotiations might require Germany to express its determination to

175

take the ultimate step. 'And if this is to be effective, we must be inwardly determined to do so.'[70]

In his meeting with Cambon on 20 July Kiderlen expressed just such a threat: if the conversations failed, Germany would demand a return to the provisions of Algeciras and would, if necessary, 'go to extreme lengths'. Cambon responded that France would go as far as Germany.[71] When Britain looked to a general conference in the event of a breakdown, Kiderlen envisaged a bilateral confrontation: the gulf between British and German expectations was about to impinge dramatically on the crisis. Sensing this divergence, on 21 July Grey warned the German ambassador, Count Paul Metternich, that 'it must be clearly understood that we should recognise no settlement in Morocco in which we had not a voice'.[72]

An accident of timing now powerfully reinforced the intended warning signal, momentarily threatening a grave Anglo-German crisis. David Lloyd George, Chancellor of the Exchequer and a supporter of the radical Liberals wary of commitments to France, was to speak that evening at the Mansion House. He obtained the agreement of the Prime Minister and Foreign Secretary to include in his address a passage on foreign affairs, a passage which was likened by one critic to Gramont's rhetoric in July 1870. Having extolled Britain's contributions to Europe and to human liberty, and expressed his own commitment to the preservation of peace, he went on:

> But if a situation were to be forced upon us in which peace could only be preserved ... by allowing Britain to be treated, when her interests were vitally affected, as if she were of no account in the Cabinet of nations, then I say emphatically that peace at that price would be intolerable for a great country like ours to endure.[73]

The speech inflamed the press in all three nations, heartening the 'French colonial Chauvinists' and provoking a 'wave of indignation' in Germany, where it was portrayed as 'a stroke of lightning in the night which has shown the entire German people where its enemy stands'.[74]

Kiderlen now reassured the British government that Germany did not seek territory in Morocco, but elsewhere. In view of Lloyd George's speech, however, this could not be made public because it would appear to be yielding to a threat: Britain's recourse to public diplomacy risked a violent explosion; and he rejected the idea of a general conference. Grey was alarmed that Germany might launch a surprise attack on the Fleet. It was placed on increased readiness and a northern cruise was cancelled, sparking rumours and speculation.[75]

The tension quickly eased: Kiderlen authorised Britain to state that the Franco-German negotiations did not touch British interests and requested Britain to state that it would welcome their successful conclusion. Prime Minister Asquith incorporated the suggestions in a parliamentary statement on 27 July which offered general support to France, but Britain once again declined to enter into commitments for specific contingencies.[76]

Meanwhile Kiderlen maintained Germany's demand for the whole of the Congo, repeating the threat to go to 'extreme lengths' on 28 July, when Bethmann dined with Kiderlen in an attempt to ascertain his objective. The result was a sleepless night: 'the Chancellor believes Kiderlen not only considers the possibility of war but wants it'.[77] Kiderlen may have been encouraged by a further unofficial offer from Caillaux, through intermediaries: while France could not part with the whole of the Congo, it could concede a substantial portion, including access to the Congo river, the frontier with the Belgian Congo. The deciphering of this communication by the French security services heightened tension between Caillaux and de Selves.[78]

On 29 July Bethmann-Hollweg and Kiderlen met the Kaiser at Swinemünde. Although there is no record of their discussion, there is good reason to see the meeting as a crucial turning-point in which the Kaiser, his long-standing caution over Morocco reinforced by Britain's public stance, now overruled Kiderlen, insisting that Morocco was not worth the risk of war, and still less the Congo.[79] The most convincing evidence is the shift in Germany's negotiating position which followed the meeting. Germany now demanded only a portion of the Congo, and the threats and war scares in the ensuing phase were no more than tactical bluffs and patently false alarms. The phase of brinkmanship came to an end when the policies of the two rivals came under the decisive restraining influence of Caillaux and the Kaiser, both unwilling to press the dispute to 'extreme lengths'. The German nationalist press, suspecting such a softening of policy, engaged in unprecedented personal attacks on the Kaiser but failed to pressure the government to resume a stronger line.[80] The bitterness of some members of his entourage was expressed by the Chief of Staff, Helmuth von Moltke, in a letter to his wife:

> If once again we crawl out of this affair with our tail between our legs ... then I shall quit. But before that I shall propose that we do away with the army and place ourselves under the protection of Japan; then we can concentrate on making money and develop into ninnies.[81]

Phase 3: The diplomacy of attrition (August–November)

On 1 August Cambon and Kiderlen agreed, as 'a basis of negotiations', that Germany would receive part of the Congo. Kiderlen's insistence that it include access to the sea and to the river Congo now created problems. Caillaux, finding it politically difficult to implement his earlier unofficial proposal, engaged in several manoeuvres to demonstrate his vigorous defence of French interests. He issued orders foreshadowing mobilisation, intended to impress the Germans but provoking such alarm that he was compelled to issue a denial. He overruled de Selves, now willing to accept German access to the Congo, insisting on holding this crucial concession for future bargaining. And on 4 August he threatened that French and British warships would move to Agadir unless there was progress towards a settlement within eight days. The Kaiser, outraged by this apparent ultimatum, supported Kiderlen's threat to break off the negotiations unless it was withdrawn; Caillaux, his bluff called, claimed to have been misreported.[82] He also inquired of General Joffre whether France would have a 70 per cent chance of victory if it came to war, and used his negative response to justify the need for negotiations. Coming so late, this must be seen as no more than a move to buttress his policy against criticism.[83]

August saw further incidents and manoeuvring for position: there were still no formal draft proposals. On 17 August Cambon was recalled for discussions and Kiderlen left on vacation, remarking: 'Return to Berlin on the 28th and we will decide whether war or peace.'[84] The publication of the Pan-German League's pamphlet *West Marokko Deutsch* had revived agitation and French fears of a sudden landing at Agadir, and led to a further unsuccessful attempt to commit the British to sending ships. Further incidents and rumours concerning army manoeuvres maintained tension at a high level.[85] A three-day postponement of the negotiations scheduled to resume on 1 September led to a spectacular collapse of the German stock exchange. There were financial reasons for the crash, but it was rumoured to have been caused by the withdrawal of French funds, and it remains unclear whether or not Caillaux played a role in precipitating it.[86]

When the negotiations resumed on 4 September Kiderlen conceded priority to the Moroccan accord, but introduced contentious claims for privileges for road construction in the south, which delayed progress. The two edged towards a Moroccan agreement, initialled on 12 October, which amounted to German acceptance of a French protectorate. The Congo agreement required further hard bargaining as Caillaux resisted access to the Congo river, pointing to the threat to his ministry's continuation in office, while Kiderlen, equally vulnerable to public criticism, succeeded in achieving his demand at the price of concessions elsewhere. Agreement was reached on 2 November, and the two treaties were signed on 4 November.[87]

The agreement of the signatories of the Act of Algeciras was achieved with little difficulty except for Austria, which sought financial compensation, and more importantly Spain which, with British backing, secured coastal territory which increased the agreement's unpopularity in France. Parliamentary ratification of the treaties encountered greater difficulties. The Reichstag approved it on 12 November, after several days of debate during which the Chancellor was jeered and the government was subjected to a barrage of criticism. The process in France was even more dramatic: Caillaux's non-official negotiations were exposed and his government fell, but his successor Poincaré marshalled the votes for ratification on 10 February 1912.[88]

Conclusion

In retrospect, Kiderlen has been severely criticised for his choice of strategy: it is argued that he was insensitive to the inevitable French response to being threatened, that he missed the opportunity for compromise when a new ministry was formed under Caillaux, and that he obtained less compensation than if he had never sent the *Panther* to Agadir.[89] This line of criticism, however, overlooks French obduracy in the face of repeated German warnings in May and the political influence of the colonial lobby and of nationalistic officials. Moreover, according to Caillaux's biographer, the new premier shared his colleagues' illusions in June, failing to perceive the situation as a crisis. The Chancellor, his perceptive assistant Kurt Riezler and the Foreign Office staff shared Kiderlen's belief that the French would make concessions only under strong pressure.[90] Unlike other colonial powers, Germany could not lay claim to territory not yet annexed by Europeans, but sought compensation within existing French colonies, provoking intense resistance from the interests affected by the claim. Purely diplomatic pressure offered little prospect of success. Conceivably Kiderlen missed a brief moment of opportunity in the days before the occupation of Fez when France may have been willing to offer concessions elsewhere, but the evidence is not compelling.[91] The Kaiser subsequently pointed to a lost opportunity but not, as Kiderlen correctly noted, at the relevant time.

Subsequent discussion will focus especially on two aspects of the crisis, bargaining and internal politics. Kiderlen's attempt at coercive bargaining illustrates three general problems: the likelihood that threats may provoke resistance, not induce compliance; the difficulty of achieving governmental unity behind high-risk strategies for questionable stakes; and the danger that the confrontation may escape from the control of the bargainers, becoming more like a hostility spiral. The major role of internal political pressures and divided governments merits further attention, as does the question of goals: while the immediate goals on both sides appear relatively clear, their larger rationale is not, raising the question, especially for Germany at that time, whether there was any such rationale.

9 PEARL HARBOR AND THE BERLIN CRISES

The United States was the principal actor in the final three cases included in the study: the US–Japan crisis in 1940–41, the Berlin blockade and the protracted Berlin crisis between 1958 and 1962. The cases offer three 'snapshots' in which it is possible to discern something of the evolution of the American conduct of foreign policy, but this is incidental to the present themes. Only the first of the three can be reconstructed from the perspective of both key actors. The paucity of Soviet sources limits the extent to which the Berlin cases can be used for comparative analysis, but they are important in illustrating the effects of nuclear weapons on crisis diplomacy.

The US–Japan crisis, 1940–1941

That the outcome of this protracted crisis would be war appeared increasingly probable to decision makers on both sides during 1941. Although it was played down by some of them in 1940, the risk of war was already evident during most of that year, but there was no clear starting point, no sudden precipitant of the crisis. Arguably, however, the repercussions of Germany's invasion of France, Belgium and the Netherlands in May 1940 were such as to intensify the conflict between the United States and Japan to the level of crisis: Japan was emboldened to consider steps which could lead to war, even though both sides hoped to avoid it. Each sought to deter the other, but most of their moves proved counter-productive, enhancing rather than reducing the perceived likelihood of war. May 1940 is therefore taken as the starting point. Some of the policy dilemmas of the crisis had already been addressed, but now they presented themselves with much greater urgency than before.

There are two radically different interpretations of the crisis. On the one hand, it is seen as a process which gradually revealed that the goals of the two adversaries were fundamentally incompatible: Japan was determined to gain control over the resources and societies of East

181

and Southeast Asia, and the United States was determined to prevent its doing so. War could be hastened or delayed, but could not in the end be averted. Snyder and Diesing, reflecting much of the earlier scholarship, present the crisis in this way, as do recent works by Michael Barnhart and Waldo Heinrichs.[1] On the other hand, a significant minority of scholars have argued that certain key policy choices were of far greater consequence. According to this view, the course of events was greatly influenced by confusion, misperception and questionable decisions. Different policies might well have postponed or even averted the diplomatic deadlock which was reached in November 1941. Among those who argue along these lines are Paul Schroeder, Chihiro Hosoya, Robert Butow and Abraham Ben-Zvi.[2] Both interpretations afford valuable insights, and neither can be conclusively refuted.[3]

The setting

Tension between the US and Japan dated from the latter's invasion of Manchuria in 1931 and its creation of a dependent regime, Manchukuo in 1932, which the US declined to recognise; but the immediate setting for the crisis was Japan's invasion of China in 1937. During the 1930s, as Japan faced international difficulties, in particular high tariff barriers against its exports, its politics became dominated by the military and by right-wing nationalists who had no scruple in using violence against their political adversaries. By the start of the European war Japan had occupied northern and eastern China but was unable to break the resistance of Chiang Kai-shek's Kuomintang government, now based in Chungking.

The US condemned the invasion of China and was antagonised by the damage to its commercial interests, but until 1940 its response was limited to diplomatic protest and a 'moral embargo' on the export of military aircraft and weapons which was announced in June 1938. In July 1939 the government gave the requisite six-month notice that it would terminate the Treaty of Commerce and Navigation with Japan. This permitted it to control exports after January 1940, but no immediate use was made of these powers. An embargo on the export of key resources needed for Japan's war economy, oil and scrap iron, would have been popular, but the President accepted Secretary of State Cordell Hull's advice that the risk of provoking further Japanese aggression was too great.[4]

The initial effect of the outbreak of war in Europe was not favourable to Japan: it was severely embarrassed by the Nazi–Soviet Pact in

August 1939, negotiated in extreme secrecy without informing Japan, which rendered meaningless its own agreement with Germany, the Anti-Comintern Pact. Two relatively moderate governments which followed, under Prime Ministers Abe and Yonai, sought to avoid clashes with the US but remained committed to victory in China and the creation of a 'New Order in East Asia'. Germany's victories in May 1940, however, created a new strategic situation. The defeat of France and the Netherlands left their colonial possessions in Southeast Asia vulnerable to Japan, and the loss of Malaya would seriously weaken Britain. The Roosevelt Administration was resolved to assist Britain against Germany, short of involvement in war, but the priority which it accorded to Europe and the Atlantic severely constrained its options vis-à-vis Japan.

The ensuing crisis may be divided into four phases. During the first, May–September 1940, Japan advanced into northern Indo-China but no further, the US imposed significant trade restrictions and Japan entered into the Tripartite Pact. These measures, whatever their deterrent objective, increased the level of mutual hostility. The second phase (October 1940–June 1941) amounted to a pause during which Japan failed to win major gains in the Netherlands East Indies through diplomatic pressure, and opened exploratory negotiations with the US. The third phase, July 1941, saw decisive moves: Japan's occupation of southern Indo-China and the US imposition of an oil embargo; and in the final phase (August–November 1941) Japan prepared for war but also pursued the option of accommodation until the breakdown of the negotiations at the end of November.

Phase 1: Towards confrontation (May–September 1940)

The repercussions in Asia of Germany's invasion of France, Belgium and the Netherlands in May 1940 became clear only gradually. Japan, initially alarmed that one of the other powers might pre-empt it by gaining control over the Netherlands East Indies (NEI), soon regained confidence. Talks between Foreign Minister Arita and US ambassador Grew in May–June established that there was no basis for agreement on the principles of an East Asian settlement between the US and the moderate Yonai ministry. In June Japan sought to block assistance to China, demanding that Indo-China, Hong Kong and Burma close their respective frontiers. The authorities in Indo-China complied, and Britain reluctantly agreed to close the Burma Road for three months. A Japanese mission to the NEI obtained increased oil deliveries but was denied access for Japanese enterprises and migrants.[5]

On 2 July, after several weeks of debate, Congress authorised the President to restrict exports essential to American defence, but initially few items were placed under licence. On 26 July, after a sharp dispute among Roosevelt's advisers, an embargo, intended to affect Japan, was imposed on aviation fuel and steel scrap, but not on its most crucial imports. Secretaries Stimson, Knox and Morgenthau had advocated a complete embargo on oil exports to Japan, but Roosevelt was persuaded that the risk of provoking a Japanese move into Southeast Asia was too great.[6] The restrictions were not prompted by any such Japanese move, but by a sharp increase in its purchases of aviation fuel.

In Japan, military pressure led to Yonai's replacement by Prince Konoye on 17 July. The new Cabinet agreed to seek a quicker victory in China and to take stronger measures in the 'south', short of risking war with Britain and the US. The Navy still ruled out such a war, while demanding greater resources in order to place itself in a position to fight it.[7] In September, seeking the use of airfields and the right to station troops in northern Indo-China, Japan engaged in limited military incursions. On 26 September the US signalled its hostility to further southward aggression by embargoing the export of scrap iron, thereby imposing serious costs on Japan's economy.[8]

During the same month Japan, Germany and Italy negotiated the Tripartite Pact, signed on 27 September. The parties acknowledged one another's spheres of influence in Europe and East Asia and undertook 'to assist one another with all political, economic and military means' if any one were attacked by the United States. The question whether a party had been attacked within the meaning of the treaty was to be determined by consultation, but the Privy Council, and later the Americans, were assured that Japan was free to decide independently. Intended to deter the US from entering into war against any of the parties, the Pact's main effect was to intensify American suspicion and hostility towards Japan.[9]

Phase 2: Pause (October 1940–June 1941)

During the following nine months Japan made no further military move in Southeast Asia, despite strong German prompting to attack Singapore. One reason was the caution of the Navy, which had concluded in November 1940 that the US would support Britain if it were attacked in the region, and was not yet ready for war with the US. New appointments were changing the balance of power within the Navy, however, in favour of middle-level staff officers ready to risk war and perceiving greater danger in waiting until the US build-up outstripped the Japanese.[10] Japan sought to associate the Soviet Union with the Tripartite Pact but, in view of emerging tensions between Berlin and Moscow, settled eventually for the Neutrality Pact with the Soviet Union, signed in April 1941.[11] Japan's attempt to achieve its goals in Southeast Asia through non-military means had only marginal success: Indo-China and Thailand accepted it as a mediator over disputed frontier issues, but the colonial government of the NEI rebuffed the more important initiative whereby Japan sought to establish an economic presence in the colony, and drove hard bargains over export contracts, leaving oil agreements to the companies which, under US influence, rejected increased deliveries.[12]

American policy during this period was constrained by the 1940 election campaign in which both Roosevelt and his opponent, Wendell Willkie, advocated all support to Britain short of war, and indeed as a way of keeping the US out of war.[13] Still in the early stages of its military build-up and with its Atlantic priority, the US nonetheless signalled its strategic interests in the Pacific through the naval presence in Pearl Harbor and through reinforcing its token military units in the Philippines, but rejected urgent British pleas to support Singapore in early 1941. Nonetheless, Anglo-American staff talks provided for coordination of naval activity should both be engaged in war in the Pacific, even though the conditions under which the US might support Britain remained unclear. The licensing of exports of materials needed for US defence was extended during this period to cover most items of importance to Japan – iron ore, pig iron, steel and copper – but not oil, which remained unrestricted except for high-grade aviation fuel.

Diplomatic conversations began in March between Hull and the newly appointed Japanese ambassador, Admiral Nomura, who was associated with the elder naval officers opposed to war with the US. Nomura's lack of diplomatic experience and his conception of his role, charitably described as 'mediator' between the two governments rather than 'communicator', ensured that the talks generated a degree of confusion and misperception, especially in Tokyo, such that to refer to them as 'negotiations' would be a misnomer.[14] The idea of a broad settlement of Japanese–American differences had arisen in unofficial discussions in Tokyo with two Catholic missionaries, Bishop Walsh and Father Drought, who subsequently communicated with Roosevelt through an intermediary. Roosevelt and Hull encouraged the two to continue discussions with Japanese representatives in Washington with a view to eliciting a Japanese proposal which could serve as a basis for negotiations. Despite Hull's pessimism concerning the

185

outcome, it was held that even the slightest possibility of averting war should be pursued, and the negotiations might buy time while the US mobilised its miltitary potential.[15]

Following these discussions, Japanese officials formulated a 'Draft Understanding', a relatively moderate statement of Japanese proposals on China, the Pacific, trade and the interpretation of the Tripartite Pact, which was presented to Hull on 9 April. He sought from Nomura confirmation that this was the Japanese official position, and acquainted him with the four principles which the US held to be essential for a broad settlement: respect for territorial integrity, non-interference in internal affairs, equality of commercial opportunity and non-disturbance of the status quo by violent means. Nomura did not communicate the four principles, and the ambiguity of his report led the Japanese government to regard the Draft Understanding as an exploratory American proposal. Tokyo thus seriously misunderstood American views, and not surprisingly formulated a 'harder' set of proposals (12 May), which was scrutinised coldly by the Americans before presenting their own 'hard' counter-proposals on 21 June.[16] The misperception of US policy between April and June encouraged an expectation that the US would acquiesce in Japan's next move, into southern Indo-China.

Phase 3: Decisive moves (June–July 1941)

Japan's decision to occupy southern Indo-China was taken incrementally in the weeks preceding the Imperial Conference of 2 July which ratified it. Germany's invasion of the Soviet Union on 22 June, which transformed the geopolitical prospects, did not prompt a careful review of Japan's options but rather what Roosevelt termed 'a real drag-down and knock-out fight ... trying to decide which way they are going to jump – attack Russia, attack the South Seas ... or sit on the fence and be more friendly with us'.[17] The commitment to advance 'south', short of risking war, dated from July 1940. The willingness to risk war increased as the US extended its embargoes and the Navy, having achieved an increased share in key resources, moved towards the state of preparedness which it had declared necessary. The Army, concerned over threats to essential resources, became increasingly insistent on gaining control of southern Indo-China as the essential springboard for any further advance.

The breakdown of the negotiations with the NEI in June, spelling the end of hopes of peaceful penetration or even increased supplies of its resources, influenced the timing of the crucial decision. On 11 June the Liaison Conference (meeting of senior ministers with the chiefs of staff) decided to recall the delegation to the NEI and the following day it approved an 'acceleration of policy concerning the South', providing for an early occupation of southern Indo-China, if necessary using force, and even if Britain and the US were to intervene.[18] Foreign Minister Matsuoka, aware of the forthcoming invasion of the Soviet Union, then sought to defer this move, championing an attack 'north' in order to exploit the expected German victory. The Navy, averse to fighting a third major power or to losing its hard-won share of resources, was the most determined opponent of a 'northern' strategy. Matsuoka attracted some Army support, but the General Staff, concerned over the demands of the China war and the threats to resources, remained committed to the move into Indo-China. Konoye failed to win support for a tentative proposal for an approach to the US. Neither he nor Matsuoka could induce the Liaison Conference to contemplate a radical response to the new strategic situation: the narrow priorities of the services – a coincidence of interests, not a consensus – prevailed.[19]

Before the decision on southern Indo-China could be implemented, however, conflict between Matsuoka and his colleagues over his proposal to break off the negotiations with the US led to the resignation of the Cabinet (16 July) which was reappointed with a new Foreign Minister, Admiral Toyoda. The Vichy government now yielded to Japan's ultimatum demanding bases in the south: their occupation began on 24 July. The decision, the ultimatum and the date of the occupation were known to the US through intercepted diplomatic cables.[20]

Despite this forewarning, the US made no attempt to deter Japan's move. While it could not threaten the use of force, it could have credibly threatened a complete embargo of oil exports. The option of 'immediate preventative action' was considered by the State Department, but appears not to have been examined at the political level.[21] This may have been because of the unresolved controversy between those advocating an oil embargo as a deterrent to further Japanese aggression and those who feared that it would provoke an attack on the NEI. Roosevelt had thus far supported the latter. In mid-July he still maintained that a complete embargo 'would probably precipitate an outbreak of war in the Pacific', and officials prepared plans which, while freezing Japanese funds, would establish a quota for oil exports based on the 'normal years' 1935 and 1936.[22] The Navy continued to oppose a complete embargo.

Orders freezing Japanese assets were issued on 26 July, but nothing was said on the permitted quota of oil exports, nor on the release of funds for approved exports. The intention was to keep Japan in a state of uncertainty while administrative procedures were worked out; governments seeking to concert policy with the US were kept in equal uncertainty. Initially, no export licences were issued and no funds released, and this practice was extended during Roosevelt's absence for his first meeting with Churchill in early August. Those implementing the policy favoured restrictiveness: requests for licences or funds were met with evasion and procrastination, and the impression was created that the policy was indeed a total embargo. On 5 September Roosevelt and Hull confirmed that this was now the case.[23]

Whether the embargo was a 'bureaucratic reflex' (Anderson) or 'a decision closely held and deviously managed' (Heinrichs)[24] is a question of interpretation which is not crucial to an understanding of the case. The former view is the more plausible: Roosevelt and Hull remained concerned to avoid a confrontation with Japan, as their toning down of the warning which Roosevelt promised Churchill he would deliver serves to indicate. As he and Hull became aware that the implementation of the policy went beyond their intentions, they also recognised that to relax it would be controversial and would send an undesired signal to friends and adversaries alike. There is no compelling evidence for the alternative view that Roosevelt, monitoring global developments as a whole, favoured the tacit stiffening of policy to the extent that it actually occurred. The embargo was a victory, of sorts, for the 'hard-liners' who had long advocated it, but was not imposed because their policy was finally accepted, but because of the way in which an ambiguous decision was implemented. Most failed to perceive the consequences; the resistance of those who did had been worn down by the momentum of events, the incremental imposition of partial embargoes and the perception of Japan as bent on aggression regardless of the US response.

Phase 4: The failure of negotiations (August–November 1941)

The freeze and embargo, unexpected by most Japanese decision makers, introduced a new urgency, even desperation, into their deliberations: it was no longer a question of seizing the best opportunity, but of striking while Japan still held adequate oil reserves and before the US could mobilise its vastly superior potential. Seasonal considerations pointed to November 1941 as the time, and the need to secure key resources pointed to Malaya and the NEI as the targets. The Army reached these decisions in early August, deferring the 'northern' attack for the time being, and the Navy, having insisted on the inclusion of the Philippines and an expansion of the force committed to the invasion, agreed by the end of the month to begin military operations in late October if Japan's demands were not accepted by that month.[25] Prime Minister Konoye and, it would appear, the Emperor, wished to see greater emphasis on diplomacy: when the programme was approved by an Imperial Conference on 6 September it was stated that the attempt to achieve agreement through diplomacy would come first, but this was perceived essentially as the acceptance of Japan's demands.[26]

The main demands were that the US and Britain cease assisting China, refrain from increasing their forces in the Pacific or deploying them beyond their own territories, restore normal trade and assist Japan's economic cooperation with the NEI. In return, Japan would undertake not to advance further beyond Indo-China, to guarantee the neutrality of the Philippines and to withdraw from Indo-China after a settlement with China had been achieved. On the Tripartite Pact it would not go beyond stating that it would decide independently on its interpretation should the US become involved in the European war.[27] The US was being asked to make major concessions of substance and principle in return, it appeared, for mere promises. It reaffirmed that any settlement must be based on Hull's four principles – implying Japan's renunciation of its 'new order' and its withdrawal from China as well as Indo-China.[28]

Konoye sought to break the deadlock by proposing a meeting with Roosevelt. The latter, initially attracted by the idea, was persuaded by Hull and his advisers that the meeting should take place only if a basis for agreement could be established in advance. Not surprisingly, this proved impossible. The projected meeting, strongly urged by Ambassador Grew, has remained a topic of speculation. Clearly, if the two had remained tied to their existing negotiating positions, it could have resolved nothing.[29] But the question was whether they might have found a new approach, setting aside the vain hope of a comprehensive settlement, and limiting themselves to the urgent and immediate: Japan's threat to Southeast Asia, and the US and its associates' restrictions on trade. In failing to explore such options, as in its earlier failure to seek to deter the advance into southern Indo-China, the US denied itself the possibility of strengthening those Japanese decision makers who were deeply apprehensive over engaging in war with so formidable a rival.

This apprehension was evident in the discussions between ministers and service chiefs during the first half of October when Oikawa, the

Minister for the Navy, could not be brought to agree that the deadline had arrived and Konoye, seeking ways of narrowing down the issues with the US, raised the possibility of reviewing the decisions of 6 September. The Cabinet's inability to reach a decision led to Konoye's resignation on 16 October, and his replacement by Tojo, Minister for War and leading spokesman of the need for an immmediate decision.[30]

On some readings, Tojo's appointment or even the preceding impasse in the negotiations signified that war had become inevitable.[31] This, however, is an oversimplification. Tojo was appointed on the understanding that his ministry was not bound by previous decisions but would undertake a thorough review of Japan's options and, in the light of that review, reach a decision as promptly as possible. The record suggests that the review was taken very seriously.[32] The dilemma created by Japan's shrinking resources, its dependence on the outcome of the European war, the prospects for early military success but the uncertainties of a long war against the US, was once again confronted, and was addressed more systematically than before. The new Foreign Minister, Togo, won time for a further diplomatic effort by threatening to resign, thus raising the prospect of further indecision. Togo's Proposal A reiterated familiar proposals, but his Proposal B broke new ground: although one-sided, for the first time it formulated an interim proposal, a potential short-term bargain. Japan would withdraw from southern Indo-China provided its assets were unfrozen and a 'required' amount of oil were supplied; the two would cooperate in relation to the NEI, both would undertake not to advance militarily and the US would cease its aid to China.[33]

On Roosevelt's suggestion, Hull prepared a simpler proposal for a three-month *modus vivendi*. Japan would withdraw from southern Indo-China and reduce its forces in northern Indo-China to the pre-July level. Both would pledge not to advance militarily; the US would supply limited amounts of key resources and would encourage Britain, Australia and the Netherlands to do likewise. Thanks to protest from China, questioning from Britain, the fear of domestic criticism and Hull's own deep suspicion of Japanese intentions, the *modus vivendi* was never put forward. Instead, on 26 November Hull presented to the Japanese envoys a ten-point restatement of the basic American standpoint, thus giving a thoroughgoing rejection of both their proposals.[34] Perceived by the Japanese decision makers, even by those who shared Togo's aversion to war, as a humiliating ultimatum, it united them in the belief that Japan now had no alternative.[35] The decision to attack was endorsed by an Imperial Conference on 1

December. The sharp questioning by the President of the Privy Council, Hara, on behalf of the Emperor, characteristic of earlier Imperial Conferences, was absent. The Emperor 'nodded in agreement with the statements being made, and displayed no signs of uneasiness. He seemed to be in an excellent mood, and we were filled with awe.'[36]

Conclusion

By 1941 the pressures of Japanese expansionism had become extremely difficult to contain. The political elite as a whole was committed to imperial expansion and autarky, the 'new order'. The armed forces were impatient for action while strategic conditions remained favourable. Could the Pacific War have been avoided, or at least deferred?

The narrative has identified a number of key choices: Japan's occupation of southern Indo-China; the US failure to attempt to deter that move; the transformation of the assets freeze into a complete oil embargo; the rejection of the proposed Roosevelt–Konoye meeting and the failure to pursue a *modus vivendi*. More generally, US policy was passive and reactive: it sought to buy time but waited on events, proceeding on the assumption that Japanese intentions were settled and that its military preparations signified a firm intent to attack; thus there was extreme suspicion of its diplomacy. There was no attempt to bargain, to exploit Japan's fears of a Pacific war, to seek to avert it, at least until the outcome of the European war was clearer. In July 1941 US policy suddenly switched from avoiding the kind of decisive economic pressure which had been deemed likely to provoke an attack in Southeast Asia to maximising such pressure, with no clear rationale and with little awareness of the significance of the shift. Policy was not informed by a larger strategic vision: the hard-line assumption that Japan would yield to pressure coexisted uneasily with the perception that it was committed to military aggression, regardless of US actions.

The US, then, failed to find ways of exploiting its overwhelming resources to diplomatic ends, relying in the end on one crude instrument, massive economic pressure. A different approach might not have succeeded in averting the war, but would have maximised the chances of doing so. Resource flows could have been permitted to continue at moderate levels subject to conditions. Japan's aversion to war would have been accorded greater weight in policy deliberations if those naval and court circles capable of taking a longer view of its interests had been strengthened as against the prevailing military preoccupation with short-term strategic 'imperatives'. Neither government achieved an integrated view of its larger interests in the conflict

191

nor devised a course of action well attuned to those interests. The Japanese were united in the end by their perception of Hull's ultimatum, and in the US Roosevelt's pragmatism imposed a modicum of coherence but no sense of purposeful direction. The depth of mutual incomprehension at the end of the crisis points to a singular failure of crisis diplomacy.[37]

The subsequent analysis will focus on the absence of bargaining and, since it was the US which had the greater options, will place some emphasis on American goals and perceptions, and in particular on the consequences of the persistence of unresolved policy differences.

The Berlin blockade, 1948–1949

The Berlin blockade was the first major East–West confrontation in which Western policy makers were required to grapple with choices which risked war, not yet against a nuclear-armed 'superpower' but against a power capable of overrunning Western Europe. Hindsight confirms that Western leaders were correct in assuming that the Soviet government was extremely reluctant to risk war, but this does not mean that the crisis was without danger. For the first time, policy makers addressed the problems of unintended war in the nuclear age, the risk that moves perceived as provocations could trigger unexpected escalation, and the opposite risk that too accommodating a posture could encourage unacceptable demands, leading to 'war through miscalculation'. Thanks to the airlift, Western policy makers were able to improvise a prudent course of action which avoided both extremes, but hindsight is deceptive if it suggests that this choice was obvious, the outcome predictable, the crisis easily 'managed'.

Initially, none believed that the airlift could supply the city's needs: it was perceived as a means of 'buying time' in which to seek a diplomatic solution, and if this had not been achieved the West would have been faced with far more difficult and divisive policy choices: whether to abandon the plans for the formation of West Germany, or to withdraw from Berlin, or to demonstrate resolution through a show of force, risking war where the Soviet Union enjoyed massive local military superiority. Soviet calculations are still not known. It is plausible that the initial assumption was that the blockade would place it in a position to secure political gains in Germany as a whole or at least in Berlin, and it is clear that when it failed to achieve such ends, it was not willing to increase the stakes and risks. But it is not known how it may have responded if the West had undertaken the kind of military

192

gestures advocated by General Lucius Clay, the American military governor, or if the crisis had taken a different course.

The blockade set important precedents for Cold War crisis diplomacy through the balance between prudence and 'firmness' which was achieved on both sides. Other choices might have been far more divisive. The significance of what was achieved requires an understanding of the complexities and uncertainties confronting the decision makers, and of the differing perspectives of the three Western actors, the US, Britain and France, whose alignment was consolidated by the crisis, although this could not have been confidently predicted in advance.[38] In the absence of direct evidence of the perceptions and calculations of the other actor, the Soviet Union, plausible inferences may be drawn from its actions and statements, but the earlier cases show that such evidence is often seriously incomplete.

The setting

The gradual breakdown of postwar Soviet–Western cooperation in Germany posed serious problems for Berlin, one hundred miles inside the Soviet-occupied zone, and administered by the four occupying powers which controlled their separate zones within the city. Cooperation had always been limited, France having initially prevented the formation of centralised administrative institutions. By late 1946 the US was giving priority to German economic recovery and the American and British zones were merged for economic purposes. By early 1947 the paralysis of the Western European economies led to the proposal of the Marshall Plan, while the four-power Council of Foreign Ministers was unable to reach agreement either on current disputes or on the basic framework for German political institutions for the future. The logic of American and British policy now pointed towards the creation of a separate state in West Germany, seen as a prerequisite for the revival of the German economy, itself in turn the key to the revival of Western Europe. France was unwilling to accept this logic, however, and Britain not yet ready to do so openly. Moves towards the formation of West Germany followed only after a second deadlocked Council of Foreign Ministers, meeting in December, had demonstrated that four-power agreement was unattainable. Negotiations on Germany between the three Western occupying powers and the Benelux nations began in London in February 1948, continuing until June.

On 20 March the Soviet military governor, Marshal Sokolovsky, denouncing the separate Western negotiations as a violation of the

193

German occupation agreements, walked out of the Allied Control Council at what proved to be its last meeting. The following days witnessed a series of moves, a 'mini-blockade', which foreshadowed the blockade proper and the Western response to it.

On 1 April the Soviet authorities introduced new controls on military personnel and goods moving between the Western zones and Berlin. After discussions involving the President, Clay was authorised to reject Soviet demands to inspect American trains but not, as he had requested, to increase the number of armed guards nor to authorise them to fire unless fired upon.[39] In the event, the Soviets did not enforce their demands for inspection, but nor did they permit the trains to proceed. Clay rejected a British suggestion that inspection be permitted before trains entered the Soviet zone, on the analogy of customs inspection. Washington in turn rejected Clay's suggestion that an armed truck convoy be forced through a Soviet checkpoint – even though no restrictions had yet been imposed on such traffic.[40] On 5 April a British transport plane crashed after being buzzed by a Soviet fighter, a threat to the airlift which had been introduced to replace the blocked rail transport. All three Western governors threatened to provide fighter escorts unless satisfactory assurances of safety were given. Although the incident was not fully resolved, there was no further intrusion into the air corridors, and the new restrictions on rail freight were tacitly withdrawn a few days later.[41]

Although there had been warnings of the possibility of Soviet restrictions on access to Berlin, there had been no thorough studies of Western options. The response was therefore improvised, in accordance with the general British and American preference for resisting perceived Soviet threats or pressures but ruling out the more forceful initiatives advocated by Clay and his political adviser, Robert Murphy.[42] As British Foreign Secretary Bevin put it, firmness must be combined with 'a determination not to be provoked into any ill-considered action which might result in an impossible position from which it would be difficult to retreat'.[43]

Despite public American and British pledges to remain in Berlin, serious doubts were expressed privately as to the feasibility of doing so. The mini-crisis did not lead to a major policy review in either capital, but General Bradley, reflecting concerns in military circles, suggested to Clay on 10 April that since it was open to the Russians to render the Western position untenable, and 'we doubt whether our people are prepared to start a war in order to maintain our position in Berlin and Vienna', it might be preferable to withdraw voluntarily: Frankfurt might at the same time become the Western capital.[44] Clay vigorously opposed withdrawal unless there was a Soviet ultimatum or a total blockade – neither of which he expected – but the logic of his further comment, an early expression of the 'domino' theory, pointed to making a stand in Berlin even in these circumstances:

> After Berlin will come Western Germany and our strength there is no greater and our position no more tenable than in Berlin. If we mean that we are to hold Europe against communism, we must not budge. .. If America does not know this ... then it never will and communism will run rampant.[45]

General Robertson, the British military governor, was reported as sharing the view that Berlin was untenable.[46] Britain was prepared to commit itself in general terms to remaining there, and to the use of fighter escorts in certain circumstances, but not to the use of force irrespective of circumstances.[47] It does not appear, however, that there was any general Anglo-American divergence on remaining in Berlin: Bevin and Marshall agreed on the need to convince the Soviet government of their determination, even though there was no plan of action if their bluff was called.[48] The French, on the other hand, made clear their reluctance to risk any confrontation.

The blockade was precipitated by the extension of the currency reform in the Western zones, announced on 20 June, to the Western sectors of Berlin on 23 June. Long perceived as a prerequisite for German economic recovery, currency reform was initially envisaged on a four-power basis, but after the breakdown of the Allied Control Council, planning was limited to the Western zones. In April Clay stated a preference for a common currency in Berlin, even that of the Soviet zone, provided its issue in Berlin was controlled by the four-power Kommandatura. Washington, while leaving him some discretion, preferred to extend the Western currency reform into the Western sectors of Berlin.[49] The West finally moved towards implementing the reform after the London Conference agreed (2 June) that an assembly be convened to draft a constitution for West Germany. On 16 June, two days before Sokolovsky was informed of the impending currency reform, the Soviet delegation walked out of the Berlin Kommandatura, effectively terminating it, and thus undermining Clay's preferred option. Evidently well prepared, Sokolovsky foreshadowed a currency reform in the Soviet zone, claiming the right to extend it to the whole of Berlin.[50]

The crisis was at hand. After an unsuccessful meeting of currency experts of the four powers on 22 June the Soviets proclaimed the new Soviet-zone currency the sole legal tender in Berlin. On 23 June, without further reference back to their governments, the three

195

Western military governors announced the introduction of the new deutschmark into the Western sectors of Berlin; France, however, expressed reservations and dissociated itself from the consequences.[51] The Berlin City Assembly, defying Soviet attempts at intimidation, resolved to accept the instructions of the occupying powers responsible for their respective sectors. On 24 June, pleading technical difficulties, the Soviets suspended all rail and barge traffic into Berlin and cut off the supply of electricity and food.

Whether or not Soviet perceptions of the foregoing reached the level of crisis cannot be known; on balance, Western perceptions fell short of it. The ensuing crisis may be divided into four phases: (1) 24 June–22 July, Western decisions on the response to the blockade; (2) 23 July–18 September, negotiations in Moscow; (3) 19 September–31 January, stalemate and United Nations diplomacy; and (4) resolution (1 February–5 May). In contrast to most crises, the first phase was, at least in the Western perception, the most intense, with the level of tension declining in each successive phase.

Phase 1: The response to the blockade (24 June–22 July)

The initial British response was clearer than the American.[52] Foreign Secretary Bevin and his advisers had resolved to remain in Berlin: they perceived Soviet policy as essentially political intimidation rather than the threat of war, although the latter could not be ruled out altogether. They differed from Clay over the method of resistance, rejecting as before his preference for attempting to break the blockade; instead Robertson proposed to Clay on 25 June that an airlift be initiated and its full potential be investigated urgently.[53] Both governments rejected a Soviet invitation to return to four-power diplomacy: the uniting of the Western zones was not open to negotiation.

By 27 June three options had crystallised in Washington: to withdraw from Berlin at an appropriate time; to defend it by all possible means including those recommended by Clay; and to maintain an unprovocative but firm stand while postponing final decisions.[54] The first enjoyed strong support among Army planners, convinced that the Western position in Berlin was untenable. Clay's proposal to break the blockade won little support, but there was no agreement on an alternative course of action prior to an *ad hoc* meeting between Truman and three top advisers – Forrestal, Lovett and Royall – on 28 June.[55] Truman cut short the discussion of options – 'there was no discussion on that point, we were going to stay, period' – but his decision was perceived as endorsing the third option, not the second. 'We were in

Berlin by terms of an agreement and the Russians had no right to get us out by either direct or indirect pressure', but Royall understood that the decision was open to review, and Army planners continued to focus on the contingency of withdrawal.[56]

The crucial positive step, the initiation of the airlift, was taken in two stages. On 25 June, after discussion with Robertson and the Berlin socialist leader Ernst Reuter, Clay ordered that all available transport aircraft begin airlifting food supplies; on 26 June Truman endorsed the airlift and ordered the allocation of further aircraft to it. Clay acted unilaterally after his staff had been unable to agree on a course of action; Truman after little or no canvassing of options.[57] These were, as often noted, striking instances of decisive leadership – reflecting deep-seated beliefs in the nature of the conflict with the Soviet Union – but it should also be noted that the airlift was uncontroversial. There was a precedent in the April mini-airlift, and while giving substance to the third option – a firm but unprovocative stand – it left the other options open. None at this stage supposed that it would supply Berlin's needs indefinitely, but it would buy time for diplomacy.

There was little immediate prospect for diplomatic progress, however: a meeting of the zonal commanders in Berlin on 3 July confirmed that the Soviet concern was much less the currency issue than the plans to unite the Western zones. Western notes to Moscow (6 July) reaffirmed the occupation rights and offered four-power talks only after the lifting of the blockade. The Soviet reply (14 July) maintained that the policy of dividing Germany removed the basis for the Western presence in Berlin. On 15 July the US sought to enhance the credibility of the Western stand by announcing that two groups of B-29 bombers would be deployed in Britain – a move which Bevin had proposed on 26 June. Though the B-29s were regarded as nuclear-capable, it is now known that these particular aircraft had not been configured to carry nuclear weapons. Whether the Soviet leaders realised this is not known, but the perception elsewhere had the effect of enhancing Western confidence at a tense moment.[58]

American policy makers now addressed the two main options for remaining in Berlin: an armed convoy or an expanded airlift. The former, again pressed by Clay, might have been popular with American public opinion but not in Europe.[59] Marshall opposed Clay's proposal, and the Joint Chiefs of Staff withheld support on the ground that the US could not adequately reinforce its greatly outnumbered units in Germany. Clay was invited to the crucial National Security Council meeting on 22 July, at which he acknowledged that his proposal could incur greater risk than relying on the airlift. General

Vandenberg, Air Force Chief of Staff, opposed expanding the airlift on the ground that it would deprive the US of the capacity to respond to any other emergency, but was overruled by Truman.[60] With reinforcement, the airlift could supply Berlin until winter. Having reached a firm decision on the strategy for remaining in Berlin, the NSC also endorsed a diplomatic approach to Stalin, subject to British and French agreement.

Phase 2: The Moscow negotiations (23 July–18 September)

British agreement was by no means automatic. There had been recent embarrassment over contacts with Moscow, and Bevin now argued that an approach to Stalin would strengthen his bargaining position. The Americans, maintaining that this alone offered a way of exploring any potential flexibility in the Soviet position, eventually prevailed, but not without friction. Tactical disagreements were magnified in the perception of some of the participants, and despite the wealth of evidence to the contrary, the British approach was perceived as 'redolent with appeasement'.[61]

The American, British and French ambassadors met with Stalin on 2 August, in a surprisingly cordial atmosphere. After initially insisting on Soviet objections to a separate state in West Germany and proposing the suspension of the London agreements, Stalin concluded by offering a far more favourable proposal, namely, the removal of the 'transport restrictions' in exchange for the withdrawal of the Western currency from Berlin. Deferral of the London agreements would merely be noted as the 'insistent wish' of the Soviet government.[62] Marshall endorsed Clay's insistence on the original Western condition that the issue of Soviet-zone currency in Berlin should be subject to four-power control. The ambassadors' subsequent negotiations with Foreign Minister Molotov became deadlocked over these issues. During a further meeting with Stalin, on 21 August, he agreed that the bank which issued the currency should be placed under the control of the four commanders in Berlin, but differences re-emerged in negotiating a directive to the military governors for implementing the agreement. Rather surprisingly, although there was no agreement on a communiqué, on 30 August Molotov and the ambassadors agreed on a directive: the governors were to formulate proposals on the lifting of the blockade and the new currency regulations by 7 September.[63]

They were unable to reach an agreement. Differences remained over three issues: Soviet insistence on controlling trade with Berlin; new restrictions on air transport; and above all, the relationship of the four-power commission to the Bank of Emission.[64] The three ambassadors presented these issues to Molotov on 14 September, claiming that Sokolovsky had gone back on the agreed points in the Moscow directive. Molotov responded on 18 September that it was the Western powers which were seeking to go beyond the directive.[65] Both claims were misplaced: whereas the language of the directive was general and imprecise, the military governors sought to introduce precision in ways which reflected the two sides' conflicting interests. The underlying issue was evident: Soviet control over Berlin's currency and trade would be a major step towards incorporating the city into the Soviet zone, whereas four-power control would mean that the Western powers would retain control over the economy of their sectors – always assuming that paralysis could be avoided at the four-power level. The breakdown of the existing four-power institutions, however, suggested that the real alternative to a Soviet-controlled Berlin was the splitting of the city into Soviet and Western sectors, parallel to the larger division of Germany.

This was becoming clear at the local level in late August–early September. Violence and intimidation prevented the Berlin Assembly from meeting in the City Hall (in the Soviet zone), and there were fears that the city government, the Magistrat, might be taken over by force. After the Assembly was prevented from convening on 6 September it met for the first time in the Western sector, the communist deputies continuing to meet in the City Hall. A mass demonstration in the Western sector on 9 September led to clashes with Soviet troops near the Brandenburg Gate; the majority party, the Social Democrats, began to establish a separate administration in the Western sector.[66] Thus the local separation preceded the effective abandonment of the Moscow negotiations. It is unlikely that the Soviet leaders saw the separation as lasting: if neither diplomacy nor local intimidation could bring about the incorporation of Berlin into the Soviet zone, then the blockade would eventually do so. The US, however, reinforcing the airlift once again on 7 September, was becoming confident that it could sustain Berlin through the winter.[67]

Phase 3: Stalemate (19 September–31 January)

The central issue during the ensuing months was which of these expectations was to be realised. After a further increase in the airlift in October, the daily tonnage was sufficient to supply Berlin's minimum winter needs, but severe interruptions due to fog in the early winter revived anxieties which were not dispelled until January. Soviet expectations, it must be presumed, moved in the opposite direction. The US placed the dispute before the United Nations, where 'neutral' members of the Security Council subsequently pursued a settlement in the face of increasing American reluctance to compromise. Whereas the Moscow negotiations had been in search of a settlement, and this was the ostensible aim of recourse to the UN, it is difficult to contest Shlaim's contention that 'American behaviour in the later months of 1948 tends to support the view that the overriding reason for going to the UN was to gain time rather than to work for a negotiated solution'.[68] Initially the airlift had been seen as buying time for diplomacy; now diplomacy was to buy time for the airlift to demonstrate its effectiveness. This, of course, could not be said openly. To maintain the airlift while making no attempt to achieve a settlement would have been politically difficult, not least in the US at the time of the Presidential election. Expressions of scepticism that the US was indeed seeking a settlement created pressure to appear to be doing so. American policy makers also hoped that the UN might endorse the Western legal position and condemn the blockade. The lack of clarity over US objectives was reflected in Marshall's assurance to UN delegate Philip Jessup that 'he would back up any action he took, provided it was not appeasement'.[69]

The six 'neutral' members of the Council proposed a variant of the earlier Moscow agreement: the lifting of all traffic and trade restrictions, a resumption of currency talks and a reconvening of the Council of Foreign Ministers. Accepted by the Western powers on 25 October, this was vetoed by the Soviet Union. The US rejected a proposal to resume four-power talks, now demanding the prior lifting of the blockade, but agreed in late November to the UN's establishing a committee of experts to make proposals on four-power control over Soviet-zone currency in Berlin, the previous stumbling block.[70]

While US and British policy was now premised on increasing confidence in the airlift, the whole approach was subjected to fundamental questioning in Washington during October–November. George Kennan, who had been asked to re-examine policy on Germany as a whole, drew attention to awkward questions: why should the Russians accept continued quadripartite control in Berlin when it had been abandoned by the Western powers in Germany as a whole? Should policy not consider seriously the conditions under which a government could be formed for a united Germany? The top decision makers declined to enter into such far-reaching discussion.[71] The Joint Chiefs of Staff could not be ignored, however, when they maintained that the airlift was adversely affecting their ability to meet their primary responsibilities, and sought a decision either to increase military preparations for the eventuality of war, or to prepare to withdraw from Berlin. Their concern over the risk of war was supported by an analysis of the difficulty of countering a range of measures by which the Soviets could interfere with the airlift. On 21 October the National Security Council, presided over by Truman and attended by Clay, reaffirmed the existing policy and resolved on a further increase in the airlift.[72]

The UN expert committee's proposals on Berlin's currency were made known on 22 December. Britain and France were prepared to consider them, but the US now argued that the splitting of the city rendered them untenable. The split had indeed deepened several weeks earlier: a new Magistrat for Berlin as a whole had been proclaimed in East Berlin on 30 November, and on 5 December elections in the Western sector had returned the Social Democrats, committed to the separate political development of the sector, with an increased majority. The split, however, had been a reality since September. The new US approach reflected a further hardening of policy after Truman's unexpected re-election. Rejecting the expert report on 15 January, the US now proposed that the deutschmark be the sole currency in the Western sectors.[73]

On 31 January Stalin gave the first signal of a change of policy, though this did not become clear for several weeks. In reply to a question by American journalist Kingsbury Smith on the conditions for lifting the blockade, he alluded to a meeting of the Council of Foreign Ministers and emphasised the lifting of Western trade restrictions (the 'counter-blockade'), but made no mention of the ostensible crux of the dispute, the currency issue.[74]

Phase 4: Resolution (1 February–5 May)

Stalin's comment aroused immediate interest in the State Department. Jessup, the chosen channel for communication, sounding out Soviet UN representative Jacob Malik on 15 February, found that he had to refer back to Moscow: a month later he informed Jessup that the omission of the currency issue was 'not accidental'. Secret negotiations now began in earnest.[75] The US obtained Soviet agreement to lift the blockade before the proposed meeting of the Council of Foreign Ministers, and rejected Soviet suggestions that further moves towards the formation of a West German state be suspended until that meeting. Bevin and French Foreign Minister Schuman, informed of the negotiations for the first time on 1 April, endorsed the American approach, which was not made known to the Defense Department, nor even Clay, until the second half of April. The currency issue, excluded from the negotiations, had finally been resolved in March by a decision of the three Western military governors that the deutschmark would be the sole legal tender in the Western sectors.[76] Last-minute differences among the Western governments delayed the agreement – a simple undertaking to end all traffic and trade restrictions and to hold a meeting of the Council of Foreign Ministers – until 5 May. The blockade was lifted on 12 May, and the meeting convened on 23 May, without further complication.

Soviet agreement to end the blockade with no more than a face-saving meeting of foreign ministers is usually explained in terms of two considerations: the economic costs of the counter-blockade and the adverse political effects of the blockade in Germany and in Western Europe as a whole. The former, the eventual cessation of most trade between the Western and Soviet zones, has been little studied, but undoubtedly caused serious economic dislocation.[77] The latter became increasingly evident as the blockade was invoked in marshalling support for the North Atlantic Treaty and the formation of West Germany. While Soviet policy continued to seek ways of postponing and complicating the latter, the chances of success must have appeared slight by early 1949. The acceptance of a split city also signified the Soviet failure to achieve the lesser objective of incorporating Berlin into the Soviet zone. The absence from the agreement of any reaffirmation of Western rights of access to Berlin, however, left the Western sectors, soon to be known as West Berlin, exposed to future pressures at a time when the circumstances might be less favourable.

Conclusion

The actions of both sides demonstrated extreme aversion to war. What part nuclear weapons played in this remains unclear: both sides had compelling reasons for avoiding major war. There was no explicit nuclear threat, and the Western governments sought to avoid rousing the European dread of war by avoiding such language, or indeed any mention of war. They were acutely aware that the Soviet army could easily overrun West Germany and probably also France, but the Soviet leaders had to contemplate the prospect of war against the sole nuclear power.

Whatever its sources, the mutual fear of war served to promote practices which became important precedents for later nuclear-age crises. The blockade and the airlift both exemplified the tactic, later widely discussed, of placing the onus of risk and escalation on the other side. Both sides not only avoided firing at one another's armed forces, but also avoided moves which would have increased the pressure on the other side to do so: an attempt to break the blockade or interference with the airlift. Such practices were not new, but now became regarded as precedents. Clay's bold proposals may or may not have succeeded in calling the Soviet bluff, but over and above the immediate risk, the experience of the crises before 1914 suggests that success through such moves tends to increase the level of risk in ensuing crises, encouraging their repetition but increasing the determination not to yield to them. The Cold War was saved from such destabilising precedents.

At the same time, there was an asymmetry with respect to political goals: the US and Britain, and eventually France, were prepared to maintain their programme to create a West German state, even at the risk that this might prove a *casus belli* for the Soviet Union, whereas the latter proved willing to abandon its political goals in Germany, and even in Berlin. Underlying this, however, was the further fundamental Cold War practice of accepting the 1945 territorial division: if desired changes could not be brought about through diplomatic means, there was no recourse to military means. This had worked in favour of the Soviet Union in Eastern Europe, but favoured the Western powers in Germany.

The caution of the bargaining and the asymmetry of the evidence limit comparison with the earlier cases, but the reasons, over and above the airlift, why the potential for danger was never realised will be examined further. These appear to include relatively favourable internal political conditions and the circumstance that although there was notably little reflection on crisis goals, overall Western goals and priorities had been clarified in the preceding period.

The Berlin crisis, 1958–1962

The protracted crisis which began in November 1958 was the most serious clash between the superpowers and their allies in Europe, the central arena of the Cold War. In contrast to 1948–49, both sides were now heavily armed and exposed to a nuclear attack. The crisis offers the classic case of an attempt to achieve political gain through exploiting the fear of nuclear war – through a demand backed not by the direct threat of war but by the threat that its rejection would lead to a situation perilously close to war. Western decision makers faced the same dilemma as in the blockade crisis, but in a more acute form: how to avoid both unintended war (through an unnecessary confrontation or provocation) and war through miscalculation (through Soviet underestimation of Western resolve). Unlike the 1948 proposals to use force to break the blockade, there was no specific focus for the choice, but it was constantly raised in contingency planning and in the issue of whether to negotiate or openly to call Khrushchev's bluff.

There were no such actions as the blockade and airlift to give continuing form to the crisis, but continuity was provided by Khrushchev's threat to sign a separate peace treaty with East Germany, with the unstated corollary that this could well lead to a blockade in circumstances far more dangerous than those of 1948–49. Just as the larger goal of the blockade had been to reopen the German question as a whole, Khrushchev sought to bring about a solution to the German question – peace treaties with both German states – highly favourable to the Soviet Union. But whereas the blockade appeared to offer Stalin a low-risk second-best option, to gain control of Berlin if the West rejected his larger demands, the threat of a separate peace treaty promised no such low-risk gain if the West rejected Khrushchev's proposals, but rather a *shared* risk that placing the control over access to Berlin in the hands of the East German government would lead to war – hence the suspicion that Khrushchev was bluffing. Up to a point, just as the airlift had circumvented the blockade, the Western governments were able to circumvent Khrushchev's threat by agreeing to negotiate provided he lifted his successive deadlines, but keeping the agenda strictly limited. In contrast to 1948–49, however, there was one important Soviet gain, the 'closing of the East German border' through the construction of the Berlin Wall in August 1961.

As before, information on Soviet thinking and decisions remains seriously incomplete, in particular with respect to the perception of options and risks, including the perception of the 'resolve' of key Western decision makers. The relevant decision making processes are little known, and thus so is the context for assessing such issues as the extent to which Khrushchev was bluffing.[78]

The setting

The years of the crisis and those preceding it were among the more turbulent of the Cold War. The suppression of the Hungarian revolution in 1956 was followed by the Soviet launching of the Sputnik and the first ICBM in 1957, and by NATO's response – stationing American intermediate-range missiles in Europe and deploying tactical nuclear weapons in Germany. In 1958, before Khrushchev initiated the Berlin crisis in November, there were crises in the Middle East and over the Chinese offshore islands. The seriousness of the Sino-Soviet split became known only gradually, but the U-2 incident, the Bay of Pigs landing, and the construction of the Berlin Wall maintained the sense of crisis, culminating in the Cuban missile confrontation in October 1962. Western Europe's vulnerability to Soviet missiles, Khrushchev's claims that the strategic balance was shifting decisively, and American fears of a 'missile gap' heightened Western apprehensions, especially before US intelligence exposed the falsity of the latter claim in autumn 1961.[79]

Continuity in Western policy throughout these disturbances was sustained by what came to be termed the Cold War consensus, but there were glimpses of what came to be termed détente, an expression then used freely only by de Gaulle, confident that in the long run nationalism would prevail over ideology.[80] Macmillan stretched the consensus through his promotion of regular meetings of world leaders and his support for arms control, which also attracted Eisenhower during his final two years as President, in particular the goal of a nuclear test ban as the first step towards bringing the arms race under control.[81]

Khrushchev's stance during the years of the crisis was open to conflicting interpretations. His doctrine of peaceful coexistence, the radical arms reductions announced in January 1960, the round of high-level visits in 1959–60, and his differences with China pointed towards a decisive break with Cold War orthodoxies. But there were indications that he was committed to pursuing the 'world communist' agenda, perhaps even more intensively than before: Soviet backing for radical forces in the Third World, his claims that the balance of forces was moving in favour of the Soviet Union, his recourse to threatening language and his apparently simplistic Marxist–Leninist creed.[82] Not surprisingly, the 'Cold War mind set' was constantly reinforced in Western policy making circles.

The immediate setting for the Berlin crisis may be traced from the 1957 missile decisions. NATO's response to the Soviet ICBM included arming West Germany with tactical nuclear delivery vehicles. Even though the warheads were to remain under US control, from the Soviet perspective there was no assurance that this would remain the case. Moscow's response, the 'Rapacki Plan' for the denuclearisation of both Germanies, Poland and Czechoslovakia, aroused interest but was vehemently opposed by the Adenauer government and rejected by the US.[83] Soviet diplomacy also pressed for the acceptance of two Germanies – the abandonment of the claim that the Federal Republic was 'the only German Government freely and legitimately constituted and ... the representative of the German people in international affairs'.[84]

The crisis saw many variations in intensity, but since there were significant differences between the responses of the Eisenhower and the Kennedy Administrations, it is divided into only two phases, 1958–60 and 1961–62, the periods of greatest tension being the early weeks of the first phase, the days preceding and following the Paris summit conference of May 1960, and the months between June and October 1961.[85]

The Eisenhower Presidency

The crisis was initiated by a Soviet note of 27 November 1958, addressed to West Germany as well as the three occupying powers, declaring that Western violations had rendered the occupation agreements on Berlin null and void, stating that the Soviet government intended to transfer its functions in regulating access to Berlin to East Germany, and proposing that West Berlin become a demilitarised Free City. If such an agreement could not be reached within six months, it would unilaterally transfer these functions to East Germany. On 10 January 1959 the proposal was broadened to include the Berlin settlement within a draft peace treaty between the four occupying powers and the two Germanies, which would be demilitarised and might subsequently negotiate bilaterally on reunification. If the West declined such an agreement Moscow would sign a separate treaty with East Germany which, as before, would terminate its responsibilities for Berlin.[86]

In reply, the Western powers reaffirmed their rights, but also signalled their willingness to discuss Berlin in the context of an overall German settlement, nonetheless refusing to negotiate under the threat of a deadline. Secretary of State Dulles – who appears to have assumed that the Soviets could not be prevented from handing over the regulation of traffic to the East Germans – showed unexpected flexibility in indicating that East German officials might be regarded as agents of the Soviet Union.[87] This foreshadowed a fundamental premise of the Western response which was to be articulated by the Kennedy Administration – that the West should not insist on upholding the status quo in every detail, but should define the essential interests on behalf of which it was prepared to incur the ultimate risk. A little later de Gaulle, in similar fashion, recommended that the Oder–Neisse line – still formally recognised only by the Eastern bloc – be accepted as the frontier of a united Germany.[88]

In contrast to the Kennedy period, military responses were played down by the Eisenhower Administration. At the outset General Norstad, Supreme Allied Commander in Europe, proposed to test Soviet intentions by sending an armed convoy to Berlin if normal access was obstructed, but the European allies had reservations. In January Eisenhower agreed to an unobtrusive reinforcement of American units in Europe, bringing them up to full strength, but supported Dulles in overruling a proposal by the Joint Chiefs of Staff to prepare for a response at division strength if a truck convoy was stopped, on the ground that this was too weak to be militarily effective but far more than was necessary to demonstrate determination. He approved plans for a small 'probe' by an armed convoy if East German officials were substituted for the Soviets, but in the event of actual obstruction the matter would be placed before the United Nations before considering the use of additional force.[89] These were unilateral American decisions: subsequently Prime Minister Macmillan was relieved to learn from Dulles that the 'Pentagon plan' to use a division to enforce access had been 'completely abandoned'.[90]

Consistent with the Eisenhower Administration's strategic doctrine and confidence in deterrence, there appears to have been no attempt to engage in detailed planning for the worst case, nor to formulate a coherent 'declaratory policy' beyond insisting that the US would stand firm, would insist on its rights and would carry out its responsibilities. Ruling out a ground war in Europe, Eisenhower relied on the uncertainty created by vague and confusing references to nuclear war, confident that Khrushchev would draw back from the ultimate risk: 'There is nothing in the world that the Communists want badly enough to risk losing the Kremlin.'[91]

It gradually became clear that the principal Western response during the Eisenhower period was to negotiate, in varying fora and with varying agendas, not restricted to Berlin and Germany, but always with the proviso that there be no deadline. This pattern became clear only after the event: the specific moves were improvised under pressure and generated considerable inter-allied friction, especially between Britain and West Germany.[92] Initially the deadline exerted considerable pressure: even after informal Soviet assurances of flexibility, there was no formal retraction of the 27 May deadline.[93] Macmillan, fearing unintended war and apprehensive over American contingency planning, caused consternation in Bonn through his visit to Moscow in February. Reaffirming the Western commitment to Berlin, he obtained a more explicit lifting of the deadline and Khrushchev's agreement to a conference of foreign ministers, in exchange supporting Khrushchev's demand for a summit conference which – Eisenhower continued to insist – could take place only after progress had been achieved at the foreign minister level.[94]

That conference took place in Geneva from 11 May to 5 August 1959, between the four occupying powers, with representatives of both German states occasionally participating by invitation. The conference remains a controversial episode and was not repeated, but in retrospect West German fears of a dangerous weakening of the Western position had little foundation. After confirming the incompatibility of Soviet and Western views on the German question as a whole – the West insisting on free all-German elections as the final step in a phased reunification process, the Soviets on a treaty with the two existing states – the powers explored the possibility of a settlement limited to Berlin. However, the kind of bargain which the West was prepared to offer – an updated agreement on access in exchange for acceptance of the notion of East Germans as agents for the Soviet Union – fell so far short of Soviet aims that the conference adjourned without agreement.[95]

Arguably, as Schick maintains, Soviet Foreign Minister Gromyko held the diplomatic initiative and the conference 'increased Soviet momentum in the crisis'.[96] The immediate sequel was Eisenhower's unexpected invitation to Khrushchev to visit the United States without the foreign ministers' having met his condition that some progress be made.[97] An alternative reading, however, would be that the West had blunted the Soviet diplomatic offensive, demonstrated its determination to remain in Berlin and to restrict bargaining within narrow limits, and had for the time being defused the crisis, drawing Khrushchev into personal diplomacy incompatible with crude threats and intimidation.

Khrushchev's visit to the United States in September amounted to a bid for détente on Soviet terms. Extensive media coverage briefly introduced a new atmosphere into Soviet–American relations, and the meeting with Eisenhower at Camp David created an impression of greater agreement than had actually been achieved. The communiqué referred to an 'understanding' that negotiations on Berlin 'would be reopened with a view to achieving a solution ... in accordance with the interests of all concerned', and both leaders indicated that there would be no fixed time limit but that the negotiations would not be prolonged indefinitely.[98] Other issues were canvassed, and it was agreed that disarmament 'dwarfed every other problem'. Eisenhower's impression that Khrushchev had 'recognised his determination' on Berlin and 'was relieved at having found a way out with reasonable dignity' was a misreading:[99] Khrushchev revived the threat of a separate treaty in January 1960. His *Foreign Affairs* article 'On Peaceful Coexistence' (October 1959) – which marked a new openness in US–Soviet relations – may indicate the rationale for his approach. His categorical rejection of preserving the 'existing status quo' in Berlin is argued within the context of a plea for 'friendship' with the United States, premised on a confident projection that history was demonstrating the superiority of socialism over capitalism.[100]

Between Khrushchev's American visit and the abortive Paris summit conference of May 1960 the various parties' public stands on Berlin remained inflexible. A 'Western summit' in December 1959 reaffirmed the existing all-German proposals. In January Khrushchev reaffirmed the Soviet peace treaty proposals, but with no deadline, and reiterated them in subsequent weeks; during his visit to France in March de Gaulle sought unsuccessfully to dissuade him from pressing the issue. The Western position on Berlin and Germany was reaffirmed by Secretary of State Herter and in more polemical terms by Under Secretary Dillon in April, leading to polemical responses by Mikoyan and Khrushchev.[101] Thus there was little prospect for agreement on Berlin at the Paris summit, nor indeed on other issues, despite British interest in a nuclear test ban, which Eisenhower had come to share. Pressure to achieve specific agreements, however, had been reduced by the general acceptance of Macmillan's suggestion that there be a series of summit meetings, but the 'success' of the summit depended on maintaining the semblance of civility in the relations among its participants.

This was shattered by the public handling of the U-2 incident – the shooting down of a U-2 aircraft over the Soviet Union on 1 May.[102] Khrushchev's announcement of the capture of the pilot and his display of the wreckage of the aircraft shocked and embarrassed the Americans, exposing their initial 'cover story'. Mounting pressure on the Administration led to the public justification of the espionage flights and the President's acceptance of responsibility for them. Khrushchev's response in Paris – his demands that Eisenhower apologise for the flights and punish those responsible for them, his use of insulting language – showed that in these circumstances he preferred to break up the conference and call off the incipient détente with the United States. On the other hand, he visited East Berlin to announce the postponement of the separate treaty, holding out the prospect of high-level talks with the next US administration to resolve the Berlin issue. While the crisis was deferred at the four-power level, East German leader Ulbricht introduced new administrative controls on

travel to East Berlin by West Germans and West Berliners, foreshadowing the unilateral closing of the border which was to be implemented
in August 1961.[103]

The Kennedy Presidency

Khrushchev signalled his intention to revive the Berlin issue on a
number of occasions in the early months of 1961,[104] but did not raise it
formally with the United States until his meeting with Kennedy in
Vienna on 3–4 June. The meeting, proposed by Kennedy in February,
took place in circumstances unfavourable to the United States, following the loss of prestige incurred by the Bay of Pigs fiasco in April. If this
encouraged Khrushchev to apply strong pressure, plans announced
by the new Administration to expand the US strategic and conventional forces provided him with an incentive not to delay further. At
Vienna he revived the proposal for treaties with both German states
and for West Berlin to become a Free City unless the Germans could
agree on a method of reunification within six months, and soon
afterwards he once again threatened to sign a separate treaty with East
Germany unless an agreement was reached by the end of the year. The
main effect of the meeting was his success in convincing Kennedy that
he was impervious to the latter's arguments and determined to press
on. Having sought the meeting in order to avert miscalculation,
Kennedy became more concerned that Khrushchev might indeed
miscalculate.[105]

In contrast to Eisenhower, Kennedy's initial response emphasised
military measures and contingency planning. This was partly due to a
fundamental change in strategic doctrine: Kennedy's advisers rejected
Dulles' 'massive retaliation' doctrine, advocating what came to be
termed 'flexible response', a doctrine of raising the nuclear threshold
through preparedness to mount a substantial conventional defence.
Whereas Eisenhower was satisfied that the risk of nuclear war was
sufficient to deter Khrushchev from dangerous moves over Berlin, his
successors were not persuaded that the threat of early use of nuclear
weapons was sufficiently credible. For them it was imperative to
strengthen NATO's non-nuclear capabilities. The European allies'
reluctance to follow this logic meant that the build-up remained
essentially American.[106]

Second, the military response was played up, and the diplomatic
response played down, due to Dean Acheson's role in shaping the
policy agenda from February, when Kennedy sought his advice on
Berlin, until July. Perceiving Berlin as essentially the occasion for a test

of will between the superpowers, Acheson urged that the US make its determination unmistakably clear by measures going as far as a declaration of national emergency and a major military build-up in Europe. Acheson's approach was analogous to Clay's in 1948, allowing for the changed strategic context. Central to his thinking was the need to be in a position to break any new blockade with a force of at least two divisions, sufficient to ensure that Soviet forces would become engaged, and thus a convincing indication of the US willingness to run the ultimate risk. In Acheson's view negotiation would be futile, and indeed dangerous, until Khrushchev had been 'faced down' at whatever level of confrontation proved necessary, and would then amount to face-saving to cover his withdrawal of the challenge.[107]

Acheson's views were contested by advisers who argued that in emphasising the worst case and military options he failed to address Khrushchev's political demands, neglected lesser contingencies and the option of defusing the crisis through negotiation, and risked provoking an uncontrollable escalation of threat and counter-threat.[108] Policy makers were not divided into two clearly-defined groups, and it was misleading to postulate that the essential divergence was over whether Soviet aims were perceived as offensive or defensive. The differences turned, rather, on whether the conflict was perceived in one dimension, as a test of will, or as complex and multidimensional, and perhaps on differences in temperament and philosophy between what came to be termed 'hawks' and 'owls', the former predisposed to clarity and confrontation, the latter fully aware of uncertainty and the dangers of unintended war and of foreclosing options.[109]

In these terms Kennedy was an owl, suspicious of contingency planning which might lock him into a predetermined response.[110] After extensive deliberations he announced the American policy on 25 July. Rejecting a full mobilisation or declaration of emergency, he nonetheless announced significant measures to increase the readiness of the non-nuclear forces and their deployment in Europe, also indicating that the response to any Soviet move might not be confined to central Europe but would take account of Soviet vulnerabilities elsewhere. He made explicit the long-standing tacit definition of the essential American interests in Berlin: a continued military presence in West Berlin, unimpeded access for those forces and the security and viability of West Berlin itself. Finally, recognising 'a duty to mankind to seek a peaceful solution', he intended to continue negotiations. It was the military measures, however, which dominated the American public's perception of the response.[111]

There was now a sense that the crisis was escalating. On 8 July

211

Khrushchev, referring to the earlier increases in American defence appropriations, announced a 34 per cent increase in Soviet military expenditure, reversing his policy of the previous year.[112] Tension had increased in East Germany following a press conference on 15 June, little noticed in the West, in which Ulbricht denied any intention of building a wall in Berlin.[113] The steady flow of refugees to the West through the city increased to the point of constituting a crisis within the overall crisis (30,000 in July, 20,000 in the first twelve days of August).

The idea of a wall appears to have originated in the 1950s, but was said to have been vetoed by the Soviet Union in favour of Khrushchev's Berlin proposals.[114] It is not known when it was reconsidered. In July East Germany introduced new restrictions on movement into East Berlin and between East and West Berlin, but these failed to halt the refugee flow. The construction of the Wall was approved at a meeting of the Warsaw Pact in Moscow on 3–5 August, and the operation began on 13 August, first consisting of barbed wire barriers, followed by the beginning of the Wall a few days later.[115]

Western 'signals' were such as to encourage the Soviet leadership to expect that the Wall would not be challenged. Kennedy's statement of the 'three essentials' omitted mention of the freedom of movement in Berlin. The Administration did not unambiguously dissociate itself from Senator Fulbright's comment on 30 July that the border might be closed without violating any treaty.[116] The Western governments, while not anticipating the precise form of the sealing of the border, expected the East German government to act to halt the refugee outflow. They were concerned to do nothing to encourage an uprising in East Germany which, accepting the precedents of East Berlin in 1953 and Hungary in 1956, they would not have assisted. Intelligence analysts advised that stringent controls on movement from East Germany into East Berlin were more likely than a physical barrier through the city, which they regarded as too costly to the East German government's prestige, but a more accurate prediction would not have influenced the Western response. A high-level working-group meeting in Paris in early August decided to hold major economic sanctions such as a trade embargo in reserve unless there was interference with Western access to the city.[117] Kennedy's view is best indicated in his conversation with Walt Rostow, also in early August: 'Khrushchev would have to do something internally to re-establish control over the situation – and if he did, we would not be able to do a thing about it ... it was not a vital interest for the United States.'[118]

Tension remained at a high level for two months, until Khrushchev withdrew the 31 December deadline in his opening statement to the Soviet Party Congress on 17 October.[119] The passivity of the Western response to the Wall created a crisis of confidence in West Berlin, which Kennedy countered by sending Vice-President Lyndon Johnson to the city, ordering a battle group to reinforce the Berlin contingent, and appointing General Clay as his special representative for several months. A Soviet note on 23 August accused the West of violating the agreements on air access, and occasional harassment took place during the following weeks.[120] Contrary to earlier undertakings, Soviet nuclear testing was resumed on 30 August, culminating in a fifty-megaton explosion in October. Soviet statements continued to insist on the urgent need for a peace treaty. Exploratory talks with Gromyko, in the US for the United Nations session, were unpromising: he was, in Kennedy's view, seeking to 'trade an apple for an orchard'; the US remained equally unresponsive to the Soviet diplomatic agenda.[121] However, in late September Khrushchev initiated what was to become an important private correspondence with Kennedy.[122]

It is not clear whether Khrushchev's withdrawal of the deadline was more greatly influenced by the US military response or by its willingness to negotiate, but some aspects of the overall context throw light on the Soviet decision to de-escalate the crisis. The construction of the Wall, probably not part of the initial Soviet strategy in 1961, reduced the incentive to press for the peace treaty. The unyielding Western reaction to harassment in the air corridors and to Gromyko's diplomatic soundings showed that there was no responsiveness to the demand for the peace treaty. To have reaffirmed the deadline would have greatly exacerbated the crisis, while actually to have carried out the threat to sign a separate treaty would have placed Ulbricht in a position to exercise inordinate influence over the course of events. In retrospect, a further escalation at this point would have been surprising.

In its penultimate phase, from October 1961 to May 1962, the crisis reverted to a situation analogous to the early months of 1959 – a search for agreement among the Western powers on a basis for negotiation. The search was now accompanied by US–Soviet talks in Washington, Moscow and Geneva, indicating a change in the overall pattern of relationships. Strained US relations with France and West Germany rendered it far more difficult than in 1959.[123] France was pursuing close partnership with Bonn and, claiming to lack confidence in the American nuclear umbrella, was committed to achieving nuclear independence. It opposed negotiations outright, arguing that they were premature and would encourage Khrushchev to miscalculate – an argument more plausible before 17 October than after. Bonn was alienated by the Kennedy Administration's setting aside of German reunification and its pragmatic approach to the issue of recognising East Germany, in contrast to its own legalistic–moralistic approach; on the right of the CDU there was a strong sense that the Kennedy Administration suffered from divided counsels and was insufficiently 'hard' in defending German interests.[124]

The negotiations never reached the point of the exchange of formal proposals: the Soviets never relaxed their demand that West Berlin become a Free City, while the US sought an updated agreement on access which presupposed the continuation of the Western rights as occupying powers. In November Adenauer succeeded in limiting the scope of negotiation to Berlin, excluding European arms control, and subsequently signalled West German disquiet in ways which may have failed to attract Washington's attention.[125] In February–March Soviet aircraft undertook their most sustained campaign of harassment in the air corridors, to which the West responded in low key, maintaining civilian schedules and military transports but not introducing combat aircraft.[126] When this ceased, the US formulated a proposal for an international access authority, details of which were promptly leaked in Bonn. In the recriminations which followed, any faint hopes of movement towards agreement disappeared entirely: Adenauer publicly criticised the proposals, and Soviet ambiguity towards the American overtures hardened into a reiteration of familiar demands.[127]

During the summer the demand for a peace treaty was revived sporadically, and the office of Soviet Commandant in Berlin was abolished. In the autumn Washington officials, suspicious of Soviet arms shipments to Cuba, feared a renewed crisis over Berlin; their concerns were strengthened by a Soviet undertaking in September to postpone any further Berlin initiative until after the congressional elections.[128] One of the major concerns during the Cuban missile crisis was that the Soviets might move against access to Berlin in response to US moves in the Caribbean. Khrushchev's first comment on Berlin after the Cuban crisis remained defiant, but his speech to the East German Party Congress on 16 January 1963 may be taken as terminating the crisis. While a peace treaty remained desirable, Khrushchev sought to persuade his audience that it was no longer urgent in view of the gains from the closing of the border. The East German government had already adjusted its expectations accordingly.[129] The situation was not ripe for resolution in 1963: the Quadripartite Agreement on Berlin of 1971 was finally negotiated in the very different context of the agreements achieved through Brandt's Ostpolitik.

Conclusion

In contrast to the blockade crisis, the presence of nuclear weapons and the risk of nuclear war were now uppermost in the concerns of policy makers, and the central theme of the crisis was the way in which each side sought to utilise this risk in order to manoeuvre the adversary into accepting its preferred outcome – a classic instance of 'bargaining' in the sense which has become current in the nuclear age. Khrushchev's bargaining was mainly tacit: if the West were to accept his version of the issues the risk would not arise. Eisenhower's response also amounted to tacit bargaining: to play down the dangers, to avoid creating public alarm, and quietly to reaffirm the Western position in the confidence that Khrushchev would avoid the ultimate risk. In Kennedy's response the bargaining was much more explicit: Western interests were articulated more precisely, military preparations were made and risks confronted more openly: the level of public concern and the overall sense of the seriousness of the crisis were greatly enhanced.

As in 1948–49 the principle of accepting the postwar territorial division remained fundamental: whereas it had then favoured the West it now permitted the construction of the Berlin Wall. As before, each side sought to place the onus of risk for escalating the crisis on the other. The scope of harassment in the air corridors was kept limited, and the response remained low-key: neither side wanted to be responsible for a serious incident, and both exercised strict control over operations. Similarly, neither side wanted to be the one which refused or broke off negotiations. Indeed, although it was obscured at the time by acrimony over the format and content of negotiations, the Western success in defusing successive deadlines by recourse to exploratory discussions and personal diplomacy, and by placing conditions on the holding of formal conferences, could be seen as a positive 'lesson' of the crisis and a potential precedent for future crisis diplomacy.[130]

The crisis thus repays attention as a source of insights for the practice of crisis diplomacy, not least because protracted uncertainties are more frequently encountered than the high drama of the Cuban crisis. The actors' goals as well as bargaining will receive further attention, as will internal politics, the pressures of which were by no means negligible in Europe, though marginal in the US.

PART III

10 CRISES AND THE INTERNATIONAL SYSTEM: ARENAS, ALIGNMENTS AND NORMS

The present chapter examines one dimension of the setting in which crises occur, namely, the international system. A second dimension, the historical background – the specific developments which explain why a particular conflict becomes so acute as to precipitate a crisis – is outlined in each of the case studies, and its significance in determining the outcome of the crises is examined in Chapter 15. It has come to be recognised that crises are influenced by the character of the changing international system, but precisely in what ways has been unclear. This chapter attempts to clarify the nature of that influence.

Two approaches to the study of the international system may be distinguished: the work of theorists of system structure in the 'neo-realist' school, such as Kenneth Waltz, Glenn Snyder and Paul Diesing, and the more heterogeneous body of writing which may be termed historical sociology, which includes earlier works by F.H. Hinsley and Richard Rosecrance, and more recent contributions by Paul Schroeder, Gordon Craig and Alexander George.[1]

Waltz does not seek to relate crises to international systems, but his comments on war would apply equally to crises:

> A theory of international politics will, for example, explain why war recurs, and it will indicate some of the conditions that make war more or less likely; but it will not predict the outbreak of particular wars ... Within a system, a theory explains recurrences and repetitions, not change.[2]

Waltz's theory is at a level of generality which does not address the issues of concern to the present study. Whether a crisis occurs, and whether it leads to war, will depend on those unit-level factors with which his systemic theory is not concerned. Contrary to some interpretations, he should not be read as a structural determinist;[3] nor should Snyder and Diesing, whose concept of system structure, like Waltz's, is parsimonious – 'the number of major actors and the gross distribution of military power among them'[4] – and who see structures as constraining the actors' options, but not determining specific outcomes. Snyder and Diesing examine, for example, ways in which the system structure affects the significance of alliances. In multipolar systems, alliances are relatively unstable but of crucial importance to the actors, whose choices are highly dependent on the alignment of the other powers. In bipolar systems alliances are relatively stable but less crucial to the actors.[5]

Major changes in the international system may take place, however, even though its structure in this sense (bipolar or multipolar) remains constant. The historical sociologists are interested in such variations, especially between relatively stable and unstable phases of the system, that is, between phases conducive to peace or to war. They take account of a wider range of variables than the theorists of system structure, but nonetheless seek to identify the salient variables, not to describe the system in its complex detail. Though the focus is broad, it is limited to the proximate causes of the stability or instability of the *international* system. These authors do not attempt to explain the forces behind the proximate causes, for example, modern industrial society, global capitalism, or the world system – 'historical sociology' in another sense.

This school is no more deterministic than the system structure theorists, but suggests that variables at this level can predispose the system towards war or towards peace, leaving some scope for state-craft – for policy choices and diplomacy. Schroeder's analysis of the reasons for the relative stability of the international system in the nineteenth century, in contrast to the eighteenth, illustrates this approach. He finds the explanation in three long-term changes, which he terms 'structural'.[6] First, whereas European conflicts in the eighteenth century were intensified by imperial conflicts in the rest of the world, the European states system was, relatively speaking, insulated from conflicts outside Europe after 1815. Second, whereas the smaller European states were little more than pawns or victims of the great powers in the former century, they functioned more as buffers or intermediaries thereafter. Finally, international politics in the nineteenth century was constrained by the acceptance of certain rules of the game and a common conception of the rights and duties of the great powers, which had not previously been the case.

The present analysis is at the level of generality of the historical sociologists. Greater differentiation among systems than is offered by the neo-realist school is needed to explain why war is relatively probable – why crises are more difficult to resolve peacefully – in some systemic contexts than in others. Moreover, the state of the international system not only influences the outcome of crises, but also affects their general character, for example through socialisation processes, alignment patterns or norms which influence the conduct of policy.

Three kinds of changes at the systemic level are especially relevant to crises during the period covered by this study: those kinds which relate to the arena, alignments and norms, respectively. The concept of the 'arena' includes two variables. Like the first of Schroeder's distinctions – whether conflicts among the European powers were intensified by imperial rivalries or relatively insulated from them – it refers to the geographical extent of the principal great-power conflicts. But it also refers to the location of the powers. The revival of imperial rivalries in the early twentieth century amounted to a partial return to the eighteenth-century pattern, but a more fundamental change in the arena was the emergence of new powers outside Europe, the United States and Japan. Problems presented by the changing arena include the uneven 'socialisation' of such states into the role of the great power, and the reluctance of some of the established powers to acknowledge them as such.[7] The term 'alignment' is broader than 'alliance'. It refers to the overall pattern of coalitions, including both formal alliances and informal collaboration. In a crisis it is the effective alignments which are important, not their formal status.

If arenas and alignments may be regarded as further specifications of the structure of international systems, the norms observed by the powers represent a different kind of contextual influence on crises. In the longer term norms are 'chosen', not 'given': they are accepted or rejected by governments. But from the standpoint of decision makers in a crisis, the prevailing acceptance or rejection of particular systemic norms is a 'given', which needs to be taken into account. The changing systemic context of the cases can be explicated in terms of these three concepts.

The changing arena

Although the basic 'multipolar' structure of the international system persisted from the 1830s to the 1930s, variations within this configuration affected the conduct of international relations, and thus crisis diplomacy, very significantly. Until the late nineteenth century the arena remained essentially European, but by the turn of the century the rise of two extra-European powers, Japan and the United States, coinciding with the intensification of imperial rivalries, made for uncertainty and instability. The change from a European to a global arena was generally acknowledged in the interwar period, but the system became even more unstable.

221

During the first of these phases the 'insulation' of Europe from conflicts elsewhere, while never complete, stands out in comparison with earlier and later periods. Anglo-Russian rivalry outside Europe, for example, created one of the principal cleavages among the powers throughout the nineteenth century. But European conflicts were not constantly exacerbated by imperial rivalries, and there were no great powers outside Europe. The arena in the case of the first three crises studied here was the long-familiar world of the five European powers. These conditions had been transformed by the early twentieth century. The Russo-Japanese crisis can be seen as a crisis of the expansion of the system of great powers, with Japan insisting on being accepted into the club, and Russia declining to acknowledge its credentials. In the case of Agadir, while the protagonists were European, the issues were of a colonial/imperial character, indicating that the insulation of European from imperial conflicts was breaking down. In the interwar period there was no longer any question that the system had become global. Although the protagonists at Munich were European, British policy throughout the 1930s was constrained by awareness of the vulnerability of the Empire, above all to an extra-European power, Japan. The Pearl Harbor crisis was between two of the 'new' powers, neither of them fully socialised into the 'European' system of great-power diplomacy. The expanding arena contributed to the increasing instability of the multipolar system in the twentieth century, not simply because there were more powers, but because this enhanced uncertainties over alignments and further eroded the limited consensus over norms which had characterised the nineteenth-century system.

Planning for the postwar world assumed that the arena would be global, and the design for the United Nations provided for five great powers – the permanent members of the Security Council. The bipolar power structure of the Cold War and its relative stability became clear only gradually. At the time of the Berlin blockade the focus of the superpower conflict was so sharply on European issues that it appeared conceivable that the effective arena might again contract, but the Korean war confirmed that it would remain global. The Berlin crises illustrate two contrasting phases of the post-1945 arena: the heightening of tension and perceived instability at the time of the blockade, the uneven movement towards détente during the later crisis.

Alignments

Snyder and Diesing have shown that alignment considerations are far more significant in crises in multipolar than in bipolar systems. The support of allies in the former case is crucial but is never fully assured: dealignment or even realignment can never be entirely ruled out. They offer an illuminating discussion of the options and dilemmas of the supporting ally, the incentives to refrain from unambiguous commitments, and the dynamics of realignment.[8] Their discussion, however, presupposes the existence of alliances, and most of their examples are drawn from the period 1880–1914, when alliances were a dominant feature of international politics.[9] This is only one of three distinct phases of the multipolar system during the period covered here. Before 1880 alignments were typically informal and *ad hoc*, not formal and long-term. The interwar period saw certain limited alliances, but the striking feature was the relative absence of firm alignments at a time when cleavages were far more acute than in the Concert period. Changes in alignment are often seen as the means by which the actors in a multipolar system adjust to changes in relative power, but if the period 1880–1914 is open to this kind of interpretation, the interwar period shows that this balancing mechanism can be overridden by other considerations. Some contrasts may be drawn between the three phases.

Despite the absence of alliances in the first phase, some of the observations of Snyder and Diesing are of relevance. The Eastern crisis provides a striking example of successful crisis diplomacy through the collaboration of the two long-term adversaries, Britain and Russia. Alignment considerations – Russia's concern to break up the incipient three-power coalition against it – provided a major incentive for this collaboration. The pattern of alignments in the Crimean crisis, on the other hand, impeded its diplomatic resolution. The only firm coalition was that between Britain and France, but the latter, the 'supporting ally', was unable to restrain Britain during the later phases of the crisis, owing to its fear of isolation. Austria, though preferring an intermediate position, was eventually drawn into the 'Crimean' coalition against Russia, the grouping which that power had circumvented in the previous crisis.

In 1870 Prussia and Russia shared certain common interests, as did France and Austria, but in neither case had these led to the formation of an alliance. Russia and Prussia had on occasion come close to a classical 'balance of power' understanding that each would support the other if it were at war with two powers. In this way, the supporting ally of one party sought to deter the other party's ally from intervening, but also signalled that in the last resort it would fight to prevent its ally's total defeat. Russia in fact made such a commitment to Prussia in 1870, but only after it had become evident that war was

223

imminent, and thus did not influence Prussia's decisions. Austria sought to disabuse France of any over-confident expectations, and Britain, not even informally aligned, did not intervene. Alignments, then, played only a slight role in the brief crisis.

The two crises during the second phase, the period of alliances, illustrate some of the Snyder–Diesing hypotheses, as well as the effects of the classic balance of power alliance of the type just noted. The Anglo-Japanese alliance was precisely of this type, each power undertaking to remain neutral if the other were at war with one other power, but to assist it if it were at war with two powers. In the event, it achieved its deterrent purpose. Japan could conduct its crisis diplomacy with the reassurance that no other power was likely to intervene. Alliance with Russia provided France with an incentive to avert a war which would weaken Russia's weight in the European balance; but even so, France was slow to initiate diplomatic conversations.

The Agadir crisis illustrates the situation where the ally whose commitment is ambiguous has a greater incentive to offer support to the crisis protagonist than has the firmly committed ally.[10] Russia could avoid involvement without placing its alliance with France at risk. Britain, whose commitment to the entente was more qualified, feared that unless it demonstrated its support, the entente might become so discredited in France that Germany would secure a far greater prize than colonial territory – the breakup of the opposing coalition, leaving Britain in an exposed position. Agadir also illustrates the tendency, discussed below, for the powers not directly involved to refrain from intervention. Despite Europe's polarisation between two alliances, only Britain became briefly involved: Germany's allies, Austria and Italy, were no more involved than Russia. Alignments played a surprisingly limited role in the crisis.

The problems created by the absence of firm alignments were manifest in the Sudeten crisis. The potential alliance of the three 'revisionist' powers, Germany, Italy and Japan, threatened the existing 'balance', as well as the security of the British Empire. The only firm alignment on the other side was Britain's informal guarantee to support France against Germany. It was the non-alignment of the other two powers (potentially the greatest two), the United States and the Soviet Union, which prevented the formation of a balance of power along traditional lines. If the former was non-aligned by choice, the latter was by deliberate exclusion, reflecting the depth of the ideological cleavage between Moscow and the Western democracies, as perceived by the conservative leadership of the time. This constellation of forces amounted to a powerful constraint on British policy, though it did not wholly determine policy – or Britain could not have fought in 1939.

The context of the Pearl Harbor crisis was quite different: the powers not involved were already at war, or had been defeated. There was no doubt on which side Japan or the United States would be fighting, if it came to war between them, and it was becoming clear that on the Axis side the alignment would be informal and opportunistic, but more closely integrated in the case of the US and Britain.

The role of alignments in the Berlin crises confirms that they are indeed less central in a bipolar system. The second crisis provides the clearest illustration: the disputes among the Western powers over the handling of the crisis were embittered, but this reflected the awareness of the European allies that they had no option of dealignment, but could only attempt to influence the dominant partner, the United States. The blockade crisis provides a less clear example, because the bipolar system was still in the process of formation. Especially in the early phase, British and French decisions were of real consequence. If they had decided not to accept the risk of remaining in Berlin, or had withdrawn their support for the creation of a separate state in West Germany, the US would have been unable to achieve its larger goals in Germany, and it is unlikely that it could have long remained in Berlin without the support of the other Western occupying powers. On the other hand, although there was as yet no alliance, there was a close Anglo-American alignment in Germany and elsewhere, reflecting those structural influences which were transforming the system in the direction of bipolarity. France's resistance to these tendencies was declining. To the extent that their freedom of choice was more apparent than real, even the blockade crisis illustrates the lessened role of allies in a system of incipient bipolarity.

The role of 'outsiders'

The preceding discussion has drawn attention to a little-noted tendency for powers not directly involved in a crisis to remain uninvolved – to limit themselves to diplomatic exchanges which avoid commitment. If the Eastern and Berlin crises, where several powers were involved from the outset, are excluded, four of the remaining five cases amounted essentially to a 'duel' between two powers within a multipolar setting, and the other case, the Sudeten crisis, exhibits some of the same characteristics. It is true that in certain other cases such as the first Moroccan crisis or July 1914 other powers did become involved, but the phenomenon of the duel, in which they remain on the sidelines, is sufficiently striking to warrant further discussion. The analogy with the duel may indeed offer clues to the reasons why the interests both of protagonists and outsiders are served by the latter's non-involvement. A duellist and his supporters have distinct roles: having taken up the challenge, he cannot seek their active intervention or mediation. A supporter will be wary of appearing to meddle, and would not be accepted as a neutral party by the other side.

The two Franco-German cases approximate most closely to the ideal type of the duel. The 1870 crisis witnessed the provocation and the taking up of the challenge, the moment of apparent compromise and the decision to fight. The outsiders counselled caution but did not seek to mediate, to call a conference or to deter. Austria refused to offer France the support which it expected. The fast-moving crisis left outsiders little time to intervene, but more importantly, none of them saw a sufficiently clear threat to its interests or to the overall balance to convince it that the risks of intervention would be less than the risks of allowing the duel to proceed.

The Agadir crisis began as a duel, this time a dramatic German response to a silent French provocation. After the experience of a conference in the first Moroccan crisis, Germany preferred bilateral diplomacy. France showed the same preference: bargaining over compensation in French colonial Africa aroused sensitivities which were likely to be exacerbated by the involvement of any further party, whose own interests, moreover, might introduce further issues and complications. Lloyd George's Mansion House speech indicates the explosiveness of third-party intervention: it offered every prospect of 'burnt fingers' and little corresponding gain.

The duel analogy remains pertinent in the Russo-Japanese case. Russia, the established power seeking to rebuff the Japanese challenge, could admit no need of support. French diplomatic involvement was in the guise of good offices, not mediation. It offered the Russian Foreign Minister the chance of a face-saving compromise, but aroused predictable Japanese suspicion as a partisan intervention. It was even more necessary for Japan, the aspiring great power, to act independently, and it was convenient for Britain to respect this preference, since it had no interest in involvement in Japan's regional conflicts. The other major outsider, Germany, could view Russia's Far Eastern entanglement with equanimity. Non-involvement served the interests of all.

Although the Sudeten crisis was not a duel, some of the same incentives were present. Germany sought the non-involvement of all the powers. France, the victim's ally, had no stomach for a duel, but left the initiative to Britain, which sought a local accommodation, preferring that no other power was involved and even coordinating with France as little as possible. The only power which expressed an interest in involvement was the Soviet Union, which was rebuffed by Britain and its nominal ally, France.

In the case of Pearl Harbor, most of the powers were not in a position to become involved in the crisis diplomacy. Britain could have been, but the US decision makers were unwilling to further complicate the process of resolving their internal differences by consulting an associate which was likely to have firm views of its own.

So small a number of cases does not permit generalisation, but the cases do suggest that in the case of crises between two powers, where the others have no direct interests, the incentives to avoid third party involvement are considerable. Potential adverse consequences such as threats to the global or regional balance, being uncertain, are readily discounted. There may be an unstated norm that others do not intervene when sensitive issues are under discussion between two powers; indeed, resentment over such meddling suggests the perception of such a norm. In addition to the reluctance to incur a rebuff, the risks of involvement may appear greater than those of non-involvement. In the case of the protagonists, considerations of prestige count against accepting support, while the delicate search for accommodation is likely to be impeded by the presence of others, who are unlikely to be accepted as impartial or to renounce self-interested demands. Strong incentives would be required, it would appear, if these disincentives are to be overridden.[11]

Norms

The focus of the present discussion is not the role of general normative ideals, but the norms which actually underlie governmental practice, and only secondarily on how these relate to the public rhetoric of the time. Moreover, it is the norms that relate to the international system, not those at the national level which may influence policy makers' goals and perceptions. Systemic norms relating to international order may be widely shared, or may be an important source of conflict among the powers. The identification of norms of this kind is a matter of historical interpretation, that is to say, a matter of judging whether or not governments act in accordance with certain norms in a given period.

Although interpretations differ in detail, there is a fair measure of agreement that with respect to major normative changes, as in the case of alliances, the period of this study may be divided into four phases. The first, the Concert of Europe, was shorter than the others, ending with the Crimean war. It was in this phase that the powers were closest to a normative consensus. The Concert norms survived in a greatly attenuated form during the second phase, from the Crimean war to 1914, alongside norms of great-power autonomy and self-assertion which became increasingly dominant. The interwar period was one of extreme normative confusion and dissension, at the level of policy making as much as that of publicly proclaimed ideals. In such a situation it is evident that these two levels cannot be entirely separated, and remain intertwined. Finally, the relations of the superpowers after 1945 were characterised by persisting ideological and normative differences at the public level, qualified by the development of prudential norms for the conduct of their practical relations.

The Concert of Europe

Certain background reasons are usually advanced to explain why the relations of the great powers during the four decades after 1815 were not merely peaceful – this was also true of the four decades after 1870 – but were characterised by a degree of normative consensus not approached before or since that period. Following a generation of war and revolution, historians suggest, European elites were prepared to subordinate national rivalries in the interests of social conservatism and peace. While this is broadly correct, it can be overstated. Aspirations of this kind are often expressed, but do not readily overcome particular differences. Such differences among the powers, both ideological and geopolitical, were not infrequent during this period. It is therefore necessary to examine the norms and mechanisms which assisted the powers to realise their aspiration to resolve such issues 'in concert'.

The 1815 peace settlement had been drawn up by diplomats who accepted the principle of the balance of power as the framework for territorial arrangements, and there was broad agreement on criteria for its practical application.[12] France, despite its vague revisionist aspirations, was able to accept a role as one of the great powers responsible for maintaining the system. No power was in a position to make a bid for hegemony. The balance of power may be regarded, in this period, both as a generally accepted norm and as one of the background conditions which rendered the Concert possible.

Though historians are agreed that there *were* effective norms of Concert diplomacy, they vary in their understanding of these norms, as is to be expected when it is not a matter of a formal, written code but of discerning the effective norms which regulate practice. It is agreed, however, that the great powers accepted a common responsibility for maintaining the territorial settlement and for finding solutions to international problems through consultation among themselves.[13] Other states were sometimes consulted, and their consent was sometimes important, but it was the great powers which conferred and reached decisions. Second, there was an effective norm ruling out unilateral changes in the status quo; Schroeder sees this as extending to a renunciation of war for territorial gain in Europe. Whether or not one construes the norm in this sense, the important point is that the management of conflict was seen as a collective responsibility of the powers: the norm of great-power autonomy which became prominent later in the century was strikingly absent. As the case studies have illustrated, the norms regarding conferences – the machinery for collaboration – were open to casuistry. While it was agreed in principle that issues should be resolved through conference diplomacy, there was scope for delay and for disputes over the venue and the agenda. Consensus was often strained to the breaking-point. Such as it was, the consensus was procedural and practical, not ideological: the attempt to achieve a common policy based on a shared conservative ideology had broken down very early.

Schroeder postulates one important norm which is absent from some analyses – the avoidance of direct challenges or confrontations among the powers – 'thou shalt not threaten or humiliate'.[14] This was in accordance with the general logic of the Concert, and may have been normal practice, but Schroeder's view requires qualification. The 1839–41 crisis is rightly seen as a success for Concert diplomacy, yet the exclusion of France from the negotiation of the 1840 Convention broke one of the Concert rules, and led to a confrontation between France and the other powers. The example illustrates the pressures to set aside the Concert restraints, even though they were observed in large measure during the crisis. As we have seen, Schroeder makes a powerful case for the thesis that it was Britain's abandonment of the Concert norms which prevented a diplomatic resolution of the Crimean crisis. Nonetheless, the crisis was shaped by the practices of Concert diplomacy, even though they proved unable to avert the drift to war. Given this failure, it is not surprising that the Concert norms were ignored during the following two decades. More fundamentally, however, the great issues of those decades, the unification of Italy and Germany, involved territorial changes on a scale which Concert diplomacy could not have been expected to regulate. Such changes could be brought about only by the unilateral action which the Concert norms sought to rule out, and no new normative system emerged during those years.

1870–1914

Shared norms and diplomatic cooperation among the European great powers played a much smaller role in the long peace after 1870 than in that after 1815. It is true that the Concert approach underwent something of a revival in the 1870s, with the conference in 1871 to legitimise Russia's denunciation of the Black Sea clauses in the treaty of 1856, and the Congress of Berlin on the Eastern question in 1878. But there was no general return to conference diplomacy, and no assumption that international questions were to be resolved by agreement among the great powers.

A number of reasons for this may be suggested. Most of the issues which arose in the three decades after 1880 were outside Europe, and thus did not directly affect the European balance. Within Europe, Bismarck sought to stabilise Germany's strengthened position – in many eyes, a hegemonial position – through a system of defensive alliances, which proved too complex for his successors to maintain. By the turn of the century rival alliances dominated the political landscape, and however defensive their intent, their offensive potential was a source of concern. In place of the Concert norm that the powers shared a common responsibility for resolving international conflicts, norms asserting the primacy of the nation-state or the autonomy of the great power were among the 'unspoken assumptions' of the decision makers.[15] The influence of social Darwinism in the era of nationalism and imperialism has been widely noted.

Balance of power assumptions and norms were a stabilising influence, but were breaking down by the turn of the century. They were rejected by liberals and socialists, and governments no longer shared a common conception of the balance. German commentators, in particular, came to perceive it quite differently from their British counterparts. For Britain, membership of the Triple Entente was necessary as a counter to Germany's increasing weight in the European balance; for Germany, it signified Britain's determination to prevent it acquiring the status of a world power.[16] Some have argued that the balance was becoming unstable precisely because the two opposing alliances were so evenly matched. While this remains debatable, the increasing divergence in the kind of balance that was perceived by the principal adversaries was unquestionably a source of instability. Paradoxically, it was the global power, Britain, which perceived the balance in traditional European terms, while it was the continental power, Germany, which perceived it as a global balance among 'world powers'.

Conference diplomacy was not completely abandoned during this period, but was resorted to as a convenient way of handling certain specific issues, not as a general diplomatic practice. The Algeciras conference on Morocco in 1906 and the London conference during the Balkan wars of 1912–13 provide examples. The cases studied here (1870, the Russo-Japanese and Agadir) are more typical of the period, illustrating the tendency to restrict crisis diplomacy to the powers directly involved. If the norms of the earlier period had remained effective, there would have been an expectation that the other powers would be involved. The effective norms during these crises legitimised the assertion of national self-interest, narrowly conceived. This led *inter alia* to deception and a readiness to humiliate the adversary in 1870, disdain on Russia's part for Japan's claims to equal standing in 1903, and a not dissimilar attempt by France to set aside Germany's claims in 1911, provoking a crudely coercive German response. The crises illustrate the weakness of normative restraints in the period before 1914.

The interwar period

A comparison of the second and third periods, however, brings out the extent to which there was a measure of normative agreement before 1914, albeit on norms which legitimised national self-interest and the notion of a balance of power, even though the latter was conceived in different ways. The interwar period saw a radical breakdown of normative consensus, part cause and part effect of the absence of stable alignments or of a *de facto* balance of power.

The peace settlement of 1919 was based on norms of national self-determination, non-aggression and the peaceful settlement of disputes. Sanctions against aggression were among the central provisions of the League of Nations, but the absence of several of the great powers from the League at all times symbolised the lack of normative consensus among them. The uneven application of the principle of self-determination was one source of Germany's grievances against the Treaty of Versailles, and of British questioning of its legitimacy. The League enjoyed strong public support in Britain and in some of the smaller member-states, but was viewed sceptically in France, which favoured maintaining the status quo through alliances. Public support for the League principles in the United States was of little consequence, since the US never became a member. In Britain there was scepticism towards the League at the governmental level, where some looked to the reconstruction of a balance of power while others supported a watered-down version of the League norm, retaining the principle of peaceful change without the attempt to provide for international sanctions.

If support for the peace settlement and the League was very narrowly based, there was even less support for a return to alliances or, more fundamentally, to the balance of power. A handful of diplomats may have sought to reconstruct a balance, and certain governments may at times have acted in terms of balance of power reflexes, but there was no substantial support for any actual or desired equilibrium. The main challenge in the 1930s was the ambition of the three revisionist powers, Germany, Italy and Japan, to bring about territorial changes amounting to a fundamental restructuring of the system. In principle, the revisionist powers could have been restrained by a superior coalition, but this would have presupposed far greater support for balance of power norms than was present. The abstention of the United States meant that at the practical diplomatic level it shared no effective norms with the relatively like-minded powers, Britain and France. The other great outsider, the Soviet Union, may by then have sought to act on balance of power instincts, but the hostility and suspicion of the leaders of the Western powers inhibited any positive response. Moreover, the Soviet record as a whole raises major questions as to the long-term feasibility of a balance of power coalition.

The Sudeten crisis illustrates the effect of the foregoing normative dissonance. Britain, having abandoned any hope in the League, was committed to the norm of peaceful change but also to preserving the broad outlines of the status quo. However, having abandoned the balance of power approach, it relied on the hope that Germany could be persuaded to exercise restraint. (Its willingness to go to war on behalf of these principles and interests became evident only in 1939.) France, recognising the erosion of its alliance system, followed the British lead, albeit with little conviction. The normative chasm that separated the British leaders from the German has frequently been noted, though Hitler was able for the last time to exploit his public espousal of the norm of self-determination. There was no normative basis for agreement between Hitler and the Western powers: any accommodation would be for reasons of short-term expediency.

The same was true of Japan and the United States in 1941. During the protracted negotiations each side reiterated conflicting sets of principles – non-discrimination, non-aggression, and self-determination, on the one hand; secure access to resources and US non-involvement in Japan's prospective sphere of influence, on the other. The principles of global liberalism were at odds with those of regional hegemony. Short-term accommodation was conceivable, but the conflicting visions of international order were incompatible.

Post-1945

The normative conflict between the United States and the Soviet Union over Eastern Europe was similar to that between the US and Japan over East Asia a few years earlier. American universalism, a commitment to non-discrimination (the 'open door'), to self-determination and to the principle that governments should be freely elected, clashed with Soviet insistence that its security required the presence of 'friendly' governments in Eastern Europe. Both sides could point to formulations at the Yalta conference which provided some justification for their differing stances. Only much later was the Soviet position reinforced by normative claims relating to the socialist community of states.

There were two essential differences between the American conflict with Japan and the later Cold War. First, the Soviet sphere of influence in eastern Europe was a *fait accompli* achieved through military occupation, whereas in 1941 Japan's occupation of part of China was contested, and it had not then occupied most of Southeast Asia. Second, in 1945 there was an extreme aversion to war on all sides. This later came to be perceived largely in terms of nuclear deterrence, but in the early postwar years war was virtually unthinkable for a variety of more immediate reasons, including material devastation and social dislocation throughout Europe. The normative cleavage between East and West provided the basic justifications for political strategies which had become reasonably well defined on both sides by the time of the Berlin blockade. In addition, differences over compliance with the Potsdam agreement provided a further area of dispute, but these were of secondary importance relative to the basic Cold War normative issues.

The term 'cold war' signifies, in part, precisely this kind of normative impasse. The scope for agreement was limited to procedural norms for accommodation and restraint. In contrast to 1938–41, however, the presence of nuclear weapons required that such accommodation be not merely temporary, but of indefinite duration. In the view of some scholars, such procedures came to be institutionalised to the extent that one may speak of conventions regulating superpower conflict. The Berlin case studies offer little support to this contention, but

233

provide abundant evidence of prudent, risk-reducing behaviour within the context of serious conflicts of interests and objectives.

Conclusion

The systemic setting of crises stems from the interaction of all three developments: in the arena, the pattern of alignments, and norms. During the first phase studied here the arena, familiar to all the actors, was readily conceptualised as the balance of power. There were no firm alignments, but the background influences making for stability were enhanced by a high degree of normative consensus, unsurpassed before or since that period. The expansion of the arena in the second phase saw the formation of major 'balance of power' alliances in Europe, but the new external powers were not yet fully part of the central balance. The expansion of the arena led to differing conceptions of the balance, European or global, and led Germans, in particular, to formulate a distinction between global and purely European powers which was little understood elsewhere. There was still a measure of normative consensus, but this amounted to the legitimisation of national self-assertion, and the new, external powers were only partially accepted by the old, and only partially 'socialised' into the system.

These disruptive tendencies were greatly exacerbated in the third phase: the expanded arena now became unmanageable. Norms of nationalist self-assertion were espoused in a more extreme form by the revisionist powers. Liberal norms were embodied in the League of Nations but enjoyed little effective support. The prerequisites for the re-creation of a balance of power were absent, both at the European and the global level, and divergences in the perceived interests of the powers as well as in their normative commitments precluded the emergence of firm alignments.

The emergence of the superpowers, and thus an essentially bipolar system, together with the development of nuclear weapons, introduced a new manageability into the post-1945 arena, but this was not initially evident. The fundamental normative conflict between the superpowers did not, like the ideological conflicts of the 1930s, foreshadow general war, but was constrained to the level of Cold War. The alliances in Europe played a significant part in this process of stabilisation, which became sufficiently assured that the realignment of so major a power as China could be accommodated without calling it in question. Normative consensus, however, remained narrow in scope, limited to practical rules of accommodation – thus not extending, as in the initial period, to agreement on the principles of international order.

234

The systemic context was of greater importance in influencing the general character of crises than in determining their outcomes, the explanation of which, it has become clear, must be sought mainly at the level of the actors' goals, strategies and interactions. The Eastern and Crimean crises both revolved around Concert diplomacy: in both cases the conventions of the Concert were placed under extreme stress, and there was a breach between one of the powers and a coalition of several of the others. That the outcome was war in the one case but merely a change of government in the other was due to a variety of specific factors affecting the policies of the key actors.

The three cases during the period 1870–1914 illustrate different ways in which the multipolar system, in the absence of norms of collective diplomacy, permitted crises to be resolved bilaterally. In 1870 the external powers had their specific reasons for non-intervention, and also the more general reason that the crisis provided no clear and present danger to the balance of power. The Russo-Japanese crisis was a consequence of the expansion of the system – the emergence of an aspiring imperial power claiming equal status with its nearest imperial rival, which the latter denied it. Again, the other powers perceived no overriding reason for intervention. Agadir illustrates both the tensions accompanying the polarisation of alliances before 1914 and the complex dynamics of those alliances, which for the most part also favoured non-intervention in the particular circumstances of the crisis.

The Sudeten crisis can be interpreted as the outcome, in a particular constellation of circumstances, of the multiple cleavages – geopolitical, economic and normative – which signified the breakdown of any system of international order in the 1930s; its denouement, seemingly so momentous at the time, was almost at once overtaken by indications of further impending crises. The US–Japan crisis, involving the two outlying powers not yet drawn into the European war, was a clash between powers upholding inflexible normative systems whose practical consequences were governed by changing strategic calculations.

The Berlin blockade was both a consequence of the division of Europe into two rival socio-economic-political systems, and a process tending to consolidate those systems, their institutions and norms, in a setting where both sides were determined to avoid war. The second Berlin crisis served to further consolidate the two blocs, and demonstrated the paradoxical character of the thermonuclear systemic context: the actors were even more determined to avoid war, yet could not avoid the risk of fatal miscalculation. In each of the cases the modes of crisis diplomacy and the magnitude of the stakes were a function of the changing international system.

235

11 THE CHOICE OF GOALS: VALUES, INTERESTS AND OBJECTIVES

The case studies suggest that, in general, crisis diplomacy is an intentional, goal-seeking form of behaviour, the pursuit of policies or strategies aimed at achieving certain ends or avoiding certain outcomes. Yet the study of goals, and in particular their rationales and the processes by which they are chosen, is a neglected area of crisis research. They are often taken for granted, or treated as 'givens', and are seldom studied in depth. They are presupposed in the bargaining approach, and largely submerged in analyses of stress or the hostility spiral. This chapter makes neither kind of assumption, but treats the extent to which crisis behaviour is goal-driven as a question to be investigated.

One approach to the discussion of goals, that of formal rational-choice theory, borrows its key concepts – utilities and preferences – from economics and game theory. Some problems in applying formal theory to foreign policy decisions were noted in Chapter 2, above. The present chapter will follow a different approach, one which is closer to the terminology used by the actors, and which allows for the heterogeneity of goals, and for the difficulty and stress in choosing among core values under conditions of uncertainty – problems which are assumed away by the concept of maximising utility. It will seek to develop what was earlier termed an informal rational-choice theory, that is to say, a systematic analysis of goals and their rationales, in a way which is more concrete and differentiated than the abstractions of utility maximising. The level of generality is thus similar to the historical sociology of the international system, discussed in the previous chapter, and it is also in line with the way in which goals have been discussed in a number of classic studies. Morgenthau emphasises the diversity of foreign policy goals; Aron, acknowledging this, classifies them under three broad headings: power, glory and idea.[1] Wolfers, and more recently George and Keohane, distinguish between possession and milieu goals.[2] The present study, dealing with the choices between peace and war, is concerned with 'core' values which have traditionally been considered under such headings as 'survival' or 'security', but the case studies show that economic goals (resources and capabilities) and milieu goals (views of international order) are often inseparable from the way in which governments conceive of security and survival.

This chapter will discuss two sets of issues concerning the actors' goals. The first section will examine their immediate goals, here termed 'objectives'. The 'core' values which motivate their policies are too general and abstract to determine their specific choices. These, it is suggested, are shaped by immediate, concrete objectives, such as the control over particular territory, the acceptance or renunciation of specific rights, and the like. It is evident that the parties' objectives have a major part in 'structuring' crises – determining their acuteness, the main lines of development, and the outcome.

First and foremost, the degree of compatibility or incompatibility between the parties' objectives points towards the likelihood of war: changes of objective, either softening or hardening them, may be of crucial significance. Certain other characteristics of objectives are also important: the extent to which they are limited or open-ended, and the extent to which it is necessary to distinguish between ostensible and 'real' objectives. However, the precise significance of objectives in 'structuring' crises is a matter for investigation. Other major influences are noted, for exploration in later chapters. And the extent to which the parties have clear objectives, or indeed any identifiable objectives, is of major consequence. The case studies, it will be argued, suggest that while objectives are normally a crucial structuring influence, the inability of even one government to agree on its objectives introduces major perturbations.

The second section of the chapter looks behind the immediate goals, inquiring how and why they came to be chosen. It treats the choice of objectives as problematic: they have *some* relationship to the basic, core foreign policy values, but what is the nature of this relationship, and how does it vary from case to case? The answer most familiar to students of international relations is that the objectives reflect the national interest; but the case studies show that on almost every occasion there were differences in the way in which decision makers perceived that interest. Thus, if the concept of national interest is to remain relevant, it must refer to particular decision makers' *sense* (or perception) of it.

The chapter explores the extent to which governmental objectives can reasonably be construed as having a national interest rationale, rather than having other sources – norms, habits, or *ad hoc* reactions to internal or external pressures. In other words, the discussion inquires

237

into relevant aspects of informal rationality: prima facie, goal-seeking behaviour is rational, but is the choice of goals in crises actually in accordance with the standard assumptions of rationality? To what extent is it the case that, while individual decision makers have their goals, a government has no identifiable goal?

Before entering into the discussion of these two issues, however, the concepts employed in the analysis – values, objectives and interests – need to be further explicated.

Concepts

Values are defined as the basic, long-term goals of foreign policy, expressed in general terms such as security, autonomy, empire or international order. Expressions of values are often aspirational, but the term is used here to refer to values which guide policy, for which there is a willingness to incur high costs. Values, however, are not formulated precisely or concretely: trade-offs are not often confronted, even though they may be implied. In some of the case studies, nonetheless, deep divisions over values can be discerned.

Objectives, as we have seen, are defined as the immediate, concrete goals which governments actually pursue in a crisis. They can sometimes be equated with demands, but only if the demands formulate the goals towards which policy is directed. Demands advanced for bargaining purposes or to satisfy an internal constituency may amount to no more than tactical ploys or statements of aspirations. Palmerston's objective in 1840, or Japan's objective in 1903, were identical with what was demanded. In the Sudeten crisis, on the other hand, the objectives of the British and German governments, even though they were not expressed as demands, can be inferred from their words and actions.

It might be inquired whether the immediate goals might be better conceptualised as preferences among a range of outcomes rather than as objectives, which often amount to a single outcome or end. Game theorists have shown that much can be learned by modelling crises in terms of preferences among outcomes, but these preferences can be formed only after certain options are defined as the crisis unfolds. Initial preferences are likely to be more ambitious but less clearly defined, and the formulation of 'realistic' preferences is often deferred, since it involves painful trade-offs. Thus the study of preferences during the whole of a crisis may be difficult or unilluminating. Most crucially, it will be less relevant than a study of the goals which are actually chosen, and thus guide and direct policy. The Kennedy Administration had a variety of preferences at the outset of the Cuban missile crisis: what shaped its policy was the choice of an objective, the withdrawal of the missiles. Cases in which objectives are absent appear anomalous, requiring special explanation, whereas cases in which realistic preferences cannot be identified are frequent.[3]

The concept of *interest* may be construed to provide the link between the generality of values and the concreteness of objectives. Eyre Crowe's memorandum of January 1907, it is often suggested, advanced a conception of British interests which guided policy before 1914, and George Kennan's 'X' article offered a formulation of American interests which provided a general rationale for specific policy choices in the early Cold War.[4] The term 'interest', however, has many meanings. It is often used to refer to specific, concrete assets or concerns, which may be economic, political or strategic, as in 'British interests in the Middle East' or 'French interests in Morocco'. It can also be used, however, as in the above examples, in a broader, aggregative sense, often termed the 'national interest', the problematic nature of which is familiar, yet which survives in new formulations. It refers, essentially, to a ranking of values and interests (in the narrower sense) in a specific context: for Britain and the US, in the examples noted, in a newly threatening geopolitical context. Trade-offs among values are involved: the process of formulating a conception of the 'national interest' may be described as the ranking of values in the context of perceived circumstances, taking account of costs and constraints, and the prescription of a general course of action for the attainment of those values. Terms such as *raison d'état* and, indeed, 'national interest' itself suggest a greater determinacy than is actually present. Crowe's and Kennan's conceptions were contested, as are all such conceptions. This is evident in the case studies, where such differences were pervasive. They show that foreign policy interests are not, as is sometimes claimed, *determined* by a state's geopolitical situation. It will, of course, constrain the choice of goals, but is always open to different readings.

In practice, the ranking of values is closely linked to the choice of a course of action intended to promote them. As Friedrich Kratochwil points out with respect to the analogous concept of 'public interest':

> a public interest claim has to satisfy another formal requirement, that of considering the consequences, which involves us in the arduous task of providing data for assessing the impact of various policies upon community values.[5]

In international crises where 'vital' interests are at stake, decision makers do not make a once-for-all choice of a 'payoff': rather, they choose a course of action which is deemed to offer the best chance of preserving their core values. The ranking of values is bound up with their beliefs about the consequences of different courses of action: whether painful trade-offs are necessary depends on whether or not there appears to be a course of action which can avoid them. The ranking of values and choice of a course of action are interdependent. Expectations about the latter depend on a multiplicity of causal judgments, or assumptions, some kinds of which are examined in the following chapter.

The concept of aggregate interest or national interest, as employed here, is both descriptive and evaluative. Descriptively, it serves to distinguish cases where policies have a coherent rationale in terms of the central values at stake (ranked, at least implicitly) and a reasonably comprehensive view of the situation and the available courses of action, from cases in which crucial values are neglected or policy does not address the actual situation. The concept is also evaluative: only if policy making is guided by such a conception does it meet the normal criteria of rationality: in essence, that it seeks to achieve highly valued ends by well-judged means.[6] In this evaluative use, the concept cannot provide a criterion for the choice of a 'correct' policy, because there are always 'legitimate' differences over the ranking of values and over the consequences of potential courses of action. However, it can serve to evaluate the policy process, which will meet the criteria for rationality provided the central values are addressed and an appropriate course of action, given the available information, is chosen.

Objectives and the 'structure' of crises

To the extent that crises can be construed as interactions among rational actors, their objectives provide the central element in explaining the course of events – the acuteness of the conflict, the main developments and the outcome. In essence, the acuteness of the crisis will depend on the extent to which the adversaries' objectives are mutually incompatible. Six of the case studies illustrate this pattern: the Eastern, Franco-Prussian, Agadir, Sudeten and both Berlin crises were 'driven' mainly by conflicts over objectives. The remaining three crises – the Crimean, Russo-Japanese and US–Japan – illustrate a contrasting pattern, where it was the *absence* of an agreed governmental objective in the case of at least one of the main actors which was crucial. However purposeful the diplomacy of the others may have been, this 'logic' could not prevail in the face of the non-purposive behaviour of the one. No significance attaches to the numbers in each category: the important point is the distinction between the two categories.

240

Table 11.1. Objectives and incompatibilities

Case	Actor		Objective	Incompatibilities
(a) Crises shaped by objectives				
Eastern	Britain		restrict Mehemet Ali	Britain/France incompatible
	France		support Mehemet Ali	
	Russia		avoid hostile coalition	
	Austria		Concert solution	
Franco-Prussian	France	*early*	withdraw Hohenzollern candidacy	*early*: compatible
		late	formal guarantees, 'apology'	*late*: incompatible
	Prussia	*early*	face-saving settlement	
		late	maintain prestige	
Agadir	France	*early*	gain Morocco unilaterally	*early*: potentially incompatible
		late	negotiate compensation	*late*: compatible
	Germany	*early*	major compensation	
		late	acceptable compensation	
Sudeten	Britain	*early*	avoid crisis	incompatible
		late	negotiated settlement	
	Germany	*early*	crisis in favourable circumstances	
		late	localised war	
Berlin blockade	Soviet Union		prevent formation of West Germany *or* gain Berlin	incompatible
	US and allies		create West Germany *and* remain in Berlin	
Berlin 1958–62	Soviet Union		broad negotiations on Germany, 'neutralise' Berlin	incompatible
	US and allies		narrow negotiations, remain in Berlin	
(b) Crises not shaped by objectives				
Crimean	Britain		no agreed objectives	not clear
	France		support Britain; impose a settlement	
	Russia		face-saving settlement	
	Austria		Concert solution	
Russo-Japanese	Japan		spheres of influence agreement, or war	not clear
	Russia		no agreed objectives	
US–Japan	Japan		agreement on control over resources, or war	long-term, incompatible
	US		deny Japanese claims, but no agreed diplomatic objective	short-term, not clear

Governmental objectives in crises tend to be highly contingent – dependent on the views and experience of those who happen to be in control at a particular time, and also on other circumstances such as the way a crisis comes about. Where a government is unified and has clearly defined objectives, these will explain the general direction of its policy. Where it is seriously divided, the conflicting objectives of key decision makers may explain its policy vicissitudes, and in the extreme case, unresolved conflicts may lead to stalemate or to the absence of an identifiable policy.

Incompatibility of objectives

In the case of the six crises structured by conflicts over objectives – the 'normal' pattern – the adversaries' immediate goals were incompatible (Table 11.1). The acuteness of the Eastern crisis in 1840 resulted from the tenacity with which Palmerston and Thiers pursued incompatible objectives over the extent of Mehemet Ali's rule. When this issue was resolved by excluding France from the negotiation, the outcome depended on what goal France would set itself: would it seek redress for its humiliation, or would it accept a face-saving return to the Concert? The choice depended on who was to control French policy. The two phases of the Franco-Prussian crisis, culminating in diplomatic compromise and in war respectively, were distinguished by a change in French objectives. Once the compromise was achieved, the French government was 'captured' by those whose objective – a humiliating public renunciation of the Hohenzollern candidacy by the King of Prussia – was incompatible with Prussia's basic values, thus ruling out a peaceful settlement. In the Agadir crisis, between the same two adversaries, the control over policy in both governments shifted in the opposite direction, from hard-line, confrontationist decision makers seeking incompatible goals to others willing to accept the best available negotiated compromise.

Until its final phase, the Sudeten crisis was structured by the elaborate attempts by Britain and Germany to achieve incompatible goals – on the one hand, to avoid a confrontation over Czechoslovakia, on the other, to promote conditions favourable to German invasion. The course of events of the final phase depended on the improvisation of new objectives. In the case of the Berlin blockade, Soviet and Western objectives with respect to the creation of the Federal Republic and the control of Berlin were incompatible, hence the protracted crisis, but it was resolved through Soviet acquiescence in their eventual inability to achieve either objective except at the cost of war. The objectives of the adversaries in the protracted Berlin crisis (1958–62) were more complex, but can be construed as a range of incompatible preferences with respect to Berlin and the overall German question, pursued tenaciously but again short of incurring a perceived risk of war. These incompatibilities account for the protracted diplomatic deadlock and the difficulty of terminating the crisis.

The other three cases, however, show that this simple pattern is not universal. In the instances where a government failed to define its objectives, two further patterns may be discerned. In the Crimean and Pearl Harbor crises, in the cases of the British and American governments respectively, this was because of differences among the decision makers. In the Russo-Japanese crisis the main reason was the Russian misperception of Japan, resulting in a failure to perceive the situation as a crisis.

In the Crimean case, the lack of clearly defined Russian objectives in the initial phase precipitated an acute crisis. More crucially, however, internal differences over Britain's interests and objectives rendered British diplomacy directionless, hampering the search for a settlement in the second phase and opening the way to an uncontrollable escalation in the third. In the US–Japan crisis the underlying conflict of interests was indeed far-reaching, but it was the inability of the divided American government to define clear objectives which decisively influenced the course of the crisis and the timing of the war. While the Russo-Japanese crisis might be taken as a further instance of the pattern – divided counsels did indeed provide part of the explanation for Russia's failure to formulate definite objectives – the main reason, it has been argued, was a shared misperception of the seriousness of Japan's challenge. This may be taken as identifying a third pattern.

Thus far, it has been argued that the central strand in the narrative of many crises and the starting-point for an explanation is the degree of incompatibility of the parties' objectives, and changes of objective usually resulting from changes in the control over policy. In a significant minority of cases, however, the absence of such objectives on the part of one of the key actors opens the way to other 'structuring' influences such as internal conflicts, misperception or escalatory processes beyond the control of governments. Moreover, incompatibilities are not always self-evident, and much may depend on how they are perceived; it is therefore necessary to turn to other characteristics of objectives.

Limited versus open-ended objectives, and the question of ostensible objectives

Contemporary thinking on crisis management, as we have seen, emphasises the limitation of objectives. Similar concerns were evident

243

Table 11.2. *Limited vs open-ended objectives and ostensible vs latent objectives*

Case	Actor	Limited or open-ended	Latent objective	Gravity of crisis
Eastern	Britain	L	—	moderate
	France	L	brinkmanship	
	Russia	L	alignment concerns	
	Austria	L	—	
Crimean	Britain	became O-E by default	—	became extreme
	France	L	disrupt status quo	
	Russia	initially O-E	—	
	Austria	L	—	
Franco-Prussian	France	ostensibly L	pretext for war	extreme
	Prussia	ostensibly L	promote German unification	
Russso-Japanese	Japan	L	—	became extreme
	Russia	unclear	—	
Agadir	France	L	prestige rivalry	moderate, potential
	Germany	initially O-E	prestige rivalry	for escalation
Sudeten	Britain	L	—	became extreme
	Germany	L (immediate) O-E	—	
US–Japan	Japan	O-E	—	extreme
	US	ostensibly O-E	—	
Berlin blockade	Soviet Union	L	⎱ German and	moderate
	US and allies	L	⎰ European balance	
Berlin 1958–62	Soviet Union	appeared O-E	German balance	moderate
	US and allies	L	German balance	

in the 1930s, when British policy depended on whether Hitler's objectives were perceived as limited or unlimited. It is doubtful, however, whether any government pursues literally unlimited objectives. Governments frequently pursue goals with no clearly defined limits, more ambitious than they wish to acknowledge: such objectives may be termed 'open-ended'. The concept of limited objectives, also, is not without problems. The ostensible objective may be limited, but it may be a cover for more far-reaching objectives, or it may have far-reaching implications for the prestige or credibility of those concerned. The ostensibly limited French demand in 1870 for formal guarantees from the King of Prussia was of this kind. Such consequences or side-effects may be perceived as the 'real' objective, and even when they are not, it is the perceived 'larger' objective which influences the course of the crisis.

Table 11.2 summarises the findings of the cases in these respects.

Whereas the pursuit of open-ended or maximal goals tends to exacerbate disputes, the choice of a limited objective is not always conducive to resolving them. It will not promote a settlement if it is incompatible with the objective of another of the actors, as is illustrated by the case of Palmerston and Thiers. Open-ended objectives, however, regularly heightened tensions. Menshikov's proposals in 1853 transformed a low-key conflict into a crisis, and it was the open-ended character of Kiderlen's demands which explains the acuteness of the Agadir confrontation. The evident open-endedness of Japan's goals in 1941 precluded a settlement, and the impression of open-endedness in Khrushchev's goals in 1958–62, which may be contrasted with Stalin's circumspection in 1948, was a constant concern in the later Berlin crisis.

In general, the prospects for a settlement depend greatly on whether a challenge is perceived as limited. If not, as in Britain in 1853, negotiation will be half-hearted; needless to say, unless the perception is broadly correct, a settlement will remain elusive.

The willingness to risk war

Thus far, objectives have been considered independently of the willingness to go to war in order to achieve them. In some few instances, such as Japan's challenge to Russia in 1903, the *casus belli* is defined in advance, but decision makers are normally reluctant to tie their hands until the specific circumstances are clear: the consequences are momentous, and there is a risk of opening up internal conflicts. Nonetheless, the parties' willingness to risk war crucially affects the seriousness of a crisis. If it were readily ascertainable, it might provide the principal clue to understanding crises, if not at the time – because it is often not clear – then at least when the evidence becomes available. Unfortunately, however, it often remains unclear. It is convenient to examine the significance of the willingness to risk war, firstly, in relation to the six cases which were structured by incompatible objectives.

In the two Berlin crises there was extreme reluctance to go to war on both sides, even though the adversaries' goals were incompatible and highly consequential. Nonetheless, both were serious crises: there were major concerns over miscalculation, and some policy makers favoured confrontationist moves – claimed to be safer in the long run – which might in fact have heightened the dangers. Aversion to war does not in itself ensure that volatile situations will remain under policy makers' control.

Three of the cases – the Eastern, Franco-Prussian and Agadir crises –

illustrate the difficulty of ascertaining the level of risk which particular decision makers were willing to run. Palmerston, Thiers, Bismarck and Kiderlen engaged in brinkmanship, each assuring his risk-averse monarch or colleagues that there was no risk of war. It is impossible to determine what risk each of the four was prepared to run, but their protestations cannot be taken at face value, and Bismarck's assurances to the King that the Hohenzollern candidacy would not lead to complications were patently insincere. In each case, the government's threshold of risk depended crucially on who exercised control over policy at different moments; Thiers or Louis-Philippe, Bismarck or the King, Kiderlen or the Kaiser. The seriousness of the crises depended also, however, on the potential 'loss of control over events' or the dynamics of the hostility spiral. The Sudeten crisis illustrates the way in which extremely risk-averse decision makers, the British, were brought to the point of war by Hitler's aggressive tactics and expanding demands, showing that 'willingness to risk war' is not a static disposition, but is subject to sudden eruptions under the pressures of crisis.

If the Berlin crises represent the extreme of unwillingness to risk war, France in 1870 illustrates the opposite. At the extremes, the effects of the willingness, or unwillingness, to go to war can be distinguished from the conflict over incompatible goals, in determining the structure of a crisis. In general, however, the conflict over objectives provides the fuller explanation of the course of events and even the seriousness of a crisis, given that, once the contest has been joined, the risk of war cannot be excluded, whatever the parties' preferences.

But what can be said of the three cases – each, in the present sample, leading to war – which were not structured by a conflict over objectives? Was the willingness to go to war clearer and more crucial in these cases? In 1903, as noted above, Japan was unusually explicit in defining the *casus belli*, but the Russian government's willingness to go to war was never clarified. Rather similarly, in 1941 Japan was resolved to risk war with the US if it could not gain control over the resources of Southeast Asia by diplomatic means, but the US leaders, unable to threaten or initiate war, could not define the *casus belli*. In these cases, both Japan's goals and its conditional willingness to go to war explain its policies in the crisis, but its adversaries' willingness to go to war is no clearer than their objectives. In the Crimean case, on the other hand, where the absence of governmental objectives on Britain's part was a major disturbing influence, the increasing belligerence of the British public was a crucial influence in the later phase of the crisis.

We may conclude that, while the willingness of one or more parties to engage in war is always important, it may be difficult or even impossible to establish. Careful analysis of the parties' objectives – or of the consequences of their failure to define them – provides a better general explanation of the unfolding of a crisis.

Are matters different when it comes to the final outcome of a crisis? When 'the chips are down' – when the issues and options are clear – may not the willingness to risk war prove decisive? A review of the cases suggests that while it can indeed be isolated as a major determinant of the outcome, the relationships involved are more complex than a purely logical analysis might suggest. The logic of the situation, it might appear, is that war is to be expected when two adversaries are ready to go to war, a diplomatic resolution when both are reluctant to do so, and capitulation by the reluctant party when there is a major asymmetry in risk-taking.

In practice, the situation is far more complex. Firstly, governments are often seriously divided over the *casus belli*: what will be crucial is which decision maker, or groups, can gain control of policy. The internal political balance can move in either direction: in favour of the 'war party', as in Britain in 1853 or France in 1870 or, with greater difficulty, against war as in the Agadir crisis. A second complication is that a government which is extremely reluctant to go to war over the issues in dispute may be faced with demands which its honour, prestige or credibility prevent it from accepting, like Russia in 1854 or Britain in 1938. Or a power can compel its adversary to fight by attacking it, as Japan did in 1904 and 1941. War may be likely if only one of the adversaries is willing to fight.

The only case in which both adversaries were, at the end, highly willing to fight over the issues in dispute was the Franco-Prussian, and even here this was only because the French 'war party' was able to seize control over policy. The other three cases resulting in war show a marked asymmetry in the parties' relative acceptance of war. Britain in 1853, and Japan in 1903 and 1941 were resolved to fight over the given *casus belli*; the other powers were reluctant in 1853 and although the preferences of Japan's adversaries remained unclear, they were evidently far more reluctant than Japan to engage in war. It is noteworthy that, except for the Franco-Prussian, the crises which resulted in war were those in which one of the actors had failed to define its objectives – in 1853 the more belligerent party, in the other cases the party more averse to war.

In contrast to the cases which led to war, all five that were resolved peacefully were characterised by the pursuit of relatively clear objectives by all the parties, even though in some instances these changed

247

along with the control of policy, or were formulated only during the crisis, as in US policy in the Berlin blockade. The willingness to risk war was usually low, but there were major exceptions or uncertainties, notably Thiers, Kiderlen and Hitler. In all these instances, except Hitler in 1938, leaders averse to war were in control by the end of the crises. With hindsight, it is evident that the reluctance to risk war proved decisive in the concluding stages of the five cases, but this could not be known at the time.

In the sample of nine cases, there are two contrasts between those which led to war and those which were resolved peacefully. First, the policies of all the actors were more purposeful, more clearly directed to specific goals, in the cases where diplomacy succeeded in avoiding war. In three of the four cases which led to war, one of the principal actors lacked such objectives. Second, at least one, and usually only one, of the actors was relatively willing to go to war in those cases, but not in the concluding phase of those which were resolved peacefully. The two factors varied independently. Purposeful diplomacy led to peace when it was sought by all, and to war when the adversaries wanted it; but in the three anomalous cases, confusion over objectives was as much part of the process leading to war as deliberate choice.

The nexus between values, interests and objectives

What lies behind the choice of objectives? The political processes that determine which particular decision makers will be in a position to choose are considered in Chapter 14, below. The present discussion inquires into the rationales for the objectives: to what extent are they derived from conceptions of the national interest, as defined above – from a weighing of the values at stake, the costs and constraints, and the consequences of relevant courses of action? If governments are to be deemed rational actors, this is how they must proceed, and there will be a close nexus between values, interests and objectives. Moreover, the rational actor must be capable of resolving the differences among decision makers – frequently over differing conceptions of the national interest – which we have seen are pervasive.

National interest rationales

It is evident from the case studies that most decision makers had rationales for the chosen course of action, and that these were usually expressed as claims about expected consequences for certain values or interests. The calculus of values and interests, however, was often

Table 11.3. *National interest rationales*

Case	Actor	Whether articulated	Comments
Eastern	Britain	√	by Palmerston
	France	—	no overall rationale
	Russia	√	by Nesselrode
	Austria	√	by Metternich
Crimean	Britain	(√)	conflicting views
	France	√	plausibly imputed to Napoleon
	Russia	√	partially, by Nesselrode
	Austria	√	by Buol
Franco-Prussian	France	(√)	conflicting views
	Prussia	√	plausibly imputed to Bismarck
Russo-Japanese	Japan	√	substantial consensus achieved
	Russia	—	relevant issues not addressed
Agadir	France	√	by Caillaux
	Germany	—	no overall rationale
Sudeten	Britain	√	thorough prior assessment
	Germany	√	by Hitler
US–Japan	Japan	√	extensively discussed, quasi-consensus
	US	(√)	conflicting partial views
Berlin blockade	US	√	broad policies clearly defined, not specific implications
	Soviet Union	√	plausibly imputed to Stalin
Berlin 1958–62	US	√	Cold War consensus
	Soviet Union	?	uncertain

implicit or incomplete. If trade-offs were recognised, it was often by implication. If limited claims about consequences are construed as an implicit calculus of interests, a 'rational actor' may be read into processes which actually proceed along different lines – for example, those of Steinbruner's cognitive paradigm or Jervis's irrational consistency.[7] When do rationales degenerate into rationalisations?

To pursue this line of inquiry fully would require a major research undertaking. But the case studies, supplemented by their sources, permit certain judgments. They suggest that, even though the immediate policy rationales were often incomplete, they were, more often than not, grounded in a larger rationale of the national interest at the time, analogous to those offered by Eyre Crowe and by Kennan. In three instances, although competing rationales were articulated, policy was not based on any one of them, and in three other instances it appears, on the available evidence, that there was little or no attempt to formulate a relevant conception of the overall national interest.

The atypical cases may be considered first (Table 11.3). The governments of Britain in 1853 and the United States in 1941 were unable to resolve the differences between the competing conceptions of their decision makers – hence, as noted above, they lacked clear objectives or policy. In 1870 differing views of France's interests in relation to Germany had been articulated during the preceding years, but Napoleon and his ministers did not address these, but improvised in different directions. Russia's neglect of Japan in its policy deliberations in 1903 provides the clearest instance of failure to formulate an overall conception of the national interest – again, leaving its objectives undefined. Thiers and Kiderlen, on the other hand, had clear objectives and engaged in elaborate tactical calculations, but there is no indication of a larger conception guiding the policy. Kiderlen had the misfortune to serve at a time marked by unusual incoherence of policy in Germany: the services proceeded autonomously, successive Chancellors were politically weak, and the Kaiser lacked the personal qualities to impose coherence. There is insufficient evidence to show whether Khrushchev's Berlin policy was also of this kind.

In most instances, however, the evidence suggests that objectives were derived from reasonably clear and wide-ranging conceptions of the interests at stake. They did not always prove well-founded in the event, but they satisfied the normal criteria for 'rational' decision making. In the Eastern crisis, for example, Palmerston, Nesselrode and Metternich achieved a high degree of 'rationality': each had a well-developed view of the respective national interest on the Eastern question and of the associated costs and risks, and each devised a course of action well adjusted to the particular circumstances. In the Crimean crisis Nesselrode's general conception was essentially unchanged, and Buol's coincided with that of Metternich, but they were unable to devise an effective course of action, partly because of the lack of clear direction in British policy. Napoleon and Bismarck are more difficult to evaluate in these terms, both because they concealed much of their reasoning and because their conception of the national interest was so strongly coloured by their interest in maintaining their personal ascendancy.

Japan in 1903 provides a model of procedural rationality, but the same could be said of Britain in 1938, where policy was based on a series of wide-ranging prior assessments. The Berlin crises offer some interesting contrasts. Only the Kennedy Administration engaged in a thoroughgoing review of options and costs, but although Eisenhower did not so fully articulate his rationales, it seems clear that his policy was well thought out in the light of a broad overview of the issues. The

Truman Administration had engaged in the major post-1945 appraisal of US interests in Western Europe as well as in relation to the Soviet Union, but had avoided addressing the awkward situation of Berlin. Objectives and policies were therefore improvised, their success being due not only to the superiority of American power resources but also to the strength of the overall policy conception which emerged from the preceding reviews.

The resolution of differences

It appears likely that the resolution of differences among decision makers would be most difficult if those differences are at the level of basic values. Striking differences in foreign policy goals became evident with the emergence of ideological conflict in nineteenth-century Europe and were at their most intense in the interwar period. Such differences, however, had surprisingly little direct impact on the conduct of foreign policy. Governments were insulated from much of the ideological debate, either by electoral majorities, by traditions which excluded foreign policy from democratic control, or by authoritarian modes of government. In the 1920s, both Germany and Japan were deeply divided over foreign policy values, a reflection of broad ideological divisions, but dissent was suppressed in the 1930s by the National Socialist regime and by Japan's nationalist and military-dominated governments. During this period both Britain and France experienced wide-ranging foreign policy debates, heavily influenced by the ideological conflicts of the time, but only intermittently affecting governmental policies. Both governments were relatively united during the Sudeten crisis, and relatively insulated from public controversies, in Britain because Chamberlain's approach enjoyed wide public support, in France because the Cabinet was able to restrict the flow of information and thus limit public debate.

A less familiar type of conflict at this level recurs in most of the cases before World War Two, a conflict between the more nationalistic and the more system-oriented, coinciding with a greater or lesser readiness to go to war on behalf of exclusive national goals. The conflict appears in perhaps its purest form in the bitter rivalry between Nesselrode and the Russian nationalists in the decades before the Crimean war, the former oriented towards the Concert of Europe and cosmopolitan values, the latter exclusively to the expansion of the Russian Empire. It is found in different forms in France in the crises of 1840, 1870 and 1911. In 1840 Thiers appeared willing to arouse radical, Bonapartist nationalism for a war to recover territories lost to the Germans; Louis-

251

Philippe accepted the constraints of the Concert system along with its benefit, peace. In 1870 Napoleon III could accept a reconstruction of Europe along national lines, but the 'nationalists' preferred to go to war rather than see France take second place to a united Germany in such a system. In 1911 'nationalist' officials could contemplate the prospect of a war to recover Alsace-Lorraine, at a time when most strands in French politics preferred to maintain peace, accepting war only in clear self-defence. The pattern should not, however, be over-generalised. The differences between Bismarck and the King, or between Kiderlen and the Kaiser, did not reflect such differences over values, and those between the political generations in Japan in 1903 were over emphasis, not over fundamentals.

Where such differences over values were present they could be resolved only by the exercise of authority, either to maintain a policy – the Tsar endorsing Nesselrode – or to change it – the dismissal of Thiers. But this was also the case, for the most part, where differences over national interest claims were based on differences over the consequences of rival policies, not on values. In 1840, to take a typical example, although Palmerston and his critics agreed that it was a major British strategic interest that Russia should be prevented from controlling Constantinople, they differed over the means for achieving it. By preserving the Ottoman Empire and restricting Mehemet Ali? Or by supporting Mehemet Ali as a stronger bulwark against Russia? Was it worth a major quarrel with France in order to coerce him? Or were the French merely bluffing? Here were contrary predictions about an unstable region and contrary assessments of a volatile neighbouring power. Despite its inability to resolve these issues through discussion, the British government was able to pursue a clearly defined objective, the restriction of Mehemet Ali, at the cost of a strained relationship with France. In other words the Cabinet, with whatever stress and delay, endorsed Palmerston's calculus of interests, overruling his critics. One view prevailed, and the objectives and policy followed logically from it. This is the pattern which recurs most frequently: one of the competing views of how the national interest can best be promoted is shared, or endorsed, by the final authority, as in Austria in 1853, in both Britain and Germany in 1938, and in the US in the Berlin crises.

A variant of this pattern, also encountered frequently, is that the control over policy changes, usually only once in a crisis, from those supporting one of the contending views of the interests at stake to those supporting another. Under the pressures of crisis the differences often come to focus on the *casus belli*: a monarch, a key decision maker or a Cabinet majority feels strongly enough and is in a position to overrule or replace those hitherto in control of policy. This worked against war in France in 1840 and 1911, and in Germany in 1911. It made for war in France in 1870, and a last-minute increase in the risk of war when the British Cabinet partially overruled Chamberlain, in 1938.

Japan in 1903 provides the sole instance where major differences over the national interest – that is, whether or not Japan was justified in going to war with Russia over its demands in Northeast Asia – were resolved by discussion, resulting in an agreement to pursue the diplomatic option initially but to go to war if it failed. The lesser differences in the US over Berlin were clarified and possibly narrowed down in discussion, but were resolved through presidential decision.

In relatively few instances, coinciding with those in which a government was unable to define its objectives, differences were not resolved, and minimal policy coherence was not achieved: Britain in 1853, Russia in 1903 and the US in 1941. In the first and third of these, there was no lack of conflicting articulations of Britain's (or the United States') interests, but the Cabinet, in the former case, was unable to agree to follow any one of them, and the President, in the latter, was unwilling to impose a specific view. In 1903, on the other hand, expressions of Russia's relevant interests remained limited and tentative, and the decision makers as a whole failed to address them.

Rational actors?

To sum up: in most instances, a rationale for a government's objectives in crises is expressed in terms that can be construed as national interest claims. These are always open to question, and in practice are usually challenged within decision making circles and beyond. Nonetheless, in most cases governments behave essentially as unitary actors, pursuing their objectives with a reasonable degree of coherence. Usually, then, governments appear to be 'rational actors'. Their coherence and purposefulness, however, are usually precarious: there are nearly always individuals who, influenced by a different rationale, aspire to change the objectives, and not infrequently the pressures of crisis provide opportunities for a change of control over policy.

There is often the potential, in the internal political balance, for such a change of direction, and in the more extreme cases for paralysis or stalemate, where the contenders are powerful enough to block one another's policy, but none can gain control and thus impose his own. A change of control does not negate rationality: just as it is quite rational for an individual to change his/her mind in the light of new circumstances or a greater awareness of what is at stake, so may a government. Usually, however, this is not a result of a collective review of the relevant considerations, but of one actor's seizing control from another. A government, a collective actor, cannot, as the rational-choice theorists show, act rationally in the same sense as an individual: *it* does not have a rationale for *its* actions, except insofar as one individual succeeds in imposing a rationale, or another in changing it.[8] In this sense, governments may, in the normal case, be deemed to be rational actors.

Although only three instances have been found where a government did not meet the minimal criteria for the unitary, rational actor, these are important, for several reasons. First, they reveal two different types of breakdown of rationality: policy stalemate due to a stand-off between advocates of incompatible views, on the one hand, and a shared failure to address the relevant issues, on the other. In a small sample of cases, the fact that these represent only a low fraction of the total number is of limited significance: far more significant is the identification of two different paths to the breakdown of rationality. Second, the breakdowns of rationality had major consequences: all three of the instances are among the cases which led to war, and in two of the three, as was suggested in the case studies and will be further discussed below, these were 'unnecessary wars', in the sense that they were not necessitated by basic incompatibilities between the goals of the adversaries. Third, it has been suggested that these three instances are by no means mere aberrations, but illustrate the extremes in a range, the instances where processes which always threaten the unity and coherence of governmental action overcame the forces which, in the majority of instances, were sufficient to maintain that coherence.

The next chapter will take up one of the findings of this one, the ubiquity of differences over national interest claims. These claims, we have seen, represent aggregate judgments which combine value rankings with assessments – or assumptions – concerning courses of action intended to promote the preferred values. These assessments rest on a complex array of perceptions: it is these which will now be examined.

12 SELECTIVE PERCEPTION AND MISPERCEPTION

Perception and misperception have a prominent place in decision making studies, yet there are major differences over their significance – in particular over whether misperception is of real consequence in determining the course of events. The primary aim of this chapter is to assess the significance of misperception in crises in the light of the case studies, but as in those studies themselves it will first consider the less familiar topic of differing perceptions among decision makers. These, as we have seen, underlie many of the differences over national interests and objectives. The previous chapter noted certain patterns in the way in which these differences are resolved, but did not explore the reasons for these patterns. A study of the related perceptions may throw some light on the reasons. Furthermore, in several of the case studies it was seen to be difficult to distinguish between selective perception and outright misperception. It is appropriate to consider first the more general phenomenon, differences of perception, before that which is encountered much less frequently, misperception. Finally, the chapter will inquire which of the two principal modes of explanation of misperception, the cognitive and the motivational, is best supported by the findings.

The term 'perception' is used as the most convenient general term to refer to decision makers' views of the international situation which confronts them. It does not exclude analysis and assessment, but it also includes images, assumptions and the 'instant perception' of situations. It identifies a broad cognitive category, and carries the implication that even the most sophisticated assessments rest on assumptions and images. Perception is necessarily selective: actors perceive different aspects of a complex reality, reflecting *inter alia* their national perspective, their expectations and policy preferences, their personal experience and cognitive style, their reading of past events, and the uneven availability and flow of information. Moreover, although it is largely neglected, individuals differ significantly in perceptiveness.

The boundary lines between selective perception, inattention and misperception are not always clear. The term 'misperception' refers to the faulty, inaccurate or incorrect perception of a situation: it is perceived to have characteristics which are not present, or which are present to a significantly lesser or greater extent than perceived. Beyond narrow limits the distinction between 'correct' and 'incorrect' perception may be problematic. It is relatively straightforward, for example, in the case of basic military capabilities, such as the number of formations or of weapons systems, but may be open to different interpretations in such cases as perceiving the meaning of a diplomatic communication or the intent behind a sequence of actions.[1]

Misperception cannot be identified with cognitive processes or emotions with which it is often associated. Faulty inference from the available evidence does not establish misperception any more than sound inference ensures correct perception. Jervis emphasises the difficulty of establishing special cognitive features of misperception.

> Scholars often have been unsympathetic with people whom history has proven wrong, implying that only a person unreasonably wedded to his views could have warded off the correct information. But in most cases those who were right showed no more openness to new information nor willingness to modify their images than did those who were wrong.[2]

In order to identify misperception, then, it is necessary to have independent evidence both of the perception and of the situation with which it is compared.

However, a number of authors have drawn attention to methodological problems in evaluating the evidence for perceptions.[3] This consists mainly of statements, which may be public or private, direct or indirect (for example, accounts of a conversation in which a decision maker is said to have expressed a particular view). Public statements may record true perceptions, but they have many other purposes; asides may sometimes be more revealing than the prepared text. There can also be reasons for distortion in the case of private statements: they may, for example, be attempts at persuasion or self-protection. Statements, minutes, diary entries and the like recorded before a decision are more reliable than those recorded afterwards, when there may be both political and cognitive reasons for distortion, but even the former may be essentially 'for the record', not frank reports. Inconsistent statements may indicate changes of perception or other motivations along these lines. For all these reasons, the evidence for perceptions needs especially careful assessment.

It is convenient to divide perceptions into certain categories. Perceptions of capabilities and intentions, as Jack Levy notes, are the primary concerns of intelligence analysis and provide essential premises for crisis decision making.[4] Both are to be construed broadly. Capabilities include not only quantifiable military power, but also economic resources and political variables such as cohesion and leadership. Intentions include not only immediate aims but the larger interests which they serve and the resolve with which they are pursued. Although it is sometimes equated with the perception of intentions, we shall see that the perception of the effects of one's own actions on others is best treated as a special category. Two further, more complex categories are the perception of new developments and of the risk of war.

Differences of perception

The perception of capabilities

The capabilities of the actors – more precisely, the perceived capabilities of the principal adversary, or coalition, relative to one's own – represent the principal constraint in crisis decision making. They identify the expected cost of war, and the limit of what appears feasible. Great-power capabilities are usually understood as military power and potential; in the case of local actors, they also often include political capabilities. Differences over the latter were important in British policy discussions in the Eastern crises but not in the Sudeten case. Although Czechoslovakia's political viability (as well as its democratic credentials) was a major issue in the public debate, decision makers minimised any sense of trade-offs by seeing that state as an artificial construct unlikely to survive under pressure.

The case studies show few differences in the perception of great-power capabilities at the decision making level. Shared assumptions were far more characteristic. Dissenting views were expressed by well-informed officials such as the French military representative in Berlin in 1870 or the British and French military attachés in Prague in 1938, but these were disregarded by the respective governments. The most interesting case is the Sudeten crisis. With hindsight, the crucial issue concerning capabilities was whether Britain and France were in a stronger position *vis-à-vis* Germany in 1938 than a year later, but this was not a salient issue in the policy discussions during the crisis. British decision makers readily assumed that the strengthening of Britain's own forces would be tantamount to an improvement in its overall position. The differences between Hitler and the generals were not, essentially, over the assessment of capabilities but over intentions – the will to use the capabilities.

Differences in the perception of military capabilities, then, were seldom a major factor in policy making. Because of inherent uncertainties they can seldom be readily resolved, established images are difficult to challenge effectively, and claims over capabilities provide a strong component in the rationale for policy choices. It is perhaps for these reasons that dissenting views were not merely overridden but were usually disregarded by the leading decision makers.

The perception of intentions

Differences in the perception of adversary intentions – inherently more uncertain and subjective – were far more frequent, for example in Britain in the Eastern, Agadir and Sudeten crises, in France and Germany in 1938, in Japan in 1903 and to a lesser extent in 1940–41 (the question of American resolve), in the US in 1940–41 and, of narrower scope, in the second Berlin crisis. Very rarely, as we have seen, are these put to the test of experience, as by Japan in 1903 when, ironically, apparently incontrovertible evidence led to a misreading of Russian intentions. Occasionally, as in 1853, differences over an actor's intentions (Russia in this case) were resolved, except in Britain, by the accumulating evidence that the Tsar was seeking a diplomatic solution.

Typically, however, events during crises provide ambiguous evidence of intentions, offering little to resolve such differences. These often stem from long-standing images of the state in question, and actors have no difficulty in construing new evidence in terms of their respective images. These differences are sometimes sharply focused but may also form part of a complex and deeply held set of beliefs about the international milieu, threats to the national interest and appropriate norms of conduct. Furthermore, differences over adversary intentions are often bound up with political rivalry – sometimes for office, always for influence over policy.

British policy making in the Sudeten crisis offers illustrations of most of these themes. The evidence of Hitler's intentions remained open to debate. Although the public debate was intense and wide-ranging, most of those involved had reached their conclusions much earlier, and these reflected interrelated beliefs and values. Dissenters, who threatened the policy and, in the longer run, the decision makers' continuation in office, were excluded or marginalised, and there was a high level of agreement within the decision making group.

258

These considerations suggest reasons for the patterns for resolving differences which were noted earlier. The circumstances of crises are not conducive to resolving important differences over intentions through discussion or by putting them to the test. Resting on long-standing and deeply held assumptions, differing perceptions are maintained vigorously, sometimes to the point that the ensuing policy loses coherence. More often, however, either after extensive discussion or with little of it, one view prevails, either by the exercise of authority or through the exclusion of dissenters from the decision making group.

The perception of the effects of one's own actions

The perception of the effects of one's own actions is related to the perception of the adversary's intentions, but the focus of attention is not the general direction of his intentions, but how firm they are, whether they are open to influence by one's own actions, and in what ways. In the Berlin blockade, for example, Clay perceived Soviet intentions as settled in advance, others as potentially reactive to Western moves. In some contexts, the adversary's intentions become secondary, the crucial question being the likely reactions to one's own tactical choices. Would a further warning provoke or deter Hitler? Would American willingness to negotiate lead Khrushchev to miscalculate the risks in Berlin? Discussion was often limited to the effects of coercion, as in Britain in 1853 or Germany in 1911. Shared misperceptions were often more consequential than the choice among the perceptions which were expressed.

The differences stem more from decision makers' general propensities, philosophies or 'operational codes' than from close observation of the actor to be influenced. Except in the case of spectacular miscalculations, the consequences in question are difficult to disentangle. The advice of ambassadors was often disregarded when it ran counter to the prevailing governmental view (for example, the senior French ambassadors in early 1911, François-Poncet in 1938 or Grew in 1940–41). Independent expertise was rarely utilised, and searching discussion was rare, the one notable exception being from the thermonuclear age, the Kennedy Administration's deliberations in the Berlin crisis. Not surprisingly, resolution of differences of this kind by any other means than the assertion of authority or the sheer overriding of dissent was even more infrequent than in the case of differences over intentions.

The perception of new developments

The element of surprise, the unexpected, figures prominently in crises. It can take many forms, ranging from dramatic events requiring immediate response to diplomatic initiatives requiring careful scrutiny of the fine print. When rapid decisions are needed the perception of the meaning of new events causes stress and perceptual distortion. Frequently, however, decisions are taken more rapidly than the circumstances dictate. Most of the present examples were situations of moderate, but not extreme stress.

The Russian naval victory at Sinope in November 1853 was the single event of the Crimean crisis which most dangerously raised the level of tension. Reactions ranged from rejoicing in St Petersburg to alarm or gloom in other capitals, but the most significant divergence was between the British perception of a 'massacre' and the perception of decision makers elsewhere, shared by a minority in London, that it was a legitimate act of war. Palmerston and Russell were willing to exploit this sentiment to overwhelm their colleagues' hesitation. A sense of urgency was generated, due not to a strategic requirement for a prompt response but to public pressure for one. Similarly in July 1870, while Napoleon and a minority in Paris shared the prevailing European perception that the withdrawal of the Hohenzollern candidacy was a remarkable success for French diplomacy, Gramont was able to exploit the emotional nationalist perception that the terms of the withdrawal were inadequate, committing the government to escalate the crisis when there was no external time pressure.

Professional diplomats can also differ strikingly in their perception of dramatic events. At the climax of the Sudeten crisis François-Poncet offered perceptive analyses, placing his government in a position to anticipate Hitler's likely moves, whereas Henderson offered no such guidance, despite – or because of – his eagerness to assume the role of policy advocate.

The cases offer many examples of differing perceptions of the meaning of new diplomatic developments: in the Crimean crisis, for example, with respect to Menshikov's original proposals, Turkey's amendments to the Vienna Note, Nesselrode's 'violent interpretation' of the Note and the Tsar's Olmütz proposals. Except for the first of these, where there was some questioning and discussion, meanings were ascribed almost instantly to complex communications, not because of time pressure but due to fixed images and in some cases strong public emotion. Similarly, differing American and West German perceptions of the Kennedy Administration's proposals on access to

Berlin, equally beyond deliberation, generated an intense dispute over their significance.

The examples illustrate how an initial perception of new events or proposals, often emotionally charged, instantly ascribed meaning to developments. Differing national perspectives explain some of the divergences, but most arose also within the relevant governments. In all the examples mentioned there was time for discussion, but it was seldom utilised; in most cases the protagonists were not open to persuasion, and thus differences would have to be settled by other means. The potential benefits of differences of perception, such as openness to new evidence and caution in the face of uncertainty, were not realised. The perception which quickly prevailed reflected established images and expectations. But the perceptions were also formed under pressures generated by strong political emotions: Temperley's image of the 'simmering cauldron of evil passions in which public opinion is brewed' could apply to French elites in 1870 as much as the British press in 1853, and strong feeling is evident in several of the other examples.[5]

The perception of the risk of war

Differences and fluctuations in the perception of the likelihood of war are found throughout the cases. This perception is sometimes derived from an actor's perception of long-term considerations: the interests at stake, the adversary's intentions and the consequences of one's own policies. At the other extreme, it may be based entirely on immediate observation: the level of perceived tension, and friendly or hostile reactions. The Eastern crisis illustrates the two extremes. Palmerston, Nesselrode and Metternich reasoned from their perception of the basic intentions of the potential adversary, France, reaching different conclusions because they took account of different considerations. The war scare in England and Germany, on the other hand, derived from the sudden perception of French hostility, not from analysis of what might lie behind it. Normally, however, the perceptions of decision makers reflect both long-term analysis and short-term observation. Their expectations relating to war in crises are perhaps less stable than the consistency of their images and beliefs might lead one to expect.

This may, however, be seen as a virtue, insofar as it suggests that decision makers do not impose a spurious certainty on the uncertainties inherent in crises, and that they are aware that war can come about not only intentionally but also through the unintended consequences

261

of their choices or through overreactions to perceived provocations. The case studies offer no support for the general proposition that decision makers cannot tolerate uncertainty. When they are over-confident, it is a consequence of specific misperceptions. The public controversy over appeasement in 1938 might appear to offer an example of undue certainty in the face of appalling choices, such as certain cognitive theories predict. On the one hand, 'peace for our time', on the other, 'the unnecessary war: there never was a war more easy to stop'. These familiar claims, however, are atypical and were made after the event. The statements of the participants during the crisis, and their private communications, acknowledged uncertainty, not claiming a high degree of confidence that war could be averted.

Differing perceptions of the probability of war are found throughout. Where they derive from different national perspectives on the crisis it is sometimes because more information is available to one of the governments on salient aspects of the crisis, as in Britain in 1853. In certain cases the risks were largely under the control of one party. This was true of Japan in 1903, when the situation was com-pletely misperceived by the adversary, Russia, whereas in 1938, where the choice for war was with Hitler, the British and French perception of the immediate dangers was quite realistic. The striking differences in 1840 among the leading decision makers outside France reflected different individual belief systems, not national perspectives. The case studies, then, show no general pattern.

Within governments, the more intractable differences derive from the perception of the stakes and of the adversary's intentions, but even where decision makers are agreed on fundamentals, differences over which tactical choices will tend to increase or decrease the risk of war may not be open to resolution through discussion of the available evidence. Public opinion, influenced mainly by immediate tension and the emotion which it arouses, may influence decision makers' per-ceptions more than they like to acknowledge, or more than is always apparent from the record.

In most of the earlier cases different perceptions of the risk of war led to discussion among decision makers, but the dissenting per-ception was usually set aside. In the later cases, from the time of the Agadir crisis, there was more extensive discussion, except in Germany in 1938, and, with the same exception, this led to increased caution in policy formulation. It did not, however, regularly lead to greater openness to new evidence: decision makers remained reluctant to question their images and policy preferences.

262

Overview

Except for the perception of military capabilities, where they were rarely expressed at the decision making level, differences of each category of perception were very frequent. Those over the adversary's intentions arose mainly from long-term images and expectations, which also entered in varying degree into the other types. The more complex perceptions reflected both long-term images and the meaning ascribed to immediate events, in varying proportions. Their high degree of variation is therefore not surprising.

Of the many reasons why differences were seldom resolved by discussion, perhaps the most important was that they normally pre-dated the crises and were based on incompatible assumptions. Those in control normally preferred to avoid the discussion of alternatives; the maintenance or change of a policy depended more on who was in control than on the merits of the argument. In effect, decision makers endorsed Dean Acheson's contention that it is more important to reassure the President than to warn him. One way of expressing this conclusion would be to say that the limited rationality of policy coherence was normally preferred to the chance of achieving a better policy through searching discussion, at the risk of incoherence through the clash of incompatible views. While this provides a ration-ale for a widely observed pattern of behaviour, it abstracts from more immediate institutional and political reasons for curtailing discussion. Some institutions, such as the European monarchies, did not provide for the canvassing of different views: the minister was expected to advise the monarch and was solely responsible for the conduct of policy, subject only to a degree of monarchical constraint. In other cases, leadership style curtailed the discussion of options: with respect to Berlin, for example, Truman and Eisenhower heard a limited range of views but relied largely on their own judgment. Not infrequently, as in most of the British examples, alternative views were sponsored by rivals for the leadership. Political reasons such as these strongly reinforced the cognitive reasons for limiting the scope of discussion of differing perceptions.

The question of the relative importance of cognitive and political/ motivational determinants of perception is taken up after the discuss-ion of misperception. The significance of images is evident in the preceding discussion, not only in the perception of relatively stable factors such as capabilities and intentions but also in forming impres-sions of new and unexpected events. On the other hand, in cases where strong emotion overwhelms judgment, motivational theories may be required to complete the explanation. Moreover, the images which shape perceptions are often themselves emotionally charged, evoking powerful historical memories. Cognitive and motivational influences on perception may not always be separable in practice.

The consequences of misperception

Differing views

There is no consensus on the significance of misperception in international relations, but rather a polarisation of views. For the realist school and for rational-choice theory its consequences are marginal, but for those who emphasise the psychological dimension of foreign policy they are of the greatest importance. It should be noted, however, that the frequent occurrence of misperception does not entail that it has important consequences. Snyder and Diesing, as we have seen, hold that there is usually extensive misperception at the outset of international crises but that, since it is largely corrected through bargaining, its consequences are ultimately quite limited.[6]

For realists, serious tensions arise not because the parties misperceive their interests, or fail to perceive common ground, but because at times there are indeed serious conflicts between the interests of states, occasions when their fundamental goals are incompatible. A Napoleon or a Hitler, for example, may seek to achieve hegemony over the entire states system while their opponents seek to maintain a system of independent states. At other times the common interests of states permit long periods of peace. In crises, as Snyder and Diesing express it, by the end of the bargaining process:

> the parties' perceptions of the crisis structure roughly correspond to the actual structure ... The relative bargaining power then stands revealed, and the crisis is ripe for resolution. The parties then do what they can or must – yield, stand firm, compromise or perhaps fight.[7]

Likewise, Arthur Stein concludes on the basis of a game-theoretic analysis that misperception can affect actors' choices and outcomes in only a narrow range of circumstances.[8]

There is greater diversity among those who see misperception as having important consequences. Liberal and idealist thinkers of the nineteenth and early twentieth centuries depicted war as the 'great illusion'. International conflicts were not serious enough to justify the inordinate cost of war: if it occurred, it could only be because governments misperceived their true interests. Some contemporary social scientists, such as Robert White, John Stoessinger and Stephen Van Evera, who adopt a very broad concept of misperception – including, for example, the misjudging of long-term consequences and the black-and-white images associated with acute conflict – view it as a primary cause of war in the twentieth century.[9] Others such as Jervis and Lebow adopt a narrower concept but even so see misperception as having very significant consequences: Jervis identifies a variety of distortions of policy, and Lebow sees it as a major reason why brinkmanship crises are initiated and can result in war.[10]

The present inquiry seeks to show, under the variety of conditions present in the case studies, the extent to which misperception played an important part in the origin, course and outcome of the crises. The Berlin cases are omitted because of the absence of crucial evidence on Soviet perceptions. Such findings cannot fully resolve the foregoing differences, but they can offer systematic historical analyses of the conditions under which misperception can have important consequences.

Identifying consequential misperceptions

The case for the limited significance of misperception is argued by Stein on theoretical grounds. Misperception, he maintains, can affect choices and outcomes in only a narrow range of circumstances. While this may be persuasive within the universe of game-theoretic models, however, the narrow range of circumstances coincides closely with the typical circumstances of international relations, especially the relations of the great powers. According to Stein, misperception will be significant only if the actors are interdependent – if 'world politics revolves primarily around a few major powers and approximates an oligopolistic market'.[11] Moreover, 'the belief that misperception is important necessarily implies that international politics is a variable-sum game',[12] but this is precisely how the traditional balance of power has been understood, as has nuclear deterrence. The true implication, then, is that misperception may well be consequential in typical international conflicts.

Snyder and Diesing's argument is both theoretical and empirical. According to their findings, the misinterpretation of diplomatic messages and signals is more frequent than their correct interpretation, yet by the end of the crises included in their sample, most interpretations were corrected in the course of the bargaining process.[13] Rational bargainers adjust their assumptions in the light of their repeated failure, and decision makers who refuse to adjust are usually replaced or overridden. The present case studies cast doubt on the generality of these findings. In this chapter it is argued that misperceptions were quite frequently more consequential than they allow, and the following chapter suggests reasons why bargaining may be less effective.

Jack Levy offers some plausible hypotheses concerning the most significant effects of misperception, namely, those which lead to war. He suggests that two types of misperception lead directly to decisions to go to war: military overconfidence, 'the underestimation of the adversary's capabilities relative to one's own'; and overestimation of the adversary's hostility, which may lead to the acceptance of war, the perception of its inevitability.[14] Other kinds of misperception are linked indirectly with decisions to go to war: the overestimation of the adversary's capabilities may lead to arms races and hostility spirals, and the underestimation of its hostility may lead to undue complacency and unpreparedness, or alternatively to an unwillingness to compromise. Because the causal links in the latter cases are more distant in time and other major considerations may intervene, Levy places the emphasis on the former categories of misperception.[15]

This provides a useful starting-point for conceptualising the effects of misperception, as well as plausible reasons for holding that they are likely to be significant, but some qualifications may be suggested. First, there may be other significant effects of misperception, over and above those which lead directly to war: for example, diplomats may fail to perceive opportunities for resolving disputes for quite different reasons from those which Levy's schema takes into account. Second, and most crucially, it is not sufficient, in order to establish the causal significance of misperception in a particular instance, to show that it was present before a relevant decision was made. It should also be shown that it was a necessary condition for the decision. While this is sometimes difficult or impossible to establish, it needs to be shown that the misperception was an important consideration. This can be illustrated by means of a negative example, Hitler's decision to invade Poland in August 1939. The evidence is usually taken to show that Hitler did not expect Britain and France to go to war – he misperceived their intentions – but also that he had decided to attack even if they should. His decision did not depend on his misperception.[16]

The opposite kind of situation provides the clearest causal link between misperception and decision. If it can be shown that a misperception provided a crucial premise for a decision, without which the actors would certainly have chosen differently, then we can say that the misperception, being necessary for the decision, indeed had major consequences. In the extreme case, misperception may be essential to a decision which leads directly to war. In other cases it may be clear that, if the situation had been perceived differently, another course of action would have been chosen, but impossible to know what this would have been. Due to the misperception, other options may not have been seriously examined, or decision makers may not have expressed their preferences in relation to the unexpected contingency in the way that Hitler did in August 1939. There are also intermediate cases. The evidence may not be full enough to show precisely how a misperception affected the decision making process, or there may be so many other considerations favouring the decision that its significance cannot be determined at all precisely.

These considerations lead to a third qualification of Levy's framework. A misperception may be directly related to a decision, yet its causal significance may be slight; on the other hand, the linkage may be indirect and relatively remote in time, yet the misperception may be of crucial importance in setting off the sequence of events which leads to the decision in question.

The findings of the case studies can best be examined in terms of the simpler and more basic categories used above: capabilities, intentions, and the effects of one's own actions; in addition, local actors are treated as a separate category. The causal judgments are drawn from the interpretations in the case studies.

The misperception of capabilities

Capabilities were misperceived less frequently than intentions. When both were misperceived, the perception of capabilities had the greater influence on decisions in 1870 and 1903 but less in 1938, and the relative significance of the two is difficult to disentangle in 1840. In two instances, French policy in 1840 and 1870, the significance of misperception is complicated by the decision makers' high willingness to run risks. In only one instance, Russia in 1903, was the misperception of capabilities clearly and unequivocally a primary determinant of the course of events. The misperception of capabilities, then, affected policy in quite different ways in each of the four cases where it was significant.

In 1840 Thiers' overestimate of Mehemet Ali's capacity to resist British naval power was one of several mutually reinforcing misperceptions which emboldened him to undertake his risky policy. Since there were strong political incentives to maintain the policy and there was a high level of uncertainty over the military prospects, there is no reason to regard this particular misperception as having major causal importance. French misperception of the military balance in 1870 was more significant. Although Napoleon took expert assessments of French weaknesses seriously, the image of French military superiority was deeply embedded and was endorsed by the Council of Ministers at the outset of the crisis. However, the decision makers and those who urged them on were highly ready to risk war, which many saw as inevitable. In this climate of opinion, while a sounder perception of the military balance must have made for greater awareness of the risks in escalating the crisis, it might not have much reduced the 'war party's' willingness to put the military uncertainties to the test of battle, or its capacity to mobilise support. The misperception made for haste and over-confidence, but may not have been crucial in determining French decisions.

In Britain in 1938 there were some specific misperceptions such as the overestimate of Germany's bombing capability, but it has been argued that the overall image of the military balance amounted to selective perception, not misperception. Further, although assumptions about the military balance played their part in shaping policy – they were not merely rationalisations for policies chosen for other reasons – the primary motivation for policy was the determination to avoid war until all legitimate means for doing so had been exhausted.

The sole instance in which over-confidence resulting from the misperception of capabilities was the primary reason for the policies which led to war was Russia in 1903. This was the fundamental misperception: from it resulted the underestimate of Japan's resolve and the misreading of its intentions. Here there was no readiness to risk war. The stakes in Korea were not regarded as serious enough to constitute the *casus belli* and the Russians were willing to bargain once they were convinced of Japan's seriousness. This is not to claim that sounder perception would have ensured the avoidance of war, but rather that Russia's misperception was of crucial importance in determining the course of events that actually ensued.

The misperception of intentions

This is the type of misperception most frequently encountered in the case studies: it is present in all seven of those under review and is deemed to have been of major significance in three of them, the Crimean, Russo-Japanese and Sudeten crises, although in the latter case in a more complex manner than is usually realised. Quite frequently more than one actor misperceived the intentions of others. It is not surprising, in view of the greater ambiguity of the evidence, that intentions should be misperceived more than capabilities. As in the former case, the significance of misperception is more difficult to assess when there is a high level of uncertainty or a high willingness to risk war.

Where misperception was of limited significance it was usually part of an overall constellation of factors influencing policy, its direct influence being difficult to discern. For example, Thiers appears to have overestimated the strength of Palmerston's opponents in London and also Austria's determination to include France in any agreement, but these misperceptions were related to his view of the military prospects, and may be seen as further reasons for maintaining a policy originally chosen for other reasons. Rather similarly, France's unwarranted expectations of alliance with Austria and support from the south German states in 1870, despite explicit Austrian warnings and the likelihood that the crisis would bring German nationalist sentiment to the fore, have the air of reasons or rationalisations bolstering a policy stance already chosen for other reasons – the desire to reassert French supremacy over Prussia and its premise, France's military capacity to do so.

The context of the misperception of intentions in the Agadir crisis was quite different, its effects relatively straightforward. The level of tension was intensified by French and British misperception of Kiderlen's intentions – the French fearing that his real aim was to gain control of part of Morocco, the British that it was to break up the Anglo-French entente. It was part of Kiderlen's tactics to stimulate the former fear; the second was almost entirely groundless. The consequences of French and British overreaction, potentially a further escalation of hostile signals and threats, were limited by the Kaiser's determination not to engage in a further round of such threats. Japan in 1941 offers a relatively straightforward example of quite a different kind. There are indications that some underestimated American resolve, contrasting Japanese 'moral spirit' with American material values, and such images may have encouraged those advocating war, especially in the earlier stages, but the misperception never became the premise for policy making. The image of Japan as a patient suffering from a serious illness, choosing between a gradual decline and a risky operation, better summed up the decision makers' perception of their choice.

In the cases where the misperception of intentions was of greater consequence, the causal patterns were also highly differentiated. In the Crimean crisis the British decision makers were unable to withstand political pressure from the vocal and influential section of the public imbued with a stereotype of the Russian aggressor threatening the gallant Turk, and the associated perception of the moral issues. The decision makers did not share this perception, but in accommodating it they followed a diplomacy of unconditional support for Turkey, rejection of Russian attempts at compromise and eventually the making of unacceptable demands. The misperception of Russian intentions, then, can be seen as a direct and primary reason for the later phases of the escalation of the crisis. Other misperceptions such as the Tsar's overestimate of the extent of Austrian and British friendship were of relatively limited consequence, conforming to the pattern of providing one of a number of reasons for underestimating the risks of a chosen course of action.

The misperception of Japanese intentions in 1903 directly affected Russian diplomacy, but insofar as it was a consequence of the more basic misperception of Japan's capabilities, the latter was the more crucial. But Japan's secondary misperception – its failure to discern or even to consider the possibility that the apparently decisive evidence of Russian intentions was misleading – was also a crucial ingredient in the crisis. If this possibility had been allowed for, the position of those favouring further negotiation would have been greatly strengthened. This is the only instance of this kind: an instance where the evidence for intentions appeared unusually clear and compelling, and where there were none of the usual cognitive features of misperception – yet a crucial misperception occurred nonetheless.

The most complex instance concerns Britain and France, especially the former, in the Sudeten crisis. This was not, as we have seen, the classic case of misperceiving Hitler's intentions as limited to self-determination for neighbouring German minorities, but rather a policy premised on uncertainty as to Hitler's ultimate intentions. The misperception that is of interest was the failure to discern Hitler's immediate intentions and strategy. The British assumed that the immediate crisis was over the Sudetenland, not suspecting that Hitler hoped to use this issue to bring about the immediate disintegration of Czechoslovakia. Britain's strategy of defusing the crisis through an internal settlement depended on this specific misperception. Thus although the final outcome depended on a quite different set of considerations, Britain's misperception shaped the course of events until the final confrontation.

The causal patterns, then, were extremely varied. Two of the major instances, Britain in 1853 and Japan in 1903, were in accord with Levy's hypothesis that the overestimation of an adversary's hostility can lead to war, and Agadir provides an instance where this process was checked short of war. Britain's misperception in the Sudeten crisis was important for quite different reasons, and in the other cases the misperception of intentions tended to buttress the choice of a policy preferred or adopted for a variety of other reasons.

The misperception of the effects of one's own actions

In international crises as in other situations, actors frequently misjudge the effects of their own actions. Such misjudgments are often corrected promptly in the light of responses to the original action, but the case studies suggest that quite frequently a misjudgment is not corrected and comes to have significant consequences, or its immediate consequences are significant, even if it is soon corrected. This form of misperception was of major significance in three of the cases, the Crimean crisis, Agadir and Pearl Harbor, and is of interest in several of the others.

Jervis discusses one type of misperception along these lines, the tendency to overestimate the extent to which the hostile behaviour of others is due to their autonomous intentions, and thus to underestimate the extent to which it is a response to one's own actions.[17] The same tendency may be observed in the perception of friendly or acquiescent behaviour. A further category of misperception occurs when the actor, correctly assuming that the other's intentions are open to influence, misjudges the effects of the particular means chosen in attempting to influence them.

The second of these categories – the neglect of the extent to which the passive or friendly behaviour of others depends on one's own actions – is most frequently encountered in the case studies. In 1853 the Tsar and Nesselrode greatly underestimated the potentially explosive consequences of their initial demands. Even if Menshikov had succeeded in creating a *fait accompli*, he would also have created an issue between Russia and the other powers. Whereas the Tsar hoped that by cultivating good relations with Austria and Britain he could defuse the issue, the reactions to the Menshikov proposals showed that, on the contrary, the issue was more likely to disrupt the good relationships which he wished to maintain. Failing to see that these relationships depended on Russia's perceived moderation, he precipitated an acute crisis. Rather similarly, in 1870 the French misread the attitudes of the south German states, perceiving them as indifferent to the issue of the Hohenzollern candidacy, but failing to perceive that they might react very strongly against the French reaction to the candidacy. And in 1903 the Russians, perceiving Japan as lacking both the capability and the will to engage in war, entirely failed to perceive the effects of their own

271

military and diplomatic signals on Japanese intentions. Unlike Nicholas, who thought that he could reassure Britain and Austria, France and Russia did not even perceive the need to offer reassurance. These two instances were of lesser consequence in that the misperception in question was a corollary of a more fundamental misperception. More significant was Hitler's failure to perceive that British and French acquiescence in his demands on Czechoslovakia had its limits, since it precipitated the confrontation in the final days of the Sudeten crisis.

The most striking examples of the third category – misjudging the effects of one's own attempts to influence others – are provided by the Agadir crisis. Kiderlen's initial miscalculation, which defined the general 'shape' of the crisis, was the most significant. Intended to induce the French to offer concessions, his threats in fact made this more difficult. Lloyd George's Mansion House speech, the British warning to Germany, may not have missed its mark so completely, but it heightened tension in a way that could have proved dangerous. Kiderlen's misperception was along familiar lines: 'they respond only to pressure'. The British appear, quite mistakenly, to have considered a speech less provocative than a formal communication.

The instance with the greatest consequences, and the main example of the first category, above, was the failure of the United States government to perceive the effects on Japan of the oil embargo imposed in July 1941. The embargo was to structure the choices of Japan's decision makers in the months that followed, creating a situation in which a continuation of the status quo, with dwindling oil reserves and a declining capacity to maintain Japan's position as a major power, was unacceptable to them. Not all the American decision makers were blind to these consequences, and the implementation of the embargo went far beyond the immediate intentions of Roosevelt and his advisers. In subsequently endorsing the implementation of a total embargo, however, Roosevelt confirmed the decision which transformed the options of the Japanese leaders, without realising that this was the case. The reasons were complex, but included the pessimistic assumption that Japan was likely to engage in unacceptable aggression, irrespective of US actions – a good illustration of Jervis's hypothesis – and also the typical 'hard-line' misperception that the adversary's intentions can indeed be influenced, but only by coercive moves.[18]

The misperception of local actors and issues

Local actors played a significant part in only three of the cases: the Eastern, Crimean and Sudeten crises. In all three, the perception of the local actor was vague and incomplete on the part of at least one of the great powers, and this was conducive to specific misperceptions, which had important consequences in two of the three cases. The exception was Thiers' over-optimism concerning the prospects of a direct settlement between Mehemet Ali and the Ottoman government. Its consequences were rather marginal, in that he had already committed himself to a course of action based on his perception of other features of the situation.

In the earlier phases of the Crimean crisis, despite their long familiarity with the Eastern question, the British decision makers were not only vague about the provisions of the existing treaties and the nuances of terminology, but also remarkably insensitive to the questions of prestige raised by the procedure that was adopted towards the Ottoman government. Had they been more clear-headed, they should either have pressed the other powers to be more responsive to Turkey's proposals or else, having opted for the Vienna Note, should have seen the need to concert with the other powers to press for its acceptance. Nesselrode's subsequent advice to the Tsar was based on his expectation that there would be several months of inaction, offering ample opportunity for further diplomacy. He failed to perceive that this might be disrupted by Turkish initiatives, which in fact were to bring about the escalation which the governments could not control. Failures of perception thus played their part in determining the ineffectiveness of Concert diplomacy and the prolongation of the crisis into a more dangerous phase.

Rather similarly, in 1938 the image of Czechoslovakia in the minds of British decision makers was vague and incomplete and, given their prior policy commitments, they had little incentive to acquire fuller information. Dubious advice which supported their underestimate of Czech military capabilities was preferred to that of the best-informed official, the military attaché in Prague. This lends support to the view that perceptions of Czech capabilities were accepted because they served to reinforce existing policy, rather than entering into policy formulation in the first place. The misreading of Henlein's intentions, on the other hand, did have important consequences. Had his strategy of escalating his demands in order to prevent any agreement with Benes been perceived, or even suspected, the British attitude to developments in Czechoslovakia would have been different.

Although drawn from few cases, the processes which are identified here appear to be typical features of great-power perceptions of local actors. The governments of great powers tend to be poorly informed and frequently appear to lack incentive to become well informed,

Table 12.1. *Instances of misperception*

		Capabilities	Intentions	Effects of own actions	Local actor
1840	France	√	√		√
1853	Britain		√√	√	√
	Russia		√	√√	√
1870	France	√√	√	√	
1903	Russia	√√	√	√	
	Japan		√√		
1911	Germany			√√	
	Britain		√	√	
	France		√	√	
1938	Britain/France	√	√√		√
	Germany		√	√	
1941	Japan		√		
	US			√√	

Note: Major instances are shown thus: √√

especially if this might require them to revise their established images. Relevant information is frequently available, but is not sought or considered. Frequently great-power governments do not appear to consider local actors important enough to warrant very much time in their policy deliberations. The consequences can be of major importance. The great-power governments will not perceive their options clearly and will fail to anticipate the reactions of the local actor, with adverse consequences for their interests. Opportunities may be missed, as in the case of British and Russian actions with respect to the Vienna Note, or a whole line of policy may be based on a false premise, as in the case of Britain *vis-à-vis* Henlein in 1938.

Consequential misperceptions

The first conclusion to be drawn from the preceding analysis is that, contrary to the realist and rational-choice views noted at the outset, misperception quite frequently has important consequences for the course of events and the outcome of crises – sufficiently important to complicate the overall causal 'structuring' of crises in terms of the actors' goals. This conclusion does not negate realist or rational-choice theory as such, but requires that they be formulated in such a way as to allow for consequential misperceptions.

Table 12.1 summarises the examples of misperception discussed above. It is not exhaustive, but further instances had less important consequences or are less adequately documented. All the instances deemed to have had major consequences are included. There is a high incidence of the misperception of intentions and of the effects of one's own actions. The misperception of capabilities is less frequent but, if this sample is representative, more likely to have major consequences when it does occur.

In general, as we have seen, the effects of misperception were in the direction postulated by Levy, although the causal patterns were more varied than he suggests. An underestimate of the adversary's capabilities encouraged France to accept war in 1870, and Russia to disregard Japan's demands in 1903. An overestimate of Germany's immediate capabilities in 1938 enhanced British and French willingness to concede. Overestimates of Russian hostility, by Britain in 1853 and Japan in 1903, led both to accept war, as Levy hypothesises, but his schema does not provide for the way in which the misperception of Hitler's and Henlein's immediate intentions in 1938 enabled Britain and France to maintain their search for a settlement.

It can be seen that the misperception of the effects of one's own actions is a distinct type, not just a sub-category of the misperception of intentions. Kiderlen's 'hard-line' misperception that the French would respond only to threats, for example, did not depend on any specific view of their intentions, and the crucial Russian misperception in 1853 was not so much the Tsar's over-confidence in British friendship but the lack of awareness of the provocative character of Menshikov's demands and tactics. Whereas the misperception of intentions leads to the choice of a general course of action, the misperception of the effects of one's own actions leads to specific moves. The former points to the problems of the security dilemma, the latter the hostility spiral.

Does the analysis suggest under what conditions misperceptions play an important part in determining the course of action in a crisis, and its outcome? Two situations may be distinguished. First, a misperception which is a necessary premise for an actor's policy remains uncorrected throughout a crisis, contrary to Snyder and Diesing's contention that the bargaining process leads to the correction of such misperceptions. In two of the present cases, in Britain in 1853 and Russia in 1903, a misperception which remained uncorrected was at the basis of a policy which led to war. The circumstances of the crises prevented their correction, but these varied from case to case.

In the second kind of situation, a misperception occurs at a crucial moment in a crisis, with major consequences for the subsequent course

275

of events – in the present cases, intensifying the crisis. Even if the misperception is subsequently corrected, its consequences cannot be undone. Several months of accommodative diplomacy on Russia's part in 1853 could not resolve the diplomatic imbroglio created by the Menshikov mission; Agadir became an acute crisis because Kiderlen misjudged the effects of his style of coercion; and the US, through its oil embargo in 1941, unknowingly transformed Japan's perception of its options in favour of war.

The consequences of misperception, then, enter into the overall causal 'structure' of crises in two ways: through the persistence of a crucial misperception until the final outcome or through actions at crucial moments which shape the future course of events. But how are the misperceptions themselves to be explained, and why (in the former set of instances) did they remain uncorrected? Was it because of the ambiguity of the evidence, or the hold of established images, or were they politically motivated? The latter two are the principal theoretical explanations, but the case studies suggest that in some instances it may not be necessary to look beyond the former.

Explaining misperception

The tension between cognitive and motivational explanations of misperception was discussed in Chapter 2. Jervis, it will be recalled, looks primarily to such cognitive factors as the influence of established images and expectations and the reluctance to acknowledge trade-offs, but allows that political pressures can lead to distorted perception.[19] Lebow argues that both cognitive and political factors are important, but that 'political needs' sometimes provide a better explanation, and that when images and needs point in different directions, needs tend to prevail.[20] Jervis argues, quite correctly, that misperception does not serve actors' interests. Political 'needs' or 'compulsions', however, are not to be equated with what proves to be in the actor's interest. He is on stronger ground in insisting that beliefs or images are not a function of actors' perceived needs, but have a life of their own: it is because of a belief such as the domino theory, for example, that certain perceived interests or needs have the influence which they do.

Lebow develops his explanation through a close analysis of two cases, the American misperception of China's commitment to intervene in the Korean war in 1950, and India's similar misperception of China's stand on the frontier dispute in 1962. In both cases, he argues, the evidence of China's intentions was so clear that its denial pointed to politically motivated defensive avoidance. The domestic political

276

cost of a change of policy, necessitated by a realistic perception of China's intentions, was so great that the decision makers persuaded themselves that China would acquiesce in their territorial advances. Their images of China by no means necessitated this conclusion, but it met their political 'needs' under severe domestic pressures.[21]

The major instances of misperception in the present case studies were not precisely of this type, but the first of the general categories noted above resembles Lebow's cases in that a crucial misperception remained uncorrected throughout a crisis. In two instances (Japan in 1903 and Britain/France in 1938) there was little evidence of the adversary's immediate intentions, thus no reason to correct the misperception. In the three instances where, as in Lebow's cases, ample evidence was available but was disregarded, it is possible to find both cognitive and political explanations for the misperception, and difficult to separate them.

Britain in 1853 differed from Lebow's examples in that the decision makers acted in accordance with pressures from advocates of the popular anti-Russian stereotype without actually sharing that stereotype. The political motivation was even clearer than in Lebow's examples. Clarendon's perception of the inevitability of war and Aberdeen's rationalisations amounted to ways of responding to domestic political pressures. At the level of the press and public attitudes, familiar cognitive principles can be seen in the way in which Russian actions which confirmed the stereotype were emphasised and those which ran counter to it were ignored, but political motivation amplified these effects. The stereotype could be exploited only because it had become part of the British public's view of the world, but an explanation of this, in turn, would have to combine cognitive elements (the British reading of earlier events) with political elements (the attitudes of the anti-Russian elites).

The interaction of cognitive and political factors is also evident in France's misperception of Prussian capabilities in 1870. Sounder perception might have led to military reforms sufficient to restrain Prussia from provoking such a crisis. Military over-confidence, however, was 'built into' the prevailing French self-image, and Prussia's advances in training and organisation were not so visible as to compel attention – in contrast, for example, to Germany's naval challenge to Britain in the early 1900s. The unpopularity of conscription and increased military expenditure provided political reinforcement for the prevailing image, and Napoleon's inability to challenge it reflected a political imperative, the need to sustain the Bonapartist myths on which his legitimacy depended. France's secondary misperceptions, its disregard for explicit Austrian warnings and its groundless optimism concerning the reactions of the south German states – contrary to Napoleon's general views on the force of nationalism – defy explanation in terms of rationality or political 'need', and appear to require a hypothesis that perception was distorted by high emotion. This aside, however, in the overall explanation sketch offered here, cognitive and political elements were intertwined, but the reasons for the power of the traditional self-image and its resistance to challenge were primarily political.

Cognitive variables were of greater importance in explaining Russia's misperception of Japan in 1903, but were nonetheless underpinned by political attitudes. The traditional image of unquestioned superiority over Japan had been confirmed by Japan's recent acquiescence in Russia's rebuffing of its diplomatic initiatives. It should be noted, however, that France before 1870 had had the opposite experience, being several times rebuffed by Prussia, but this had not led to a questioning of the image of French superiority, but rather to discontent with the government's diplomatic performance. Too much significance should not be read into such diplomatic experience, in either direction. Attitudes such as imperial and racial arrogance in part constituted and in part sustained Russia's established image. It may be inquired, however, why the other European powers, which shared these attitudes, were more ready to perceive Japan's emerging capabilities in their true light. The reasons appear to be both psychological and political: only Russia was in a potential adversary relationship to Japan, engaging emotions of pride and imperial prestige; involvement of the self-image may impede sound perception. The military evidence which might have led Russia to correct its image of Japan was probably less than that which was available to France before 1870: the latter was correctly perceived by some few expert observers, whereas the Russian misperception of the quality of the Japanese forces was less challenged.

Comparing the three cases, it is evident that political and cognitive theories point towards different elements which can sometimes be viewed separately but were often mutually interdependent. Both types of theory are necessary in order to explain the persistence of the misperceptions in question. In line with Lebow's findings, political variables 'explain more' in the Crimean case, and arguably in the Franco-Prussian case, but not in the Russo-Japanese. The complementarity of the two kinds of explanation remains the principal general finding.

In the second kind of situation distinguished above, misperception at a crucial moment had major consequences because the decision makers were unaware of the provocative character of their actions. Such failures of perception or judgment can be readily explained, in the first instance, in terms of hypotheses drawn from attribution theory, according to which decision makers tend to reason in terms of simplified causal inferences, neglecting relevant contextual considerations.[22]

The Tsar's confidence that he could rely on Aberdeen's sympathy for Russia to ensure British support for the goals of the Menshikov mission illustrates both excessive reliance on personal relationships and a perception of another state's reaction in terms of those relationships, and the neglect of the British Cabinet system, the suspicions of other British leaders and public attitudes – a striking illustration of the simplified causal schema postulated by attribution theory. Nesselrode, however, was well aware of the contextual influences but failed to warn the Tsar of the provocative aspects of the mission. The evidence does not show whether this was a case of defensive avoidance ('bolstering' the chances of success of his preferred option), or whether Nesselrode perceived the dangers but could do nothing to avert them.

The 'hard-line' misperception which underlay Kiderlen's gunboat diplomacy reflected a different kind of simplified causal schema: since the French would respond only to coercion, a German threat would enable the French government to justify concessions which would otherwise be blocked by interested parties. This 'overestimate of one's importance as influence'[23] disregarded two contextual factors: that the interested parties could arouse nationalist feeling against yielding to threats, and that even leaders inclined to cooperate with Germany would have to heed such nationalism. That Kiderlen was consciously appealing to such sentiment in Germany while overlooking it in France points to a high degree of perceptual distortion.

In implementing the decision to license oil exports to Japan as a total embargo, US officials acted without awareness of the consequences for Japan's decision makers. Some assumed that Japan's intentions were aggressive, irrespective of US actions, others that it could be deterred by firmness, and others again acted from internal concerns such as the need to conserve oil supplies for the US itself – some, then, in terms of a rigid image, others in terms of the causal schemas of attribution theory.

The theory, however, postulates that an individual thinks in terms of a plurality of loosely connected beliefs and causal schemas,[24] but does not explain why a particular schema is chosen in a particular situation. The choice of a particular schema may reflect emotion or political motivation. It is difficult to test this hypothesis in the case of the US in 1941, but it offers plausible explanations in the other two instances.

The Tsar 'needed' to restore his prestige in Constantinople, not only to secure Russia's interests but to satisfy nationalist sentiment as well as his own wounded pride. It was politically and emotionally congenial to assume that the sympathetic Aberdeen would acquiesce in his seeking to achieve these goals through a forceful display of Russia's diplomatic prowess. Causal attribution might equally have led him to reason that it was necessary to avoid giving his old adversaries, Palmerston and Stratford, an opportunity to arouse British sentiment against him. He chose the more appealing causal schema.

In Kiderlen's case, where the German government was under pressure to achieve a striking political success, it was congenial to opt for a causal hypothesis according to which the kind of public challenge which would maximise the political benefit in Germany would also achieve the desired effect in Paris. The precedent of the first Moroccan crisis or the memory of 1870 should have led German policy makers to the opposite hypothesis, that threats tended to arouse French anger and resistance. It is plausible to attribute Kiderlen's choice of a causal schema more to personal ambition and political convenience than to 'cold' cognitive processes.

As in the case of the persistence of crucial misperceptions, cognitive and political explanations complement one another. However, reviewing the cases as a whole, one may reasonably give greater weight to political motivation for major distortions of perception than to purely cognitive explanations, especially when the decision maker is in a position to choose among different images and causal schemas. This conclusion is strengthened when examples of selective perception, short of outright misperception, such as the British perception of relative military capabilities in 1938, are taken into account. Finally, it should be recalled that some highly consequential cases of misperception require no explanation beyond the incompleteness or ambiguity of the evidence available at the time.[25] The need on some occasions to act under conditions of extreme uncertainty ensures that some choices will be based on faulty premises, and the variability of contexts and contingencies ensures that some such choices will be of major consequence.

13 CRISIS BARGAINING

The case studies confirm the importance of bargaining as a form of crisis interaction, but its centrality has been treated as hypothesis, not assumption. The main questions addressed in the case studies were the extent to which the parties followed coherent bargaining strategies and the overall significance of bargaining in each of the cases, and the findings point to limitations of a bargaining analysis. The aims of this chapter are (1) to suggest ways in which it may be necessary to qualify the hypothesis that bargaining is the primary form of interaction in crises, and (2) to explore what this implies for the explanation of crisis outcomes. Further, although the case studies do not suggest that the hostility spiral could replace bargaining as a general theory of crisis interaction, the chapter will inquire to what extent it may supplement a bargaining analysis. First, however, it is necessary to explain further the way in which the terms 'bargaining' and 'bargaining strategy' are used in the present work.

Bargaining is seldom defined explicitly in the international relations literature, but the concept employed in the present study – attempting to influence the decisions of others through strategies of coercion and accommodation – is consistent with the usage of the term by Thomas Schelling and by Snyder and Diesing. There is, however, an important distinction between the way in which Schelling employs the term and its use by the latter authors. Schelling, who emphasises tacit bargaining and signalling, explicitly excludes from bargaining actions which are 'disconnected from any conscious process of coercion, persuasion or communication of intent' – for example, gratuitous acts of violence, reflex actions or responses to purely internal pressures.[1] Snyder and Diesing do not restrict the term in this way. Although they do not explicitly equate international interaction with bargaining, they provide no criterion for distinguishing bargaining from other modes of interaction, and in practice they appear to construe all interaction in terms of the assumptions of bargaining theory.[2] Whatever is done is understood as part of a strategy – a coercive, accommodative or mixed

281

strategy, a complete or incomplete strategy – a usage which leaves no place, for example, for reflex actions or for *ad hoc* or incoherent responses to conflicting pressures.[3]

In the present study, 'bargaining' is restricted, in accordance with Schelling's criterion, to actions guided by a conscious strategy of coercion, accommodation, persuasion or communication of intent. Similarly, a 'bargaining strategy' is not just a summary term to describe the general tenor of a policy – coercive or accommodating, hard-line or soft-line – but is understood as presupposing a number of conditions:

1   A government's goals are reasonably clearly defined. Unless its actions are directed towards achieving identifiable goals they will not amount to a bargaining strategy.

2   However serious its differences with its adversaries, it prefers to resolve them short of war. If it prefers war, or believes it inevitable, its crisis diplomacy will not consist of bargaining but will be essentially a search for a pretext in order to legitimise war.

3   In the interests of resolving differences, it is willing to bargain with the other parties. If it seeks its goals solely through unilateral action, it is not bargaining.

4   Its actions can be shown to be part of a reasonably coherent and realistic strategy, oriented towards other governments. Even if a government has certain goals, if it lacks a general plan of action for achieving them, or is unaware of the interests of other parties, it cannot be said to have a bargaining strategy.

Where these preconditions are met, it is likely that a crisis will consist essentially of bargaining among adversaries with competing strategies. But this is only one of several possibilities which may be set out as ideal types, starting with that of the pure bargaining crisis, with each successive ideal type diverging further from the original. Actual cases may not fall squarely within one of the ideal types, but they serve to clarify a number of different ways in which crisis interaction may diverge from bargaining.[4]

Type 1: Pure bargaining
The principal moves are in accordance with rational bargaining strategies. This assumes, to recapitulate, that governments resolve internal differences such that they behave as unitary actors with agreed goals, that they are willing to bargain with one another in the hope of realising their objectives short of war, and that their strategies are

reasonably coherent and realistic. The assumptions of this ideal type do not require 'correct' perception, but are compatible with Snyder and Diesing's view that bargaining tends to correct the misperception which is frequently present at the outset of crises.

Type 2: Strategy without bargaining

As in type 1, there is a high level of rationality and the parties follow coherent strategies, but at least one of them does not bargain. Two sub-categories may be distinguished. First, the party in question may prefer war to any conceivable settlement; its diplomacy seeks to establish a pretext for war. While in principle the distinction between genuine bargaining and negotiation for side-effects – in this case to legitimise a war – may be clear, it may be difficult to draw in practice, since both motivations may be present in some degree, varying between different decision makers and different phases of a crisis. Second, one or more parties, while preferring a settlement to war, may have a strategy of avoiding bargaining. It may engage in unilateral action, treating the issue as falling within its 'sphere of influence' or demanding a 'free hand'. Bargaining will ensue only if one of the other parties can insist that it is indeed a party whose interests must be taken into account. Again, there may be no bargaining because one party prefers to wait for the situation to change in its favour, or until it can be successfully manipulated. This may appear difficult to distinguish from 'waiting' as a well-known bargaining tactic, but the case envisaged is that in which a party circumvents the bargaining process altogether until an outcome becomes tacitly accepted or is imposed unilaterally.

It may be objected that there is a sense in which all such 'non-bargaining' strategies can be seen as part of a wider bargaining process.[5] Declining to treat another party as having legitimate interests can be construed as a demand supported by a tacit threat or challenge (the other will not or cannot forcibly intervene). Even the preference for war in a particular situation can be construed as a demand for a change in the terms of a relationship, backed by the willingness to incur the costs and risks of war. The history of the relations of the powers can be written in terms of the concepts of bargaining theory – their changing bargaining assets and liabilities, their images, prestige, the availability of resources and allies, and so forth. While such extensions of the concept may be illuminating in the study of long-term relationships, they obscure distinctions which are important in short-term contexts such as crises. In the case of crises, distinctions such as those between genuine negotiation and the establishing of a pretext

283

for war, or whether or not a state is accepted as a party in the crisis diplomacy, are of crucial importance. Within the time-frame of the crisis and its resolution, the distinction between bargaining and uni-lateral strategies may have major consequences.

Type 3: Bargaining negated by misperception

Crisis interactions may fall short of bargaining because, in the case of at least one actor, misperception amounts to a pervasive unrealism, too deep-seated for the bargaining process to correct it. There may be quasi-bargaining – negotiation at cross-purposes, in which the parties talk past one another and threats miss their mark. In this type of crisis, misunderstanding is not occasional (as is true of any bargaining situation) but is a pervasive, dominant feature of the interaction.

Type 4: Divided actors

Crisis interaction may also fall short of bargaining because one or more actors are not sufficiently unitary. Differences among decision makers and those who influence them may prevent a government from adhering to a consistent line of policy. The point here is not the mere presence of differences, but an inability to resolve them.

Type 5: The hostility spiral

Whereas in types 3 and 4 there may be elements of bargaining, in the fifth type interactions follow an entirely different logic, or illogic. As noted earlier, the most familiar alternative is the hostility spiral, domi-nated by reflex reactions, not calculation, and often associated with decision making under stress.[6] It may also be associated with decision making which is more responsive to internal than to external pressures, where policy is shaped by conventional norms and expecta-tions or internal political 'compulsions', with little realistic orientation to external actors.

The characteristics which distinguish between the ideal types are at the level of the state, not the international system. Most crises illus-trate a combination of types, but one is normally predominant. A case will fall wholly within one type only if all the main actors have the characteristics of that type. This is especially true of type 1, *pure bargaining*: if even one major actor falls within one of the other types, effective bargaining may become impossible. The judgments which assign cases to types are based on the case study interpre-tations.

The role of bargaining: the typology illustrated

The first ideal type (pure bargaining) is predominant in three cases – the Eastern crisis, Agadir and Berlin (1958–62) – as is the second (strategy without bargaining): the Franco-Prussian crisis, the Sudeten crisis and the Berlin blockade. The third ideal type (misperception) is predominant in only one case, the Russo-Japanese crisis, and the fourth (divided decision making) in two, the Crimean crisis and Pearl Harbor. There is no case in which the fifth ideal type (hostility spiral) is predominant, but it is present as a complicating factor in several. In every case there are elements of at least one further ideal type, often more than one, but not all five. In view of the small sample of cases, the numbers in each type are not significant. What is of interest is the different processes which may be involved when crises diverge from bargaining.

Pure bargaining

The Eastern crisis
The crisis is judged to be one in which bargaining was predominant (type 1) with certain elements of strategy without bargaining (type 2) and limitations imposed by divisions among decision makers (type 4). Early bargaining over coalition formation set the parameters for the restricted bargaining over the conditions to be imposed on Mehemet Ali; leadership divisions in France and Britain figured prominently but their overall impact was surprisingly limited.

The rapid formation of a three-power coalition (Britain, France and Austria) not only deterred Russia from any residual intent to act unilaterally, but also prompted it to initiate the partnership with Britain which secured its own position and placed Palmerston in a favourable position to impose his preferred terms on Mehemet Ali, given Austria's interest in mediating between the principal adversaries, and Prussia's passive role.

Palmerston followed an ostensibly non-bargaining strategy in insisting on extreme terms and imposing them on Mehemet Ali by force, but he was sensitive to possible changes in the positions of the powers and offered concessions to France just sufficient to retain the support of Austria and of his own Cabinet. Thiers' apparent non-bargaining strategy was also formulated with an eye to the overall bargaining context: he privately sought to induce Mehemet Ali to compromise, and in the phase of French isolation after the four-power Convention, he consciously sought to use the risk of war to induce the other powers

285

to improve their offer to Mehemet Ali. Thiers' strategy, however, was not played out to its logical conclusion. When it appeared that he might not be able to keep the risks under control, Louis-Philippe engineered his resignation. Internal divisions, in which the more cautious decision maker held the stronger position, cut short a strategy of high-risk bargaining.

Internal divisions constantly threatened to undermine Palmerston's strategy. Allowing full credit for his persistence and skills, an unusual combination of political circumstances was required to enable him to pursue so coherent a strategy in the face of such sustained internal opposition as he experienced. Moreover, he enjoyed a measure of luck in that the protracted delays caused by the internal divisions did not negate the chances of a settlement among the powers. The potentiality for the collapse of Palmerston's strategy was evident, but the crisis would probably have remained of the bargaining type, with different bargainers, as it did after the collapse of Thiers' strategy.

The Agadir crisis

Agadir provides the second example, but the bargaining was less skilful than in the Eastern crisis, and more seriously affected by divisions among decision makers – most obvious in the case of Germany, but also significant in France. Moreover, the reactions to some of the coercive moves showed that there was a danger that the unintended consequences of what were intended as bargaining moves could have transformed the crisis into a hostility spiral.

France initially followed a non-bargaining strategy, in the hope that Germany would acquiesce in a *fait accompli* in Morocco, but switched rapidly to a bargaining strategy when challenged by Germany. Bargaining was complicated by differences over tactics among the decision makers, by the weakness of French parliamentary governments in this period and by divisions among those seeking to influence policy. The dilemma for the policy makers was that the Assembly might reject a settlement perceived as too accommodating to Germany, yet a 'stronger', nationalist approach risked provoking German reactions which could have brought about a hostility spiral.

On the German side, Kiderlen had a clearly defined coercive bargaining strategy, based on the assumption that France would offer significant concessions only under threat, and which required Germany to appear willing to risk war. In some quarters Kiderlen's tactics enhanced the readiness to make concessions, but in others the determination to resist. Moreover, his attempt to restrict the conflict to the bilateral relationship, France–Germany, had the effect of provoking

British intervention in a way which increased the perceived fear of a hostility spiral. The Kaiser's determination not to risk war, however, placed a major constraint on Kiderlen's strategy: it was not pressed to its logical conclusion – a diplomatic triumph, or war. After the initial coercive gestures, German policy settled down into much the same bargaining style as the French, haggling over details while aroused interest groups found fault with every proposed compromise. Since neither side was prepared to risk war, however, a compromise was eventually reached, by a process of attrition. Above all, the crisis illustrates how readily a case which exemplifies type 1, pure bargaining, might be transformed into another type, either because leadership divisions negate a bargaining strategy or, more dramatically, because bargaining itself degenerates into a hostility spiral.

The Berlin crisis

In contrast to the blockade, discussed below, Berlin 1958–62 was essentially a bargaining crisis, type 1, in which the Soviet Union sought to use the risk and fear of war to pressure the West to accept significant changes, while the West sought to demonstrate its commitment to the essentials of the status quo, bargaining only over what most decision makers regarded as secondary issues. Unilateral strategies were significant, but were pursued within a bargaining context. Divisions among decision makers played a prominent part in Western policy making, but did not in the end greatly modify the bargaining approach preferred by the key American decision makers.

There was no direct threat of war by the Soviet Union, but this was not needed: the situation itself ensured that the risk of war was uppermost in the minds of Western policy makers. Khrushchev offered them a choice between an agreement which would undermine their legal position in Berlin and at the same time upgrade the status of East Germany, and the risk that he would unilaterally repudiate the existing arrangements on Berlin, with all the uncertainties that this might entail. In the more acute phases he set certain deadlines for reaching agreement, but was persuaded rather easily to relax them.

The Western governments sought to defuse the crisis through negotiation, rejecting Khrushchev's deadlines and preferring to negotiate on other issues, but were prepared in the last analysis to offer limited counter-proposals which, in the majority view, would have preserved the basic Western rights unchanged. The minority view, that the Soviet bluff should be called, never prevailed; intermittent bargaining over secondary issues took place, but the two sides remained far from agreement. There was no clear-cut termination of the crisis, but

Soviet pressures and Western offers ceased after the Cuban missile crisis.

The decision to construct the Wall was taken in the light of the bargaining process, after Soviet and East German probing and a variety of Western 'signals' had indicated that it was unlikely to be resisted. Unilateral Western policies, in particular changes in NATO strategy, entered into the bargaining as measures intended to strengthen the Western commitment to Berlin, but were also pursued for their own sake, especially by the Kennedy Administration. Despite these elements of type 2, this was the crisis in which bargaining was most clearly predominant, cautious and inconclusive though it was.

Overview

The first two cases not only illustrate the difficulty of maintaining a coherent strategy in the light of serious differences within governments, but they show that certain preconditions for bargaining were frequently endangered. In a multipolar system, coalitions provide the essential framework for bargaining, but mid-nineteenth-century coalitions were unstable, raising the prospect of a sudden change in the bargaining context, and some in 1911 perceived the coalition structure (the Entente) as a major stake in the crisis. Other threats to the bargaining process were even more far-reaching, and could quite plausibly have changed the whole nature of the 'game', even precipitating a shift to a hostility spiral.

The dangers of the loss of a coherent bargaining approach and the risk of a hostility spiral were most evident in the Agadir crisis. Governmental divisions and instability were a constant problem for French diplomacy at the time, and German policy was noted for its fragmentation. Minimal coherence was maintained, however, because of the Kaiser's determination to limit Kiderlen's use of threatening tactics, which had the potential to exacerbate internal divisions precisely because they aroused plausible fears of a hostility spiral. The risk of a spiral also emerged briefly in the Eastern crisis. Louis-Philippe had good reason to fear Thiers' Schelling-type risky tactics: the threat that the crisis might escape control was all too plausible. Nationalist passions and ambitions in both France and Germany, in the context of French political instability, could have generated uncontrollable reactions.

Bargaining in the Berlin crisis avoided provocative tactics, and it is difficult to envisage a political context in the nuclear age in which internal political emotion might precipitate a hostility spiral. But were Western policy makers, in rejecting the dangers in openly calling the

Soviet bluff, risking that the Soviets might miscalculate – misperceiving Western prudence as weakness? The incompleteness of information on Soviet decision making precludes a firm judgment, but it may be said that, in contrast to the two other cases, the main hazards of the Berlin crisis were intrinsic to the bargaining process.

Strategy without bargaining

The Franco-Prussian crisis

If the Franco-Prussian crisis had been resolved by the withdrawal of the Hohenzollern candidacy, it would have been a clear case of bargaining (type 1). As it was, the crisis is deemed to have been predominantly type 2 – strategy without bargaining – with a substantial type 1 dimension in the early stages, and elements of type 5, the hostility spiral.

French diplomacy up to 11 July, the withdrawal of the candidacy, is consistent with a bargaining interpretation. Gramont's inflammatory speech of 6 July had exacerbated public feeling and had placed the Empire's prestige at stake, maximising the pressure behind the demand for the withdrawal. Diplomacy sought to bring this pressure to bear on the decision makers most likely to be responsive – the King of Prussia and Prince Karl Anton, the candidate's father – offering them a face-saving mode of withdrawal insofar as it could be presented as a private family decision.

Prussian diplomacy, insofar as it also depicted the issue as one in which the state had no involvement, allowed for the possibility of such a fall-back position. But it is more plausible to interpret Prussian policy in the crisis as a non-bargaining strategy. By denying all involvement, Bismarck appears to have wanted the crisis to run its course without official Prussian participation. France would either have to acquiesce in a distasteful *fait accompli* or else it might provoke a crisis or even a war, but in a way which the other powers would perceive as overreacting, or as reasserting ancient claims to hegemony. The evidence suggests that Bismarck wanted a crisis which could revive the movement for German national unity, and that he was prepared to run a high risk of war; there is no indication that he envisaged bargaining in order to avert it.

With the demand for guarantees, French policy in the later phase of the crisis also falls under type 2, strategy without bargaining, with some overlap with the pretext-for-war category of crisis, insofar as no realistic decision maker could have regarded the new French demands as acceptable. However, it would be an overstatement to say that the

289

French leaders had resolved on war on 11 July, when due account is taken of the emotionally charged atmosphere in which they formulated their new demand and its somewhat incremental character, viewed from their perspective. Their initial bargaining strategy had already shown signs of recklessness, leaving little room for manoeuvre. While it could be construed as a Schelling-type, high-risk strategy of commitment, it could also be seen as one which risked provoking a hostility spiral at the outset. Thus the crisis was predominantly of type 2: it was Bismarck's ostensible approach throughout, and the French approach in the decisive second phase.

The Sudeten crisis
From the standpoint of the great powers, this was a non-bargaining crisis, except for a period of confused bargaining in the last phase. Until the Berchtesgaden meeting, both Germany and Britain followed well-defined non-bargaining strategies, with France following Britain's lead. Germany sought to isolate and subvert Czechoslovakia and thus to avoid bargaining with its ally, France, or with Britain. Britain, having failed to draw Germany into broad negotiations or into talks on the Sudeten issue, sought to avoid an acute crisis by pressing the Czechoslovakian government to come to a settlement with the Sudeten Germans.

Germany had only limited means of bargaining to achieve its preferred position, that Britain grant it a free hand in central and eastern Europe, but it could reject negotiation, instead placing Czechoslovakia under increasing pressure, in the hope that either its 'intransigence' would lead France and Britain to withdraw their support, or else internal instability would furnish a pretext for German intervention. Although Britain, in pursuit of its crisis avoidance strategy, applied pressure on Czechoslovakia systematically, coordination with France was uneven and no settlement was achieved. As the prospect of violence and German intervention increased, Chamberlain compelled Hitler to enter into bargaining through his surprise initiative of visiting Germany. Neither side had a well-defined strategy for the ensuing bargaining; Hitler initially improvised more successfully, but overplayed his hand and was compelled to settle for an outcome which could have been negotiated without the final confrontation.

The case can be classified as predominantly type 2, strategy without bargaining. Although there was an element of bargaining in Britain's warning to Germany, its main goal was to avert a crisis through influencing the local actor, Czechoslovakia, just as Germany sought to bring about its preferred, localised crisis by the same means. Divisions among decision makers had little impact on policy. Fear of a hostility spiral influenced British and French decision makers, but a spiral itself was easily avoided, with the partial exception of Hitler's reaction to the May crisis, which was not well understood by the other powers.

The Berlin blockade

The blockade combined substantial elements of bargaining with strategies which relied on unilateral action, that is to say, the maintenance of the blockade on the one side, its circumvention by the airlift on the other. Since the outcome of the crisis depended essentially on the latter, the case is deemed to have been predominantly type 2. Divisions within the Western governments were resolved without impairing their overall strategies, and there was no hostility spiral. The crisis illustrates a relatively simple combination of two types 2 and 1.

The evidence suggests that the imposition of the blockade was initially part of a Soviet strategy to reopen the larger German question, in particular to prevent the establishment of a separate state in West Germany. After it became clear that Berlin did not offer sufficient leverage for this purpose, the bargaining briefly focused on an agreement linking the lifting of the blockade with the introduction of the currency of the Soviet zone into Berlin. After talks on implementing this broke down, negotiation was downgraded by the Western governments as the capabilities of the airlift improved. So long as they feared that the Western zones of Berlin could be supplied for only a limited period, the Western governments had been willing to enter into a bargain which could have weakened their long-term position in Berlin. This became less and less the case.

The Western governments, then, came to rely essentially on their capacity to sustain Berlin, using negotiations to embarrass the Soviet Union and later to devise a face-saving formula for lifting the blockade, but no longer to bargain on any of the original issues. Soviet policy, once the weakness of the initial ambitious bargaining strategy was clear, made little effort to achieve the potential advantages of an ambiguous all-Berlin agreement, but turned to the political consolidation of the Soviet zone. The predominance of unilateral approaches is clear.

Overview

Strategy without bargaining can be attempted in several contexts: an actor may have a general preference for unilateral action, or may believe that particular goals are attainable without bargaining, or that it can maximise its control over events through a posture of non-involvement while seeking to manipulate a conflict indirectly. It is instructive that not even Bismarck or Hitler could successfully control their crises in this way, Bismarck because circumstances required the King to act independently, Hitler because Chamberlain negated his unilateral strategy by flying to Germany. A non-bargaining stance may reflect a readiness to risk war (both parties in 1870, Hitler with respect to a local war in 1938), but it can also reflect a perception that one is in a strong position and the risk of war safely remote (the West in the later phase of the Berlin blockade).

The cases point to the difficulty of sustaining the strategy in the face of pressures to bargain – thus there is an admixture of type 1 in each of the type 2 cases. They do not provide such clear evidence as the type 1 examples of potentialities leading towards the further types. In France in 1870, however, there was a complex linkage between the 'war party's' non-bargaining strategy and aspects of the hostility spiral and the pretext-for-war type of crisis. Both the strategy and the pretext required a mood of patriotic emotion and outrage – attitudes whose expression tends to provoke counter-expression, thus an 'escalation' towards war. This kind of political climate was entirely absent in the other two cases: there is no general association between non-bargaining and escalation.

Bargaining negated by misperception: the Russo-Japanese crisis

It has been argued that while Japan followed a coherent bargaining strategy, the course of the crisis and its outcome were determined by the absence of bargaining on the part of the other main actor, Russia, and that while divisions over strategy were significant, the principal reason for Russia's failure to bargain was its misperception of Japan's capabilities and resolve. Thus the crisis is classified as type 3, with elements of types 1 and 4.

The overall effect of Russian policy was *as if* Russia was following a strategy of playing for time – until the completion of the Trans-Siberian railway would improve its capacity to reinforce its armed forces in the region – meanwhile deterring Japan by harsh signals. Russian decision making, however, shows no evidence of such a strategy. Only Alekseiev was opposed to a negotiated settlement with Japan and favoured relying wholly on deterrence. The Tsar endorsed the negotiations, but rejected all suggestions for accommodating Japan's concerns, seeing no need to do so. Until December Russia followed no strategy and engaged in no bargaining; the low-key diplomatic confrontation then brought about a reconsideration, too late to avert Japan's decision for war.

Only one crisis is predominantly of type 3, though misperception was also a major factor in the Crimean crisis (judged to be, on balance, type 4). In both cases the effects of a deep-seated misperception on the part of one actor were sufficient to render the bargaining of others ineffective. In both cases war was the outcome, whereas it was a reasonable expectation that a diplomatic settlement could have been achieved if bargaining had not been negated by misperception. The case studies do not offer an example of the opposite: that is, a crisis ending in a diplomatic settlement where war might have been expected if crucial misperceptions had been corrected. The Sudeten crisis is often regarded as such an example, but the case study has argued that this is a faulty interpretation, since British decisions were not based on a misperception of Hitler's intentions but on uncertainty over them.

Divided actors

The Crimean crisis

This case is deemed to have been predominantly of type 4, where the crisis interactions fall short of bargaining because at least one actor is not sufficiently unitary, as was true of Britain in this instance. Russian divisions were of some significance in the early phase, and Austrian divisions were prominent but of little ultimate consequence. It is Britain's crucial role in the crisis which justifies giving such weight to unresolved differences among its decision makers. Elements of other ideal types were also prominent. British policy was constrained by the strength of public support for a misleading stereotype of Russia (type 3), and some of the main 'escalatory' moves were not so much part of a bargaining strategy as quasi-reflex actions, conventional moves with little thought to the context, potentially making for a 'hostility spiral' rather than calculated bargaining (type 5). The predominance of type 4 is not immediately evident, but emerges from a review of the obstacles to bargaining in the crisis.

Following France's disturbing of the uneasy balance in the Near East, Russia initially followed a familiar type of bargaining strategy, placing pressure on Constantinople in order to redress its position, seeking a *fait accompli* but also seeking to reassure Britain, the power most likely to object. Clumsy execution of the strategy, and the open-ended character of Russia's demands, led to a deadlock and opened a more acute phase of the crisis. Thereafter, Russia's mixture of coercive and accommodative moves did not amount to a coherent strategy. Its attempt to reach an accommodation through Concert diplomacy was vitiated partly by its overestimate of the time available for negotiation, but more by Britain's unresponsiveness. France sought to follow a bargaining approach, intending to negotiate from strength, but Napoleon's unwillingness to break with Britain left him with no effective means of constraining it to adopt the same approach. Austria followed a mediating role, as in 1840, its influence based on its readiness to grant or withhold its support, but was ultimately unable to offset the pressures to escalate.

It was Britain's failure to pursue a coherent strategy, either of deterrence or of Concert diplomacy, which decisively affected the course and outcome of the crisis. Britain did not combine its coercive and accommodative moves effectively. The principal coercive moves, the advancing of the fleet, were not designed to influence Russia or Turkey in the desired direction, but were essentially responses to domestic expectations. And the increasing unwillingness to restrain Turkey rendered Britain unable to formulate a diplomatic strategy or to respond constructively to the initiatives of others.

The characteristics of types 3, 4 and 5 are prominent in British policy. The escalatory moves were more in accordance with the 'hostility spiral' than with the logic of bargaining, even though some of them were rationalised in bargaining terms; and during the later phases, the strength of the public's commitment to a misleading stereotype of Russian aggression was a major constraint on the government's capacity to bargain. However, the crisis is deemed to have been primarily of type 4, owing to the causal priority of divisions among the decision makers, which prevented Britain from adopting a bargaining approach which would have greatly improved the chances of the powers' achieving their preferred outcome, a diplomatic settlement. A Palmerstonian strategy from the outset offered some prospect of moderating the early Russian demands, and a resourceful Concert strategy in the next phase offered a good chance of achieving a settlement. But Aberdeen neither controlled the policy nor fully understood the issues, and Clarendon, swayed by conflicting pressures, was increasingly reluctant to risk popular disapproval. The argument, then, is that it was Britain's inability to adopt a coherent strategy in the earlier and middle phases which opened the way to the hostility spiral and the dominance of public emotion in the later phase, and which justifies treating the crisis as predominantly type 4.

Pearl Harbor

In the case of the protracted US–Japan crisis leading to Pearl Harbor, it is not easy to discern which was the predominant type. During the first confrontation phase (May–September 1940) each made unsuccessful attempts to deter the other, but with very limited bargaining (types 1 or 2). In the decisive confrontation of July 1941, Japan moved unilaterally and the American response, the oil embargo, was neither designed to deter nor implemented with full awareness of its consequences. There were elements of misperception and of divided decision making on both sides (types 3 and 4). The negotiations during 1941 confirmed that a long-term settlement was impossible, but despite some interest in both governments in postponing the recourse to war, there was little sustained pursuit of a *modus vivendi* – in large measure due to internal divisions. Indeed, unresolved differences on both sides provide a common thread, such that on balance the case may be regarded as predominantly type 4.

For example, the graduated US response to Japan's early advances reflected divisions among hard-line and more cautious policy makers more than a clear strategy. At the time of the decisive moves in July 1941 there was a relative lack of awareness of the consequences on both sides, but this reflected not so much sheer obtuseness as the persistence of important divisions among decision makers, resolved not by argument and analysis but more by a process of attrition. As the probability of war became increasingly evident, some decision makers on both sides saw advantage in postponing it, but there was little American support for the first initiative to this end, a proposed summit meeting, and scarcely more support for a *modus vivendi*, when Japan for the first time adopted a clear bargaining stance. The failure even to define a short-term diplomatic option for further postponing the conflict points to the pervasiveness of unresolved differences among American decision makers.

Overview

Divisions of opinion, present in all governments, are normally resolved sufficiently to permit minimal consistency in objectives and strategy. The divided actors considered here were unable to achieve this. One consequence was incrementalism, as policy gradually hardened in response to competing pressures which reflected the greater political power of the 'hard-liners' in each of the governments in question. The persistence of unresolved differences involved the persistence of competing images and perceptions. The absence of bargaining removed that potential source for the correction of misperception:

295

extreme images tended to persist in the minds of opposed schools of thought in each government. Options and choices were not clarified. In the Crimean case these failings contributed to an 'unnecessary war'; in the Pearl Harbor case they eliminated the option of further stalling for time which clearer bargaining would have identified in the late phase of the crisis.

The hostility spiral

Although none of the cases exemplifies the ideal type of the hostility spiral, fears of such a spiral were present in most of them: there was concern that particular leaders might act dangerously, and more diffuse fears that events might get out of control. Frequently crisis decision makers express some kind of perception of an 'escalation dynamic', and the foregoing analysis suggests that this is often well founded. Yet in most cases these pressures were kept under control, and decisions for war were more a function of the actors' goals than of a hostility spiral.

Theory in this area is underdeveloped. Neither Hermann and Brady's 'hostile interaction model' of crisis behaviour, nor Jervis's account of the security dilemma, discussed in Chapter 2, explains under what conditions a hostility spiral is to be expected. Suggestions along these lines may be found, however, in Richard Smoke's discussion of the dynamics of escalation. Although his main focus is on war, he pays some attention to crises, and his findings are highly relevant to the present inquiry. He identifies a number of sources of escalation: the desire to prevail, or to avoid losing; the tendency for the stakes to increase (as prestige, for example, becomes more engaged); leaders' personal identification with national goals; tactical and military considerations; and the activation of 'latencies' – broader interests of the original actors or of third parties.[7] To prevent these pressures from generating an uncontrollable spiral of reactions, he suggests, requires unusual conceptual skills, in particular the capacity to anticipate sequences of events, not merely the next move, and to grasp the frame of reference of other parties, not merely their goals but their expectations. In the absence of thought at this level, the lower-level pressures of cognitive consistency tend to reinforce narrowly defined national perspectives and the screening out of options.[8]

Smoke provides an illuminating analysis of the strategic and cognitive dimensions of escalation, but his omission of internal politics – except insofar as it may sometimes be included under 'latencies' –

proves to be a crucial one in relation to the present case studies, in several of which internal politics was the principal source of pressures making for a hostility spiral. This was especially true of the earlier cases. In the Eastern crisis it was the prospect of an internal eruption in France which created a fear of escalating nationalist provocations. In the Crimean case a major cause of the escalation was the arousing of anti-Russian sentiment in Britain, compelling the government to respond as in the spiral model, pressuring it into military moves while inhibiting diplomatic bargaining. In July 1870 the crucial escalation of French demands was not in accordance with the spiral model – the major Prussian concession should have evoked an accommodating response – but was explicable in terms of the political strength of the 'war party' within a regime weakened by internal conflicts, in a moment of high public emotion. Finally, during the Agadir crisis the fear was that coercive moves could spiral out of control because nationalist lobbies could demand such responses, precluding the kind of bargaining which might resolve the dispute.

Fears of a hostility spiral in the later cases were focused on governmental reactions. The concern in the Sudeten crisis was that Hitler or the supposed extremists in his entourage might be so readily provoked that threats or warnings would be counter-productive. In the US in 1940–41 fears of provoking Japan were for long a powerful obstacle to proposals for an embargo on crucial resources as a form of deterrent. In both Berlin crises there was concern that moves intended to force a quick resolution (Clay's proposed armoured column in 1948, and proposals to call Khrushchev's bluff in 1961) could instead bring about a sudden escalation; there were also fears of escalation from quite a different source, a military incident.

The cases, then, suggest the multiplicity of factors which can make for escalation or its avoidance. The exceptional intellectual capacities which Smoke sees as necessary for the control of escalation are important, but in most of the present cases aversion to war was the essential reason for the rejection of steps perceived as likely to provoke a spiral. Of the cases that led to war, 'spiral' dynamics were prominent in only one, the Crimean. The spiral is not irrelevant in 1941 insofar as the decisive American embargo left the Japanese with a changed cost-benefit calculus which simplified their choice for war, but that choice can also be seen as the culmination of a sequence of acts of aggression as the advocates of military expansion became increasingly dominant in policy making. In general, then, the spiral model illuminates important potentialities of crises, but the present cases suggest that it rarely identifies the primary causal processes.

Ideal types and crisis outcomes

Outcomes are examined more fully in Chapter 15, but at this stage we may compare the present findings with those of Snyder and Diesing, who derive their explanation of crisis outcomes from their analysis of bargaining in terms of game-theoretic models. Game theory, as they apply it, explains crisis outcomes in terms of the actors' preferences in the final phase of a crisis. Since the options confronting the actors in that phase, and their preferences, are treated as given, not themselves explained, a more complete explanation of crisis outcomes will have to add to the game-theoretic models, drawing on other theories.

The two-person game models which provide the basis for their explanation are essentially an economical way of presenting 'the ordinal ranking, by the crisis participants, of their values for each of the four gross outcomes: win, lose, compromise or breakdown'.[9] Since it can be assumed that all participants rank win, compromise and lose in that order, the crucial variable which determines the different game structures is the ranking of war. If an actor prefers to lose, that is to say, to concede the issue in dispute, rather than go to war, its preference structure is that which is modelled in the game 'Chicken'. If it is prepared to go to war rather than concede the issue ('lose'), but prefers compromise to war, its preference structure is that of the game 'Prisoner's Dilemma'. In addition to these well-known game models, Snyder and Diesing devise two further models suggested by their subject matter. If the actor prefers to go to war in order to 'win', rather than accept any feasible compromise, its preference structure is, in their terminology, 'Bully'. If it prefers war to winning without war, the preference ranking is termed 'Big Bully'.

Where a conflict (game) as a whole is termed 'Chicken' or 'Prisoner's Dilemma', this means that both parties have the preference ranking in question. Where both parties prefer war to compromise ('Bully'), the game as a whole, in Snyder–Diesing terminology, is 'Deadlock'. The *game* 'Bully' refers to the case where one party is 'in Bully', the other 'in Chicken'. Other asymmetrical games which they identify are 'Called Bluff', where one party is in Prisoner's Dilemma, preferring war to conceding, the other in Chicken, with the reverse preference; and Bully–Prisoner's Dilemma, a self-explanatory combination of those two preference rankings.[10]

In applying these models to international crises Snyder and Diesing vary some of the standard assumptions of game theory. Classical game theory assumes a single game in which the parties make simultaneous choices without communication. The search for information is assumed to have taken place before the game. The game itself consists of choosing the strategy which is expected to achieve the most advantageous of the available payoffs. Snyder and Diesing vary the assumptions of non-communication and simultaneous choice. For them, the game consists of a series of moves which include communication, not a once-for-all choice of an optimal strategy.[11]

These variations have major consequences for the player's choice of a strategy, and thus the expected outcome of the game, which can best be shown by reference to the game Prisoner's Dilemma, the source of extensive applications of game theory in many contexts. Using the conventions explained in note 10, the game is depicted as follows:

Player B

		C	D
	C	3,3	1,4
Player A			
	D	4,1	2,2

Under the standard assumption of the single choice, each player will rationally choose strategy D, because the payoff is preferable to the C payoff, irrespective of the other's choice of strategy. The structure of the game constrains the players to choose DD, for each a worse payoff than could have been achieved if collaboration were possible. Under Snyder and Diesing's assumptions the players can communicate and make a sequence of moves before the decisive choice, or can choose incrementally. They can, for example, threaten to respond to strategy D in kind or offer to reciprocate strategy C. A compromise CC is not the automatic outcome, but depends on each following an appropriate strategy (excessively conciliatory moves may prompt the other to defect, and too 'hard' a stance may prevent agreement). But whereas 2,2, through mutual defection, is the logical outcome of the standard game, 3,3 (compromise) is the expected outcome, after bargaining has established that each is likely to go to war rather than to concede, but would prefer to compromise – this is based on Snyder and Diesing's assumptions.[12]

The expected outcomes for the various games, given these assumptions, are as follows:[13]

Preference structure	Typical outcome
Chicken	one side capitulates
Prisoner's Dilemma	compromise
Deadlock	war
Called Bluff	capitulation by Chicken party
Bully	capitulation by Chicken party
Bully–Prisoner's Dilemma	war
Big Bully	war

Certain of these outcomes require no further explanation: where war is preferred to compromise, war can be expected, and when only one of the parties has Chicken rankings, it can be expected to capitulate to its more determined adversary. The outcome in the case of Chicken, however, as in the case of Prisoner's Dilemma, is not self-explanatory. Why is it not compromise? The rationale for one-sided outcomes is that once one of the parties has revealed its unwillingness to fight, it loses bargaining power, and the other, even though itself bluffing, has no incentive to compromise but is encouraged to press for its full demands.

The interpretation of a case as exemplifying one or other model requires judgments of a complex kind. The models are essentially ideal types. Decision makers within governments are rarely in complete accord on the issues of peace and war, and the preferences of individual decision makers are not always clear and consistent. Nonetheless, most cases can be classified as approximating to one of the game models, sometimes changing from one to another model in the course of the crisis.

The expected and the actual outcome

Table 13.1 presents, for each of the cases included in the present study, the game type, the expected outcome according to Snyder and Diesing's theory, and the actual outcome. Explanations for the assignment of game types are provided in an appendix to the chapter. For the five later cases the types coincide with Snyder and Diesing's classifications, except for the Sudeten crisis, where the case study argues that Britain and France did indeed risk war, however reluctantly – hence were in Prisoner's Dilemma, not Chicken.[14] In the case of Pearl Harbor and the Berlin blockade, alternative interpretations appear possible, as indicated in the appendix. The most difficult case to interpret in these terms is the Franco-Prussian.

In only four of the cases was the outcome unambiguously as

Table 13.1. *Crisis outcomes*

Case	Game type	Expected outcome	Outcome
Eastern	Chicken	capitulation	capitulation
Crimean	*early*: PD	compromise	war
	late: Bully–PD	war	
Franco-Prussian	*early*: PD(?)	compromise	war
	late: Deadlock	war	
Russo-Japanese	PD	compromise	war
Agadir	PD	compromise	compromise
Sudeten	*early*: Chicken	capitulation	compromise
	late: Called Bluff		
Pearl Harbor	*short-term*: PD	compromise	war
	long-term: Deadlock	war	
Berlin blockade	Chicken *or* Called Bluff	capitulation	capitulation
Berlin 1958–62	PD	compromise	compromise

Note: PD Prisoner's Dilemma.

predicted by the theory (the Eastern crisis, Agadir and the two Berlin crises). A fifth, the Franco-Prussian crisis, might be added insofar as the classification of the early phase as Prisoner's Dilemma is one of the least certain, and the final phase was undoubtedly Deadlock, which led to the predicted outcome, war. The Sudeten crisis is also one which is difficult to classify in terms of a single game model. According to the present case study, however, in the final phase it was Called Bluff. This should have led to capitulation by the Chicken party, Hitler. His bluff was called so reluctantly, however, that the compromise outcome was in his favour (though by much less, in terms of the parties' evaluations, than in the familiar hindsight view).

In the cases which led to war, however, with the exception of the Franco-Prussian crisis, the outcome was not as the theory would predict. In the Crimean crisis, the early Prisoner's Dilemma game, favouring compromise, was transformed only gradually into Bully–PD, as Britain's preferences, not wholly consciously, shifted to Bully. (In contrast, the French shift to Bully in 1870 was sudden and dramatic, and may have reflected the latent preference from the outset.) The Bully–PD conflict led, as predicted, to war, but what requires explanation is why the original PD conflict led not to the expected compromise but to Bully–PD. The same outcome was arrived at by a different route in the case of the Russo-Japanese crisis: once again, a Prisoner's Dilemma conflict did not show the expected move towards compromise, but rather towards war. In the case of Pearl Harbor, while the long-term preference rankings pointed towards war, significant short-term preferences favoured an agreement that would have postponed the recourse to war – compromise of a sort. Yet this was not achieved. The most challenging cases which require further explanation are those which led to war, despite initial preference structures favouring compromise. Do the ideal types, discussed above, provide this further explanation?

The five cases in which the outcome was in accordance with Snyder and Diesing's theory were instances of ideal types 1 and 2 (pure bargaining or strategy without bargaining). The Sudeten crisis (ideal type 2) may be regarded in this context so much as *sui generis* that it shows little more than that crises shaped by well-defined strategies can have unexpected outcomes. The three instances of unexpected wars (unexpected, that is to say, in terms of the original preference structures in two cases; in terms of timing, in the third) exemplify ideal types 3 or 4, where bargaining is undermined by pervasive misperception or by unresolved differences among decision makers, or both.

The ideal types provide the materials for explaining the unexpected outcome. Whereas 'efficient' bargaining in the Crimean crisis should have clarified the original Prisoner's Dilemma preferences, divisions among the British decision makers prevented this, opening the way for a partial hostility spiral premised on misleading stereotypes, which led to an incremental shift in Britain's preferences from Prisoner's Dilemma to Bully. The outcome was in accordance with the new preference structure. In the Russo-Japanese case, the absence of bargaining by Russia was the direct consequence of a pervasive misperception. There was no change in the Russian preference structure: the game remained Prisoner's Dilemma, but the outcome was war because one side declined to bargain. The Pearl Harbor case was similar, to the extent that in the absence of bargaining by the Americans over a short-term compromise, the Prisoner's Dilemma preference of certain US decision makers could not become effective.

Single cases cannot support universal generalisations, but they can illuminate potentialities. If an unnecessary war is one in which the basic values (the preference structures) of the actors are consistent with an expectation of a peaceful outcome, then the Crimean and Russo-Japanese cases demonstrate that unnecessary wars are possible.

The present findings require a reformulation of Snyder and Diesing's conclusions concerning the role of bargaining in crises. Whereas they see bargaining as the central process in crises except for certain limited categories (war scare and pretext for war) the present analysis sees this as true only in cases which fall within the first of the five ideal types. Where a crisis is essentially of this type, bargaining has, in general, the function which Snyder and Diesing ascribe to it, that is to say, it tends to correct misperceptions such that, by the time the crisis is ready for resolution, the parties have a sound perception of one another's preference structures. But in the case of the four other ideal types, bargaining does not have this effect, either because there is little or none of it (types 2 and 5) or because divisions among decision makers or deep-seated misperceptions render it ineffective. Nine cases provide no basis for conclusions about the incidence of the five potential types of crises, but the breakdown supports Smoke's contention that bargaining is a variable, not a constant. Snyder and Diesing's analysis of crisis bargaining remains fundamental, but the other variables discussed above are not minor perturbations, but need to be incorporated into the theoretical analysis of crises.

Appendix: Interpreting the cases in terms of game models

The *Eastern crisis* is classified as Chicken. None of the actors perceived the issues over Mehemet Ali as sufficient to justify a European war, but the issues were substantial enough for them to engage in a protracted diplomatic contest and the local use of force. However, the humiliation of France through its exclusion from the four-power Convention raised the stakes by involving French prestige. If the control of French policy had passed into the hands of radical nationalists the original issue would have ceased to be relevant and an entirely new 'game' would have begun, conceivably a 'pretext-for-war' crisis between popular nationalism in France and Germany.

The *Crimean war crisis* was at the outset essentially a Prisoner's Dilemma game in which Britain and France sought to restrain Russia from gaining disproportionate influence in Constantinople. All the governments preferred a diplomatic settlement to war. However, the fighting between Russia and Turkey, and Britain's increasing diplomatic support for Turkey and hostility towards Russia led to a situation in which British preferences became effectively Bully, a situation somewhat disguised insofar as Russia was perceived as aggressive, and war as inevitable. Since the preferences of the other powers did not change, the game thus ended as Bully–Prisoner's Dilemma.

The early phase of the *Franco-Prussian crisis* is more difficult to classify. France appeared to be in Prisoner's Dilemma: the threat to go to war unless the Hohenzollern candidacy was withdrawn appeared to signify a preference for peace if it was withdrawn. The readiness with which France increased its demands after the *de facto* withdrawal, however, suggests that the effective preference of some of its leaders was Bully – to seize an unexpected opportunity for war. The Prussian King was in Prisoner's Dilemma, preferring an honourable settlement. Bismarck did not reveal his preferences, but would probably have rejected a simple ranking of war over compromise: either a favourable diplomatic outcome or a war in which France was isolated were preferable to an adverse diplomatic outcome or a war in which Prussia faced a dangerous coalition. He preferred the prospective war to the King's compromise. In the later phase of the crisis, both governments having Bully preferences, the game became Deadlock.

The *Russo-Japanese* crisis is best interpreted as Prisoner's Dilemma. This was explicit in Japan, but did not become clear in Russia because Japan's preferences were perceived as Chicken, and thus could be safely disregarded. Since Russia's preferences were not clarified, it cannot be completely ruled out that they were Bully – a preference for war over the yielding of any imperial interest – but the case study argues that they were Prisoner's Dilemma – a preference for compromise.

The *Agadir crisis* was a clearer case of Prisoner's Dilemma preferences on the part of those in control of policy. There was a point beyond which they would not concede – if France had refused all compensation, on the one hand, or Germany had insisted on a share in Morocco, on the other – but the preference for compromise was evident. Those prepared to use threatening tactics which risked changing the game were restrained by the predominant decision makers.

In the *Sudeten crisis* Hitler's preferences were a combination of Bully or even Big Bully in relation to Czechoslovakia and Chicken in relation to Britain and France. Although he expected war with the latter in the long run, he accepted that Germany was not yet ready for it. Perceiving his preferences as Prisoner's Dilemma, however, and recognising that there were circumstances in which they could be drawn into war, Britain and France were prepared to go very far in compromising. Hitler was not interested: his game was to 'win' through a combination of Bully and Chicken, playing on their aversion to war. Although the outcome greatly favoured Germany, it was contrary to Hitler's preferences. The final phase was, in a paradoxical way, Called Bluff. Hitler, the Chicken party, had made extraordinary gains through his bluff, but was dissatisfied because the others risked war to insist on the formalities of a diplomatic compromise.

The effective American and Japanese preferences rendered the *Pearl Harbor crisis* Deadlock, although the potential for a further postponement of war, a short-term Prisoner's Dilemma outcome, was present late in the crisis. Japan was prepared to go to war unless it could secure sufficient resources through diplomacy, and the US became committed to war if Japan advanced beyond Indo-China. In the view of significant decision makers on both sides, however, postponement of a decision for war would have been advantageous, but since those of this persuasion were unable to prevail, the effective preferences remained Deadlock.

The *Berlin blockade* may plausibly be reconstructed as Chicken, but could have been Called Bluff. Both sides were prepared to expend political, diplomatic and economic resources but not actually to risk war. Stalin was required to make choices which support this judgment, but the Western powers were not. When the capacity of the airlift was still underestimated, they demonstrated a preference for diplomatic compromise over risking the use of force, but this does not show how they would have responded if the blockade had begun to cause severe physical hardship in Berlin. If in such a situation they had proved willing to risk war, they would have been in Prisoner's Dilemma.

Berlin 1958–62 is usually interpreted as Prisoner's Dilemma on both sides. That is to say, *some* change in the status quo was vital for the Soviet Union while the Western powers would risk war to preserve what they saw as their essential interests. Soviet preferences could, however, have been Chicken: Khrushchev's deadlines proved to be bluffs, and the construction of the Berlin Wall was undertaken with circumspection. It did, however, entail *some* risk of escalation, pointing to Prisoner's Dilemma preferences. On the Western side the need to engage in elaborate contingency planning and to reassure West Germany lent credibility to the frequent commitments to West Berlin, creating a presumption that the game was not merely Chicken but was indeed Prisoner's Dilemma.

14 INTERNAL POLITICS

It is evident from the case studies and from the preceding chapters that the 'black box' of internal politics provides the key to resolving many otherwise puzzling aspects of the cases. The goals of the actors' foreign policies depend on the power structures which sustain their rulers. Governmental stability or instability affect the capacity to respond to crises: internal politics impinge on governments' ability to pursue coherent objectives, to confront difficult choices and to bargain effectively, and can generate processes which make for the uncontrolled escalation of crises (the hostility spiral). The processes for resolving differences among decision makers vary in accordance with differing political institutions, but their effectiveness is also influenced by the level of internal political tensions.

The most dramatic changes in a state's foreign policy goals result from changes of political regime: from France under the *ancien régime* to the revolution and Empire, for example, or from Germany under the Weimar Republic to Nazism. But as the case studies have shown repeatedly, foreign policy objectives differ even between relatively like-minded decision makers: Palmerston and Aberdeen, or Kiderlen and the Kaiser. The institutions and political processes which determine who rules are major 'givens' in the case studies: they also determine whose goals will be pursued, whether their rule is stable or contested, and so forth. If explanations are sought for these 'givens', it must be in the political histories of each state, broadly understood.

It is not surprising, in view of the multi-faceted character of the 'black box', that attempts to theorise about external–internal linkages have proved frustrating.[1] Comparative politics is not a highly developed field, theoretically speaking: it consists largely of comparisons among states with similar institutions, thus generating 'narrow-gauge' theory, or, in the case of the systems approach, a heuristically productive framework for systematic description, but not an explanatory theory.[2] The study of comparative foreign policy has, as yet, little that is systematic and general to say about external–internal linkages.

A novel conceptualisation of these linkages has recently been put forward by Robert Putnam.[3] The focus is on bargaining: he formulates a 'stylised model of two-level negotiations' according to which the 'chief negotiator' is always engaged in 'games' at two levels, bargaining with other chief negotiators at one level, and with key domestic constituents and coalitions at the other. Unless he can satisfy the latter, he risks losing his place at the 'table' of the former game to a rival aspirant to his role. The detailed working out of the model, which reflects Putnam's interest in cooperation in the contemporary international political economy, is not of concern here: what is of interest is its general character. Its strength is that it offers a plausible general image of international inter-action: the model assumes, quite rightly, that a government's domestic political base and indeed the essentials of the domestic political setting can never be neglected in a satisfactory account of foreign policy. (A government is never completely 'insulated' from domestic pressures, and the degree of insulation or exposure can be explained only in terms of the 'domestic' political system.)

Putnam's analysis leads him to identify certain considerations which are always relevant to an explication of external–internal linkages, for example, whether domestic cleavages are homogeneous (hawks against doves) or heterogeneous (cross-cutting cleavages), and whether institutional arrangements which strengthen decision makers at home will strengthen or weaken their international bargaining position.[4] Insofar as they are formulated within the framework of rational-choice theory, these amount to more than a checklist. However, his model shares with that mode of theorising its tendency to treat important explanatory variables as exogenous. Focusing on the intersection of external–internal bargaining relationships, it usefully draws together the immediate causes of diplomatic behaviour, leaving their wider explanation to be sought elsewhere. It does not throw very much light on some of the central issues in the preceding chapters, in particular the reasons why a substantial number of the cases could not be explained in terms of the basic logic of bargaining.[5]

The question of the ultimate feasibility of a general theory of external–internal linkages need not be addressed here. The findings of the present study may be seen as a step towards narrow-gauge theory. They complement some of Lebow's findings, in particular on the political preconditions for successful crisis diplomacy.[6] Four aspects of internal politics are relevant to this general issue:

1   Internal politics viewed as the source of the historically 'given' characteristics of the states-as-actors, those 'fortuitous' elements, as

Lebow expresses it, which determine who rules, how secure is their hold on power, the prevailing 'political culture', and the like.

2   Governmental processes, in particular their bearing on the resolution of differences among decision makers or the failure to resolve them.

3   The effects of political instability on crisis diplomacy, and the effect, at times dramatic, of the eruption of domestic politics in the course of a crisis.

4   In the light of the foregoing, a discussion of the internal political preconditions for effective crisis diplomacy.

The historically 'given'

In the case of the systemic context of crises, it was noted that the configuration of power and the nature (or absence) of prevailing norms, although the product of countless prior decisions, amount to 'given' structures and constraints for crisis decision makers, not depriving them of choice but limiting it, opening up some opportunities while foreclosing others. The 'givens' of the internal political systems of the state-actors are even more potent, not only determining the extent of the decision makers' cohesion and control over their respective polities, but in a sense endowing them with their values and beliefs. The nature of these 'givens' can best be brought out by briefly reviewing the cases from this perspective. Since goals and perceptions have been discussed extensively in earlier chapters, the focus of these reviews is the impact of internal political forces on governments' security in power and their control over policy, noting but not elaborating on the diversity of governmental institutions.

The Eastern crisis

The government whose foreign policy was most exposed to internal pressures and constraints was that of France under Thiers. His predecessor had lost his parliamentary majority over internal issues. Thiers, who lacked a strong party base, could not rely on retaining a majority. The incentive to refrain from divisive internal measures and to seek to rally national feeling behind an assertive foreign policy was thus substantial. His bold support for Mehemet Ali's claims and his brinkmanship were readily explicable in these terms. Success held out the prospect of consolidating a parliamentary majority; 'weakness' would have endangered it. He had the most powerful incentives to pursue a high-risk foreign policy. However, this endangered the regime, the Orleanist monarchy. The arousing of radical nationalist passions might, as in July 1870, put the government under pressure to embark on war against its better judgment. Or frustrated nationalism might be turned to revolutionary ends. Louis-Philippe concluded that the lesser risk lay in pre-empting these dangers by obtaining Thiers' resignation; he judged correctly that the parliament and public would accept his calling off the confrontation.

In Britain, on the other hand, where the narrowness of its parliamentary majority created an impression of instability, the government survived despite its internal tensions. Indeed, Melbourne was able to use the slightness of its majority as an argument to deter ministerial resignations. In contrast to the unstable coalitions at the time of the Crimean crisis, there was sufficient party solidarity to sustain the Whig government against its Tory rival. Moreover, the breach with France was not an issue on which Palmerston's rivals could find support in the opposing party or in the public at large. Thus a number of factors tended to stabilise the government and enabled Palmerston to pursue a policy at odds with many of his colleagues.

Austria provides an example of a traditional monarchy with a well-entrenched Chancellor, Metternich, whose position was secure so long as he observed constraints insisted on by the powerful State Councillor, Kolowrat. The case of Russia is of greater interest. The regime, and the Tsar's position as final decision maker, were absolutely secure, but the positions of his ministers, and their policies, were subject to his satisfaction. Nesselrode had accepted office on the condition that Russia follow a basically 'European' policy, but this was endangered by the strength of the 'Russian nationalists' at the court. At the time of the crisis, however, the Tsar opted for Nesselrode's 'Concert' approach: his position as chief foreign policy adviser was not immediately threatened.

The Crimean crisis

In the next great Eastern crisis it was the British government which was most exposed to internal pressures, owing to the instability of parliamentary coalitions following the split in the Conservative Party occasioned by the dispute over the repeal of the Corn Laws. The 'Peelites', led by the Prime Minister, Lord Aberdeen, and deeply opposed to war with Russia, were an indispensable part of the governmental coalition, but were not in a position to prevail over their more numerous Whig partners, when the two best-known Whig parliamen-tarians, Palmerston and Russell, were prepared to use the threat of resignation, backed by a popular cause. Given the strength of anti-Russian sentiment, inflamed by the press, the government's incentive to opt for the more popular policy was evident. Of the two leading decision makers, Clarendon was directly swayed by these pressures, while Aberdeen engaged in rationalisation, clinging to the hope that he might be able to avert the impending war.

In the early days of the new Empire, Napoleon III was not directly exposed to internal pressures, but conflicting internal considerations appear to have influenced his calculations. One was the strong nation-wide sentiment for peace, but against this was the condemnation of Louis-Philippe for inactivity in foreign policy, and the need to estab-lish the prestige of the new Empire through successes abroad, prefer-ably through diplomacy but otherwise through a limited war which could serve to 'unfreeze' the 1815 status quo. The incentives to incur risks were not insignificant.

In the case of Austria, although Buol was a new minister, he was able to prevail in determining Austria's policy, not least because the mediating role which he favoured was in line with earlier precedent. In the case of Russia, the tension between Nesselrode and the nation-alists was in a new configuration: the situation at the outset, where unilateral initiatives had brought success to France and Austria, favoured the nationalists, who determined the style, if not the content, of the original Russian *démarche*, setting in motion a process of escala-tion which Nesselrode did not fully understand and was not able to bring under control.

The Franco-Prussian crisis

France in 1870 provides the example of greatest regime instability, even though this was expressed only in the government's dependence on the volatile mood of the parliament and the Paris crowds, not in overt moves against the regime. Napoleon had responded to pressures for internal change by introducing constitutional reforms – the 'Liberal Empire' – but the immediate pressures in the crisis came not from the liberals, but from the nationalist Right. The legitimation of the regime depended to a dangerous extent on maintaining the external prestige of the Empire. Foreign policy failures such as those since 1866 affected the standing not just of a particular government but of the Emperor, and thus of the regime. The prudence and restraint occasioned by Napoleon's awareness of the weakness of France's military capabilities were overcome by the powerful emotion of those convinced that the moment had come to re-establish French superiority over Prussia. Whereas the form of government had earlier insulated Napoleon from direct pressures, the parliamentary reforms and the nature of the issues in 1870 left him more exposed to pressure than perhaps any other government among those studied.

The Prussian monarchy, at the other extreme, was securely established, its prestige enhanced by recent victories, and the pressures of impatient German nationalists were readily restrained. It was Bismarck who sought to inflame nationalist sentiment and pressed for a stronger stand against France, not the general public. Bismarck's incentive to take risks was not due to internal pressures but rather to his ambition to unify Germany under Prussian leadership, a goal whose prospects seemed to be receding prior to the crisis. If events had turned out differently, and if Bismarck had acted on his inclination to resign, the King would have been embarrassed but the regime as such would not have been endangered.

The Russo-Japanese crisis

Attempts to explain Russia's dangerous brinkmanship in terms of internal pressures furnishing incentives for war are unconvincing. Even if the Minister for the Interior, conscious of the discontents which foreshadowed the 1905 revolution, may have seen the attractions of 'a short victorious war', neither the Tsar nor the ministers involved in the decisions wanted war, and they were not aware of the dangerous consequences of their failure to respond more positively to Japan's diplomatic initiatives. The tension between the 'Korean' lobby associated with Bezobrazov and the Tsar's ministers shows a certain parallel with the earlier rivalry between the Foreign Ministry 'Europeans' and the 'Russian nationalists', though the earlier rivalry raised far more fundamental issues. All the policy makers in 1903 were imperialists, divided mainly over timing and tactics. However, the significance of the 'Korean' group is often overstated: the shared misperception of Japan's capabilities and intentions was far more consequential.

In the case of Japan at this point in its history, internal pressures from nationalist groups and from younger officials served to strengthen the government's resolve to press its imperial claims, but were not so powerful as to compel it to act against its judgment. The potentially powerful voice of the senior military endorsed the claims but expressed caution as to the military prospects, while the circumspection of the elder statesmen commanded respect in its own right.

311

The government was in a position to balance the different pressures, not under severe constraint from any one quarter.

The Agadir crisis

Imperial Germany experienced serious internal conflict in the years before 1914. The coalition of the Right, which *inter alia* had supported the expansion of the Navy, broke up in 1909 over differences on taxation. The Social Democrats were gaining electoral support but not effective political power, since the Chancellor and other ministers were responsible to the monarch, not the parliament. Exaggerated fears of revolutionary socialism and an inclination to promote nationalist issues, either as a weapon against the socialists or as a way of integrating them into the national community, were widespread among German conservatives.[7]

Bethmann-Hollweg, appointed Chancellor in 1909, sought to reduce the internal cleavages and to restore the political unity of the Right and Centre. Having failed to promote these ends through cautious proposals for electoral reform, Bethmann turned to foreign policy. Foreign Secretary Kiderlen first sought an agreement with Britain, but was unable to obtain the support of the Secretary for the Navy, von Tirpitz. Thus in 1911 the government had an incentive to seek other opportunities. Germany did not, however, initiate the Agadir crisis, but responded to the French move on Fez in a way which was calculated to arouse German nationalist feeling. Kiderlen was fully aware of the domestic implications of this approach. His initiative was not a response to direct pressure, but rather an attempt to enhance his own, and the government's prestige and to influence domestic politics. While he failed to achieve his objectives, it is arguable that the crisis did indeed serve some of the purposes of the German Right. Insofar as nationalist feeling was aroused, and the following years saw an increased expectation and acceptance of war, a climate of opinion was generated in which attention was focused on external issues and a mood of national solidarity could be fostered.

France was not subject to the same acute political and constitutional tensions. The policy which precipitated the crisis was initiated by the political and colonial *bureaux* in the Foreign Ministry, and enjoyed the strong support of colonial interests. It illustrated the relative independence of officials and the weakness of the short-lived Monis government, but owed little to larger political pressures or considerations. Caillaux enjoyed broad support for his policy of avoiding war with Germany, but his bargaining was constrained by the strength of the colonial lobby and by diffuse national feeling provoked by Kiderlen's bullying tactics.

The Sudeten crisis

The British government enjoyed an extremely secure parliamentary majority, based on its electoral victory in 1935. Even so, it was sensitive to changes in public opinion, and Chamberlain needed to maintain the support of the majority of the Conservative Party against the alternative policy championed by Churchill and a small group of well-known dissidents. Chamberlain's general approach enjoyed broad support from the public, the great majority of the Conservative Party and most of those officials close to policy making – the military even more so than the Foreign Office. The response to Hitler's Godesberg demands provided a brief glimpse of the way in which pressures might build up for a less accommodating policy, but the crisis was resolved so rapidly that these tensions remained almost submerged. Chamberlain's dominance within the Cabinet and Party, and the secrecy of the decision making process, ensured that the process was insulated from direct political pressures.

Political tensions in France were much closer to the surface. The Popular Front, elected in 1936, had been unable to maintain its unity behind a reforming programme, and a succession of unstable governments had seen the centre of gravity shift from the Left to the centrist Radicals. Deep ideological divisions led to divisions over foreign policy, within as well as between the parties. The passivity of French policy not only reflected France's strategic dependence on British support, but also served the internal interests of the Daladier government. By refraining from overt initiatives, it avoided raising divisive issues. The differences within the Cabinet, which were much more acute than in London, were largely contained at that level. Some important decisions were taken by Daladier and Bonnet without reference to their colleagues. Thus, to a surprising extent, French policy also was largely insulated from public scrutiny and criticism. It was in accordance with the prevailing mood, as Daladier's welcome after Munich demonstrated, but his uncertainty whether he was to return in triumph or disgrace testifies to the relative isolation of the French 'political class', compared to their English counterparts.

In Germany, there was no public pressure to which Hitler had to respond, nor was he under serious pressure from within the National Socialist Party to act more rapidly than he himself might choose. The major internal constraint was the unwillingness of the military leadership to risk war with Britain and France in 1938. Thus the escalation of

313

the crisis after the Godesberg meeting created the potential for a sudden crisis for the regime, had the announcement of the Munich conference not averted the risk of war.

The Pearl Harbor crisis

Although there was little open political pressure on the Japanese government, it was subject to sustained pressure from the military, especially the Army. During the 1930s, this had sometimes been reinforced by nationalist violence against political moderates. In 1940–41 pressure mainly took the form of militant support within the officer corps for forward policies, at times against the better judgment of government ministers. During the final weeks of the crisis, when the government had to weigh the most serious risks to the nation's future under the leadership of a general widely regarded as a hard-liner, the pressures were considerably eased.

In the United States, on the other hand, public opinion set ill-defined but widely acknowledged limits to the Administration's freedom of choice. It could not take measures which appeared likely to lead to the initiation of war, but it had to avoid the appearance of appeasement. These constraints were especially compelling before the 1940 election, but remained effective after Roosevelt's re-election. In order to be able to continue his policy of assisting Britain, and to maintain national unity, Roosevelt needed to minimise public controversy and the risk that Congress might censure his policies. The embryonic China lobby ensured that the Administration would not waver in its support for the restoration of China's territorial integrity, in the interests of accommodation with Japan. There was little public support for such an accommodation; indeed a confrontation with Japan might not have been unpopular, provided the issue were such that Japan was perceived to be 'in the wrong'. But the constraint on this was not only the need to appear unprovocative, to respect the public aversion to the United States being drawn into a great war, but also the need to 'buy time' in order to improve America's state of preparedness. The cautious, temporising diplomacy of Cordell Hull in 1941 was a natural response to the conflicting pressures, internal even more than external, to which the Administration was subject.

The Berlin blockade

Although nothing was said of electoral considerations in the American deliberations on the response to the Berlin blockade, they reinforced the arguments for Truman's basic policy, to stand firm in Berlin but to avoid any action which might appear provocative or might enhance the perceived risk of war. Not to have stood firm would have risked damaging charges of appeasement; but any actual fighting would have been unpopular and would have risked heavy Western losses, with incalculable effects throughout Western Europe. It is likely that Truman's stand greatly improved his chances of re-election, generally seen as very low at the outset; electoral incentives may have reinforced the rationale for the chosen policy. There was little direct political pressure on Truman during the crucial early decisions which determined the main lines of American policy. The subsequent recourse to the United Nations had both an external and an internal rationale. It responded to the concerns of Britain, France and other UN members and, at a time when uncritical support for the UN was still widespread in the US, it averted a potential line of criticism and controversy. After Truman's re-election the attempt at UN mediation was quietly set aside in the interests of a unilateral solution.

In the case of Britain, whose Labour government enjoyed a secure parliamentary majority, a similar convergence of internal and external incentives led to support for the same policies. While aversion to war was extremely strong, the Soviet Union was not perceived as bellicose, and the perceived lessons of the 1930s weighed heavily against giving way to political intimidation. At the same time, Bevin sought to rule out moves which might be provocative, or might appear so. In France, on the other hand, there was governmental instability reflecting an absence of ideological consensus. There had been greater support for the earlier independent French policy of preventing a German revival, than there was for the new policy of working with the US and Britain to establish a state uniting the three Western zones of Germany. Likewise, the attempt to avoid commitment in the impending Cold War had been more popular than the new alignment with the West. France remained a reluctant partner in the Western response. There is insufficient information on Soviet decision making in this period to indicate to what extent, if at all, internal political pressure influenced Stalin's choices.

Berlin 1958–1962

The political climate at the time of the second Berlin crisis has come to be termed the Cold War consensus: the general public and the foreign policy elite were in agreement on the nature of the issues and the goals of policy. Most pronounced in the US, the consensus also underpinned

315

policy in Western Europe. The consensus set outer limits which were internalised by the decision makers, thus there was no sense of constraint by public opinion: on the one hand, the need to avoid 'softness' or 'appeasement', on the other hand, the need to be responsible, to avoid unnecessary provocation in the face of the dangers of the nuclear age. Remaining within this broad consensus, policy formulation was relatively insulated from political pressures. Within this overall consensus 'hard-line' and 'soft-line' US advisers differed over perceptions and strategies. The policy chosen by both the Eisenhower and Kennedy Administrations – the preference for negotiation over confrontation, but limiting the scope of the negotiations – reflected the weight of the internal arguments among policy makers. The issues did not arouse public feeling, nor were major lobbies involved.

The spectrum in Western Europe was somewhat wider. In Britain, where the climate of opinion was influenced by the Campaign for Nuclear Disarmament, Macmillan's efforts to open up communication with Moscow were popular, and wider possibilities for negotiation were canvassed in public discussion. In West Germany, on the other hand, mention of any negotiation regarding Berlin or the status of East Germany aroused acute concern, but the government felt constrained, both internally and externally, from precipitating an open breach with Washington. De Gaulle felt no such inhibition. The newly established Fifth Republic was under pressure on several issues, but the Berlin crisis was not one of them. Secure in the knowledge that the crucial decisions would be taken elsewhere, the government could demonstrate French independence from the Anglo-Saxons, winning popularity and contributing to the new Franco-German solidarity. Of the three Western European powers, the French government was the most insulated from public and sectional pressures, the West German the least, with Britain in between.

In the case of the Soviet Union, although there has been considerable discussion of internal differences and pressures – and it is clear that the Khrushchev period was one of relative governmental instability – the evidence does not permit any firm judgment on the extent to which the somewhat erratic Soviet policy was a consequence of competing internal pressures.

Governmental processes: the resolution of differences

We have seen that the failure or inability to resolve differences among decision makers has major consequences for crisis diplomacy: a government in this situation has no effective policy and cannot bargain. It is not surprising that the case studies suggest that governments place a high value on achieving policy coherence. In the three instances where this was lacking – Britain in 1853, Russia in 1903 and the US in 1940–41 – the consequences were, arguably, unnecessary wars or at least a failure to define relevant issues and options. (In the Russian case, unresolved differences were no more than a contributing reason for the weakness of the diplomacy.)

The present study does not closely examine the institutional structures within which decision makers seek to resolve their differences, but has sought to identify some distinctions among the political processes that are involved. What is striking about the instances of failure to resolve differences is the diversity of both the institutional and political contexts. The British Cabinet, the Tsarist autocracy and the American Presidency were normally capable of resolving differences among policy makers, but failed to do so on the occasions in question. The British government in 1853 was relatively unstable, as was the position of most of the Russian ministers in 1903, but there was no such governmental instability in the US in 1940–41. Its unstable parliamentary base may have rendered the British Cabinet unable to resolve its differences; in the Russian case the shared misperception made the differences appear less urgent; and the US example appears explicable in terms of Presidential choice and style. In other words, there appears to be no single political context associated with the failure to resolve differences: in each instance it was the product of a particular combination of circumstances – perceptions and personalities as well as political pressures in particular institutional settings.

Are the various processes for resolving differences more closely associated with specific institutional or political settings? Four such processes have been identified.

Intellectual processes
The Japanese leaders' decision in 1903 to put their differing views of Russian intentions to the test through negotiation is a solitary example of this approach. It is sometimes a secondary consideration, as in Cordell Hull's negotiations in 1941 or to a lesser extent Britain in 1938; Hitler's intentions, however, could not be subjected to a clear test in the Sudeten crisis. In a sense, policy assumptions are constantly being tested by events, but this is seldom the conscious aim of policy makers. Crises do not provide favourable conditions for devising tests: the need to meet deadlines and to maintain policy coherence tends to take precedence. Where there is substantial consensus on interests and objectives, as in the US in the Berlin crises, the intellectual analysis of

317

policy options may play a greater part in resolving differences, but the only substantial effort along these lines was under the Kennedy Administration. This approach is not likely to be followed unless there is governmental stability, and the cases suggest that its preconditions as a whole are not often fulfilled.

Internal bargain

Differences are occasionally resolved through an explicit internal bargain: that is to say, through the principal decision maker's accepting a constraint which meets the essential concerns of those with different views or priorities. Thus in the Eastern crisis Metternich accepted a veto by Kolowrat on policies which might incur a risk of war, and in 1938 Hitler reluctantly assured the generals that he would not risk a war with Britain and France over Czechoslovakia. Such a bargain requires governmental stability. To renege on the bargain, as the latter case suggests, risks extreme instability.

One view prevails

The most frequent pattern, in widely varying institutional settings, was the 'management' of differences by overriding dissenting views. Policy and strategy were determined by a decision maker committed to a particular view, sustained by the final decision making authority – monarch, cabinet or parliament – or by that final authority directly, for example, American Presidents in the Berlin crises. In most of these instances, policy coherence was preferred to any attempt to take account of the views of different schools of thought. In principle this might be compatible with governmental or political instability, but in practice the governments in question were relatively stable.

Changes of key decision maker

The replacement of a decision maker might indicate a change in policy, as in the case of the resignation of Thiers, but this was not necessarily the case. The appointment of Tojo in October 1941 did not, as expected, signal an immediate hardening of Japan's policy, but rather a more energetic examination of its options. The governmental crisis which brought Caillaux to the prime ministership in 1911 was of a relatively routine nature, not a consequence of the Agadir crisis. Changes in the relative influence of key decision makers sometimes had much greater impact on policy. The Kaiser intervened in policy making in 1911 in order to restrain Kiderlen; French policy in 1870 changed in the opposite direction, from the diplomatic compromise favoured by Napoleon to the confrontation which Gramont was able to precipitate.

The context was normally governmental instability, and sometimes more serious political turbulence; in the latter cases, however, a deeply divided government, having suddenly reversed its policy, was able to maintain the new policy with reasonable consistency.

None of the patterns for resolving differences, then, appears to be associated with particular institutional structures. The first three are associated with relative governmental stability, the fourth with governmental, and indeed political instability. But what can be said more generally on the effects of instability?

Internal conflict and unstable government

How does acute internal political instability affect crisis diplomacy? It is plausible to suppose that it is disruptive, but there has been little systematic study of the question. It is sometimes suggested that governments create international crises in order to divert attention from internal difficulties, but the case studies offer little support for so simple a generalisation. It has a certain plausibility in relation to Thiers in 1840 and Kiderlen in 1911, but even here it offers a misleading simplification of the pressures of internal politics, not a sound starting-point for an explanation.

Lebow offers a convincing account of the way in which internal conflict can provide a plausible explanation for crisis mismanagement. He presents two case studies in which acute political pressures endangered the position of key decision makers – Acheson in 1950 and Nehru in 1962.[8] Their insecurity was conducive to uncharacteristic cognitive rigidity, faulty judgment and risk-taking. Acheson, the focus of Republican condemnation of the Truman Administration's foreign policy, was blind to the mounting evidence of China's intervention in the Korean war and refused to countenance any modification of the policy of advancing to the Yalu. Nehru, under pressure from adversaries within the Congress Party, took up the popular nationalist cause of insisting on India's definition of the Sino-Indian frontier and ensured a foreign policy debacle by stationing outposts in the disputed areas, confident that their presence would deter the Chinese. Lebow makes a strong case that it was the exposure of each government to acute internal pressure which led it to make an ill-judged commitment to a course of action whose risks it underestimated: once committed, it steadfastly refused to acknowledge the risks.

The present case studies do not offer close parallels to such an extreme kind of miscalculation and deterrence failure, but they provide an opportunity to examine the effects of internal political conflict and governmental instability of varying acuteness. In what ways do they impair crisis decision making and diplomacy, and to what extent do they explain the major instances of misperception and mismanagement observed in the case studies?

The most striking finding is the extent to which the 'eruption' of internal political conflict affected the course of events and the outcome of the earlier crises – all of those before 1914 except the Russo-Japanese – in each case rendering it more acute, by way of escalation in 1840 (France), 1853 (Britain) and 1870 (France) and by providing incentives for provocation in 1911 (Germany). In each of these instances the government in question came to act with a parochial assertiveness which went far beyond the dictates of a sober *raison d'état*. It would be misleading, however, to depict these eruptions as early instances of 'mass politics' or the influence of public opinion: in each instance popular sentiments were aroused and manipulated by the demagoguery of a section of a narrow ruling elite.

Paradoxically, the pressures of domestic politics were 'managed' more effectively by twentieth-century democratic governmental institutions. France in the 1930s and 1940s was divided by internal cleavages as serious as those of the nineteenth century, yet French governments were able to pursue a relatively coherent foreign policy in 1938 and 1948–49. Like the British and American governments in this period, they were aware of the 'constraint' of public opinion and its electoral implications – the potential for enhanced prestige or severe embarrassment – but there was not the direct 'public' pressure of the earlier cases.

The term 'governmental instability' covers a range of possibilities. It is used here to refer to situations in which the existence of a government or a regime, or the continuation in office of a key decision maker, are endangered. Instability may be chronic, as in France under the Third and Fourth Republics, where marginal changes in parliamentary coalitions brought about frequent changes of government, or it may be acute, where a regime is under threat or a change of government is perceived to have momentous consequences, as in France in 1840 and 1870. In Germany in 1911 the conservative dominance, unchallenged since 1870, was felt to be under threat, and in Britain in 1853, unstable parliamentary majorities exposed Cabinets to unfamiliar political pressures.

Table 14.1 sets out the instances in which governments are deemed to have been unstable. Instability found different expression in different institutional contexts. In Britain (1853) and in France throughout,

Table 14.1. *Governmental instability*

Government	Degree of Instability	Consequences
France, 1840	acute	misperception, risk-taking
Britain, 1853	acute	misperception, mismanagement
Russia, 1853	latent	not clear
Austria, 1853	latent	—
France, 1870	acute	misperception, risk-taking
Russia, 1903	latent	—
France, 1911	chronic	minor
Germany, 1911	acute	miscalculation, mismanagement
France, 1938	chronic, latent	minor
Japan, 1941	chronic	minor
France, 1948	chronic	minor

governments were uncertain of retaining a parliamentary majority. In autocratic systems such as those of Austria and Russia, the principal foreign policy adviser held office at the pleasure of the emperor, and his views might be arbitrarily set aside in favour of those of rival officials, as appeared possible in 1853. Governmental instability in pre-World War Two Japan reflected shifts of power within the ruling oligarchy and pressures from the armed services.

The effects of both latent and chronic instability were relatively minor. In France in 1911, for example, the change of government brought to power a leader, Caillaux, who had his own reasons for initiating a more restrained policy than that which had provoked the crisis, but this was probably unavoidable in any case. In 1938 and in 1948–49 the potential for internal controversy was far greater, but was contained. It remains possible that latent or chronic instability may have serious consequences for crisis diplomacy, but the examples show that it need not.

The more interesting instances, those of acute instability, are precisely those noted above in which the escalation of a crisis can be traced directly to the pressures of internal politics in one of the actors. Germany in 1911 is closest to the case of a government seeking an external recourse to surmount internal difficulties even though, as noted earlier, external confrontation was not its first recourse. Electoral support for the divided conservative coalition was faltering, creating a sense of an incipient crisis for the regime, and nationalist spokesmen were fomenting a mood of both thwarted ambition and heightened alarm. The incentive to seek a striking diplomatic success was evident. The political setting in France in 1840 also created such incentives, but Thiers, unlike Kiderlen, inherited the crisis from his predecessor. He

321

needed to attract popular support outside the parliament to counter the conservative inclinations of the monarch and the majority of deputies, yet to avoid alienating them through domestic radicalism. The attractions of an assertive foreign policy were evident, yet before long this too came to endanger the regime.

In the other two cases the pressures for a confrontationist foreign policy were more direct. Britain in 1853 was not undergoing acute internal conflict but the government's precarious parliamentary base exposed it to severe pressures against its unpopular foreign policy. In yielding to these it showed some of the cognitive rigidities and defensive avoidance observed in Lebow's cases, except that, far from denying the risk of war, Clarendon arrived prematurely at the perception of its inevitability. In France in 1870 the new constitution of the 'Liberal Empire', a concession to popular pressures, was still on trial, and the Prime Minister, Ollivier, enjoyed neither a secure parliamentary majority nor the Emperor's confidence. Although Napoleon was aware of France's relative military weakness, the Bonapartist myth which legitimised the regime fostered the nationalist mood, which was exploited by the more reckless, or less clear-sighted Gramont to commit the government to a confrontationist stand which rendered the war inevitable. Nationalist frustrations and the sudden upsurge of emotion overwhelmed Napoleon's better judgment. Cognitive rigidity may have contributed to Gramont's actions, but not to Napoleon's.

In the two French examples, political turbulence provided the background against which weak governments hastily adopted ill-judged, risky policies. The influence of political pressures and emotions was evident; that of cognitive rigidity was only marginal. In Britain in 1853, the case closest to Lebow's, the pressure was sustained over a much longer period, its effects incremental, the cognitive distortions gradual. In Germany in 1911 political emotions were latent. Kiderlen was able to devise a strategy at leisure, well calculated to win domestic applause but insensitive to political reactions in Britain and France. The cognitive distortion was not so much 'rigidity' but the kind of ethnocentrism which diplomats are, supposedly, trained to avoid.

Acute internal political conflict is not, of course, the only source of crisis mismanagement. Pervasive misperceptions or unresolved differences among decision makers may be found in stable political settings. But internal political instability provides conditions in which the likelihood of crisis mismanagement is greatly increased. The views of politicians with a greater awareness of the international milieu are likely to be subordinated to the views of those more willing to appeal to popular symbols, or to the immediate preoccupations of leaders struggling to maintain their hold on office. Acute political conflict within any one of the main actors provides perhaps the most dangerous setting for international crises.

Preconditions for effective crisis diplomacy

Thus far the discussion has focused on negative influences on crisis diplomacy. Previous studies have paid little attention to positive influences: political preconditions for 'good' crisis diplomacy. Lebow once again is an exception, and his discussion provides a valuable starting-point. As he notes, much of the discussion of crisis management has sought to promote more open decision making environments – that is, procedures for ensuring that alternative premises and options are taken into account.[9] Although this is a central tenet of contemporary thinking, we have seen that it was seldom accepted by decision makers in the case studies, and thus cannot be regarded as a general precondition for effective crisis diplomacy. Lebow, who also notes the aversion of most leaders to open and critical discussion, argues that 'the really important preconditions for good decision making are an expression of underlying conditions', in particular '(1) legitimate central authority, (2) a consensus within the policy-making elite with respect to fundamental political values and procedures, and (3) freedom from domestic political pressures that compel leaders to pursue a particular foreign policy'.[10]

The rationale for each of these is fairly evident. If a government does not enjoy generally accepted legitimacy its hold on power, and thus its capacity to sustain a coherent policy, is likely to be weak. If the political elite is deeply divided over goals and norms, differences of the kind which can paralyse effective policy making are likely. And if policy is dominated by internal political imperatives, a certain blindness to external consequences is to be expected.

But are these true preconditions? Are they *necessary* for effective crisis diplomacy? The legitimacy of the central authority in France was weak in 1840, yet nonetheless it was able to assert its control, and arguably also in 1938. A consensus among policy makers over fundamental values was notably lacking in Russia in 1840, yet decision making nonetheless remained coherent and controlled; and in France in 1938 Daladier and Bonnet were able to pursue a coherent course of action which was accepted by a deeply divided Cabinet whose divisions mirrored those in the political elite as a whole. Exceptions to Lebow's third precondition are more difficult to envisage, and Britain in the Crimean crisis offers a further example in support of it. The present cases suggest, however, that 'adequate' decision making is possible under a wider range of conditions than Lebow postulates.

If clear preconditions are difficult to establish, it may be possible to distinguish conditions which are conducive to adequate crisis diplomacy from those conducive to mismanagement. The case studies suggest that adequate decision making is possible in a wide variety of institutional and political contexts, but offer substantial support for the first and third of Lebow's preconditions. That is to say, where the legitimacy or general acceptance of a government is lacking, or where public pressures seriously restrict a government's freedom of manoeuvre, 'rational' policy choices (rational in relation to a government's goals and assessments) become difficult.

In the present study France (in 1840, 1870 and 1938) provides the main examples of a regime whose legitimacy was widely questioned, Germany in 1911 a more marginal case, where the legitimacy of the norms which ensured conservative rule was under challenge. The examples confirm that concerns over legitimacy place governments at a serious disadvantage in major crises, even though they may sometimes overcome them. Daladier and Bonnet were able to take advantage of practices which weak governments had adopted in self-defence, and were able to turn France's external weakness to their advantage in internal politics. The other three examples illustrate what is probably the more typical case – the pressure to incur ill-considered risks in the hope of resolving the legitimacy problems through a dramatic stroke of policy – and they also demonstrate its dangers. One led to an ill-judged war; in the other two the monarchs were able to call off the confrontation, but only at some cost to their personal prestige.

Concerns over legitimacy, then, place crisis diplomacy under special stress. But it is arguable that acute political instability, which may, but need not be associated with weak legitimacy, offers a clearer indication of the conditions which render crises unmanageable. A regime under long-term challenge but enjoying a phase of short-term stability is better able to withstand the stresses of crises than a legitimate regime during a phase of instability. The present cases suggest that the first precondition is better defined as political stability than as legitimacy.

Britain in 1853 and France in 1870 provide the only present examples of the absence of Lebow's third precondition – freedom from 'compelling' internal pressures to pursue a particular line of policy. These two governments were unstable, but Lebow's examples show that even a stable government can be subject to such compulsions if a key leader is insecure. Such pressures are many and varied. They include not only the manipulation of popular prejudices, stereotypes and ethnocentric attitudes, most striking in 1853, 1870 and the Agadir crisis but present in most of the cases, but also the pressure of parochial and sectional interests, a prominent feature of Agadir and also, for example, in the influence of the Japanese armed services in 1940–41.

Parochial and ethnocentric attitudes of this kind are most detrimental to crisis diplomacy when they are shared by the decision makers themselves. This points to a further precondition, namely, that the decision makers are not dominated by such attitudes. Their perspectives are inevitably national, but should be qualified by broad, non-stereotyped perceptions of the external environment, qualities of mind akin to those noted by Richard Smoke as enabling policy makers to maintain control over the pressures to escalate an acute conflict. Like Lebow's preconditions, these qualities of mind are not within the control of existing governments, but they are partly a function of political institutions. That is to say, political traditions, including procedures for recruiting and socialising leaders, will affect the probability that foreign policy decision makers will bring this kind of broad perspective to their task.

Lebow's other prerequisite, consensus within the policy making elite with respect to fundamental values and procedures, is more problematic. Except at the extremes, it is difficult to establish whether or not such a consensus obtains. However, it would not appear to be a prerequisite for effective crisis diplomacy. We have seen that policy may remain coherent even where there is a notable lack of consensus on basic values, and there are instances of broad consensus on basic values where differences over the perception of specific issues and over strategy had serious effects on crisis diplomacy, most obviously in Britain in 1853 but also in the US in 1940–41, and potentially in the Berlin crises.

Consensus on fundamentals, then, is difficult to specify and of uncertain relevance to good crisis decision making. What is of greater relevance is a means for resolving differences among decision makers over immediate issues – issues which may not be 'fundamental' in the long term but may be crucial for timely decisions in a crisis. We have seen that such differences were most often resolved by neglecting or overruling dissenting views. Policy coherence does not, of course, equate with 'good' decision making, and the capacity to jettison an unsuccessful policy (which may create an impression of incoherence) may be a criterion for good crisis diplomacy. But the case studies support the view that policy coherence is necessary for effective bargaining or for any other strategy, and thus the capacity to achieve that coherence, by whatever means, is indeed a prerequisite for good crisis diplomacy.

Other factors conducive to such diplomacy will be related to specific institutional structures, but the four which have been identified here are of a more general character: first, a reasonable degree of internal political stability; second, reasonable freedom of manoeuvre in relation to domestic political pressures on foreign policy; third, a broad, non-parochial perspective on the part of decision makers, which may be fostered by appropriate traditions and socialisation procedures; and fourth, a means for resolving differences among decision makers. The absence of any of these preconditions in the case of any of the key actors greatly complicates the task of crisis diplomacy for all.

326

15 THE OUTCOME AND THE RISK OF WAR

How is the outcome of crises determined? In particular, what can now be said on the relative importance of crisis decisions and diplomacy, on the one hand, and 'structural' and other long-term determinants, on the other? Many historians place the emphasis on the long-term, 'under-lying' causes. Crises, it is suggested, resemble the tip of an iceberg: the visible tip is moved by the submerged bulk of the iceberg, responding to ocean currents invisible to the observer. Such images draw attention to the need for a thorough understanding of the background of any crisis, but the preceding analysis has shown that outcomes are not predetermined by underlying causes. A crisis is not, like the tip of an iceberg, an inert mass whose movements depend entirely on forces external to it. The question cannot be resolved so simply.

Contemporary historical scholarship amounts to an ongoing debate rather than a preferred answer to the question. This is well brought out in James Joll's reappraisal of the explanations of World War One. Some historians, he notes, favour the Marxist style of explanation in terms of 'a comparatively small number of basic factors', but this leaves a gap between the general analysis and the specific decisions taken in 1914. Another, predominantly English school goes so far as to reject attempts at long-term explanation, whether social, economic or intellectual. Joll sets aside both extreme positions in the debate:

> But even without necessarily accepting the familiar metaphors which suggest that history is a river or a gale or a railway or a runaway horse ... we nevertheless feel the need to place our explanations for the outbreak of war in 1914 within a wider perspective. Each of the crucial decisions was taken within a specific institutional and social framework. They were conditioned by a wide range of assumptions about the behaviour of individuals and governments and by values resulting from long cultural and political traditions as well as from the social and economic structure of each country.[1]

It may be necessary, he suggests, to accept a 'two-tier' view of history. In terms of the broad lines of social, economic and environmental development, a world war is only a minor episode. 'On the other hand, there is the world in which the decisions of individual leaders ... can affect the lives and happiness of millions and change the course of history for decades.'[2] The study of crises, clearly, falls within this second 'tier', but also requires an understanding of its relationship to the first.

Purely structural explanations tend to divert attention from crises. If the contradictions within and between the imperialist powers rendered war inevitable in the earlier twentieth century, the important object of study is those contradictions, not the crises which preceded the two world wars. Marxist scholars seek to uncover the class interests or the ideology which lie behind foreign policy, but are much less interested in the question why the representatives of the ruling classes choose the particular policies which they do, still less how such policies interact in particular crises. Yet the interest of the ruling class is as problematic a concept as the national interest, and the gap between that presumed interest and the actual decisions which lead to crisis or war is outside the purview of the structuralist. A rigorous theorist such as Waltz acknowledges that structural explanations can account for recurrent patterns, such as the incidence of war in the international system, but cannot explain any particular war.[3] But many structuralists resist this implication of their mode of theorising.

Similarly, a certain type of 'realist' thinking sees crises as unimportant because decision makers are assumed to act, in the last analysis, in accordance with 'compelling' national interests. If the conflicts between national interests are so serious as to be beyond compromise, there will be war; if they are not so serious as to require war, there will be a diplomatic solution. Crises, as it were, register or demonstrate the seriousness of the underlying conflicts, and may thus be regarded as 'moments of truth' which reveal the 'reality' normally concealed by half-truths and illusions. The events of the crisis do not play an important part in determining its outcome, but, properly understood, reveal the true determinants. The case studies, however, have shown that this version of realism is fundamentally flawed. Some decision makers may believe that their perception of the national interest is compelling, that they are responding to necessities, not choosing, but it is these beliefs which are illusory. In principle, there can always be different perceptions of the 'national interest' in any given setting, and in practice there are usually differences over priorities or over which course of action will best promote the national interest.

Snyder and Diesing's version of 'realism' takes these considerations into account. For them, the crucial determinants of crisis outcomes are interests and capabilities, as perceived by the decision makers who control policy: they make no claim that these reflect a wider consensus or compelling national interest. 'Comparative interests and comparative military strength, as the parties perceive them, are the basic determinants of relative bargaining power and crisis outcomes.'[4] These determine the parties' basic preference rankings, in particular their willingness to go to war. An important qualification, which limits the scope of these generalisations, is that they refer to the parties' preferences in the final phase, when a crisis is ripe for resolution. Snyder and Diesing acknowledge that preference rankings may change during a crisis, either because of changes in perception – of what is at stake, or of the adversary's intentions, or of relative capabilities, for example – or because of a change of decision makers.[5] Thus the generalisation that crisis outcomes depend on relative perceived·interests and capabilities becomes virtually a tautology: the outcome depends on the preferences of those controlling policy immediately before the outcome. But no such inferences can be drawn from preferences at the outset of a crisis.

Thus while Snyder and Diesing avoid the problems of the 'reification' of the national interest by focusing on the perceptions of decision makers, their analysis is narrower in scope than their formulations suggest. They do not claim to offer a theoretical explanation of initial preferences, and their discussion of changes of preference during a crisis is mainly concerned with the correction of misperception during the crisis bargaining. If explanations are sought for initial preferences, however, it becomes necessary to examine long-term as well as immediate influences, a task which raises the problems of historical explanation noted at the outset. Game theory offers a new angle of approach, but no new key to resolve these problems: it isolates preferences as crucial variables, but they are 'given', not explained.

The present study seeks to provide a framework which can bring out the interrelationships among long-term and short-term determinants, without extending indefinitely Joll's 'ever-widening circles of causation'. Long-term changes are seen as bringing about a state of affairs in which a crisis is likely. They may also bias the situation in favour of one outcome rather than another but, it will be argued, they never fully determine the outcome. This depends on choices during the crisis itself, which in turn depend on a multitude of variables over and above those of a structural kind. As Marx expressed it: 'Men make their own history, but they do not make it just as they please. They do not make it under circumstances chosen by themselves, but under circumstances directly encountered, given, and transmitted from the past.'[6]

The relevant findings of the preceding chapters may be summed up as follows:

1   The overall state of the international system influences the probability of great-power crises and of their peaceful resolution. It also affects their general character. For example, those in the Concert period normally took the form of collective diplomacy; those between 1856 and 1941 were quite often resolved bilaterally and depended mainly on the strategic calculations of the powers individually, with alliances playing a major role in the years 1900–1914; and those after 1945 were dominated by the shadow of nuclear war, requiring caution and prudence of a new order compared with earlier periods. The probability of the peaceful resolution of crises varies according to the relative stability of the arena, the extent to which there is a common perception of the balance of power and the degree of consensus on basic norms. But these long-term factors affect the probability of war over a certain period: the outcome of a particular crisis depends mainly on variables at other levels.

2   As a first approximation, the objectives to which governments are committed play a major part in shaping the overall development of crises, and the seriousness of a crisis depends on the extent to which the adversaries' objectives are incompatible. In an important minority of cases, including three of those which ended in war, the crises could not be understood in this way, because at least one of the parties was unable to define its objectives. In the normal case, however, where objectives can be defined, more often than not, they are found to be derived from a conception of the 'national interest', based on long-term values and beliefs. However, there are always alternative views of the national interest: in modern societies there are often differences even at the level of basic values, and there are always differences over the complex perceptions and judgments which underlie any conception of the national interest, even though some political systems may prevent their open articulation. Thus, the particular values and conceptions of those in control of policy are of crucial importance for crises and their outcomes. Explanations of 'who rules', and of the rulers' conceptions, have to be sought in the internal politics and historical experience of the actors, and normally combine long-term and short-term considerations.

3   Differences of perception, even among relatively like-minded decision makers, are one of the major sources – often *the* major source – of different conceptions of the national interest. Some of these, such as

perceptions of an adversary's capabilities or intentions, may derive mainly from images built up over a long period; others, such as perceptions of the consequences of one's own actions, or of new events, or of the risk of war, result more from immediate impressions. The capacity to resolve such differences also depends on a combination of long- and short-term factors: on political culture and institutions, and the extent of basic cleavage or consensus, on the one hand, but also on personalities and the configuration of political coalitions and rivalries, on the other. Policy coherence is valued highly, which may be a sound general preference in view of the costs, manifest in several of the cases, of failing to achieve it. The reasons for these failures, once again, must be sought in internal politics.

4   The most important forms of misperception are the under- or overestimate of adversary capabilities, the misreading of intentions and the failure to perceive the effects of one's own actions on the perceptions and reactions of others. While in no sense the primary cause of international conflict or war, misperception is quite frequently an important factor in determining the course and outcome of crises. It enters into causal relationships in complex ways, sometimes presenting difficult problems of interpretation. Its significance depends on contextual factors which vary greatly between crises, but two broad categories may be distinguished: misperceptions which constitute major policy assumptions, and remain uncorrected during much or the whole of a crisis; and misperceptions at a crucial moment, when major decisions are taken. The former points toward relatively long-term influences, the latter to a mixture of long-term (images) and short-term (adventitious circumstances). The cases lend support to both cognitive and motivational explanations of misperception, suggesting that both are necessary, but they also show that consequential misperceptions sometimes result from nothing more than the incompleteness of the evidence available at the time when decisions had to be made.

5   The greater part of international behaviour in crises can be interpreted as attempted bargaining, which constitutes the major form of interaction. Sometimes, however, actors follow unilateral strategies in preference to bargaining, and in other crises bargaining is negated because at least one actor fails to correct crucial misperceptions or is unable to resolve fundamental differences among policy makers, and thus lacks a minimally coherent strategy. None of the cases exemplified a wholly different model of crisis interaction, the hostility spiral, though the potential for uncontrolled escalation leading to such a

331

spiral was often present. Game theory models can illuminate bargaining in crises and can explain the expected outcome in terms of different game types, but these explanations hold only when bargaining, or in some cases unilateral strategies, constitute the major form of interaction, not when it is impeded through gross misperception or internal divisions. Ideal types which incorporate these variables can offer sounder explanations than game theory models alone. In the sample of cases studied, none of those which ended in war were pure bargaining crises.

6   Internal politics provides the key to many otherwise puzzling aspects of crises. Historical 'givens', internal political structures and processes, but also contingencies of personality and circumstance, determine who rules, whose goals will prevail, whether governments are stable, and sometimes whether policy coherence is attainable. The case studies confirm that where governments are unstable and vulnerable to internal political pressures, the danger of uncontrolled escalation is high: such eruptions of internal politics occurred in several of the nineteenth-century cases, whereas twentieth-century governments were more able to 'manage' opinion. Political conditions conducive to effective crisis diplomacy include, as well as relative political stability and relative freedom from acute pressures, non-parochial perspectives on the part of decision makers and effective procedures for resolving policy differences. The absence of any of these reduces the chances of controlling crises. Once again, while some of these are essentially long-term 'givens' in a crisis, others may be contingent or short-term.

The course of events and the outcome of crises, then, result from the interplay of long-term and short-term, structural and contingent factors. Metaphors such as the iceberg, river, gale or railway are misleading in their deterministic overtones. The runaway horse is a better image insofar as it suggests that the final destination may owe a good deal to short-term contingencies. There can be no complete separation between these sets of influences. Some contingent factors, such as the propensities and beliefs of individual decision makers, may be of long duration and may be explicable as responses to structural conditions – but so may be the contrasting responses of other decision makers. In political systems dominated by single leaders, who may reshape political, economic or social 'structures', it becomes difficult to distinguish between the structural and the contingent. Nonetheless, it is not impossible to form judgments concerning the relative importance of long- and short-term determinants of crisis outcomes in particular cases. An account of the situation at the outset can provide the basis for a judgment on the likely outcome – war or peaceful resolution. Such judgments can be no more than approximations, but they are needed for assessing the significance of crisis decisions and actions.

Ideal types may readily be constructed for extreme situations. If two rival powers, neither of which enjoys military superiority, are each determined to gain control of certain territory, a crisis over that issue is likely to lead to war. If they are resolved to avoid war, and prefer the territory to remain a buffer zone, it is likely that the conflict will be settled through diplomacy. It is not certain, however: one or both might perceive the other's moves as threatening; misfortune or mismanagement could lead to unintended war. In such a case, crisis decisions would be of crucial significance.

Actual conflicts are far more complex, but the same basic approach can be followed. A review of the situation at the outset of a crisis, with the emphasis on long-term structural factors and on the larger reasons for the conflict, permits a judgment on the relative likelihood that the conflict can be resolved without war (or vice versa). In cases where the actual outcome diverges from the expected one, or where the initial situation permits no firm judgment, the outcome will depend to an important extent on the events of the crisis: crisis diplomacy will matter. Even in cases where the expected outcome is realised, it does not follow that crisis diplomacy is unimportant: opportunities can be missed, or seized, and perhaps even created; misjudgments can be compounded, or retrieved, and so forth. Nonetheless, the broad distinction offers a basis for judging whether or not crisis diplomacy 'made a difference'.[7]

The most striking general finding is that in more than half of the cases the crisis proved more acute than was to be expected in the light of the initial situation – more dangerous and difficult to resolve, or even leading to war where a peaceful outcome might reasonably have been expected – an unnecessary war as defined earlier. Before discussing this general finding, however, the cases will be reviewed from this point of view, in order to make explicit the judgments on which it rests.

The cases reviewed

The cases will be examined in four groups: (1) those in which the initial situation pointed to the likelihood of war, and war indeed eventuated – the crises of 1870 and 1941; (2) those in which the initial situation pointed rather to a diplomatic solution or left the outcome entirely open, yet the outcome was war – 1853–54 and 1903–04; (3) those in which a diplomatic solution appeared likely, but where the crisis proved more dangerous than the initial situation would have suggested – 1839–41, 1911 and 1938; (4) those in which a diplomatic solution appeared the probable outcome, and in which it was achieved, in one case more easily than initially appeared likely – 1948–49 and 1958–62.

War initially probable: war the outcome

The Franco-Prussian crisis

Following Italian unification, the most prominent structural change in train was the movement of the German states towards national unity. Prussia's defeat of Austria had transformed the balance in central Europe, and a united Germany appeared likely to replace France as the strongest continental power, owing to the rate of growth of its population and industrial production. The two flanking powers, Britain and Russia, however, were not alarmed by these structural changes, perceiving advantage in the strengthening of Prussia against the potential trouble-maker, France; and the norms of the Concert, which would have required the powers to meet in conference, were in eclipse.

The Prussian government, and in particular its Chancellor, Bismarck, were in a strong position after the victories over Austria. The government of the Second Empire, on the other hand, was not. Napoleon had been compelled to agree to the strengthening of parliament, political divisions were more open, and his prestige had been reduced by reverses in foreign policy. He, and his regime, were under pressure to achieve a striking success. Nationalism was strongly promoted in both countries, pressed by the unification movement in Germany, and engendered by the nature of the regime in France. The French, nonetheless, were divided over the prospect of German unity: on the one hand, Napoleon professed to accept it in accordance with his doctrine of the remaking of Europe along national lines, while on the other hand a deep-seated French instinct and tradition saw it as a vital need for France that Germany remain divided. These underlying conditions did not necessitate a war but ensured that any Franco-Prussian crisis would be extremely dangerous.

In the crisis itself, both governments were divided between those more, and those less ready to risk war. Bismarck chose to provoke a crisis and was prepared to take a 'hard' line in brinkmanship. The unexpectedly independent role of the King of Prussia, however, permitted a transient diplomatic compromise. In France, compromise following a short phase of brinkmanship was in accordance with Napoleon's preferences: aware of French military vulnerability, he sought to avoid war. The compromise, however, though perceived in the rest of Europe as a French triumph and a severe embarrassment to Bismarck, was not sufficient to satisfy the Paris crowds, manipulated by those who perceived a golden opportunity for a preventive war to exorcise the nightmare of a united Germany. The general conditions noted earlier rendered such an outcome probable. If Napoleon had been fully in control, the outcome might have been different – but that phase of the Second Empire had passed.

The US–Japan crisis
In 1941 the international system was being reshaped by war. Germany, having violently overthrown the unstable European 'balance', began its rapid advance into the Soviet Union; Britain was under extreme pressure; the US still at an early stage of mobilisation. Japan, controlling much of China and threatening Southeast Asia, enjoyed a precarious dominance over its region – precarious in that it lacked secure access to the crucial resources needed to sustain its position. Japan's inability to subdue Chinese resistance, and the US commitment to assist China, provided a direct source of Japanese–American antagonism. The two powers espoused diametrically opposed normative principles for reshaping the international order in East Asia, the US insisting on the liberal principles of free trade, open access and self-determination, Japan looking to regional hegemony. But whereas after 1945 this kind of conflict over long-term goals led to protracted Cold War, Japan's inability to complete the conquest of China and above all its lack of control over vital resources rendered the situation in 1941 far more explosive.

Internally, Japanese politics was increasingly dominated by those favouring war, but consciousness of the risks of war with the US led the government to persevere with negotiation. The American Administration's freedom of manoeuvre, however, was restricted by its perception of the constraints imposed by public opinion. It could not adopt a clear deterrent stance, because this would have entailed a threat to go to war in a specified contingency; but any compromise of the principle of self-determination or of assistance to China would be condemned as appeasement.

The 'shape' of the crisis began to be defined when Britain and the Netherlands declined to guarantee Japanese access to the resources of their Southeast Asian dependencies. Conceivably, a threat to cut off oil supplies if Japan advanced into southern Indo-China might have deterred that crucial move, opening the way to a different outcome. The imposition of an oil embargo *after* Japan's move south greatly narrowed the options but still left open the temporary *modus vivendi* sought by Japan – it would refrain from further advances and the US would restore oil supplies. This would have met some immediate American concerns, but was not seriously entertained by Hull, fearing a negative public reaction.

Thus long-term developments brought about a protracted crisis and rendered its resolution extremely difficult. With hindsight it is possible to discern opportunities for deterrence or for postponing the diplomatic breakdown, but the cautious incrementalism which characterised American diplomacy in response to divided counsels and internal constraints rendered it unlikely that such options would be pursued. Had the two been able to reach a *modus vivendi* in 1941, however, it might have proved more durable than expected. The declining prospect of a German victory would have increased the risk in Japan's attacking the US, and World War Two might have followed a very different course.

War not initially probable: war the outcome

The Crimean crisis

After four decades, the structural continuity of the international system established in 1815 was striking. Whatever his aspirations, Napoleon III was not in a position to challenge that settlement. The five-power balance had survived the revolutions of 1848. Britain's increasing industrial pre-eminence did not translate into hegemony in Europe, and indeed the Crimean war was to expose the limitations of British power in the European context. The diplomacy of the crisis was carried on in accordance with the established procedures of the European Concert, whose norms still enjoyed general acceptance. As in the preceding Eastern crisis, the imperial interests of four of the powers generated a Prisoner's Dilemma conflict over Constantinople. All preferred the status quo, the buffer created by Ottoman control – which the Tsar now perceived as about to collapse – but they were willing to go to war to prevent its falling under the control of a rival power, though not to achieve supremacy. Their preferences, then, were conducive to compromise.[8] If long-term structural influences and the interests of the powers were to determine the outcome, a diplomatic solution like that of 1840–41 and the other Eastern crises could reasonably have been expected.

The principal reason for the outcome, it was argued, was the state of internal politics in one of the key actors, Britain. The conjunction of three circumstances – the instability of parliamentary majorities, the irreconcilability of differences within the government and the strength of public feeling against Russia – provided a setting in which the pressures to escalate the conflict increasingly outweighed the incentives to bargain towards a compromise. The inability of the British decision makers to resolve their differences left the government dangerously exposed to pressure from an ill-informed public aroused by simplistic images of Russian aggression.

Crisis diplomacy confronted a number of other difficulties. The early unilateral initiatives by France and Russia were unsettling. None of the decision makers had as clear a strategy as Palmerston or Nesselrode in the earlier Eastern crisis. Even Napoleon's brinkmanship was more opportunistic, less directed to any specific goal, than that of Thiers in 1840. The diplomats in Vienna were insensitive to Ottoman concerns. Against this setting, none of the diplomatic initiatives achieved its objective. On the other hand, inadvertent diplomatic 'signals' and military moves aimed at deterrence had the unintended consequence of 'escalating' the crisis towards war. The change in the British preference structure from Prisoner's Dilemma to Bully was not a conscious re-ranking of values, but a consequence of hardening misperception: the public's image of Russian aggression, and Clarendon's perception of the inevitability of war, which became self-fulfilling. An 'unnecessary war' was generated by the dynamics of crisis decisions, perceptions and interactions.

The Russo-Japanese crisis
The crisis was a direct consequence of structural changes in the Far East, in particular the rapid emergence of Japan as a modern power at a time when the European powers were seeking to establish their spheres of influence in China. The Anglo-Japanese alliance placed Japan in a strong position to challenge Russia in its bid for a more symmetrical relationship in Korea and Manchuria. There was little acceptance of norms for resolving differences over colonial spheres of influence, even among the European powers; such conflicts were resolved through unilateral moves and occasional confrontations, as in the Fashoda and Moroccan crises. Thus, even if Russia had been more ready to acknowledge Japan as an equal, there was no accepted normative basis for resolving their differences. Internally, both had reasonably secure governments. A change of political generations in Tokyo was placing power in the hands of more nationalistic and

337

imperialistic decision makers, responsive to even more strongly nationalistic pressure groups but still having to persuade the cautious 'elder statesmen' of the soundness of their policies. Russian policy in the region was constrained by considerations of cost, but little affected by an awareness of potential revolutionary unrest.

The values of the rival governments were clear and assertive on the one side, ambivalent on the other. The Japanese had come to a firm resolution that Japan should claim a sphere of influence in Korea and residual rights in Manchuria equal to those of Russia in Korea. This had become a 'vital interest' for which, failing a satisfactory settlement, they would go to war. The Russian decision makers never squarely addressed this issue. The Tsar and his ministers wished to avoid war in the Far East but were misled by their assumption that Japan would not dare to attack the Russian Empire. Although seeing Korea as not vital, they preferred not to limit their future options or formally to acknowledge Japan as an equal. The outcome of the crisis would depend on which way the Russians would resolve this latent conflict among their preferences.

In the event, the crisis amounted to a protracted sequence of negotiations during which the Russians continued to avoid confronting this choice. Their evasion of the issue was assisted by the cumbrousness of the decision making process. Reaching no decision on which of their relevant interests were vital, they engaged in brinkmanship, but not as an act of conscious policy, and their final consideration of compromise offers was inconclusive. Since the Russians avoided clarifying their preference structure, it is not possible to establish conclusively that the Russo-Japanese war was (as understood here) 'unnecessary', but it has been argued that this is the more plausible interpretation.

Resolved peacefully, but more acute than initially probable

The Eastern crisis

As in the Crimean case, structural continuities were much more prominent than changes. The 1815 settlement, and the five-power balance which underpinned it, was unchallenged. There was no hegemonial power in Europe: each of the powers had its own special interests and concerns, its own strengths and vulnerabilities. There were no lasting coalitions. Though always subject to stresses, the norms of Concert diplomacy created a presumption that the powers would collaborate to achieve diplomatic solutions to pressing international issues as they arose.

The differing ideologies and internal political systems of the powers were of limited relevance in this period. The salient internal factor, which profoundly affected the course of events in the crisis, was the instability of the French political system, which in the first instance provided incentives for brinkmanship and later opened up unexpected risks of war. With respect to the Eastern question, as in 1853, there was a potential Prisoner's Dilemma conflict over the control of Constantinople: all preferred the status quo, Ottoman control, but might well go to war to prevent its falling under the control of a rival. They were in agreement, further, that Mehemet Ali should not be permitted to overthrow the Ottoman Empire. Their differences over the extent of the territories which he might retain did not, at the outset, appear likely to lead to a major crisis. That they did so was a result of specific decisions, miscalculations and brinkmanship.

Within Britain and France, and potentially in Russia, the decision makers were divided over which course of action would best promote the national interest. The orientation of British and Russian policy during the crisis depended on Palmerston's and Nesselrode's remaining in control; the extent of the risk which France was prepared to incur depended on the relative power of the King and his minister, Thiers.

Britain's positive response to Russia's crucial decision to prefer a Concert solution to the assertion of its hegemonic claims averted the most serious risk of war. With this issue resolved, Britain and France gradually hardened their stand on the lesser issue of Mehemet Ali, each adopting risky strategies which, in the overall bargaining context, led to the isolation of France and the brief but serious war scare of autumn 1840. France's backing away from war was in accordance with the Chicken preference structure which may plausibly be attributed to its decision makers. At the same time, there were sufficient indications of the potential for escalation, arising from the instability of French politics, to illustrate the difficulties of controlling the risks in crises, even where all the relevant decision makers share a preference for doing so. The Crimean crisis was to show how these dangers might be realised.

The Agadir crisis

The setting was one of multidimensional structural changes. Germany, in the forefront of industrial and technological development, had outstripped Britain and its other European rivals. In some respects the European states system had become global: within the old system Germany was by far the strongest power, without having become in the full sense a 'world power'. The 'balance of power' was uncertain

339

and ambiguous; the two European alliances created a potential confrontation. The Concert norms, largely in abeyance, were invoked occasionally as a matter of convenience; balance of power norms were weakened by different images of the balance, and norms of self-assertion enjoyed increased legitimacy.

Whereas French governmental instability had become routine, the tensions affecting Germany's political system and conservative dominance placed its government under pressure to achieve popular successes. The prevailing values in France and Germany were highly nationalistic, though with a leavening of liberal, socialist and cosmopolitan values in the case of France. Considerations of national prestige were readily aroused. While these developments suggested that any crisis could be dangerous, the actual issues at stake were so limited, and so amenable to compromise, and key decision makers so averse to war for those particular stakes, that the initial situation must be seen as one in which the probability of war was low. The acuteness of the crisis must be seen as a product of mismanagement in the context of the tensions in the overall situation.

The crisis also offered possibilities of breaking up, or at least loosening up, the Anglo-French entente, and Britain's attempt to forestall this was one of several unanticipated actions which increased the level of tension and aroused fears of war out of all proportion to the moves which prompted them. The painful negotiation process exacerbated nationalist sentiment in both France and Germany, heightening feelings of enmity and expectations of war. Kiderlen's strategy of brinkmanship might conceivably have provoked a contest of prestige along the lines of 1870, had he not been constrained by the Kaiser. As it was, the lack of a clear strategy on the German side and the political constraints on the French side led to tortuous negotiations in which any chance of a Franco-German *rapprochement* receded. If the expected compromise was eventually attained, most of the further consequences of the crisis were unintended, except perhaps by extreme nationalists.

The Sudeten crisis

Structural changes in the overall balance which particularly affected the position of the crucial actors in the crisis, Britain and Germany, made for a greater degree of global instability than in any of the other cases, even Agadir. A system in which three of the powers were openly 'revisionist', two supported the status quo, one (the United States) played a major economic role but refrained from politico-military involvement, while the last, the Soviet Union, was excluded from such

340

involvement, lacked the basic configuration of a balance of power system. Britain's weakened global position constrained its options in Europe, while Germany was potentially more dominant there than ever before, even though in 1938 its rearmament had not yet advanced to the point of achieving its goals. The absence of a global balance reflected, and was exacerbated by, the absence of minimal normative agreement.

Internally, the German political system and ideology legitimised the pursuit of extreme nationalist and imperialist goals. The slowness and ambivalence of the response of the powers were partly due to their internal preoccupations but also to the systemic structural dislocation just noted. With hindsight, it is evident that Germany's goals – the achievement of *Lebensraum* in the east, entailing the overthrow of any territorial and power balance in Europe – were incompatible with Britain's insistence on retaining the essentials of the status quo. Thus the potential for a major war was evident but, again with the advantage of hindsight, it was improbable that it would begin in 1938. German capabilities were not yet ready, and the British and French were not yet convinced of the enormity of Hitler's goals, concealed as they were by the pretexts which had successfully legitimised his earlier unilateral moves and his 1938 claims for self-determination for the Sudeten Germans.

While the outcome of the crisis was in line with this expectation, its severity and the uncertainty over how close Hitler came to deciding for war show that once again a satisfactory explanation must take account of crisis decisions and interactions; in particular, of the way in which the British Cabinet and Hitler defined their immediate objectives, leading them to adopt strategies at cross-purposes with one another. Each could undermine the other's strategy, and in the hectic ensuing negotiation, ill-prepared and unorthodox bargaining brought the two sides to the brink of war before arriving at an outcome which was attainable at the outset. Moreover, misperceptions on both sides tended to enhance Hitler's willingness to take risks. For all these reasons the crisis was far more difficult to control than knowledge of the actors' preference structures would lead one to expect.

Peaceful resolution the more probable, and achieved

The Berlin blockade

The blockade crisis took place during a period of fundamental structural change in the global and European balance. The transition to the bipolar international system of the postwar period was only imperfectly understood. American goals and priorities had been defined during 1947: Western European economic recovery was to take precedence over the rapidly diminishing hope of achieving agreements with the Soviet Union on the outstanding European issues. By 1948 the US had come to see the creation of a West German state as a prerequisite for the wider economic recovery. Britain shared these priorities; France accepted them only with extreme reluctance. The inevitable Soviet response was to seek to prevent the incorporation of the larger part of Germany into an emerging Western bloc, but there was no indication what alternative Moscow could offer. Its own economic plight and its unpopularity in Germany left it with little leverage. The British government was securely in office and reasonably cohesive; the Truman Administration, though not popular, enjoyed bipartisan support for its European policies. France, on the other hand, was deeply divided internally over political and economic fundamentals, and deeply apprehensive over a potential German threat. Stalin's control over the Soviet government is usually assumed to have been unchallenged.

Berlin appeared to provide the Soviet Union with the most promising means of leverage for blocking Western plans for a separate state in Germany. The US and Britain, however, were unwilling to reconsider these plans. They were confident that the Soviet Union did not intend to initiate war, and had a common perception of the lessons of the 1930s that 'appeasement' would enhance the risk of war, not reduce it. At the same time, they endorsed the non-provocative response by way of the airlift in preference to Clay's confrontationist proposal to enforce the right of access by ordering an armoured column to break the blockade.

While hindsight might suggest that after this decision the crisis posed little risk, proceeding slowly to an outcome which reflected the Chicken preference structures of both sides, this assumes information which was not available at the time. At the outset it was assumed that West Berlin could not be sustained indefinitely by airlift. If this had been correct the Soviet position would have been much stronger, the Western governments would have faced extremely difficult choices, and the crisis would have been far more acute. This provides the only example of a crisis which proved less dangerous than an examination of the initial situation (including the actors' perceptions) would lead one to expect.

Berlin 1958–1962

The consolidation of the two blocs in Europe had proceeded a long way since the blockade crisis, but major tensions could still arise over

Germany. The integration of West Germany into the Western community was still novel, and to many it appeared fragile. The rearming of West Germany had provoked major controversies and the provision of tactical nuclear delivery vehicles to the *Bundeswehr* in 1957–58 aroused Soviet concerns. The steady drain of refugees from East Germany through Berlin was a constant reminder of the weakness of the most exposed member of the Soviet bloc; Berlin was 'a bone in the throat'. The Western powers, however, were strongly committed to remaining in West Berlin. In traditional terms, the Soviets were challenging a vital interest, and policy thinking was dominated by the ultimate threat of nuclear war.

The publicly espoused norms on the two sides offered no guidance on crisis diplomacy, but there were by now strong precedents for restraint and for avoidance of direct confrontation. None of the Western governments was under severe political pressure on the Berlin issue; the 'cold war consensus' left US Administrations relatively insulated from public pressure. The extent to which Soviet politics under Khrushchev had become unsettled remains unclear.

The crisis had no clear termination, and its only specific outcome was the construction of the Wall, which resolved the most pressing Soviet concern without challenging the interests which the West had signalled to be the most vital. It is plausible to see the outcome as determined by the conflicting imperatives of avoiding nuclear war while using the latent threat of it to bring about an imperfect accommodation of the parties' most pressing interests, leaving larger issues to the future. This, however, required crisis diplomacy which was not only cautious and responsible, but also effective. The emphasis on image building and on low-key coercive tactics demonstrated caution, but it remains unclear just how determined was the larger Soviet challenge: whether, for example, Khrushchev seriously contemplated any moves which might have triggered an escalation process, and whether he miscalculated the resolve of either American President. In the event, the tenacity and perseverance of Western diplomacy proved adequate to the task of defusing the crisis.

Overview

Two conclusions may be drawn from the foregoing analysis. First, crisis outcomes are determined by the interplay of multiple influences – long-term and short-term, structural and contingent. Long-term conditions and trends usually 'bias' the outcome in one direction or another, but crises can unfold in ways that confound the probabilities.

There can be no general answer to the question: under what conditions do crises lead to war, and when are they resolved peacefully? Nor can there be a general answer to the question: which kind of cause is more important? The occurrence of a crisis is usually explained in terms of a conjunction of relatively long-term developments, some of which may be contingent rather than structural. The crisis itself is a sequence of decisions and interactions which need to be explained in their own terms, even when they approximate to the working-out of the logic of the initial situation (an ideal type not encountered in its pure form). The diplomatic equivalent of Clausewitz's 'friction' is especially prominent in crises.

The second conclusion is that crises are frequently more acute and dangerous than the initial situation might lead one to expect. Of the four cases which ended in war, this appeared probable at the outset in only two, the Franco-Prussian and Pearl Harbor crises. Even in these cases a diplomatic solution was quite conceivable, possibly only of an interim kind, but it cannot be ruled out that the situation could have developed in ways that would render war less, rather than more probable. In the other two cases ending in war, an examination of the initial situation and the interests of the main actors would suggest that the outcome was entirely open, or even that war was not very probable. These two cases (the Crimean and Russo-Japanese crises) provide instances of 'unnecessary wars' – wars that were *not* the logical outcome of incompatible goals and the policies flowing from them, but can be attributed in large measure to 'crisis mismanagement'.

Of the five cases with peaceful outcomes, the crisis was more serious, the risk of war greater than the initial interests would have suggested, in three (the Eastern, Agadir and Sudeten crises). In each of these the incentive to avoid war – at least at that time or over that issue – appeared decisive for most of the key decision makers, yet brinkmanship brought the parties close to war in circumstances that were not at all anticipated at the outset. The dynamics of escalation, which proved stronger than the diplomatic process in the Crimean crisis, briefly threatened to take over. In only one case, the Berlin blockade, the crisis in the end proved less dangerous than the initial clash of interests might have suggested.

In the case studies, and in subsequent chapters, explanations have been sought at an intermediate level of generality. The explanation of decisions has not taken preferences or interests as given, but has looked beyond them to the general conceptions which underpin them, to the extent of support for different conceptions, and thus to internal political systems. For the most part these internal 'structures' are taken as givens for the purposes of the present inquiry. It also seeks to avoid pursuing ever-widening circles of causality by taking a number of major features of the international system since the mid-nineteenth century as given. These include the uneven development of capitalism and other potential explanations for the rapid advance of the United States, Germany and Japan as great powers; the development of nationalism; and the ideological conflicts which characterised most of the period. An explanation of these would have a prominent place in a world history, but in a study of crises they can be treated as familiar aspects of the background.

Each of the dimensions of crises studied in the preceding chapters – the international system, the actors' goals, perception and misperception, bargaining and non-bargaining, and internal politics – is relevant to the explanation of crisis outcomes. As we have seen, within each of these there are competing conceptualisations and theories. The final chapter will draw together the theoretical evaluations, and will inquire into their interrelationship.

PART IV

16 CONCLUSIONS: THEORY AND POLICY

Some assessments of the theories outlined in Chapter 2 have been offered in the preceding chapters. The present chapter will draw these together, will inquire into the interrelationships among the relevant theories, and will comment on the study's implications for policy thinking. In addition to explaining the specific findings presented in Part III, theories need to be consistent with the broader findings of the preceding chapter – that crises are frequently more dangerous than the initial conditions appear to indicate, and that explanations of their outcomes are necessarily multidimensional.

This mode of explanation is at odds with the value placed on parsimony in contemporary international relations theory but is in accordance with the practice of historical explanation and with many approaches to policy studies.[1] Parsimonious theory is of limited relevance to the central questions of the present study: under what conditions do crises lead to war and when are they resolved peacefully? To what extent does this depend on the gravity and acuteness of the initial conflict and to what extent on crisis diplomacy? The answers, as we have seen, must take account of both long- and short-term considerations. They are likely to take the form of contingent generalisations. Guided by appropriate theories, the explanatory factors may be brought together within an economical framework, but their essential multidimensionality needs to be respected, not assumed away.

In order to bring out the interrelationship among theories it is convenient to proceed from the 'macro' to the 'micro': from the international system, through internal politics, to interaction and decision making. This makes it possible to link the ensuing synthesis to developments in international relations theory and indeed in broader social theory. With minor adaptation, the theory of 'structuration' advanced by sociologist Anthony Giddens, which has recently attracted interest in international relations,[2] can provide an overall framework particularly appropriate for ordering the present findings, although they were arrived at independently of it.[3] They may be taken as supporting its empirical relevance – an issue which remains contested – and in turn, structuration could offer a meta-theoretical underpinning for the present theoretical systematisation.[4]

The essential principle of the structuration approach may be outlined quite briefly. Whereas most theories ascribe priority either to individual actors, on the one hand, or to social relationships and structures, on the other, structuration theory claims that they are mutually interdependent, 'co-determined' or 'mutually constituted'.[5] Theories based on 'methodological individualism' insist that social phenomena must be explained in terms of the activities, interests etc., of individual persons, the only 'real' actors, while structural theories in their various forms insist that the capabilities, beliefs, lifestyle etc., of individuals depend on the social wholes or structures in which they are located.[6] These differences over explanation, it is plausibly claimed, raise both epistemological and ontological issues. For structuration theory there is no such absolute priority. Social structures persist only insofar as individual actors reproduce the multiplicity of practices which together constitute the structures. They are not absolute constraints, and in modern societies practices undergo constant modification as actors choose to vary them.

Needless to say, this conception of structure is contested, in particular the question whether agents (actors) have choices to the extent which the theory appears to assume.[7] In modern societies, however, it may be suggested that decision makers are a particular class of agent whose main activity consists in choosing which practices and structures to perpetuate, which innovations to approve, and so forth. For such actors, existing structures, practices and rules may be seen as constituting 'materials' which must be recombined in new ways, since not all can be perpetuated unchanged.[8] This may be especially true of decision makers in foreign policy, who constantly face choices between seeking to adjust internal practices to meet external demands, or vice versa. While many foreign policy decisions are routine, simply perpetuating existing practices, crises lie at the other extreme, where choices of broad scope and consequence are required of decision makers.

Structures

Structural theory in international relations has been developed at the level of the international system, but national and international structures enter into the analysis and explanation of the cases in essentially the same way – as constraints, but also as the 'materials' – the capabilities, relationships, norms etc., which constitute the historically given 'conditions' for each crisis. At both levels, structures predispose but do not predetermine outcomes. The conditions are not wholly structural, but are partly contingent, including 'accidents' of timing and personality: particular leaders, and not others, happen to hold office at a given time, particular coalitions happen to be juxtaposed, and so forth. But all this takes place within certain structured contexts. Since the purpose is to explain crises, the focus is on how structures affect crises, not the reverse process, but it is assumed that crises affect structures, either dramatically or incrementally.

The international system

The most prominent contemporary theory of the international system, Waltz's neo-realist theory of systemic structure, has limited relevance to the present inquiry. We have seen that this follows from its aims, and the consequent limitations of its scope. As Waltz makes clear, it seeks to explain characteristic behaviour, recurrent patterns, and the range of possible outcomes, but not particular outcomes; to explain why wars or crises are possible, but not why a crisis had this outcome rather than that.[9]

The analysis offered in place of the neo-realist was drawn from the work of historians of the international system, which combines the historical interpretation of the way in which the system has evolved with theorising on the causes and effects of systemic change and on systemic stability and instability. The present analysis is not a history of the international system, and thus does not attempt to explain the changing phases of which the characteristics provide the systemic context for each crisis. Historians differ over explaining these phases, but there is substantial agreement on their characteristics and on their consequences for the relative stability or instability of the system, and thus on the severity of the problems for crisis diplomacy.

In the previous chapter it was argued that the relative stability of the system affects the probability of crises and war over a certain time period, but that the outcome of a specific crisis depends more on the actions and interactions of states. Crises are essentially short-term phenomena, in relation to which Morton Kaplan's view of the international system as 'sub-system dominant' is broadly correct, and the neo-realist aspiration to explain state behaviour primarily in systemic terms is out of place.[10] Although the international setting provides some of the important 'givens' – conditions, resources, practices, norms – internal conditions are even more crucial in shaping the choices and the outcome. Systemic features, nonetheless, influence the seriousness of crises: the risk of a limited war posed by the breakdown of the Concert in 1853 was of a different order of magnitude from the 'death struggle' dreaded by decision makers in 1938, let alone the spectre of a nuclear holocaust in the 1960s. We have also seen that the mode of crisis diplomacy reflected systemic factors such as prevailing practices and norms: the consultative norms of the Concert of Europe, for example, would have ruled out the bilateral handling of crises (the 'duel'), which was characteristic of the subsequent phases of the system.

What is the scope for theory at this level? The systemic setting of each crisis is historically specific. Martin Wight's well-known dictum that international relations theory *is* historical interpretation does not survive as a general claim, but has some plausibility in a context such as the present.[11] However, this need not be equated with a rejection of theory, but rather with the demand that theory do justice to specificity and that it illuminate the historical process. Even deductive theorising on the consequences of different system structures, in Waltz's sense, can offer some illumination, as Snyder and Diesing have shown, but the richer analyses of the historical sociologists can offer far more. Here the typical theoretical finding takes the form of contingent generalisations, such as George and Smoke develop in other contexts.[12] The present work has focused on ways in which three aspects of the international system which lend themselves to contingent generalisation – the changing arena, patterns of alignment and the degree of normative consensus or conflict – contributed to systemic stability or instability.

Although these particular generalisations were relatively narrow in scope, the systemic analysis presented in Chapter 10 has broader implications. It suggests, for example, that there can be no general answer to the question, of major theoretical import, whether the balance of power is stabilising or destabilising. There can even be conditions, as in the interwar period, where the question does not arise, because too many actors are unable or unwilling to pursue policies of balancing. A balance of power may be stabilising if, as in the Concert period, the actors perceive it in much the same way and are committed to preserving it, but it may be destabilising if they perceive it in terms of different arenas, as did Britain and Germany at the turn of the century. The systemic analysis suggests that balance of power theory, like theories on alignment patterns or the role of shared norms, should have the form of contingent generalisations.

Internal politics

Although there are frameworks for analysing the nexus between internal politics and foreign policy, there is no general explanatory theory comparable to Waltz's structural realism at the systemic level. The historical specificity of internal political forces and institutions, not to mention specific leaderships, is even more obtrusive than in the case of the distinctive phases of the international system. Once again, this does not preclude narrow-gauge theory, such as comparative analyses of different types of political regime or of the working of policy making institutions. The present work has drawn on political histories, comparative politics and studies of decision making institutions in attempting to assess the bearing of internal political structures and processes on the actors' foreign policies and crisis diplomacy.

Within the changing international systemic context, the sources of each state's crisis behaviour are to be found in its internal politics. Political structures and processes determine which elites or coalitions will control the government, and thus which values and conceptions of the national interest will inform its policies; the state's political history preceding the crisis will determine the degree of governmental stability and cohesion; established institutions and political culture will influence governmental perceptions and determine how decisions are made. Most of these internal influences are acknowledged in the specialist sources, but differences over their significance are not infrequent. Some aspects, such as the significance of political culture, are less well developed in the existing histories and might repay further inquiry.

The most familiar theory in this area, bureaucratic politics, offered only limited insights, even in the twentieth-century cases. Typically, the issues were such as to require the sustained attention of the political leadership, which drew on the advice of like-minded officials, setting aside dissenting views. The Sudeten crisis represents the extreme instance of this, but the pattern is found in most of the other cases. Bureaucratic inputs were important in certain specific contexts. French 'hard-line' officials precipitated the Agadir crisis, but once Kiderlen raised the stakes, the crisis was at the top of the political agenda. In pre-1941 Japan the politics of the armed services were of central importance in policy making, because of the dominant position of the military in the political system, and bureaucratic influences were also important in the US in the same crisis. Except for the Japanese instance, however, it was the wider political system which was the

353

source of major internal political inputs, the role of bureaucracies remaining secondary.

Contingent generalisations have been put forward in three areas: the processes by which governments resolve policy differences, and reasons why on some occasions they are unable to do so; the adverse consequences of political and governmental instability; and internal political preconditions for effective crisis diplomacy. The latter – in summary, the stability of the central authority, its freedom from 'compelling' internal pressures, non-parochial perspectives on the part of decision makers, and effective procedures for resolving policy differences – might indeed be regarded as preconditions for the rational conduct of foreign policy more generally, understanding 'rationality' in the sense discussed below. In this way the contingent generalisations could contribute to the development of theory in one of the least theorised areas of international relations.

Interaction

Interposed between structures and agents, interaction is not part of the structuration framework but can be readily accommodated within it. The case studies confirm that bargaining offers the best approximation to a theory of crisis interaction, but no more than that. While some crises lend themselves to interpretation in terms of the actors' bargaining strategies, there is frequently, to borrow Clausewitz's well-known image, sufficient 'friction' to qualify or even negate such strategies. If one of the key actors is unable or unwilling to bargain, it becomes difficult to reconstruct a crisis in terms of strategic interaction. This distinguishes the present analysis from that of Snyder and Diesing, for whom bargaining is the principal activity in crises, friction is marginal and the outcome normally reflects the logic of the bargaining situation.[13]

Nonetheless, despite the qualifications, it is important to recognise the central role of bargaining in 'good' crisis diplomacy. Bargaining theory identifies a crucial aspect of crisis interaction: the relationship among the preferences of the relevant actors, the governments of the crisis adversaries. Moreover, as Snyder and Diesing have shown, the use of formal models can illuminate this aspect of crises and can identify the 'rational' outcome. Where the present cases could be interpreted in these terms, the outcomes were as the models would predict. However, not all crises can be interpreted in these terms, above all when one or more actors' preferences are not sufficiently clear. In such cases explanations must be sought elsewhere.

The short-term focus of bargaining theory would be a weakness if the theory were regarded as a total explanation: the preferences, we have seen, have to be treated as given, and their explanation requires different types of theory. Its short-term focus is a strength, however, if bargaining is seen as a necessary complement to other explanations. Crisis interactions are essentially short-term, and what the theory demonstrates is that they have their own dynamic, or 'logic'. In this sense crises have a certain autonomy, requiring a different kind of theoretical explanation from the largely historical analysis which explains the underlying conflict – they are not merely 'tips of icebergs'. This is equally clear when 'friction' prevents a crisis from following the logic of bargaining to its 'rational' outcome. The discussion emphasised two kinds of friction. The first is where the workings of internal politics prevent a government from following a bargaining strategy, either because it is weakly based and thus vulnerable to pressure, or because it is unable to overcome internal divisions. Such disabilities may merge with the second source of friction, where pervasive but erroneous stereotypes – crucial misperceptions – are too deep-seated to respond to contrary evidence; the parties do not bargain, but 'talk past' one another.

Other kinds of friction have also been noted. They may lead to unexpected escalation, as in the Eastern crisis where the most dangerous confrontation was over an issue which all regarded as secondary. Contingencies of timing can disrupt a potential bargaining process, as the Crimean crisis illustrated more than once. The 'May crisis' in 1938, caused by a misperception of Germany's immediate plans, crucially affected Hitler's subsequent intentions, drastically narrowing his options. 'Friction' can sometimes be characterised as the unintended consequences of deliberate choices, but sometimes results from nothing more than diplomatic fumbling or misjudgment under conditions of uncertainty.

The final conclusion was that although the hostility spiral is not a serious alternative to bargaining as a general theory of crisis interaction, it identifies a dangerous potentiality that a crisis may degenerate into an uncontrolled sequence of escalatory reactions, a potentiality which became visible in several of the crises. That so many of them became more serious than the initial situation suggested was not due to the dynamics of a hostility spiral, however, but to the two principal sources of 'friction', internal political turbulence and deep-seated stereotypes and misconceptions.

Actors

The approaches to decision making which were outlined in Chapter 2 could be regarded as different conceptions of the agent, or actor.

Should the actor be assumed to be rational? If so, should theory move beyond informal analysis to the formalisation of expected utility theory? If the actor is taken to be non-rational, are the essential dynamics to be sought at the level of individual cognition and motivation, or at the level of complex organisations? More generally, at what level are the actors to be understood, the individual decision maker or the state?

As foreshadowed earlier, the concept of the actor which best explicates the case studies is that which was termed informal rationality. Actors meet the everyday criteria for rationality, but their reasoning is subject to a variety of limitations. Formal theory has little relevance for explaining crisis diplomacy. In this it is analogous to structural realism. On the other hand, no reason has been found to endorse the radical alternative paradigm, based on non-rational assumptions. Informal rationality is first and foremost a concept at the level of the individual actor – the tacit premise of diplomatic history – and only by extension at that of the collective actor, an organisation or government. The study of decision making cannot sensibly disregard the different conceptions which influence individual decision makers' perceptions and choices, but must give due weight to variables at this level.[14]

Formal utility theory does not explain specific decisions. Jervis notes the relevance of a comment by Herbert Simon, made in a similar context: 'Most of the work is being done by propositions that characterise the [actor's] utility function and his or her beliefs, expectations and calculations.'[15] The present discussion of goals and perceptions attempts much of this 'work'. It is not, as is sometimes suggested, a matter of 'rich contextual detail', but of providing an economical analysis at the same level of generality as the historical sociology of the international system. A second problem is the artificial homogenisation that occurs if core foreign policy values and the decision maker's own personal goals are conceptualised unproblematically as a utility function. This not only neglects potential incompatibilities among goals, but has difficulty in taking account of the sudden eruption of latent values in a crisis – for example, French nationalism in 1840 and 1870, or Cadogan's and Halifax's unexpected resistance to Hitler's Godesberg demands in 1938. Further, the language of utility maximising tends to impose a pervasive sense of rationality on events, and neglects the question whether the decision making processes actually meet the criteria for rationality. It is true that the use of expected utility theory 'to make logical sense of what otherwise seems like bizarre behaviour'[16] can be illuminating, but only if it is treated as hypothesis, not as assumption. Rationales have sometimes been advanced for British policy in the Crimean crisis, for example, and for Russian policy *vis-à-vis* Japan in 1903, but a reconstruction of the actual decision making shows them to be instructive anomalies.

The concept of informal rationality

In contrast to formal modelling, there has been little theoretical development of informal rationality (Elster's 'broad' rationality). For Elster, 'To say that truth is necessary for rational beliefs clearly is to require too much; to say that consistency is sufficient, to demand too little. Similarly, although more controversially, for rational desires: the requirement of consistency is too weak, that of ethical goodness too strong.'[17]

His criteria for broad rationality are essentially procedural, relating to the formation of beliefs and desires – 'the way in which they are shaped'. They must have the right sort of reasons, or causal history, and must respect what Jervis terms 'the generally accepted rules for drawing inferences'.[18] Elster's discussion relates to individuals, but it is evident that the same approach can be extended to the procedural rationality of institutional decision making. The informal rationality of beliefs, perception and information processing has been extensively discussed in international relations, but Elster's second category, the rationality of desires and goals, much less so.

The concept may be used both normatively and descriptively. Used normatively, for example, it enjoins individuals and institutions to adopt procedures whereby important decisions are made on a thorough assessment of the relevant information. Used descriptively, it refers to the extent to which particular actors are found to meet this and like criteria for rationality. Procedural rationality is not equated with the maximising of utility, but rather with achieving a high level of competence in the relevant activities: the assessment of evidence, the analysis of options, and so forth.

The merit of the concept of informal rationality is that it offers a general conception of the actor – the decision maker – which can be related without difficulty to the various kinds of influence which impinge on crises. It allows for distortions and anomalies. It is compatible with many, but not all, theories, and while it does not in itself explain decisions, except insofar as an explanation in terms of the actor's intentions is sufficient, it leads readily to a search for explanations in terms of the more fundamental reasons and conditions which lie behind the immediate intentions.

357

Theories: perceptions and goals

The most radical alternative to the assumption of rationality, Steinbruner's cybernetic-cognitive paradigm, was outlined in Chapter 2. Apart from his own case study on the proposed NATO multilateral force, there have been few attempts to apply his challenging theoretical construct. The present case studies support earlier findings that crisis decision making seldom departs so far from rationality as to be in accordance with Steinbruner's paradigm.[19] Competing values and goals are often considered very seriously, and policy is often based on a reasoned conception of the interests at stake. Uncertainties are often acknowledged, and stereotypes based on past experience are sometimes distorting but are seldom the straitjackets which he suggests. Since the issues receive the sustained attention of the political leadership, bureaucratic influences are less important than he postulates; the personality, experience and capacities of leaders are of greater importance. Decision making, in general, is in accordance with informal rationality, not the cybernetic-cognitive paradigm.

Informal rationality expects anomalies, and the most widely discussed of these is cognitive distortion, which as Jervis has shown occurs in definite patterns which can be explained by cognitive psychology. Some distortion is unavoidable: the same processes of simplification which make perception possible also lead to misperception, much of which is of little consequence or is eventually corrected as discrepancies are reviewed in accordance with the norms of informal rationality. No common pattern could be discerned in those – relatively few – instances where misperception was of crucial importance in a crisis. Moreover, the number of cases was too small to permit definitive testing of the competing explanations of consequential misperception – cognitive and motivational. However, there are grounds for a somewhat greater emphasis on political motivation, insofar as highly charged emotion clearly impelled the decision makers in a particular direction, whereas the diversity of cognitive mechanisms usually offered a choice among different images and courses of action.

In contrast to formal theory's maximising of (existing) utilities, and cognitive theory's emphasis on distortion, the concept of informal rationality as a high level of competence opens the way to a consideration of 'higher' intellectual qualities such as discernment, judgment, creativity and the sense of the larger context. These merit attention as desiderata in diplomacy and decision making. There is little or no relevant theory, but the cases offer certain examples. Unfortunately

Metternich and Bismarck were not sufficiently in control of their respective crises to demonstrate the range of their political and diplomatic skills. Palmerston's and Nesselrode's diplomacy in the Eastern crisis provide perhaps the clearest examples, but neither achieved the same level in the Crimean crisis. François-Poncet's understanding of the Sudeten crisis showed a rare discernment but was disregarded by the French government. Arguably, none reached quite these levels in the Berlin crises. Crises, it appears, offer limited scope for the highest qualities of diplomacy. It may well be that the capacity to discern the potential for structural changes and to shape them creatively can be exercised only in relatively 'open', favourable settings. The present cases provided few such settings, but were conducive, at worst, to serious misconceptions and, at best, to what might be termed the diplomacy of attrition.[20]

Whereas the discussion of perception (rational belief, in Elster's terminology) was able to draw on a substantial body of theory, the discussion of goals (Elster's rational desires) could not. The national interest concept remains influential in policy analysis, but has not been a focus of recent theoretical discussion.[21] The rational actor would be one who chooses goals which are appropriate in the light of the actor's basic values and the relevant circumstances. It has been found useful to adopt the usage of the national interest concept which incorporates this criterion. Clearly, the concept cannot provide a substantive criterion for the choice of policy, since there are always multiple values and many 'legitimate' ways of perceiving the issues, but it can provide a procedural criterion. Just as some forms of misperception reflect lapses of rationality, so do some choices of goals: when they are adopted unthinkingly, for example, leaving important values or considerations out of account. More often than not, however, the decision makers in the present case studies did base their policies on reasonably coherent conceptions of the national interest, in this sense. Thus, the informal concept of rationality is a reasonable initial assumption for an account of the typical crisis decision making process, but only because it also assumes gradations and lapses.

Collective actors

Many of the judgments regularly made about foreign policy apply rationality criteria to governments. According to formal rational-choice theory, this cannot be done: 'there do not exist collective desires or beliefs', and members of a group rarely have consistent preferences.[22] However, there are generally accepted norms that governments should have goals, should act consistently and the like. Indeed the goals which are ascribed to individual decision makers are those which they espouse on behalf of the government or the state, not their individual ambitions. The rationality of a government's perceptions or goals can only be considered by way of individual conceptions, but then *its* actions and policies can be examined in terms of the criteria for informal rationality. We have seen that it may fall short for one of two broad reasons: either because no satisfactory rationales are formulated, or because it is unable to resolve differences among its members whose individual, but incompatible views in themselves may satisfy the criteria, as in Britain in 1853.

At the governmental level, more obviously than at that of the individual, there may be conflicts among the criteria for rationality. To take the most striking example, the rational procedure for resolving consequential differences in perception would be by deliberation and the search for new evidence, but we have seen that this was relatively infrequent. Far more often, dissenting views were overruled; the outcome depended on the balance of influence among those with the differing perceptions. The reasons for this include time pressures, the intractability of the differences and political rivalry. However, there is also the norm of maintaining policy coherence. Trade-offs among the criteria for rationality may sometimes be necessary, just as trade-offs between the logic of economics and politics, or of internal and external goals, are sometimes necessary. There may be conflicts and dilemmas within the 'rational'.

Overview

A conception of agents and structures which coincides with structuration theory provides a framework within which the theories relevant to explicating crisis diplomacy may be interrelated. Parsimonious theories at the highest level of generality, on the other hand, address few of the questions which are raised by an inquiry into the reasons why particular crises took place or had the outcomes which they did. Game theory is an exception in that it serves as a starting-point for explaining crisis interactions, but it needs to be qualified by the kind of contingent generalisation which represents the main type of relevant theory for this inquiry. Such generalisations take account of historically changing structures at both the international and the nation-state level. The study has pursued the 'ever-widening circles of causation' as far as these structures; historical understanding could be deepened by pursuing these explanations further back, but this would be a task for another project. Understanding the crises themselves, however, will still require the kind of multi-level contingent generalisations which have been suggested. Informal rationality is a conceptualisation of the actor which provides common ground for the theories at all levels and is congruent with the form of those theories, and with an expectation that contingencies and 'friction' will have a significant part in the explanation of most crises.

Implications for policy thinking

Three unresolved problems concerning the relationship of theory to policy were noted at the outset of the inquiry. The first was George and Smoke's comment that policy ideas in international relations tend to consist of 'free-floating generalisations and isolated insights'.[23] Second, even when policy ideas are grounded in theory, the theories are mutually incompatible and none enjoys general acceptance. Finally, there is often dissonance between the theoretical analysis and the associated normative recommendations: in particular, between the emphasis on non-rational processes in decision making and recommendations presupposing rationality.

The present analysis has sought to address these problems, even though they cannot be fully resolved. The policy ideas which follow are grounded in theoretical as well as historical analysis; moreover, in striving for a theoretical evaluation and synthesis, this work joins others in seeking to move the discipline beyond the juxtaposition of incompatible theories or 'paradigms'.[24] The concept of informal rationality, building on Jervis's view of the rational and non-rational as a continuum rather than as opposites, permits the formulation of descriptive and normative theory in the same idiom. This is not to deny the strength of the pressures which may distort perception and judgment, but is to maintain that in principle the recourse to deliberation on fundamental goals, values and causal relationships can free decision makers from the hold of dogmas and stereotypes.

Policy ideas can be thought of as principles or maxims such as those discussed in Chapter 3 above, but underlying such principles are general orientations to policy: for example the problem-solving versus the fatalistic approach, the activist versus the reactive, the legalistic versus the pragmatic, and so forth. We may note some orientations to policy which may be derived from the preceding analysis.

Policy orientations

The first concerns the manageability of crises. Policy makers should not assume that crises lend themselves readily to 'management'. Their 'manageability' depends on a range of factors of which any given decision maker is likely to be only partially aware. While complete loss of control, the hostility spiral, is rare, the tendency of crises to become more dangerous than the initial conditions indicate is encountered frequently. The appropriate orientation, then, is wary – 'owl'-like.[25] Crisis diplomacy should not be thought of as crisis management.

Second, among the various dimensions of crises, foreign policy elites and decision makers tend to focus most strongly on the actors' goals and willingness to risk war, often accentuating the personal; the perception of systemic stability or instability is often intuitive or implicit, and the perception of internal structures and tensions weak or distorted, above all when the self-image becomes involved.[26] It is desirable that policy thinking focus more systematically on structural and cognitive, as well as intentional factors. Similarly, crisis diplomacy would benefit from greater awareness of the characteristic processes and problems relating to the parties' interactions: the way in which the bargaining process serves to clarify what is at stake, and thus the scope, or lack of scope, for accommodation, and the processes which lead certain crises to become more dangerous than the original stakes would indicate. Awareness of these problems does not entail their solution, but is a necessary starting-point. The 'owl'-like approach is appropriate, as are the qualities of patience and perseverance which are exemplified in several of the case studies.

Policy making communities would also benefit from heightened awareness of two further considerations: the problems and complexities relating to goals, and the intellectual demands of crisis diplomacy. As discussed further below, the principle that objectives be limited needs substantial qualification, especially with reference to the need for constant appraisal of the rationale for specific objectives in terms of the larger interests which they are deemed to promote – one of the basic norms of informal rationality. The tension between those norms and the pressure for policy coherence is not open to resolution by formula, but greater recognition of the problem is a step towards promoting creative tension rather than the mere suppression of dissenting views. Recognition, moreover, of the value of those rare intellectual qualities of discernment, imagination, creativity and sensitivity to sequences and systemic effects, would tend to promote a climate for policy making which improves the chances for constructive crisis diplomacy.

Principles for crisis diplomacy

We may now review the seven principles of crisis 'management' discussed in Chapter 3. To what extent can they be endorsed, or should they be qualified or supplemented? Five of the seven are seen to be of major importance.

Multiple advocacy in decision making

The serious consideration of different perspectives and perceptions is in accordance with the basic 'realities' of the human mind addressing complex issues. Yet this approach is adopted infrequently. Most political leaders give priority to policy coherence, perhaps sensing the costs of failure to achieve it and the difficulty of insulating multiple advocacy from political rivalry. In Britain in 1853 and the US in 1941, the potential benefits of multiple advocacy were negated by the failure to achieve policy coherence. Differences among decision makers found only limited expression in the Sudeten crisis and in Japan in 1941, and sometimes relatively narrow choices were debated after the crucial decisions had been taken with little or no debate (Britain in 1938, and the US in 1948). In some of the nineteenth-century cases policy remained firmly in the hands of a single decision maker without adverse consequences; or, as in France in 1870, the outcome might have been more favourable if this had been the case. The nature of governmental institutions and the increasing complexity of the international environment in the later twentieth century point to the greater contemporary relevance of multiple advocacy. Yet it is clear that there are major problems of institutional design if the aforementioned creative tension between its demands and those of policy coherence is to be realised in practice.

The limitation of objectives

Although it remains a valid starting-point for policy thinking, the limitation of objectives requires qualification and amplification. A limited objective which is perceived as open-ended can be just as inflammatory as an open-ended objective itself and, as the Crimean case shows, such misperceptions may not be readily corrected. War can arise over a limited issue if it is pursued with equal obstinacy on both sides or if prestige becomes heavily involved, even though it is often the case that the original limited stake is not of equally great

363

importance to both sides. For this reason it is often suggested that crisis diplomacy should take account of the relative intensity of the parties' interests.[27] Underlying this is the more basic norm emphasised here, that specific objectives be chosen and reviewed in relation to the larger values and interests at stake. Only thus can unnecessary wars be avoided.

Maintaining flexible options

The principle of maintaining flexibility requires the least qualification, but it must be noted that it refers to 'realities' more than 'appearances': governments have bargaining incentives to cultivate an aura of resolve and commitment while retaining short-term, tactical options. In general, policy makers seek to preserve freedom of manoeuvre. The tactic of tying one's hands in advance is seldom adopted, and in most instances the foregoing of options is an indication of weakness. Thiers' lack of options vis-à-vis Mehemet Ali and Britain's vis-à-vis the Ottoman Empire in 1853 seriously constrained their diplomacy, and Gramont's deliberate narrowing of French options in 1870 seriously weakened the position of those interested in a diplomatic outcome. Western decision makers in the Berlin crises were keenly aware that a confrontationist approach posed excessive dangers of narrowing the options.

The overall situation, internal and external, sets the outer limits of the options. The perceived options may be narrower, and the range of options actually available may vary considerably during a crisis. For example, the success of the airlift greatly extended Western options in the Berlin blockade, whereas developments in internal politics narrowed Britain's options in the Crimean crisis, and both French and German options in the Agadir crisis. In some of these cases political pressures caused a narrowing of goals. By way of contrast, the capacity to reformulate and broaden goals may be one of the most effective ways of opening up options.

Perception of the adversary

The cases illustrate the central importance of achieving a correct perception of the adversary, and also the difficulty of doing so, even when serious thought is given to it, which was quite often not the case. Comfortable stereotypes frequently went unquestioned, as by most French decision makers in 1870, or Russian in 1903, and British leaders in 1853 were unable or unwilling to challenge the popular stereotype of Russian aggressiveness. British decision makers in 1938 and American in 1940–41 devoted a good deal of thought to assessing the adversary, but despite a wealth of information, their understanding remained seriously incomplete. On the other hand, Western decision makers formed reasonably coherent assessments of Soviet intentions in the Berlin crises, which were consistent with the outcomes. The leaders were most familiar with one another in the Eastern and Crimean crises, but this proved of limited value in the latter case, and in the former they were better judges of persons than of the political systems and pressures which constrained their choices.

The cases point to the need to supplement the leaders' first-hand experience and direct contacts with independent expertise on the conditions and structures which influence policy. The relative stability of nineteenth-century structures provided a setting which at times permitted successful decision making by outstanding individuals: the constant structural changes in the present environment point once again to the need for multiple advocacy in order to bring to bear the best and most varied intellectual resources available to policy making. This will not ensure sound assessments but will normally be a pre-requisite for achieving them.

Communication and signalling

Problems of communication may be regarded as constituting the central dilemmas of crisis diplomacy, incapable of resolution through recourse to general principles. The ambiguity of the signals communicated by the actors ensures that the assessment of their intentions remains problematic but, short of ultimatums or declarations of war, ambiguity cannot be resolved. It results, in part, from the general preference for keeping options open, but more fundamentally is inherent in the limitations of each of the basic forms of communication – words and actions – for signalling what needs to be communicated, whether resolve or flexibility. Words are not taken at face value: conciliatory expressions are mistrusted, and statements of resolve may lack credibility (Kennedy's fear in the Berlin crisis, or Britain's and France's problem in 1938). Before 1914, Britain sought words which would restrain Germany without encouraging France to expect more than Britain wished to promise. Actions, however, are no less ambiguous, as the case studies regularly illustrate: Menshikov's bullying tactics, the Hohenzollern candidacy, Russian military gestures in 1903, the *Panther's* anchoring at Agadir, Chamberlain's flights to Germany, the blockading of Berlin – all raised but did not resolve questions about intentions.

Keeping channels of communication open is a minimal safeguard but does little to distinguish genuine messages from deception, true signals from background 'noise'. As Khrushchev showed, imperviousness to signals may be a tempting bargaining tactic. Ideological or cultural cleavages may block understanding, even when interaction is frequent, as the Sudeten crisis or those involving Japan serve to illustrate. Multiple channels, and in particular unorthodox channels of communication, may be functional but can also increase suspicion and confusion. Certain familiar maxims are relevant but in themselves of limited value: that crucial communications be clear and emphatic, for example, and that repetition may be useful. But they will be construed in the light of a record beyond the communicator's control. That the sender should seek to envisage the message in the frame of reference of the recipient is easy to enunciate but difficult to achieve. Given these limitations, awareness of the problems of communication may be the greatest need on the part of those engaged in crisis diplomacy, fostering a capacity for rapid adjustment to the unexpected.

Two of the original principles of crisis management prove to be of more limited relevance.

Close political control over policy implementation
Unlike the five preceding principles, this is generally regarded as a new requirement of nuclear-age crises. Since the case studies do not illustrate major problems in this area, this principle need not be further reviewed.

Time pressure
Time pressure is by no means a necessary feature of acute crises. A medium level of pressure, as in the Agadir crisis or the Berlin blockade, can generate serious tension, not least because of the heightened fear of incidents, but well short of a sense of imminent loss of control. In some cases of apparent time pressure, such as the 1870 crisis, a government may generate a sense of urgency by acting more hastily than circumstances require. Some of the adverse effects of acute time pressure can be seen in Britain and France in September 1938, but Hitler's attempt to manipulate it had only limited success. The case of Russia in 1903 suggests that the absence of any sense of time pressure may be counter-productive. None of these comments qualify the desirability of seeking to reduce excessive time pressure in any nuclear-age crisis, but they suggest that below that level of urgency the problems and potential responses are quite varied.

Beyond crisis management

Five of the original principles have been endorsed, but only with major qualifications. It has also been noted that there are important interconnections among them – for example, between multiple advocacy and the perception of the adversary, or between the limitation of objectives and communication, although the latter is to some extent interrelated with all the others. In general, the principles are better regarded as considerations which it is costly to neglect, than as rules or maxims on which policy makers can safely rely. That they point to dilemmas rather than maxims is clearest in the case of communication, but has some validity in all cases.

Two further principles may be suggested: the importance of timing and the need for a more clearly articulated conception of diplomacy. It is often observed that successful political leaders have a keenly developed sense of timing – *when* to raise an issue, when not to, when to press for a solution, and when to wait. William Zartman examines the way in which long-standing conflicts may undergo a process of 'ripening' such that they become capable of resolution, but in order to achieve this a sense of timing as well as an appropriate formula will be needed.[28] Snyder and Diesing show that the mistiming of moves in a crisis can impede its resolution: for example, attempts at accommodation before resolve has been adequately demonstrated may be premature: they may inadvertently mislead and thus prolong or intensify a crisis.[29]

Yet under conditions of crisis, misjudgments of timing are to be expected. The Crimean crisis offers many examples, but in certain other cases it may be more appropriate to refer to dilemmas: in the Sudeten crisis, for example, Benes might appear to have mistimed his major concession in that its impact was overwhelmed by other events, but it is not clear that there was a 'good' moment which he missed. The key actors in 1840 showed a good sense of timing in moving to resolve the crisis (Melbourne in his indirect threat to France, Louis-Philippe in risking the dismissal of Thiers). Such clear-cut examples may be rare, but it is worth noting that even in the diplomacy of attrition, as in 1911 and in the 1958–62 Berlin crisis, it is important to avoid poorly timed moves, even though the conditions for a well-timed move may not be present.

Second, the need for a more strongly delineated conception of diplomacy brings together several of the preceding themes. Diplomacy is analogous to 'grand strategy'. It consists, first and foremost, in choosing goals and appropriate courses of action. General principles of

367

crisis diplomacy are to be seen as interrelated, and as no more than guidelines whose application in any particular instance is problematic. As Snyder and Diesing show, effective bargaining requires decision makers to make the trade-offs between different principles: to achieve the 'right' balance between coercion and accommodation requires fine judgment and sensitivity to the reactions to one's moves.[30] The present study has sought to identify the high intellectual demands of crisis diplomacy, and the consequent need to have available to decision makers advisers of varied and unusual qualities of mind. Certain personal qualities are also important: they include patience and strong nerves, the capacity to avoid being pressed into hasty decisions, and perseverance (of which Palmerston, Buol and Chamberlain provide notable examples). Diplomacy is, as Max Weber said of politics in general, a matter of slow boring through hard boards.[31] In the case of democratic systems, rare political skills are required to maintain public support without incurring major diplomatic costs.

Diplomacy, then, not management, provides the appropriate over-arching concept for integrating the requirements of crisis policy making. It also points towards the continuity of crisis and non-crisis, and thus to the relationships and activities which precede and follow crises. Zartman notes that 'ripe moments' for resolving long-standing issues 'tend to come before or after but not usually during a crisis'[32] – a reminder that the conditions for constructive diplomacy are more likely to be found in other contexts: in crisis avoidance or in utilising a post-crisis atmosphere to improve the overall relationships in question. Nonetheless, as the second Berlin crisis shows, crisis diplomacy can be conducted with an eye to such improvements.

The original maxims of crisis management can be seen as having *ad hoc* relationships to particular theories, above all to bargaining theory (the limitation of objectives, flexible options, and perception of the adversary). Multiple advocacy was a way of countering cognitive distortion as well as an acknowledgment of the complexity of the foreign policy environment. The easing of time pressure was a means of warding off the hostility spiral. Close control over policy implementation addressed anomalies of bureaucratic politics.

The present discussion has not sought to establish linkages between specific theories and policy ideas, but has emphasised the interrelatedness of the latter and the importance of an appropriate overall policy orientation. It seeks to move policy thinking from reliance on maxims and from too strong a focus on the short term – on tactics and, at the level of theory, on bargaining. These are important, but need to be placed in context. Priority should go, rather, to the choice of goals and to deliberation on their rationales and on the available courses of action. While much of this must precede crises, they provide a challenge to reappraise fundamentals, not merely to take established goals and stereotypes as given. It is desirable that there be greater awareness in policy communities of the relevant theories, not because they provide ready answers to immediate questions but because the theories as a whole, and even the tensions among them, permit a fuller and more explicit understanding of both the structural and the contingent factors bearing on crisis diplomacy. Policy makers are always aware of choice and constraint, but often oversimplify or misperceive both. A more widely diffused knowledge of theory – as well as close knowledge of the specific case – can make for a sharper perception of constraints and a more discerning awareness of choices. Crises will remain dangerous, and war may sometimes be chosen deliberately and clear-sightedly, but unnecessary wars, and unnecessarily dangerous crises, will become less likely.

NOTES

1 Introduction: aims and approach

1 See, in particular, Kurt Gottfried and Bruce G. Blair, eds., *Crisis Stability and Nuclear War* (New York: Oxford University Press, 1988).

2 For a discussion of the role of the great powers, see Hedley Bull, *The Anarchical Society: A Study of Order in World Politics* (London: Macmillan, 1977), pp. 200–29. See also Bull, 'The Great Irresponsibles? The United States, the Soviet Union and World Order', *International Journal*, 35 (1980), pp. 437–47.

3 For recent examples of the debates over July 1914, see Scott D. Sagan, '1914 Revisited: Allies, Offense and Instability', *International Security*, 11 (Fall 1986), pp. 151–75, commenting on 'The Great War and the Nuclear Age', special issue, *International Security*, 9 (Summer 1984); see also Marc Trachtenberg, 'The Meaning of Mobilization in 1914' and Jack S. Levy, 'Preferences, Constraints and Choices in July 1914', *International Security*, 15 (Winter 1990/91), pp. 120–50 and 151–86. For an overview, see James Joll, *The Origins of the First World War* (London: Longman, 1984).

4 The definition of 'crisis' is discussed in the following chapter.

5 Alexander L. George, 'Case Studies and Theory Development: The Method of Structured, Focused Comparison', in P. G. Lauren, ed., *Diplomacy: New Approaches in History, Theory and Policy* (New York: Free Press, 1979), p. 50.

6 Other breakdowns are, of course, conceivable. In particular, institutional aspects or personality considerations might be seen as meriting greater emphasis. The choice of perception and bargaining reflects their theoretical significance, and the need for further theoretical analysis appears to be greatest with respect to goals and internal politics. Institutional and personality considerations may be less amenable to systematic theorising. It is hoped that their importance is sufficiently acknowledged in the individual case studies.

7 George, 'Case Studies', pp. 43–68. The approach has also been influenced by Eckstein's discussion of case study methodology and by Skocpol and Somers' analysis of different 'logics' in comparative history. See Harry Eckstein, 'Case Study and Theory in Political Science', in F. I. Greenstein and N.W. Polsby, eds., *Handbook of Political Science* (Reading, MA: Addison-Wesley, 1975), vol. VII, pp. 79–138; Theda Skocpol and Margaret Somers, 'The Uses of Comparative History in Macrosocial Inquiry', *Comparative Studies in Society and History*, 22 (1980), pp. 174–97.

370

8 Glenn H. Snyder and Paul Diesing, *Conflict Among Nations: Bargaining, Decision Making, and System Structure in International Crises* (Princeton: Princeton University Press, 1977), p. 67.

2 Theories of crisis behaviour

1 Snyder and Diesing also refer to this function of theory. 'This book ... uses several kinds of theory to *describe and* explain ... how states and statesmen behave in international crises.' Snyder and Diesing, *Conflict Among Nations*, pp. 3–4. Emphasis added.

2 For its use by historians, see Randolph Starn, 'Historians and "Crisis"', *Past and Present*, 52 (1971), pp. 3–22.

3 For discussions of the definition of crisis, each offering a different break-down, see Charles F. Hermann, 'Some Issues in the Study of International Crisis', and James A. Robinson, 'Crisis: An Appraisal of Concepts and Theories', both in Charles F. Hermann, ed., *International Crises: Insights from Behavioral Research* (New York: Free Press, 1972), pp. 6–16 and 20–7; A. J. R. Groom, 'Crisis Management in Long-Range Perspective', and Wolf-Dieter Eberwein, 'Crisis Research – The State of the Art: A Western View', both in Daniel Frei, ed., *International Crises and Crisis Management: An East–West Symposium* (Farnborough: Saxon House, 1978), pp. 101–4 and 126–9.

4 Coral Bell, *The Conventions of Crisis: A Study in Diplomatic Management* (London: Oxford University Press, 1971), pp. 7–9.

5 Michael Brecher, 'State Behavior in International Crisis', *Journal of Conflict Resolution*, 23 (1979), p. 447. Richard Ned Lebow offers a similar definition: *Between Peace and War: The Nature of International Crisis* (Baltimore: Johns Hopkins University Press, 1981), pp. 9–12.

6 Michael Brecher and his collaborators in the International Crisis Behavior Project have recently distinguished between foreign policy crises and international crises. The former, 'a crisis viewed from the perspective of an individual state', is defined in terms of the perceptions of the highest-level decision makers, as discussed above. The latter is a situational change characterised by intense disruptive interactions, a challenge to the existing system and a high probability of military hostilities or a change in the military balance. Michael Brecher, Jonathan Wilkenfeld and Sheila Moser, *Crises in the Twentieth Century*, vol. I, *Handbook of International Crises* (Oxford: Pergamon Press, 1988), p. 3.

7 Snyder and Diesing, *Conflict Among Nations*, p. 6.

8 Alastair Buchan, *Crisis Management: The New Diplomacy* (Boulogne-sur-Seine: Atlantic Institute, 1966), p. 21. Crises which lead to war are some-times named retrospectively after the war (e.g., Crimean crisis, Franco-Prussian crisis) but some of these had alternative names at the time, e.g., the Eastern crisis of 1853, the crisis of the Hohenzollern candidacy.

9 See, e.g., Bell, *Conventions of Crisis*; Buchan, *Crisis Management*; Anthony J. Wiener and Herman Kahn, *Crisis and Arms Control* (Harmon-on-Hudson, NY: Hudson Institute, 1962); Oran Young, *The Politics of Force* (Princeton: Princeton University Press, 1968).

10 See, e.g., Ole Holsti, *Crisis, Escalation, War* (Montreal: McGill–Queen's Uni-

371

versity Press, 1972); Michael Nicholson, *Conflict Analysis* (London: English Universities Press, 1970), ch. 7; Robinson, 'Crisis: Concepts and Theories'.

11 For full reference, see note 3 above.

12 Philip Williams, *Crisis Management: Confrontation and Diplomacy in the Nuclear Age* (New York: Wiley, 1976).

13 Graham T. Allison, *Essence of Decision: Explaining the Cuban Missile Crisis* (Boston: Little, Brown, 1971), p. 10.

14 *Ibid.*, pp. 36–8.

15 See, e.g., Michael Nicholson, *Formal Theories in International Relations* (Cambridge: Cambridge University Press, 1989).

16 See, e.g., R. D. Luce and H. Raiffa, *Games and Decisions* (New York: Wiley, 1957); Allison, *Essence of Decision*, pp. 28–32; John D. Steinbruner, *The Cybernetic Theory of Decision: New Dimensions of Political Analysis* (Princeton: Princeton University Press, 1974), pp. 32–6; Bruce Bueno de Mesquita, *The War Trap* (New Haven: Yale University Press, 1981), pp. 29–33.

17 Bueno de Mesquita, *War Trap*, p. 31.

18 Jon Elster, *Sour Grapes: Studies in the Subversion of Rationality* (Cambridge: Cambridge University Press, 1983), p. 15. For critical discussions of expected utility theory, see Robert Jervis, 'Realism, Game Theory, and Cooperation', *World Politics*, 40 (1988), pp. 317–49; Paul J. H. Shoemaker, 'The Expected Utility Model: Its Variants, Purposes, Evidence and Limitations', *Journal of Economic Literature*, 20 (1982), pp. 529–63.

19 See, e.g., Jon Elster, 'Introduction', in Jon Elster, ed., *Rational Choice* (Oxford: Blackwell, 1986), pp. 13–14; Jervis, 'Realism'.

20 Steinbruner, *Cybernetic Theory*, p. 35; See also Robert Jervis, *Perception and Misperception in International Politics* (Princeton: Princeton University Press, 1976), pp. 119, 174–81.

21 James March and Herbert Simon, *Organizations* (New York: Wiley, 1958), pp. 137–42; Allison, *Essence of Decision*, pp. 70–1.

22 Holsti, *Crisis, Escalation, War*, p. 35.

23 The effects of stress are discussed in Williams, *Crisis Management*, pp. 73–8, but receive little attention in Snyder and Diesing, for example, or in Lebow. For a review of the psychological literature, see Ole R. Holsti and Alexander L. George, 'The Effects of Stress on the Performance of Foreign Policymakers', *Political Science Annual*, 6 (1975), pp. 255–319.

24 For a discussion of these findings, see J. L. Richardson, 'New Insights on International Crises', *Review of International Studies*, 14 (1988), pp. 309–16; for a different assessment, Ole R. Holsti, 'Crisis Decision Making', in Philip E. Tetlock and others, *Behavior, Society and Nuclear War* (New York: Oxford University Press, 1989), pp. 25–40.

25 Steinbruner, *Cybernetic Theory*, pp. 15–18.

26 *Ibid.*, pp. 47–139.

27 Jervis, *Perception and Misperception*.

28 Lebow, *Between Peace and War*, pp. 107–19, 222–8.

29 For a recent overview, see Yaacov Y. I. Vertzberger, *The World in Their Minds: Information Processing, Cognition and Perception in Foreign Policy Decisionmaking* (Stanford: Stanford University Press, 1990).

30 Allison, *Essence of Decision*, p. 67. See also Morton H. Halperin, *Bureaucratic*

Politics and Foreign Policy (Washington, D.C.: Brookings Institution, 1974); Graham T. Allison and Morton H. Halperin, 'Bureaucratic Politics: A Paradigm and Some Policy Implications', *World Politics*, 24 (Supplement, 1972), pp. 40–79.

31 See, e.g., Zara S. Steiner, *The Foreign Office and Foreign Policy* (Cambridge: Cambridge University Press, 1969); George W. Monger, *The End of Isolation: British Foreign Policy 1900–1907* (London: Nelson, 1963); John F. V. Keiger, *France and the Origins of the First World War* (London: Macmillan, 1983).

32 Steinbruner, *Cybernetic Theory*, pp. 71–86, 124–36.

33 Snyder and Diesing, *Conflict Among Nations*, pp. 355–407.

34 Lebow, *Between Peace and War*, pp. 169–91.

35 See Snyder and Diesing, *Conflict Among Nations*, pp. 22–7. The concept is discussed in Chapter 13, below.

36 Young, *Politics of Force*; Snyder and Diesing, *Conflict Among Nations*, pp. 480–4, 488–93.

37 Jervis, *Perception and Misperception*, pp. 62–78.

38 Charles F. Hermann and Linda P. Brady, 'Alternative Models of International Crisis Behavior', in Hermann, ed., *International Crises*, pp. 291–6.

39 Thomas C. Schelling, *Arms and Influence*, (New Haven: Yale University Press, 1966), p. 97.

40 For discussions of communication and the interpretation of signals, see Bell, *Conventions of Crisis*, pp. 73–7; Schelling, *Arms and Influence*, pp. 263–86; Jervis, *Perception and Misperception*, pp. 205–16; Roberta Wohlstetter, *Pearl Harbor: Warning and Decision* (Stanford: Stanford University Press, 1962), esp. pp. 5–70, 228–78.

41 F. H. Hinsley, *Power and the Pursuit of Peace* (Cambridge: Cambridge University Press, 1963); Paul W. Schroeder, 'The 19th-Century International System: Changes in the Structure', *World Politics*, 39 (1986), pp. 1–26.

42 See, for example, Fritz Fischer, *War of Illusions: German Policies from 1911 to 1914* (London: Chatto & Windus, 1974); Gar Alperovitz, *Cold War Essays* (New York: Doubleday, 1970).

43 Lebow, *Between Peace and War*, pp. 1–3 refers to Thucydides. World War One is often interpreted as Britain's inevitable response to Germany's challenge to the balance of power; see e.g., Hinsley, *Power and Peace*, pp. 289–308. The traditional reading of Thucydides has recently been challenged. See Daniel Garst, 'Thucydides and Neorealism', *International Studies Quarterly*, 33 (1989), pp. 3–27.

44 Lebow, *Between Peace and War*, p. 19.

45 Allison, *Essence of Decision*, p. 247.

46 Snyder and Diesing, *Conflict Among Nations*, p. 67.

3 'Crisis management' versus 'crisis diplomacy'

1 Cited in Bell, *Conventions of Crisis*, p. 2. For a more extended discussion of the topic of this chapter, see J. L. Richardson, 'Crisis Management: A Critical Appraisal', in Gilbert R. Winham, ed., *New Issues in International Crisis Management* (Boulder, CO: Westview, 1988), pp. 13–36, passages from which are reprinted by permission of Westview Press.

2 The term is used in this sense by Hanspeter Neuhold, 'Principles and Implementation of Crisis Management: Lessons from the Past', in Frei, ed., *International Crises and Crisis Management*, p. 4, and by Alexander L. George, David K. Hall and William R. Simons, *The Limits of Coercive Diplomacy: Laos, Cuba, Vietnam* (Boston: Little, Brown, 1971), pp. 8–11. The latter contrast 'crisis management' with 'coercive diplomacy' – measures intended to compel the adversary to accept one's goals. Snyder and Diesing take 'crisis management' to incorporate the tension between the goals of coercive diplomacy and war-avoidance. Snyder and Diesing, *Conflict Among Nations*, p. 207.

3 Richard Ned Lebow, *Nuclear Crisis Management: A Dangerous Illusion* (Ithaca: Cornell University Press, 1987), p. 18.

4 Gilbert R. Winham, 'Conclusion', in Winham, ed., *New Issues*, p. 232.

5 McGeorge Bundy, *Danger and Survival: Choices About the Bomb in the First Fifty Years* (New York: Vintage Books, 1990), p. 459.

6 In addition to the sources in notes 1 and 2, the analysis is based on the following: Holsti, *Crisis, Escalation, War*; Williams, *Crisis Management*; Thomas Milburn, 'The Management of Crises', in Hermann, ed., *International Crises*, pp. 259–77; King-Yuh Chang, 'Practical Suggestions for Crisis Management: An Inventory', in Daniel Frei, ed., *Managing International Crises* (Beverly Hills, CA: Sage, 1982), pp. 199–209; Jonathan M. Roberts, *Decision-Making During International Crises* (London: Macmillan, 1988), pp. 94–108.

7 Robert Kennedy, *Thirteen Days: The Missile Crisis* (London: Pan, 1969), p. 109.

8 See, e.g., Alexander L. George, 'The Case for Multiple Advocacy in Making Foreign Policy', *American Political Science Review*, 66 (1972), pp. 751–85.

9 Roger Hilsman, *To Move a Nation: The Politics of Foreign Policy in the Administration of John F. Kennedy* (Garden City, NY: Doubleday, 1967), p. 213.

10 'To avoid a repeat of the Vietnam nightmare – President Johnson leaning over maps in the White House, circling specific targets – Powell had kept as much air-targeting information as possible out of Washington.' Bob Woodward, *The Commanders* (New York: Simon and Schuster, 1991), p. 368.

11 Arthur M. Schlesinger, Jr, *A Thousand Days: John F. Kennedy in the White House* (London: André Deutsch, 1965), p. 715.

12 Elie Abel, *The Missiles of October: The Story of the Cuban Missile Crisis* (London: MacGibbon & Kee, 1962), p. 78.

13 Kennedy, *Thirteen Days*, p. 71.

14 See, e.g., Ole R. Holsti, 'Time, Alternatives and Communications: The 1914 and Cuban Missile Crises', in Hermann, ed., *International Crises*, pp. 58–80.

15 Kennedy, *Thirteen Days*, p. 122.

16 Holsti, *Crisis, Escalation, War*, p. 222.

17 Kennedy, *Thirteen Days*, p. 123.

18 Here the *locus classicus* is Wohlstetter, *Pearl Harbor*.

19 Holsti, *Crisis, Escalation, War*, pp. 224–5; Chang, 'Practical Suggestions', pp. 201–3.

20 For example, Paul W. Schroeder, Review of Holsti, *Crisis, Escalation, War*, in *Journal of Modern History*, 46 (1974), pp. 537–40; Groom, 'Crisis Management

in Long-Range Perspective'; Lebow, *Nuclear Crisis Management*, and *Between Peace and War*; Arthur N. Gilbert and Paul G. Lauren, 'Crisis Management: An Assessment and Critique', *Journal of Conflict Resolution*, 26 (1980), pp. 641–64.

21 Schroeder, Review of Holsti, p. 539.

22 Thomas C. Schelling, *The Strategy of Conflict* (Cambridge, MA: Harvard University Press, 1960).

23 Henry A. Kissinger, *The White House Years* (Boston: Little, Brown, 1979), p. 622, cited in Scott D. Sagan, 'Nuclear Alerts and Crisis Management', *International Security*, 9 (Spring 1985), p. 124.

24 Eliot A. Cohen, 'Why We Should Stop Studying the Cuban Missile Crisis', *The National Interest*, 2 (1986), p. 5. Cf. also the comment of McGeorge Bundy, above.

25 Gilbert and Lauren, 'Crisis Management', pp. 649–51.

26 Bell, *Conventions of Crisis*, pp. 14–15.

27 Lebow, *Between Peace and War*, pp. 315–17, 326–33.

28 Gilbert and Lauren, 'Crisis Management', pp. 655–6.

29 Lebow, *Between Peace and War*, pp. 272, 273.

30 Snyder and Diesing, *Conflict Among Nations*, pp. 323–39, 389–98.

31 Alexander L. George and Richard Smoke, *Deterrence in American Foreign Policy: Theory and Practice* (New York: Columbia University Press, 1974), p. 620.

32 *Ibid.*, pp. 616–42.

33 Donald R. Kinder and Janet A. Weiss, 'In Lieu of Rationality: Psychological Perspectives on Foreign Policy Decision Making', *Journal of Conflict Resolution*, 22 (1978), p. 728.

4 The Eastern crisis, 1839–1841

1 For a discussion of tensions within the liberal alliance, see Roger Bullen, *Palmerston, Guizot and the Collapse of the Entente Cordiale* (London: Athlone Press, 1974), pp. 1–24. The sources for this period refer to 'Britain' and 'England' interchangeably.

2 Sir Charles Webster, *The Foreign Policy of Palmerston, 1830–1841* (London: Bell, 1951), vol. I, pp. 301–10; Kenneth Bourne, *Palmerston: The Early Years, 1784–1841* (London: Allen Lane, 1982), pp. 382–4; C. J. Bartlett, *Great Britain and Sea Power, 1815–1853* (Oxford: Clarendon Press, 1963), pp. 88–95.

3 John Howes Gleason, *The Genesis of Russophobia in Britain: A Study of the Interaction of Policy and Opinion* (Cambridge, MA: Harvard University Press, 1950), pp. 153–7, 173–204.

4 Harold N. Ingle, *Nesselrode and the Russian Rapprochement with Britain, 1836–1844* (Berkeley: University of California Press, 1976), esp. pp. 25–49; Matthew Anderson, 'Russia and the Eastern Question, 1821–41', in Alan Sked, ed., *Europe's Balance of Power, 1815–1848* (London: Macmillan, 1979), pp. 79–97.

5 For accounts of the *Vixen* affair, see Ingle, *Nesselrode*, pp. 63–72; Gleason, *Genesis of Russophobia*, pp. 192–204; Webster, *Foreign Policy*, vol. II, pp. 570–6 (subsequent references are to vol. II). The detailed chronology supports

Ingle's interpretation, that the initiative in resolving the dispute was taken by Nesselrode, rather than by Palmerston, as is claimed by Webster.

6 Ingle, *Nesselrode*, pp. 98–101; Philip E. Mosely, *Russian Diplomacy and the Opening of the Eastern Question in 1838 and 1839* (Cambridge, MA: Harvard University Press, 1934), pp. 15–18.

7 Ingle, *Nesselrode*, pp. 72–9, 83–7; Webster, *Foreign Policy*, pp. 738–52.

8 Webster, *Foreign Policy*, pp. 596–600.

9 Bourne, *Palmerston*, pp. 565–8.

10 Webster, *Foreign Policy*, p. 604.

11 Mosely, *Russian Diplomacy*, pp. 41–3. Mosely comments on a suggestion by the French ambassador, Barante, that British and French troops should be stationed close to the Dardanelles, that: 'The mere hint of such a plan would probably have brought the Russians to the Bosphorus' (p. 43).

12 Webster, *Foreign Policy*, pp. 606, 613–4.

13 Henry Dodwell, *The Founder of Modern Egypt: A Study of Mohammed Ali* (Cambridge: Cambridge University Press, 1931), p. 171.

14 Ingle, *Nesselrode*, pp. 103–8.

15 Webster, *Foreign Policy*, p. 594.

16 *Ibid.*

17 Mosely, *Russian Diplomacy*, pp. 88–9.

18 *Ibid.*, p. 135.

19 F.H. Hinsley, *Power and Peace*, p. 218.

20 Vernon J. Puryear, *International Economics and Diplomacy in the Near East* (Stanford: Stanford University Press, 1935), pp. 152–4; Webster, *Foreign Policy*, pp. 637–8.

21 Dodwell, *Mohammed Ali*, p. 171.

22 Webster, *Foreign Policy*, p. 636.

23 Theodor Schiemann, *Geschichte Russlands unter Kaiser Nicholas I*, vol. III, *1830–1840* (Berlin: George Reimer, 1913), pp. 383–90; Webster, *Foreign Policy*, pp. 646, 659, 661–2; Ingle, *Nesselrode*, pp. 111–4. Nesselrode shared the Tsar's horror at the prospect of an Anglo-French alliance, which he referred to as *fâcheuse* or more usually *funeste*. See Anatol de Nesselrode, *Lettres et Papiers du Chancelier Comte de Nesselrode, 1760–1850* (Paris: A. Lahure, 1904–11), vol. VII, *1828–1839*, p. 288; vol. VIII, *1840–46*, p. 36.

24 Webster, *Foreign Policy*, pp. 638–9. François Charles-Roux, *Thiers et Mehemet-Ali* (Paris: Libraire Plon, 1951), pp. 7–14.

25 Webster, *Foreign Policy*, p. 645; Mosely, *Russian Diplomacy*, pp. 62–3; Ingle, *Nesselrode*, pp. 115–20.

26 Webster, *Foreign Policy*, pp. 649–52.

27 *Ibid.*, p. 653.

28 *Ibid.*, pp. 670–1; Metternich, *Mémoires, Documents et Ecrits Divers* (Paris: Plon, 1883), pp. 454–64.

29 Webster, *Foreign Policy*, p. 685.

30 Dodwell, *Mohammed Ali*, p. 183.

31 Webster, *Foreign Policy*, pp. 691–3.

32 Harold Temperley, *England and the Near East: The Crimea* (London: Longmans, Green & Co., 1936), pp. 119–20.

33 *Ibid.*, pp. 120–30.

34 Bartlett, *Sea Power*, p. 141.
35 J. P. T. Bury and R. P. Tombs, *Thiers, 1797–1877: A Political Life* (London: Allen & Unwin, 1986), p. 70.
36 *Ibid.*, pp. 70–1; Charles-Roux, *Thiers*, p. 188.
37 Charles-Roux, *Thiers*, pp. 263–4.
38 Webster, *Foreign Policy*, pp. 753–76.
39 Puryear, *Economics and Diplomacy*, pp. 15–23, 44–5, 152–6.
40 *Ibid.*, pp. 107–25; Charles-Roux, *Thiers*, pp. 37–8; H. L. Hoskins, *British Routes to India* (New York: Longmans, Green, 1928), pp. 208–35, 268–70.
41 The 'francophile' sentiment of part of the Cabinet might have served as a basis for a different analysis of British interests, placing greater weight on alliance with France, but in practice it did not amount to an alternative analysis. For the pro-French views of the Whigs, see Bullen, *Entente Cordiale*, pp. 2–6.
42 See Afaf Lufti al-Sayyid Marsot, *Egypt in the Reign of Muhammad Ali* (Cambridge: Cambridge University Press, 1984), pp. 235–40, for a discussion of Palmerston's views on the economic issues.
43 W. Bruce Lincoln, *Nicholas I: Emperor and Autocrat of All the Russians* (London: Allen Lane, 1978), p. 217.
44 Ingle, *Nesselrode*, p. 27; Anderson, 'Russia and the Eastern Question', identifies the same conflict, also placing the Tsar clearly in the 'European' camp.
45 Ingle, *Nesselrode*, p. 26.
46 Temperley, *The Crimea*, pp. 57–8.
47 Ingle, *Nesselrode*, pp. 137–8.
48 Charles-Roux, *Thiers*, pp. 7–30.
49 Webster, *Foreign Policy, passim*; Henry Lytton Bulwer, *The Life of Henry John Temple, Viscount Palmerston* (Philadelphia: Lippincott, 1871), vol. II, pp. 260ff.
50 Herbert Maxwell, *The Life and Letters of George William Frederick, Fourth Earl of Clarendon* (London: Edward Arnold, 1913), vol. I, pp. 186–93; reprinted in Kenneth Bourne, *The Foreign Policy of Victorian England, 1830–1902* (Oxford: Clarendon Press, 1970), pp. 237–43.
51 Palmerston obtained information on the military prospects from several local sources: see Webster, *Foreign Policy*, p. 689; Bartlett, *Sea Power*, p. 145.
52 Bulwer, *Palmerston*, pp. 270, 277, 279, 285–6.
53 Palmerston to Queen Victoria, cited in Emile Bourgeois, *History of Modern France, 1815–1913* (Cambridge: Cambridge University Press, 1941), vol. I, p. 223. See also Herbert C.F. Bell, *Lord Palmerston*, vol. I (London: Longmans, Green, 1936), p. 311.
54 Bulwer, *Palmerston*, pp. 279–80.
55 *Ibid.*, pp. 294–6.
56 Temperley, *The Crimea*, p. 488.
57 Spencer Walpole, *The Life of Lord John Russell* (New York: Greenwood Press, 1968; first published 1889), vol. I, pp. 345–6.
58 *Ibid.*, pp. 347–9, 351.
59 *Ibid.*, pp. 355–7.
60 Webster, *Foreign Policy*, pp. 717–18.
61 Ingle, *Nesselrode*, pp. 134–5.

62 Bury and Tombs, *Thiers*, p. 70, comment on the unanimity of French expert opinion. For an example of French reasoning, see C.I. Hamilton, 'Naval Power and Diplomacy in the Nineteenth Century', *Journal of Strategic Studies*, 3 (1980), p. 82. For Thiers' calculations, Charles-Roux, *Thiers, passim*.

63 Bury and Tombs, *Thiers*, p. 73.

64 *Ibid.*, p. 70; Charles-Roux, *Thiers*, pp. 188, 231, 262.

65 Bury and Tombs, *Thiers*, p. 73.

66 *Ibid.*, pp. 77–8.

67 Charles-Roux, *Thiers*, p. 180; F. S. Rodkey, *The Turco-Egyptian Question in the Relations of England, France and Russia, 1832–1841* (New York: Russell & Russell, 1972), reprinted from *University of Illinois Studies in the Social Sciences*, 11 (1923), p. 171.

68 Bourgeois, *Modern France*, p. 222.

69 *Ibid.*

70 Metternich, *Mémoires*, pp. 432, 437–40.

71 *Ibid.*, pp. 454–64; Heinrich Ritter von Srbik, *Metternich: Der Staatsmann und der Mensch* (Munich: Verlag F. Bruckmann, A.-G., 1925), vol. I, pp. 64–82.

72 Metternich, *Mémoires*, pp. 437–40, 445–8, 486–9, 490–5.

73 John Marlowe, *Perfidious Albion: The Origins of Anglo-French Rivalry in the Levant* (London: Elek, 1971), pp. 256–7.

74 Ingle, *Nesselrode*, p. 136.

75 Webster, *Foreign Policy*, pp. 706, 714–16.

76 Bury and Tombs, *Thiers*, p. 76.

77 Palmerston claimed to his colleagues that the deposition 'has created something for the French to insist upon and for us to acquiesce in without touching the stipulations of the Treaty'. Charles R. Middleton, 'Palmerston, Ponsonby and Mehemet Ali: Some Observations on Ambassadorial Independence in the East, 1838–40', *East European Quarterly*, 15 (1982), pp. 409–24, at p. 420.

78 Bury and Tombs, *Thiers*, p. 75.

79 Gleason, *Genesis of Russophobia*, pp. 239–57.

80 Cf. Bury and Tombs, *Thiers*, p. 77.

81 C. A. Macartney, *The Hapsburg Empire, 1970–1918* (London: Weidenfeld & Nicolson, 1968), pp. 235–9, 255–8.

82 Webster, *Foreign Policy*, p. 714.

83 See the discussion in Chapter 13 below.

84 Webster, *Foreign Policy*, p. 712.

5 The Crimean war crisis, 1853–1854

1 One historian who distances herself from the 'bluffs and blunders' theory of the origins of the war is Ann Pottinger Saab, *The Origins of the Crimean Alliance* (Charlottesville: University Press of Virginia, 1977), pp. 23, 75, whose research in the Ottoman sources enables her to bring out the role of Turkish diplomacy in the escalation of the crisis, a hitherto neglected dimension. The British accounts remain within a national perspective which leaves many questions unexplored. A corrective is provided by Paul W. Schroeder's masterly *Austria, Great Britain and the Crimean War: The*

Destruction of the European Concert (Ithaca, NY: Cornell University Press, 1972), a major influence on the present interpretation, despite some differences in emphasis. Earlier historiographical debates are discussed in Brison D. Gooch, 'A Century of Historiography on the Origins of the Crimean War', *American Historical Review*, 42 (1956), pp. 33–58; more recent literature is discussed in Edgar Hösch, 'Neuere Literatur (1940–1960) über den Krimkrieg', *Jahrbücher für Geschichte Osteuropas*, Neue Folge, 9 (1961), pp. 399–434 and Winfried Baumgart, 'Probleme der Krimkriegsforschung', *ibid.*, 19 (1971), pp. 49–109, 243–64, 371–400.

2 For these claims, see Norman Rich, *Why the Crimean War? A Cautionary Tale* (Hanover, NH: University Press of New England, 1985), pp. 20–1.

3 M. S. Anderson, ed., *The Great Powers and the Near East, 1774–1923* (London: Edward Arnold, 1970), pp. 68–9.

4 Rich, *Cautionary Tale*, pp. 23–4; Charles Emerson Walker, 'The Role of Karl Nesselrode in the Formulation and Implementation of Russian Foreign Policy, 1850–1856', Ph.D. dissertation, West Virginia University, 1973, pp. 101–3.

5 Rich, *Cautionary Tale*, pp. 37–8; Walker, 'Role of Nesselrode', pp. 101, 131 cites the two texts. For Nesselrode's instructions to Menshikov, see *ibid.*, pp. 127–35; A.M. Zaionchkovskii, *Vostochnaia Voina 1853–1856* (St Petersburg: Voennoe ministerstvo, 1908), vol. I, appendix, pp. 369–87.

6 For a discussion of the treaty and its interpretation, which endorses the view above, see Roderic H. Davison, *Essays in Ottoman and Turkish History, 1774–1923: The Impact of the West* (London: Saqi Books, 1990), pp. 29–50.

7 Rich, *Cautionary Tale*, p. 25.

8 For the Seymour conversations, see *ibid.*, pp. 28–32; Temperley, *The Crimea*, pp. 270–9.

9 Walker, Role of Nesselrode, p. 165.

10 *Ibid.*, pp. 141–5. See also Nesselrode, *Lettres et Papiers*, vol. X, p. 216, Dmitri Longuinof to Count Dmitri de Nesselrode, 19 March, 1853.

11 Walker, 'Role of Nesselrode', pp. 148–9. For accounts of the Menshikov mission see Rich, *Cautionary Tale*, pp. 34–59; Temperley, *The Crimea*, pp. 304–32.

12 Rich, *Cautionary Tale*, pp. 46–7; Walker, 'Role of Nesselrode', p. 173: 'Treaty or convention, it is all much the same to me'.

13 Rich, *Cautionary Tale*, p. 48.

14 Edmond Bapst, *Les Origines de la Guerre de Crimée: La France et La Russe de 1848 à 1854* (Paris: Librairie Ch. Delagrave, 1912), p. 380.

15 For Menshikov's note, see Zaionchkovskii, *Vostochnaia Voina*, no.148, p. 436; for documents on the mission, *ibid.*, pp. 387–437.

16 For varied reactions, see *Aberdeen Correspondence, 1852–1855*, privately printed by Lord Stanmore, n.d., pp. 104–8. For accounts of this phase, see Paul W. Schroeder, *Austria*, pp. 41–82; Temperley, *The Crimea*, pp. 333–65; J. B. Conacher, *The Aberdeen Coalition, 1852–1855* (Cambridge: Cambridge University Press, 1968), pp. 148–201.

17 Temperley, *The Crimea*, pp. 333–4.

18 Stanley Lane-Poole, *The Life of the Right Honourable Stratford Canning, Viscount Stratford de Redcliffe* (London: Longmans, Green & Co., 1888), vol.II,

pp. 280–4. For a summary of eleven diplomatic proposals, between June and December, see pp. 278–9.

19 For text of the 'Turkish ultimatum' see Great Britain, House of Commons, *Accounts and Papers: Eastern Papers*, 71 (2), 1854, p. 32. Confusion appears to have arisen because Stratford did not send the Note to Vienna as soon as some of the other Turkish documents, but delayed until it received final approval (Lane-Poole, *Redcliffe*, p. 288).

20 *Eastern Papers*, 71 (1), p. 350.

21 Nesselrode, *Lettres et Papiers*, p. 251, letter to Meyendorff, 9 July, 1853; see also pp. 262–3, 267 for Nesselrode's decision to demand amendments to Clarendon's draft.

22 Text in Anderson, *Near East*, p. 78.

23 Schroeder, *Austria*, pp. 56, 58; Nesselrode, *Lettres et Papiers*, pp. 267–8.

24 Text in *Eastern Papers*, 71 (2), p. 26.

25 Nesselrode, *Lettres et Papiers*, pp. 268–9; Schroeder, *Austria*, p. 58. Saab, *Crimean Alliance*, pp. 62–75, while not persuaded that Stratford made the maximum effort, argues from the Ottoman sources that the Note was unacceptable to that government, and that even coercion by the threat to withdraw British support might not have been effective.

26 Walker, Role of Nesselrode, pp. 230–3, 237; Bapst, *Origines*, p. 438.

27 Bapst, *Origines*, pp. 441–3.

28 Temperley, *The Crimea*, p. 349; text in *Eastern Papers*, 71 (2), pp. 104–5.

29 Schroeder, *Austria*, pp. 63–73. Aberdeen's dismay over the 'violent interpretation' was genuine: see M. E. Chamberlain, *Lord Aberdeen: A Political Biography* (London: Longman, 1983), p. 486.

30 Maxwell, *Clarendon*, vol. II, p. 24.

31 *Eastern Papers*, 71 (2), p. 134.

32 Schroeder, *Austria*, pp. 77–80. Clarendon recognised that Nicholas had made a major concession. For Stratford's report that the Turks would under no circumstances sign the Vienna Note, see *Eastern Papers*, 71 (2), p. 110, dispatch of September 5, received on September 19.

33 Conacher, *Aberdeen Coalition*, pp. 195–6.

34 Texts in *Eastern Papers*, 71 (2), pp. 175–6; 200–2. For accounts of this phase see Temperley, *The Crimea*, pp. 366–84; Conacher, *Aberdeen Coalition*, pp. 201–57; Schroeder, *Austria*, pp. 83–142.

35 *Eastern Papers*, 71 (2), pp. 205, 286–8.

36 *Ibid.*, pp. 296–8.

37 *Ibid.*, pp. 334–8.

38 Schroeder, *Austria*, p. 123; Temperley, *The Crimea*, pp. 515–16; *Aberdeen Correspondence*, pp. 416–17, 425.

39 These events are passed over briefly in the British accounts, but are discussed by Schroeder, *Austria*, pp. 131–3.

40 Nicholas did not fully disclose his thinking to Seymour, especially with regard to the Principalities and the Straits. See Temperley, *The Crimea*, pp. 276–7, 461.

41 Schroeder, *Austria*, pp. 28–9.

42 For some indications, see Vernon J. Puryear, *England, Russia and the Straits Question* (Berkeley, CA: University of California Press, 1931), pp. 128–9. For

an account of Anglo-Turkish trade and its significance, see Frank Edgar Bailey, *British Policy and the Turkish Reform Movement: A Study in Anglo-Turkish Relations, 1826–1853* (Cambridge, MA: Harvard University Press, 1942), pp. 84–128.

43 See, e.g., Conacher, *Aberdeen Coalition*, p. 207.

44 Russell, quoted in *ibid.*, p. 182.

45 Schroeder, *Austria*, pp. 76, 134–5, 150–2.

46 *Ibid.*, pp. 58, 88, 125, 132–3.

47 *Ibid.*, pp. 60–5, 77–80.

48 F. A. Simpson, *Louis Napoleon and the Recovery of France, 1848–1856* (London: Longmans, Green & Co., 1923), pp. 8–12; Albert Pingaud, 'La politique extérieure du Second Empire', *Revue historique*, 156 (1927), pp. 41–68.

49 Bapst, *Origines*, pp. 357–60.

50 *Ibid.*, pp. 352–4.

51 Schroeder, *Austria*, pp. 99–103, 108.

52 *Ibid.*, pp. 131–3; Bapst, *Austria*, pp. 480–3.

53 Lynn M. Case, *French Opinion on War and Diplomacy During the Second Empire* (Philadelphia: University of Pennsylvania Press, 1954), p. 25, cites a letter from Napoleon to Hubner which suggests the possibility that he was appealing more to French opinion than to Nicholas: 'Public opinion looks for moderation in the sovereign. So I have given proof of moderation by writing a letter today to the Emperor Nicholas...'. Saab endorses the view that he preferred a diplomatic settlement (*Crimean Alliance*, p. 133).

54 Schroeder, *Austria*, pp. 42–6, 58–9, 140–1. Paul W. Schroeder, 'Bruck versus Buol: The Dispute over Austrian Eastern Policy, 1853–1855', *Journal of Modern History*, 40 (1968), pp. 193–217; Charles W. Hallberg, *Franz Joseph and Napoleon III, 1852–1864: A Study of Austro-French Relations* (New York: Bookman Associates, 1955), pp. 45–71. For a discussion of the reappraisal of Buol's diplomacy in recent scholarship, see review article, untitled, by Ann Pottinger Saab, *Central European History*, 8 (1975), pp. 51–67.

55 Schroeder, *Austria*, pp. 156–68.

56 The fullest discussion is in Kingsley Martin, *The Triumph of Lord Palmerston: A Study of Public Opinion in England before the Crimean War* (London: Hutchinson, 1924, revised edition 1963), *passim*, esp. pp. 47–74, 80–94, 107–20, 128–37, 162–78, 194–213.

57 *Ibid.*, p. 203. Can the opinion expressed by the press be identified with 'public opinion'? The press was read by only a minority, but this was the same minority which was politically active and effective.

58 *Eastern Papers*, 71 (1), pp. 50, 108.

59 *Ibid.*, pp. 128–9.

60 The document had been translated from a Turkish translation of the original. See *ibid.*, pp. 134–8 for the English translation, and Zaionchkovskii, *Vostochnaia Voina*, pp. 383, 392–3 for the original.

61 *Ibid.*, pp. 155–6.

62 Lane-Poole, *Redcliffe*, p. 263.

63 *Aberdeen Correspondence*, pp. 104, 107, 108.

64 *Eastern Papers*, 71 (1), pp. 163, 182–3.

65 *Aberdeen Correspondence*, pp. 193–4, 198; for the mishandling of the Vienna Note more generally, see Saab, *Crimean Alliance*, pp. 61–75.
66 *Aberdeen Correspondence*, pp. 134, 140.
67 *Ibid.*, pp. 150–1, 155, 164–5.
68 *Ibid.*, pp. 218, 221, 237.
69 *Ibid.*, pp. 255, 282, 290.
70 *Ibid.*, pp. 417, 425, 449–50, 456–7.
71 Evelyn Ashley, *The Life and Correspondence of Henry John Temple, Viscount Palmerston* (London: Richard Bentley & Son, 1877), vol. II, pp. 25, 33–4.
72 *Ibid.*, pp. 27–9, 36–40.
73 *Ibid.*, pp. 41–51.
74 Temperley, *The Crimea*, pp. 382–3.
75 *Aberdeen Correspondence*, pp. 104, 107.
76 Maxwell, *Clarendon*, vol. II, pp. 20, 26.
77 *Ibid.*, pp. 8, 26; Schroeder, *Austria*, pp. 62, 98.
78 Maxwell, *Clarendon*, vol. II, pp. 12, 18–32; Conacher, *Aberdeen Coalition*, pp. 148–65, 175–214; Schroeder, *Austria*, pp. 47–51, 54–81, 87–112.
79 *Aberdeen Correspondence*, pp. 244–6, 416–17, 425.
80 Bapst, *Origines*, pp. 361–4; *Aberdeen Correspondence*, p. 104.
81 F. A. Wellesley, *The Paris Embassy during the Second Empire: Selections from the Papers of Henry Richard Charles Wellesley, First Earl Cowley* (London: Thornton, Butterworth, 1928), p. 26.
82 Schroeder, *Austria*, pp. 52, 67–8, 74, 99–103, 108, 116, 123, 131. Baumgart's bibliographical review notes that much of French thinking remains unclear ('Krimkriegsforschung', pp. 76–7).
83 Temperley, *The Crimea*, p. 274.
84 John Shelton Curtiss, *Russia's Crimean War* (Durham, NC: Duke University Press, 1979), pp. 107–9. Curtiss concludes that: 'while the Russian claims to enjoy broad rights to protect the Orthodox Church, based on treaty rights with Turkey, were somewhat exaggerated, Nesselrode's position that Russia was claiming accepted rights backed by treaties was not far from the truth' (p. 109). In view of Davison's analysis of the Treaty (*Ottoman and Turkish History*), this is difficult to accept.
85 Walker, Role of Nesselrode, p. 231.
86 Nesselrode, *Lettres et Papiers*, pp. 289–90, 291, 294.
87 *Ibid.*, pp. 311–13.
88 Schroeder, *Austria*, pp. 30–1.
89 *Ibid.*, p. 58.
90 *Ibid.*, p. 130.
91 Nesselrode, *Lettres et Papiers*, pp. 216, 218; Temperley, *The Crimea*, p. 310.
92 *Eastern Papers*, 71 (1), pp. 79, 93, 102, 119–20, 141, 161–2.
93 Gavin B. Henderson, 'The Seymour Conversations', in Brison D. Gooch, ed., *The Origins of The Crimean War* (Lexington, MA: Heath, 1969), p. 16 (first published in *History* 18, October 1933).
94 Ashley, *Palmerston*, p. 25.
95 Conacher, *Aberdeen Coalition*, p. 267.
96 Schroeder, *Austria*, p. 411.
97 *Ibid.*, pp. 53–7.

98 *Eastern Papers*, 71 (2), p. 27; Schroeder, *Austria*, p. 59.

99 Maxwell, *Clarendon*, p. 20; Schroeder, *Austria*, p. 61.

100 Schroeder, *Austria*, p. 77.

101 L. Thouvenel, *Nicholas Ier et Napoléon III: Les préliminaires de la guerre de Crimée 1852–1854, d'après les papiers inédits de M. Thouvenel* (Paris: Calmann Levy, 1891), p. 181.

102 Case, *French Opinion*, pp. 15–25.

103 Simpson, *Louis Napoleon*, p. 243.

104 See Temperley, *The Crimea*, pp. 305–6; Bapst, *Origines*, p. 439; and especially Walker, Role of Nesselrode, pp. 232–3, commenting on dispatches of the French ambassador, Castelbajac.

105 Ingle, *Nesselrode*, p. 45. Translation reprinted with permission, copyright 1976, The Regents of the University of California.

106 Schroeder, *Austria*, pp. 18–21, 84–5, 139–41, 153–63; also Schroeder, 'Bruck versus Buol'.

107 Schroeder, *Austria*, p. 413.

108 Conacher, *Aberdeen Coalition*, p. 151.

109 Temperley, *The Crimea*, p. 305.

110 Schroeder, *Austria*, p. 30.

111 Richard Smoke, *War: Controlling Escalation* (Cambridge, MA: Harvard University Press, 1977), p. 154. Smoke's summary of the dynamics of escalation in the crisis complements the present analysis.

> The cycle proceeded through a combination of causes: numerous analytic failures by the Russians, French and British in assessing one another's objectives and expectations; interlocking institutional failure on the part of the Russians especially; deliberate effort by the Turks through their own inaction to draw the Western powers deeper into the situation; and an asymmetry between Western naval power and local Russian predominance on the ground. Other contributing factors included public opinion in the West ... and the sheer complexity of the interactions among the powers deeply involved (pp. 193–4).

112 Hinsley, *Power and Peace*, pp. 226–8.

113 Schroeder, *Austria*, pp. 400–15.

6 The Russo-Japanese crisis, 1903–1904

1 Ian Nish, *The Origins of the Russo-Japanese War* (London: Longman, 1985), pp. 253–5.

2 The interpretation of the crisis is based primarily on information from the following: John A. White, *The Diplomacy of the Russo-Japanese War* (Princeton: Princeton University Press, 1964), pp. 1–131; Shumpei Okamoto, *The Japanese Oligarchy and the Russo-Japanese War* (New York: Columbia University Press, 1970), pp. 69–102; Andrew Malozemoff, *Russian Far Eastern Policy, 1881–1904* (Berkeley: University of California Press, 1958); Nish, *Origins*; Ministère des Affaires Etrangères, *Documents Diplomatiques Français (1871–1914)*: 2nd series (1901–1911), vol. III (3.1.03–4.10.03) and vol. IV (5.10.03–8.4.04) (Paris, Imprimerie Nationale, 1931, 1932) (henceforth DDF).

Malozemoff's 'Bibliographical Essay' (pp. 317–31) presents a devastating analysis of the earlier historiography of the origins of the war, showing how most earlier historians remained within the confines of the original controversy between the 'traditional' (pro-Japanese) interpretation and the 'traditional Russian' interpretation which defended the 'responsible' leaders Witte and Kuropatkin, and blamed the 'adventurers' associated with Bezobrazov. B.A. Romanov, the first to make systematic use of the Russian archives, showed the unreliability of the memoirs on which the 'traditional Russian' interpretation had been based. Malozemoff, building on Romanov's research, offers questionable interpretations but a wealth of detailed evidence on Russian policy. White offers an excellent overall account, drawing on the diplomatic documents and archives of all the powers, the Japanese and French material being especially useful. Nish is especially valuable on internal politics and the decision making processes. Okamoto offers a sophisticated analysis of Japanese decision-making. A bibliographical essay by Hosoya Chihiro, 'Japan's Policies Toward Russia', in James W. Morley, ed., *Japan's Foreign Policy 1868–1941: A Research Guide* (New York: Columbia University Press, 1974), confined mainly to Japanese sources, does not refer to Okamoto, but offers a similar interpretation. Of the more readily available of the diplomatic documents, the French are by far the most informative. White does not fully exploit them on some aspects of the crisis.

Many legends about the crisis live on, unaffected by modern scholarship. The colourful account in David Walder, *The Short Victorious War* (London: Hutchinson, 1973) oversimplifies Russian misperceptions. These, like the policy conflicts among the Russian leaders, were more complex, and more instructive, than the traditional interpretations suggest. Lebow retains the 'traditional Russian' interpretation: *Between Peace and War*, pp. 74–9.

3 Nish, *Origins*, p. 242.

4 This section is based primarily on White, *Diplomacy*, pp. 1–94, and Malozemoff, *Far Eastern Policy*, pp. 51–207.

5 Bezobrazov, a retired officer, played an active part in Russian policy-making, thanks to his personal favour with the Tsar. Malozemoff shows that his influence and that of his 'circle' has been exaggerated in the 'traditional Russian' account, but may overstate the opposite case. White is more balanced, suggesting that, while some of Bezobrazov's schemes may have been as 'hare-brained' as his critics alleged, he was also able to offer shrewd strategic assessments. Nish, taking a similar position, notes the Tsar's practice of balancing the influence of different factions.

6 Malozemoff, *Far Eastern Policy*, pp. 205–7, 228.

7 White, *Diplomacy*, p. 60. This contrasts with the earlier claim by foreign minister Muraviev, with respect to Port Arthur: 'One flag and one sentry, the prestige of Russia will do the rest.' (Cited in Lebow, *Between Peace and War*, p. 76).

8 Okamoto, *Japanese Oligarchy*, pp. 70–6; White, *Diplomacy*, pp. 95–6.

9 Okamoto, *Japanese Oligarchy*, p. 69; Nish, *Origins*, p. 153.

10 Okamoto, *Japanese Oligarchy*, pp. 76–7; for the text of Komura's memorandum, Ian H. Nish, *Japanese Foreign Policy, 1869–1942* (London: RKP, 1977), pp. 277–8.

11 Observers differed over the military balance between Russia and Japan, but

it was clear that Japan's naval position had improved, and it now enjoyed the protection conferred by the Anglo-Japanese alliance. For discussions of the military balance, see Denis and Peggy Warner, *The Tide at Sunrise: A History of the Russo-Japanese War, 1904–1905* (New York: Charterhouse, 1974), pp. 163–6, 173; also White, *Diplomacy*, pp. 135–48; Nish, *Origins*, pp. 198–9.

12 K. Asakawa, *The Russo-Japanese Conflict* (Port Washington, New York and London: Kennikat Press, 1970; first published 1904), pp. 298–9.

13 For the text of the successive proposals, see White, *Diplomacy*, appendix 1, pp. 351–8.

14 *Ibid.*, pp. 349–51.

15 *Ibid.*, pp. 102–5.

16 For the Tsar's draft, see Malozemoff, *Far Eastern Policy*, p. 240.

17 White, *Diplomacy*, p. 106.

18 Okamoto, *Japanese Oligarchy*, pp. 97–8.

19 White, *Diplomacy*, p. 111; Malozemoff, *Far Eastern Policy*, pp. 242–4.

20 Bompard to Delcassé, 4 December 1903, 7 January 1904, DDF IV, pp. 161, 223; also Delcassé to Cogordan, 6 January 1904, p. 220. Both report the extreme disappointment of the Japanese diplomats over this reversal.

21 Okamoto, *Japanese Oligarchy*, pp. 98–9.

22 *Ibid.*; White, *Diplomacy*, pp. 114–16. Military planning had been in train for some time: it was now a question of actual war preparations. The Navy required more time than the Army. See Nish, *Origins*, pp. 193, 197–200.

23 White, *Diplomacy*, pp. 112–14; Malozemoff, *Far Eastern Policy*, pp. 244–6.

24 Okamoto, *Japanese Oligarchy*, p. 100; White, *Diplomacy*, pp. 120–1.

25 White, *Diplomacy*, pp. 126–7.

26 Bompard to Delcassé, 16 January 1904; 18 January 1904; 20 January 1904; 22 January 1904; 24 January 1904, DDF IV, pp. 259–62; 271; 278–9; 281; 284–5.

27 Malozemoff, *Far Eastern Policy*, pp. 248–9; White, *Diplomacy*, p. 129; Bompard to Delcassé, 4 February 1904, DDF IV, p. 318.

28 White, *Diplomacy*, pp. 123–4, 130.

29 Okamoto, *Japanese Oligarchy*, pp. 101–2.

30 White, *Diplomacy*, pp. 129–30; Nish, *Origins*, pp. 206–21; 253–5.

31 Okamoto, *Japanese Oligarchy*, p. 100.

32 A. J. P. Taylor, *The Struggle for Mastery in Europe, 1848–1918* (Oxford: Oxford University Press, 1954), pp. 412–17; Christopher Andrew, *Théophile Delcassé and the Making of the Entente Cordiale* (London: Macmillan, 1968), pp. 180–215.

33 White, *Diplomacy*, p. 93; Richard Storry, *Japan and the Decline of the West in Asia, 1894–1943* (London: Macmillan, 1979), p. 41.

34 Blanche Dugdale, *Arthur James Balfour* (London: Hutchinson, 1936), vol. I, pp. 282–8; George W. Monger, *The End of Isolation: British Foreign Policy 1900–1907* (London: Nelson, 1963), pp. 147–53.

35 Ian H. Nish, *The Anglo-Japanese Alliance* (London: Athlone Press, 1966), pp. 267, 273–8, 281–2; White, *Diplomacy*, pp. 116–18.

36 Raymond Esthus, *Theodore Roosevelt and Japan* (Seattle: University of Washington Press, 1967), pp. 3–23.

37 Okamoto, *Japanese Oligarchy*, pp. 11–54; Storry, *Japan*, pp. 54–6; Roger F.

Hackett, *Yamagata Aritomo in the Rise of Modern Japan, 1838–1922* (Cambridge, MA: Harvard University Press, 1971), pp. 212–33.

38 Okamoto, *Japanese Oligarchy*, pp. 69–78; White, *Diplomacy*, pp. 95–102; Delcassé to Bompard, 23 January 1904, DDF IV, p. 282. As Nish shows, Japan's interests in Manchuria sometimes appeared to be accorded greater weight, but the above best sums up the position at the end of the negotiations.

39 On 'Witte's Manchurian empire', see White, *Diplomacy*, pp. 12–22; on its cost, Malozemoff, *Far Eastern Policy*, pp. 186–96.

40 White, *Diplomacy*, p. 47.

41 *Ibid.*, p. 64; DDF III, p. 265.

42 Malozemoff, *Far Eastern Policy*, pp. 236–7.

43 Nish, *Origins*, p. 210.

44 Malozemoff, *Far Eastern Policy*, p. 243.

45 White, *Diplomacy*, pp. 142–5; Warner, *Tide at Sunrise*, pp. 159–60; Baron Rosen, *Forty Years of Diplomacy* (London: Allen & Unwin, 1922), vol. I, p. 213.

46 Alexei N. Kuropatkin, *The Russian Army and the Japanese War*, trans. A.B. Lindsay (London: John Murray, 1909), vol. I, pp. 214–15.

47 Nish, *Origins*, p. 168.

48 White, *Diplomacy*, p. 127.

49 Kuropatkin, *Russian Army*, p. 194.

50 *Ibid.*, p. 176.

51 Asakawa, *Russo-Japanese Conflict*, p. 299.

52 *Ibid.*, pp. 298–9.

53 *Ibid.*, p. 332.

54 White, *Diplomacy*, p. 358.

55 Rosen, *Forty Years*, p. 230; Graf Witte, *Erinnerungen* (Berlin: Verlag Ullstein, 1923), p. 159; G. P. Gooch and Harold Temperley, eds., *British Documents on the Origins of the War, 1898–1914*, vol. II (London: HMSO, 1927), p. 265 (Lansdowne to MacDonald, 30 December 1903) (henceforth BD).

56 White, *Diplomacy*, pp. 106–7, 111; Kuropatkin, *Russian Army*, p. 188.

57 Witte, *Erinnerungen*, pp. 150–1; Rosen, *Forty Years*, pp. 224–7; White, *Diplomacy*, pp. 47–9. For doubts on the reliability of Rosen's account, see Nish, *Origins*, p. 249.

58 See, e.g., comments that Kuropatkin's entourage was pessimistic. Moulin to André, 30 September 1903; 20 October 1903, DDF III, p. 595; IV, p. 35.

59 Rosen, *Forty Years*, pp. 167–8.

60 MacDonald to Lansdowne, 29 October 1903, BD II, p. 220; see also G. A. Lensen, ed., *The D'Anethan Dispatches from Japan, 1894–1910* (Tokyo: Sophia University, 1967), pp. 167–8.

61 White, *Diplomacy*, pp. 102–7; Asakawa, *Russo-Japanese Conflict*, pp. 292–4, 318–22.

62 Bompard to Delcassé, 14 August 1903, DDF III, pp. 535–6.

63 Lensen, *D'Anethan Dispatches*, p. 166.

64 Rosen, *Forty Years*, p. 210.

65 Okamoto, *Japanese Oligarchy*, pp. 71–6.

66 *Ibid.*, p. 101.

67 *Ibid.*, pp. 101–2.

68 Monger, *End of Isolation*, pp. 147–52; Dugdale, *Balfour*, pp. 283–8; Nish,

Anglo-Japanese Alliance, pp. 273–6; for a contemporary military assessment, BD II, pp. 211–12.

69 MacDonald to Lansdowne, 27 October 1903; 29 October 1903, BD II, pp. 219, 220.

70 BD II, pp. 227–41, especially Lansdowne to MacDonald, 30 December 1903; 29 January 1904, pp. 227–8; 241.

71 Boutiron to Delcassé, 9 October 1903; 23 October 1903, DDF IV, pp. 10–12, 46–8; Harmand to Delcassé, 29 October 1903, *ibid.*, p. 70.

72 DDF IV, pp. 220–85 *passim*; Harmand to Delcassé, 28 January 1904, pp. 299–300.

73 Von Alvensleben to Bülow, 20 December 1903; Aufzeichnung Lichnowski, 15 January 1904; von Alvensleben to Auswärtiges Amt, 27 January 1904; Metternich to Auswärtiges Amt, 8 February 1904; in J. Lepsius, A. M. Bartholdy and F. Thimme, eds., *Die Grosse Politik der Europäischen Kabinette* (Berlin: Deutsche Verlagsgesellschaft für Politik und Geschichte, 1925), vol. XIX, no. 1, pp. 17–19, 29, 53–4, 58–9.

74 *Papers Relating to the Foreign Relations of the United States, 1903* (Washington, D.C.: Government Printing Office, 1904; Krauss Reprint, 1969), pp. 615–22.

75 See, e.g., *ibid.*, p. 622; Lensen, *D'Anethan Dispatches*, pp. 163–4, 168–9, 171–3; MacDonald to Lansdowne, 1 October 1903, BD II, p. 217; White, *Diplomacy*, pp. 120–1.

76 The concept of bargaining is discussed in Chapter 13, below.

77 White, *Diplomacy*, pp. 112–13.

78 On Kuropatkin's strategy, *ibid.*, pp. 47–9, 113–14; Malozemoff, *Far Eastern Policy*, pp. 168–9, 203–5, 243; Kuropatkin, *Russian Army*, pp. 160–7.

79 Raymond A. Esthus, 'Nicholas II and the Russo-Japanese War', *Russian Review*, 40 (1981), p. 397. Esthus argues that during the war he showed 'stubborn resolve ... doggedness and consistency' but agrees that before the war he 'completely misread' the situation. The evidence does not support a contemporary comment that he was 'the head and front of the war party' (cited in Nish, *Origins*, p. 247). Malozemoff, cited above, offers substantial evidence to the contrary.

80 Snyder and Diesing, *Conflict Among Nations*, p. 489.

81 Walder, *Short Victorious War*, p. 56. The remark was attributed to him by Witte, his rival.

82 Dietrich Geyer, *Russian Imperialism: The Interaction of Domestic and Foreign Policy 1860–1914*, translated by Bruce Little (Leamington Spa: Berg, 1987), pp. 218–19.

83 Public pressure on the Japanese government is discussed in Okamoto, *Japanese Oligarchy*, pp. 57–69, 81–96; the role of the general staff, pp. 71–6. See also Lensen, *D'Anethan Dispatches*, pp. 163–73.

84 Nish, *Origins*, pp. 8–9.

85 The best account is Okamoto, *Japanese Oligarchy*, pp. 69–80, 96–102.

86 White, *Diplomacy*, p. 75.

87 For a good account, see Nish, *Origins*, pp. 3–8.

88 For example, Geyer, *Russian Imperialism*, pp. 212–19; Esthus, 'Nicholas II'.

89 Nish, *Origins*, p. 241.

90 *Ibid.*, pp. 242, 253–5.

7 The Sudeten crisis, 1938

1 Recent scholarship is reviewed in J. L. Richardson, 'New Perspectives on Appeasement: Some Implications for International Relations', *World Politics*, 40 (1988), pp. 289–316. See also Gerhard L. Weinberg, 'Munich After 50 Years', *Foreign Affairs*, 67 (1988), pp. 165–78.

2 Keith Middlemas, *Diplomacy of Illusion: The British Government and Germany 1937–39* (London: Weidenfeld & Nicolson, 1972), pp. 32–7, 116–28; Paul M. Kennedy, '"Appeasement" and British Defence Policy in the Inter-war Years', *British Journal of International Studies*, 4 (1978), pp. 161–77.

3 Middlemas, *Diplomacy of Illusion*, pp. 70–3, 128–43.

4 *Ibid.*, pp. 110–56; Maurice Cowling, *The Impact of Hitler: British Politics and British Policy* (Cambridge: Cambridge University Press, 1975), pp. 177–9.

5 Middlemas, *Diplomacy of Illusion*, pp. 133–7; Josef Henke, *England in Hitlers Politischem Kalkül, 1935–1939* (Boppard: Harald Boldt Verlag, 1975), pp. 111–19; Telford Taylor, *Munich: The Price of Peace* (Garden City, NY: Doubleday, 1979), pp. 308–12. Reinhard Meyers, 'International Paradigms, Concepts of Peace, and the Policy of Appeasement', *War and Society*, 1 (1983), pp. 57–8, discusses the different worlds of Hitler and Halifax as revealed in this meeting. For the official record, *Documents on German Foreign Policy, 1981–1945*, series D, vol. I (London: HMSO, 1949), no.31 (19.11.37). Cited below as DGFP, I, etc. (all references are to series D).

6 Middlemas, *Diplomacy of Illusion*, p. 155; Henke, *England*, pp. 127–33; Taylor, *Munich*, pp. 571–5; DGFP, I, no.138 (3.3.38).

7 See especially Henke, *England*, pp. 99–107; Andreas Hillgruber, 'England in Hitlers Aussenpolitischer Konzeption', *Historische Zeitschrift*, 218 (1974), pp. 65–84.

8 Alan Bullock, *Hitler: A Study in Tyranny*, revised edition (London: Penguin, 1962), pp. 367–71; Taylor, *Munich*, pp. 299–307; DGFP, I, no. 18 (10.11.37).

9 Bullock, *Hitler*, pp. 420–35.

10 Boris Celovsky, *Das Münchener Abkommen* (Stuttgart: Deutsche Verlags-Anstalt, 1958), pp. 128–9.

11 DGFP, II, no.107 (28.3.38).

12 Summary in *ibid.*, no.135 (25.4.38); for a discussion, see Gerhard L. Weinberg, *The Foreign Policy of Hitler's Germany: Starting World War II, 1937–1939* (Chicago: Chicago University Press, 1980), pp. 334–6.

13 DGFP, II, nos.132, 133, 176 (22.4.38; 20.5.38); discussed in Weinberg, *Foreign Policy*, pp. 336–40, 364–6; Taylor, *Munich*, pp. 380–90.

14 Middlemas, *Diplomacy of Illusion*, pp. 184–7; Taylor, *Munich*, pp. 618–35. Middlemas's contention that the Government's decisions were contrary to the advice of the Foreign Office is at variance with the evidence which he presents. See also David Dilks, ed., *The Diaries of Sir Alexander Cadogan, 1938–1945* (London: Cassell, 1971), pp. 62–4.

15 Middlemas, *Diplomacy of Illusion*, p. 202.

16 *Ibid.*, pp. 226–8; Taylor, *Munich*, pp. 507–10. For the formation of the Daladier government and its foreign policy, see Anthony Adamthwaite, *France and the Coming of the Second World War, 1936–1939* (London: Cass, 1977), pp. 95–110, 175–9.

17 Middlemas, *Diplomacy of Illusion*, pp. 230–1; Weinberg, *Foreign Policy*, pp. 361–2; DGFP, II, nos.143, 144, 147, 152 (30.4.38; 1.5.38; 6.5.38; 11.5.38).

18 *Documents on British Foreign Policy*, 3rd series, vol. I (London: HMSO, 1949). Cited below as DBFP, I etc. (all references are to 3rd series), nos.171, 191–2, 204–5 (4.5.38; 8.5.38; 11.5.38).

19 Celovsky, *Münchener Abkommen*, pp. 209–14; Henderson B. Braddick, *Germany, Czechoslovakia and the 'Grand Alliance' in the May Crisis, 1938*, Monograph Series in World Affairs, vol. 6, no.2, 1968–69 (Denver, CO: University of Denver, 1969), pp. 15–18.

20 DBFP, I, nos.287, 289 (23.5.38); Ministère des Affaires Etrangères, *Documents Diplomatiques Français, 1932–1939*, 2nd series, vol. IX (Paris: Imprimerie Nationale, 1974), no. 426 (23.5.38). Cited below as DDF, IX etc. (all references are to 2nd series). Braddick, *May Crisis*, pp. 15–16, 23; Weinberg, *Foreign Policy*, pp. 367–9; Christopher Andrew, *Secret Service: The Making of the British Intelligence Community* (London: Sceptre, 1986), pp. 553–5. DBFP, II, no.823 (10.9.38).

21 DBFP, I, no.250 (21.5.38).

22 DGFP, II, nos.176, 221 (20.5.38; 30.5.38).

23 Middlemas, *Diplomacy of Illusion*, pp. 239–40, 272, 325; Andrew, *Secret Service*, p. 555; Sir Nevile Henderson, *Failure of a Mission* (London: Hodder & Stoughton, 1940), pp. 139–40, 146–7.

24 DDF, IX, no.535 (9.6.38).

25 DGFP, II, no.210 (26.5.38).

26 DDF, X, nos.235, 238, 242, 245 (20.7.38; 21.7.38).

27 DBFP, I, no.521 (20.7.38).

28 DBFP, II, nos.753, 758 (3.9.38; 4.9.38).

29 For the Sudeten German reactions, see Celovsky, *Münchener Abkommen*, pp. 294–7; Ronald Smelser, *The Sudeten Problem 1933–1938: Volkstumpolitik and the Formulation of Nazi Foreign Policy* (Middletown, CT: Wesleyan University Press, 1975), pp. 237–40.

30 John W. Wheeler-Bennett, *Munich: Prologue to Tragedy* (London: Macmillan, 1948), pp. 95–7; Middlemas, *Diplomacy of Illusion*, pp. 323–4.

31 Middlemas, *Diplomacy of Illusion*, pp. 275–8; David Dilks, 'Appeasement and "Intelligence"', in David Dilks, ed., *Retreat from Power: Studies in Britain's Foreign Policy in the Twentieth Century*, vol. I, *1906–1939* (London: Macmillan, 1981), pp. 147–8.

32 Middlemas, *Diplomacy of Illusion*, pp. 296–300, 319–22; Taylor, *Munich*, pp. 669–74.

33 Middlemas, *Diplomacy of Illusion*, p. 325.

34 DBFP, II, no.823 (10.9.38).

35 Smelser, *Sudeten Problem*, pp. 237–40.

36 Middlemas, *Diplomacy of Illusion*, pp. 331–3; Adamthwaite, *France*, pp. 210–11.

37 Middlemas, *Diplomacy of Illusion*, p. 334; Cowling, *Impact of Hitler*, pp. 186–7.

38 Smelser, *Sudeten Problem*, pp. 237–41 sees weaknesses in Henlein's position, but Celovsky, *Münchener Abkommen*, pp. 334–5 supports the contemporary view of François-Poncet that he executed a skilful manoeuvre. See DDF, XI, no.171 (15.9.38).

39 L. E. Hill, ed., *Die Weizsäcker-Papiere, 1933–1950* (Frankfurt: Ullstein, Pro-pyläen-Verlag, 1974), p. 143; for the official record of the talks, DGFP, II, no.487 (15.9.38); for Chamberlain's and Wilson's notes, DBFP, II, nos.895, 897 (15–16.9.38).

40 Middlemas, *Diplomacy of Illusion*, p. 346–54; Taylor, *Munich*, pp. 747–52; DBFP, II, no.928 (18.9.38).

41 DDF, XI, nos.222, 232 (19.9.38; 20.9.38).

42 Celovsky, *Münchener Abkommen*, p. 383; Taylor, *Munich*, pp. 804–5; D.C. Watt, 'Introduction', in D. Irving, ed., *Breach of Security: The German Secret Intelligence File on Events Leading to the Second World War* (London: Kimber, 1968), pp. 15–42.

43 Henke, *England*, pp. 176–7; Weinberg, *Foreign Policy*, pp. 432–7.

44 DDF, XI, nos.183, 203, 237, 245, 254, 291 (17.9.38; 18.9.38; 20.9.38; 21.9.38; 22.9.38).

45 Middlemas, *Diplomacy of Illusion*, pp. 360–4; Cowling, *Impact of Hitler*, p. 193; Taylor, *Munich*, pp. 795–8.

46 Middlemas, *Diplomacy of Illusion*, pp. 370–3; Taylor, *Munich*, pp. 810–13.

47 Dilks, *Cadogan Diaries*, pp. 102–3.

48 Celovsky, *Münchener Abkommen*, pp. 414–15; Adamthwaite, *France*, pp. 177–8, 217.

49 DBFP, II, no.1093 (25.9.38). For French military plans, see Adamthwaite, *France*, pp. 226–32, and Taylor, *Munich*, pp. 859–61. France might undertake a limited attack, but the plans were essentially defensive.

50 Middlemas, *Diplomacy of Illusion*, pp. 386–7.

51 DBFP, II, no.1118 (26.9.38).

52 Bullock, *Hitler*, pp. 461–5; for the Berliners' reaction, see William L. Shirer, *Berlin Diary* (New York: Knopf, 1942), pp. 142–3; Paul Schmidt, *Statist auf Diplomatischer Bühne* (Bonn: Athenum, 1949), p. 410.

53 DGFP, II, no.635 (27.9.38); Dilks, *Cadogan Diaries*, p. 109.

54 Adamthwaite, *France*, pp. 221–2. See also Celovsky, *Münchener Abkommen*, p. 426; DDF, XI, no.400 (27.9.38). These accounts demonstrate the lack of reliable information on French Cabinet meetings and leave unanswered the question whether Bonnet had Daladier's authorisation for the major concession he was about to offer.

55 Middlemas, *Diplomacy of Illusion*, pp. 391–4.

56 Middlemas's account (pp. 390–6) is confusing: Halifax did not agree to 'force the Godesberg terms on the Czechs', as is later made clear (p. 396), and as is confirmed by *Cadogan Diaries*, p. 107. See also Taylor, *Munich*, pp. 870–5; 877–8; 881–9.

57 DDF, no.413 (28.9.38); René Girault, 'La décision gouvernementale en politique extérieure', in René Rémond and Janine Bourdin, eds., *Edouard Daladier, Chef du Gouvernement* (Paris: Presses de la fondation nationale des sciences politiques, 1977), p. 217.

58 Taylor, *Munich*, pp. 884–5.

59 DBFP, II, nos.1158, 1159 (28.9.38).

60 *Ibid.*, nos.1180–2 (28.9.38); Bullock, *Hitler*, p. 467; Taylor, *Munich*, p. 894.

61 There is no official record, but for Wilson's account, see DBFP, II, no.1227 (29–30.9.38). The fullest account is in Taylor, *Munich*, pp. 14–57.

62 Taylor, *Munich*, p. 60.
63 See e.g., Bullock, *Hitler*; Klaus Hildebrand, *The Foreign Policy of the Third Reich* (Berkeley: University of California Press, 1973).
64 Taylor, *Munich*, pp. 681–706; Robert J. O'Neill, *The German Army and the Nazi Party, 1933–1939* (London: Corgi, 1968), pp. 211–32.
65 DGFP, II, no.175 (20.5.38).
66 O'Neill, *German Army*, p. 223.
67 Paul Kennedy, *Strategy and Diplomacy 1870–1945: Eight Studies* (London: Allen & Unwin, 1983), pp. 87–106.
68 Support for the balance of power was latent, not explicit: it was not part of the standard rhetoric of the time, but was evident in the willingness to support France against German attack, and in the general hostility to Germany's gaining a preponderance of power.
69 Weinberg, *Foreign Policy*, pp. 325–31.
70 See, e.g., Paul M. Kennedy, 'The Tradition of Appeasement in British Foreign Policy, 1865–1939', *British Journal of International Studies*, 2 (1976), pp. 203–15.
71 Middlemas, *Diplomacy of Illusion*, pp. 69–79; Aaron L. Goldman, 'Two Views of Germany: Nevile Henderson vs Vansittart and the Foreign Office, 1937–1939', *British Journal of International Studies*, 6 (1980), pp. 247–77.
72 Keith Feiling, *Life of Neville Chamberlain* (London: Macmillan, 1946), p. 367.
73 French objectives are discussed in Adamthwaite, *France, passim*, esp. pp. 106–9, 180–1.
74 Taylor, *Munich*, pp. 685–90, 702–6.
75 Weinberg, *Foreign Policy*, pp. 379–93, 423–4.
76 O'Neill, *German Army*, pp. 213–21, for excerpts from Beck's memoranda.
77 *Ibid.*, p. 224.
78 Adamthwaite, *France*, pp. 178–9, on Bonnet's discussions with the German Ambassador.
79 Taylor, *Munich*, pp. 624–6; Middlemas, *Diplomacy of Illusion*, pp. 186–7.
80 Feiling, *Chamberlain*, p. 297.
81 *Ibid.*, p. 357.
82 Dilks, 'Appeasement and "Intelligence"', pp. 147–8.
83 DDF XI, no.171 (15.9.38).
84 Taylor, *Munich*, pp. 820–1.
85 Dilks, *Cadogan Diaries*, p. 103.
86 See dispatches of François-Poncet between 13–27 September, DDF, XI.
87 Dilks, *Cadogan Diaries*, p. 63; Cowling, *Impact of Hitler*, p. 198.
88 Comment by General Ironside, in Brian Bond, *British Military Policy Between the Two World Wars* (Oxford: Clarendon Press, 1980), p. 278.
89 Taylor, *Munich*, pp. 834–5, and for Pownall's similar advice, pp. 886–7; see also Bond, *British Military Policy*, pp. 278, 281.
90 Taylor, *Munich*, pp. 882, 885–9; Bond, *British Military Policy*, p. 281.
91 F. H. Hinsley, *British Intelligence in the Second World War: Its Influence on Strategy and Operations* (London: HMSO, 1979), vol. I, pp. 78–9.
92 E.g., Middlemas, *Diplomacy of Illusion*, pp. 192–4; Bond, *British Military Policy*, pp. 279–82 partially supports this view. John Dunbabin argues persuasively that 'the chief military contribution ... was the establishment of

strategic parameters within which appeasement was a very natural re-action'. See his 'The British Military Establishment and the Policy of Appeasement', in Wolfgang J. Mommsen and Lothar Kettenacker, eds., *The Fascist Challenge and the Policy of Appeasement* (London: Allen & Unwin, 1983), p. 181.

93 On the last of these, see the discussion of attribution theory in Deborah Welch Larson, *Origins of Containment: A Psychological Explanation* (Princeton: Princeton University Press, 1985), pp. 34–42.

94 Adamthwaite, *France*, pp. 238–41.

95 In contrast to Britain, there was no Cabinet secretariat and no formal record of Cabinet meetings. *Ibid*, pp. 111, 397–402.

96 D. C. Watt, 'British Intelligence and the Coming of the Second World War in Europe', in Ernest R. May, ed., *Knowing One's Enemies* (Princeton: Princeton University Press, 1985), p. 263.

8 The Franco-Prussian and Agadir crises

1 In the case of the unification of Italy, France had obtained such compensation in Nice and Savoy. Following Prussia's gains in 1866, Bismarck rebuffed Napoleon's attempt to recover the frontiers of 1814 or to establish a claim over Belgium. In the crisis over Luxembourg in 1867 he may have sought to accommodate France, but the outcome was perceived in France as yet another embarrassment engineered by Bismarck. For a brief account, see M. R. D. Foot, 'The Origins of the Franco-Prussian War and the Re-making of Germany', in *New Cambridge Modern History*, vol. X (Cambridge: Cambridge University Press, 1960), pp. 577–82.

2 For French attitudes, see, e.g., Case, *French Opinion*; Elisabeth Fehrenbach, 'Preussen-Deutschland als Faktor der Französischen Aussenpolitik in der Reichsgründungszeit', *Historische Zeitschrift*, supplement 6 (new series, 1980), pp. 109–37. For Bismarck's perception, see Lothar Gall, *Bismarck: The White Revolutionary*, vol. I, *1815–1871*, translated by J. A. Underwood (London: Allen & Unwin, 1986), p. 335. Gall's interpretation is more convincing than the contrary view, asserted, e.g., by A. J. P. Taylor, *Bismarck: The Man and the Statesman* (London: Arrow Books, 1961), pp. 115–17.

3 For the failure of attempts to achieve a Franco-Austrian alliance, see Foot, 'Origins', pp. 582–4, 586; Gall, *Bismarck*, pp. 337–8; Taylor, *Struggle for Mastery*, pp. 185, 188–96.

4 *Ibid.*, pp. 175, 179–80, 183–5, 188–9, 196–8.

5 Richard Millman, *British Foreign Policy and the Coming of the Franco-Prussian War* (Oxford: Clarendon Press, 1965).

6 Foot, 'Origins', pp. 587–8; Gall, *Bismarck*, pp. 344–6, 348–50; Lawrence D. Steefel, *Bismarck, the Hohenzollern Candidacy, and the Origins of the Franco-German War of 1870* (Cambridge, MA: Harvard University Press, 1962), pp. 11–61; for the text of Bismarck's memorandum, Georges Bonnin, ed., *Bismarck and the Hohenzollern Candidature for the Spanish Throne: The Documents in the German Diplomatic Archives* (London: Chatto & Windus, 1957), pp. 68–73.

7 Gall, *Bismarck*, pp. 352–4; Steefel, *Bismarck*, pp. 61–84; Bonnin, *Hohenzollern Candidature*, pp. 73–163.

8 Steefel, *Bismarck*, pp. 84–100; Bonnin, *Hohenzollern Candidature*, pp. 163–212.

9 In addition to Steefel and Bonnin, see Josef Becker, 'Zum Problem der Bismarckschen Politik in der Spanischen Thronfrage 1870', *Historische Zeitschrift*, 212 (1971), pp. 529-607.

10 Gall, *Bismarck*, p. 349. The work was first published as *Bismarck: Der Weisse Revolutionär* (Frankfurt-on-Main: Ullstein, 1980).

11 *Ibid.*, pp. 348-51; Otto Pflanze, *Bismarck and the Development of Germany: The Period of Unification 1815-1871* (Princeton: Princeton University Press, 1963), pp. 395-418.

12 Gall, *Bismarck*, pp. 351-2.

13 Ibid., pp. 353-4; Pflanze, *Bismarck*, pp. 447-8.

14 The evidence is drawn together in Nancy Nichols Barker, *Distaff Diplomacy: The Empress Eugenie and the Foreign Policy of the Second Empire* (Austin: University of Texas Press, 1967), pp. 186-94. See also James F. McMillan, *Napoleon III* (London: Longman, 1991), pp. 154-5.

15 Gall, *Bismarck*, p. 348.

16 See, e.g., Case, *French Opinion*; Natalie Isser, *The Second Empire and the Press* (The Hague: Nijhoff, 1974), pp. 182-90.

17 Translated from Fehrenbach, 'Preussen-Deutschland', p. 134.

18 *Ibid.*, pp. 126-37.

19 Emile Ollivier, *L'Empire Libéral* (Paris: Garnier Frères, 1895-1912), vol. XIV, pp. 35-6; Case, *French Opinion*, pp. 243-4, 313.

20 Robert H. Lord, *The Origins of the War of 1870: New Documents from the German Archives* (Cambridge, MA: Harvard Historical Studies XXVIII, 1924), p. 121.

21 Foot, 'Origins', p. 590.

22 *Ibid.*

23 *Ibid.*

24 Steefel, *Bismarck*, pp. 121-5.

25 Ollivier, *L'Empire Libéral*, pp. 99-108; Steefel, *Bismarck*, pp. 112-13.

26 Barker, *Distaff Diplomacy*, p. 195.

27 Lord, *Origins*, pp. 128-32.

28 *Ibid.*, p. 155; Steefel, *Bismarck*, p. 119.

29 *Ibid.*, pp. 110-11, 120-1.

30 S. William Halperin, *Diplomat Under Stress: Visconti-Venosta and the Crisis of July 1870* (Chicago: University of Chicago Press, 1963), pp. 34-5, 42-3.

31 Steefel, *Bismarck*, p. 126. For accounts of this phase, see *Ibid.*, pp. 125-43; documents in Bonnin, *Hohenzollern Candidature*, pp. 229-52; Lord, *Origins*, pp. 154-205.

32 Bonnin, *Hohenzollern Candidature*, p. 232.

33 Steefel, *Bismarck*, p. 133.

34 *Ibid.*, pp. 137-9; Barker, *Distaff Diplomacy*, pp. 196-7. The King of Roumania was Leopold's brother: there were fears that France would seek to weaken his position. The Belgian intervention impressed Karl Anton (see Bonnin, *Hohenzollern Candidature*, p. 250).

35 Lord, *Origins*, p. 67.

36 Steefel, *Bismarck*, p. 146. The few included Thiers and Guizot.

37 Ollivier, *L'Empire Libéral*, p. 199; France, Foreign Ministry, *Les Origines Diplomatiques de la Guerre de 1870-1871* (Paris, 1910-1930), vol. XXVIII, p. 270 (Ollivier's report to Napoleon).

38 *Ibid.*, pp. 222–3, 250–1; Steefel, *Bismarck*, p. 149.
39 Millman, *British Foreign Policy*, p. 186; for Napoleon's comment, see Hermann Oncken, *Die Rheinpolitik Kaiser Napoleons III von 1863 bis 1870 und der Ursprung des Krieges von 1870/71* (Stuttgart: 1926), vol. III, p. 427.
40 Steefel, *Bismarck*, pp. 144–64; Case, *French Opinion*, pp. 251–6.
41 Steefel, *Bismarck*, pp. 178–92.
42 *Ibid.*, p. 166.
43 *Ibid.*, pp. 168–77.
44 *Ibid.*, pp. 195–8.
45 *Ibid.*, pp. 199–203.
46 *Ibid.*, pp. 203–13; Case, *French Opinion*, pp. 256–65.
47 For discussions of the idea of the necessity of war in Germany in this period, see V. R. Berghahn, *Germany and the Approach of War in 1914* (London: Macmillan, 1973), pp. 81, 165–75; Isobel V. Hull, *The Entourage of Kaiser Wilhelm II, 1888–1918* (Cambridge: Cambridge University Press, 1982), pp. 236–65.
48 The Anglo-Russian entente in 1907 complemented the Franco-Russian alliance (1892) and the Anglo-French entente (1904). The Triple Alliance between Germany, Austria and Italy dated from 1882.
49 Ima C. Barlow, *The Agadir Crisis* (Hamden, CT: Archon Books, 1971), p. 76. (First published by University of North Carolina Press, 1940.)
50 *Ibid.*, pp. 76–83; Geoffrey Barraclough, *From Agadir to Armageddon: Anatomy of a Crisis* (London: Weidenfeld and Nicolson, 1982), pp. 86–7.
51 Interpretations differ as to how far the change of government from that of Briand, in which Pichon was the long-serving Foreign Minister, to Monis, with Cruppi as Foreign Minister, marked a change in French policy. Barraclough emphasises the continuity of French pressure to gain full political control (*Ibid.*, pp. 87–94), whereas Allain argues that the new Ministry abandoned its predecessor's willingness to accept the constraint of internationally negotiated arrangements. Jean-Claude Allain, *Agadir 1911: Une crise impérialiste en Europe pour la conquête du Maroc* (Paris: Sorbonne, 1976), pp. 274–97. The difference has little bearing on the present account of the crisis.
52 Barlow, *Crisis*, pp. 178–84.
53 Allain, *Agadir*, pp. 275–6, 314–16; Barlow, *Crisis*, pp. 187, 190–5.
54 *Ibid.*, p. 195; Allain, *Agadir*, pp. 316–17. For an account of differences within the Foreign Ministry, see Keiger, *France and the Origins of the First World War*, pp. 25–43.
55 Barlow, *Crisis*, pp. 220–2; Allain, *Agadir*, pp. 322–3; Fischer, *War of Illusions*, pp. 72–3. The Kaiser shared the alarm of German conservatives over the prospect of electoral gains by the Social Democrats.
56 *Ibid.*, p. 73; Allain, *Agadir*, pp. 327, 398–400; Joanne Stafford Mortimer, 'Commercial Interests and German Diplomacy in the Agadir Crisis', *Historical Journal*, 10 (1967), pp. 442–5; Michael Balfour, *The Kaiser and his Times* (London: Cresset Press, 1964), pp. 262, 310–12.
57 Allain, *Agadir*, pp. 325–6; Barraclough, *From Agadir*, p. 101.
58 *Ibid.*, p. 103.
59 Barlow, *Crisis*, pp. 207–14; Allain, *Agadir*, pp. 327–8.

60 *Ibid.*, p. 329.
61 Fischer, *War of Illusions*, pp. 74–5; Barlow, *Crisis*, pp. 233–7.
62 Allain, *Agadir*, pp. 351–2; Barlow, *Crisis*, pp. 238–43; Samuel R. Williamson, Jr, *The Politics of Grand Strategy: Britain and France Prepare for War, 1904–1914* (Cambridge, MA: Harvard University Press, 1969), pp. 145–7.
63 Barlow, *Crisis*, pp. 243–51; Allain, *Agadir*, p. 386; Williamson, *Grand Strategy*, pp. 146–8.
64 Barlow, *Crisis*, pp. 255–60.
65 *Ibid.*, pp. 262–3; Barraclough, *From Agadir*, pp. 126–8.
66 Williamson, *Grand Strategy*, pp. 150–2; M. L. Dockrill, 'British Policy During the Agadir Crisis of 1911', in F. H. Hinsley, ed., *British Foreign Policy under Sir Edward Grey* (Cambridge: Cambridge University Press, 1977), pp. 275–7.
67 Barlow, *Crisis*, pp. 263–7.
68 'Euer Exzellenz sind ermächtigt, Verhandlungen in bisher befohlener Weise fortzuführen.' Ernst Jaeckh, ed., *Kiderlen-Wächter, Der Staatsmann und Mensch: Briefwechsel und Nachlass* (Stuttgart: Deutsche Verlags-Anstalt, 1924), vol. II, p. 134. Barlow, *Crisis*, p. 267, presents this as his authorising Kiderlen to conduct the negotiations as he deemed best; Allain, *Agadir*, p. 371 claims that he was given 'full power' to do so.
69 Translation in Fischer, *War of Illusions*, pp. 75–7; text in Jaeckh, *Kiderlen-Wächter*, pp. 128–30.
70 Translated from *Ibid.*, p. 134.
71 Barlow, *Crisis*, pp. 269–70.
72 Dockrill, 'British Policy', pp. 277–8; Williamson, *Grand Strategy*, p. 153.
73 Barlow, *Crisis*, p. 298. See also Williamson, *Grand Strategy*, pp. 153–4; Dockrill, 'British Policy', pp. 278–9; Keith Wilson, 'The Agadir Crisis, the Mansion House Speech, and the Double-Edgedness of Agreements', *Historical Journal*, 15 (1972), pp. 513–32; Timothy Boyle, 'New Light on Lloyd George's Mansion House Speech', *Historical Journal*, 23 (1980), pp. 431–3.
74 Barlow, *Crisis*, pp. 305–7; Wilson, 'Mansion House Speech', p. 521.
75 Barlow, *Crisis*, pp. 307–12. Kiderlen had earlier sought, unsuccessfully, to avoid the risk of a meeting of the fleets, at a time when such an order would have been unalarming. *Ibid.*, pp. 290–1.
76 *Ibid.*, pp. 313–16; Dockrill, 'British Policy', p. 279.
77 Konrad H. Jarausch, *The Enigmatic Chancellor: Bethmann-Hollweg and the Hubris of Imperial Germany* (New Haven: Yale University Press, 1972), pp. 122–3; Barlow, *Crisis*, pp. 325–8.
78 Barlow, *Crisis*, pp. 328–35.
79 Barraclough, *From Agadir*, pp. 134–5; Barlow, *Crisis*, pp. 338–9; Snyder and Diesing's claim that 'the German government, at the Kaiser's insistence, made a firm decision not to go to war, no matter how little France offered', goes beyond the available evidence (Snyder and Diesing, *Conflict Among Nations*, p. 544), but the Kaiser's reluctance to have Morocco become a *casus belli* is well documented. See, e.g., Balfour, *The Kaiser*, pp. 310–14.
80 For the press criticisms, see Fischer, *War of Illusions*, p. 83.
81 *Ibid.*, p. 88 (the last sentence is modified in line with the translation in Berghahn, *Germany*, p. 97).
82 Barlow, *Crisis*, pp. 339–42; Barraclough, *From Agadir*, pp. 136–7.

83 Joffre reports that the conversation took place in the first days of August. Allain argues that it was probably later – not convincingly in view of Caillaux's actions in early August (*Agadir*, p. 370).

84 Barlow, *Crisis*, p. 346.

85 *Ibid.*, pp. 343–7.

86 Barlow discounts French initiatives, suggesting that German financiers withheld their support for the market as a means of pressuring their government to be less secretive (*Ibid.*, pp. 351–5). On the other hand, Allain gives some credence to the view that Caillaux's influence on French financiers played a part. Jean-Claude Allain, *Joseph Caillaux: Le Défi Victorieux, 1863–1914* (Paris: Imprimerie Nationale, 1978), pp. 383–4.

87 Barlow, *Crisis*, pp. 363–73.

88 *Ibid.*, pp. 374–87; Keiger, *France*, pp. 47–8.

89 See, e.g., Barlow, *Crisis*, p. 374; Snyder and Diesing, *Conflict Among Nations*, p. 545.

90 Allain, *Joseph Caillaux*, pp. 377–9; Jarausch, *Enigmatic Chancellor*, pp. 121–2; Wayne C. Thompson, *In the Eye of the Storm: Kurt Riezler and the Crises of Modern Germany* (Iowa City: University of Iowa Press, 1980), p. 40.

91 For example, Dr Ludwig Delbrück, a banker, reported at that time that Germany could demand whatever colonial concessions it wished, provided it conceded Morocco. Barraclough, *From Agadir*, p. 109.

9   Pearl Harbor and the Berlin crises

1 Snyder and Diesing, *Conflict Among Nations*, pp. 553–6; Michael A. Barnhart, *Japan Prepares for Total War: The Search for Economic Security, 1919–1941* (Ithaca: Cornell University Press, 1987); Waldo Heinrichs, *Threshold of War: Franklin D. Roosevelt and American Entry into World War II* (New York: Oxford University Press, 1988).

2 Paul W. Schroeder, *The Axis Alliance and Japanese–American Relations* (Ithaca: Cornell University Press, 1958); Chihiro Hosoya, 'Miscalculations in Deterrent Policy: Japanese–US Relations, 1938–1941', *Journal of Peace Research*, 5 (1968), pp. 97–115; Robert J. C. Butow, 'The Hull–Nomura Conversations: A Fundamental Misconception', *American Historical Review*, 65 (1960), pp. 822–36; Butow, *The John Doe Associates: Backdoor Diplomacy for Peace, 1941* (Stanford: Stanford University Press, 1974); Abraham Ben-Zvi, *The Illusion of Deterrence: The Roosevelt Presidency and the Origins of the Pacific War* (Boulder, CO: Westview, 1987).

3 The contributors to *Pearl Harbor as History*, a major collaborative project by American and Japanese historians, could reach no agreement on the question whether war could have been avoided. See Richard W. Leopold, 'Historiographical Reflections', in Dorothy Borg and Shumpei Okamoto, eds., *Pearl Harbor as History: Japanese–American Relations 1931–1941* (New York: Columbia University Press, 1973), p. 20.

4 Herbert Feis, *The Road to Pearl Harbor* (New York: Atheneum, 1962, originally published by Princeton University Press, 1950), pp. 21–3, 49–50; Robert Dallek, *Franklin D. Roosevelt and American Foreign Policy, 1932–1945* (New York: Oxford University Press, 1979), pp. 193–6, 236–7.

5 For a general account of these events see Feis, *Pearl Harbor*, pp. 56–71. For the British decision on the Burma Road, which followed the US rejection of a British proposal that it send naval support to Singapore, see Peter Lowe, *Great Britain and the Origins of the Pacific War: A Study of British Policy in East Asia 1937–1941* (Oxford: Clarendon Press, 1977), pp. 136–75.

6 Feis, *Pearl Harbor*, pp. 72–5, 88–94; Dallek, *Roosevelt*, pp. 239–41; Irvine H. Anderson, Jr, 'The 1941 *De Facto* Embargo on Oil to Japan: A Bureaucratic Reflex', *Pacific Historical Review*, 44 (1975), pp. 203–10; Cordell Hull, *The Memoirs of Cordell Hull* (London: Hodder & Stoughton, 1948), vol. I, pp. 897–9.

7 Feis, *Pearl Harbor*, pp. 76–87; Barnhart, *Japan Prepares*, pp. 162–70.

8 Feis, *Pearl Harbor*, pp. 101–9.

9 *Ibid.*, pp. 110–21; James W. Morley, ed., *Deterrent Diplomacy: Japan, Germany and the USSR, 1935–1940* (New York: Columbia University Press, 1976).

10 Barnhart, *Japan Prepares*, pp. 162–75, 198–214; Asada Sadao, 'The Japanese Navy and the United States', in Borg and Okamoto, eds., *Pearl Harbor*, pp. 225–59; Tsunoda Jun, 'The Navy's Role in the Southern Strategy', in James W. Morley, ed., *The Fateful Choice: Japan's Advance into Southeast Asia, 1939–1941* (New York: Columbia University Press, 1980), pp. 241–95.

11 Feis, *Pearl Harbor*, pp. 145–9, 180–7.

12 *Ibid.*, pp. 130–1, 150–1, 207–8; Barnhart, *Japan Prepares*, pp. 165–6, 207–8, 217–18.

13 For an overview, see Feis, *Pearl Harbor*, pp. 122–32, 153–70.

14 See Butow, 'Hull–Nomura Conversations'; Hosoya Chihiro, 'The Role of Japan's Foreign Ministry and its Embassy in Washington', in Borg and Okamoto, eds., *Pearl Harbor*, pp. 149–64.

15 Hull states that: 'I estimated right at the outset that there was not one chance in twenty or one in fifty or even one in a hundred ... but if new agreements would contribute to peace in the Pacific, we believed we should not throw the chance away, however microscopic it was', Hull, *Memoirs*, vol. II, pp. 985–6.

16 For Hull's account, *ibid.*, pp. 982–1011.

17 Quoted in Feis, *Pearl Harbor*, p. 206.

18 Nobutaka Ike, *Japan's Decision for War: Records of the 1941 Policy Conferences* (Stanford: Stanford University Press, 1967), pp. 47–53.

19 *Ibid.*, pp. 53–77; Feis, *Pearl Harbor*, pp. 202–18; Barnhart, *Japan Prepares*, pp. 208–14; F. C. Jones, *Japan's New Order in East Asia* (London: Oxford University Press, 1954), pp. 455–7.

20 Ike, *Japan's Decision*, pp. 93–110; Feis, *Pearl Harbor*, pp. 219–61. For details on the intercepted messages, and how they were interpreted, see Wohlstetter, *Pearl Harbor*, pp. 98–131.

21 For a brief note on views expressed in the State Department, see United States, Department of State, *Foreign Relations of the United States, Department of State, Foreign Relations of the United States, 1941*, vol. V, p. 210, note 90 (henceforth *FRUS*).

22 Anderson, '*De Facto* Embargo', p. 219. Japan had placed orders at record levels in the preceding months, and in June, due to scarcity in the eastern states of the US, oil exports from east-coast ports had been prohibited, with the sole exception of deliveries to Britain.

23 For accounts of these developments see *ibid.*, pp. 219–30; Dallek, *Roosevelt*, pp. 274–5; Feis, *Pearl Harbor*, pp. 227–48; Heinrichs, *Threshold*, pp. 132–6, 141–2, 153, 159–60, 176–8.

24 Heinrichs, *Threshold*, p. 177. Feis anticipates, and Dallek follows Anderson's interpretation, the 'bureaucratic reflex'. For critical analyses of the 'hard-line' advocacy of an embargo, see Ben Zvi, *Illusion*, pp. 31–65; Hosoya, 'Miscalculations in Deterrent Policy'. For an account of differing views within the Navy, even though the Commander of Naval Operations, Admiral Stark, was among the strongest opponents of the embargo, see James H. Herzog, 'Influence of the United States Navy in the Embargo of Oil to Japan 1940–1941', *Pacific Historical Review*, 35 (1966), pp. 317–28.

25 Barnhart, *Japan Prepares*, pp. 237–45.

26 *Ibid.*, pp. 245–7; Feis, *Pearl Harbor*, pp. 261–7; Ike, *Japan's Decision*, pp. 124–51.

27 For the text of the demands, see *ibid.*, p. 135–6.

28 Feis, *Pearl Harbor*, pp. 271–8; Hull, *Memoirs*, pp. 1016–33; Heinrichs, *Threshold*, pp. 161–2, 183–8. For the text of the definitive statement of American policy at this stage, Hull's Oral Statement of 2 October 1941, see *FRUS: Japan 1931–1941*, vol. II, pp. 656–61.

29 This appears to be the assumption of Feis, *Pearl Harbor*, pp. 274–8; Barnhart, *Japan Prepares*, pp. 232–4; and Dallek, *Roosevelt*, pp. 301–3. For an alternative view, see Jones, *New Order*, pp. 457–9.

30 Barnhart, *Japan Prepares*, pp. 248–54; Ike *Japan's Decision*, pp. 176–85.

31 See, e.g., Feis's comment that the crisis 'brought into power a group determined to fight us rather than move further our way. Thereafter war came first, diplomacy second' (*Pearl Harbor*, p. 277).

32 See R. J. C. Butow, *Tojo and the Coming of the War* (Stanford: Stanford University Press, 1961), pp. 313–44. 'Tojo did not become premier in order to lead Japan into war. He became premier in order to break the deadlock of indecision', *ibid.*, p. 314. For a detailed interpretation along these lines, see Eugene F. Sathre, 'Communication and Conflict: Japanese Foreign Policy Leading to the Pacific War', Ph. D. thesis, University of Minnesota, 1978.

33 For the text of the proposals, see Ike, *Japan's Decision*, pp. 209–11.

34 Hull, *Memoirs*, pp. 1069–86; Feis, *Pearl Harbor*, pp. 307–21; Dallek, *Roosevelt*, pp. 3305–8; Heinrichs, *Threshold*, pp. 206–11.

35 Butow, 'Hull–Nomura Conversations', pp. 339–43; Sathre, 'Communication and Conflict', pp. 89–92, 250–2, 278–81, 292–4.

36 Ike, *Japan's Decision*, p. 283; for the Imperial Conference as a whole, *ibid.*, pp. 262–83.

37 The yardstick here is Snyder and Diesing's contention that the function of crisis bargaining is to clarify options and issues. The foregoing argument has been addressed to the question whether different policy choices might have enabled the US to achieve one of its objectives (pressed especially strongly by the military), viz. to postpone and possibly avert a Pacific war in 1941. It does not address the question whether, given all the values and interests at stake, this would have been a better outcome. Churchill was not alone in his sense of relief and satisfaction at the US entry into the war.

38 The best account of American perspectives is Avi Shlaim, *The United States and the Berlin Blockade, 1948–1949: A Study in Crisis Decision-Making* (Berk-

eley: University of California Press, 1983). The British perspective is well brought out in Alan Bullock, *Ernest Bevin: Foreign Secretary* (Oxford: Oxford University Press, 1985, first published by Heinemann, 1983), and the French in John W. Young, *France, the Cold War and the Western Alliance, 1944–49: French Foreign Policy and Post-War Europe* (Leicester: Leicester University Press, 1990). Two earlier accounts which bring out the significance of politics in Berlin itself are W. Phillips Davison, *The Berlin Blockade: A Study in Cold War Politics* (Princeton: Princeton University Press, 1958) and Philip Windsor, *City on Leave: A History of Berlin, 1945–1962* (London: Chato & Windus, 1963).

39 Shlaim, *Berlin Blockade*, pp. 121–8; Jean E. Smith, ed., *The Papers of General Lucius D. Clay: Germany 1945–1949* (Bloomington: University of Indiana Press, 1974), vol. II, pp. 599–607.

40 Shlaim, *Berlin Blockade*, pp. 128–33; Smith, *Clay Papers*, pp. 607–8.

41 Shlaim, *Berlin Blockade*, pp. 133–5; Smith, *Clay Papers*, pp. 618–21.

42 Shlaim, *Berlin Blockade*, pp. 111–12 on the nature of the earlier policy studies, and pp. 47–109 on the basic attitudes of American decision makers in this phase of the Cold War.

43 Bullock, *Ernest Bevin*, p. 557.

44 Shlaim, *Berlin Blockade*, p. 136; Smith, *Clay Papers*, p. 622.

45 Shlaim, *Berlin Blockade*, p. 136; Smith, *Clay Papers*, p. 623. Clay expressed the widely shared view that, while further moves against the access of the Western powers were likely, a full blockade of the city would be too damaging to the Soviet image in Europe for its leaders to opt for so ruthless a measure.

46 *FRUS, 1948*, vol. II, p. 894 (Murphy to Marshall, 15 April 1948).

47 *Ibid.*, pp. 899–900 (Douglas to Marshall, 28 April 1948); Shlaim, *Berlin Blockade*, p. 140.

48 *Ibid.*, p. 141.

49 *Ibid.*, pp. 151–2; Smith, *Clay Papers*, pp. 643–4.

50 Shlaim, *Berlin Blockade*, pp. 152–7.

51 Shlaim, *Berlin Blockade*, pp. 158–62 for a discussion of Clay's decision to include the Western sectors of Berlin in the currency reform. Shlaim, citing Manuel Gottlieb's critique, questions why so important a decision was not referred back to Washington. Clay's account (Smith, *Clay Papers*, pp. 697–9) shows that he saw himself as implementing established policy. The accounts in Bullock (*Ernest Bevin*, pp. 573–4) and Windsor (*City on Leave*, pp. 104–6) implicitly support the decision. For the French statement see Smith, *Clay Papers*, p. 692.

52 The best account of this phase is Shlaim, *Berlin Blockade*, pp. 171–280. For the British response see Bullock, *Ernest Bevin*, pp. 571–80.

53 Douglas to Marshall, 26 June 1948, *FRUS, 1948*, vol. II, pp. 921–6; Shlaim, *Berlin Blockade*, p. 202.

54 *Ibid.*, pp. 218–19.

55 The Secretary of Defense, Deputy Secretary of State and Secretary for the Army, respectively.

56 Shlaim, *Berlin Blockade*, pp. 220–2.

57 *Ibid.*, pp. 202–11. For a discussion of Truman's and Clay's basic images and propensities, see *ibid.*, pp. 69–84, 97–109, 174–81, 186–94.

58 *Ibid.*, pp. 229–40. Shlaim argues that the B–29 deployment may well have achieved a deterrent effect; for a more sceptical analysis, see Harry R. Borowski, 'A Narrow Victory: the Berlin Blockade and the American Military Response', *US Air University Review*, 32 (1980–81), pp. 18–30.

59 Shlaim, *Berlin Blockade*, p. 241, notes the high level of American public support for using force to break the blockade; see also *ibid.*, p. 339.

60 *Ibid.*, pp. 244–5, 259–66.

61 Bullock, *Ernest Bevin*, pp. 588–90; Marshall to Douglas, 21 July 1948, *FRUS, 1948*, vol. II, pp. 975–6, and subsequent documents, pp. 977–83.

62 Shlaim, *Berlin Blockade*, pp. 313–14.

63 *Ibid.*, pp. 314–19, 322–6. For the text of the directive, Smith, *Clay Papers*, vol. II, pp. 779–80.

64 *Ibid.*, pp. 835–7; Shlaim, *Berlin Blockade*, pp. 328–33.

65 *Ibid.*, pp. 342–4.

66 Windsor, *City on Leave*, pp. 109–15; Jean E. Smith, *The Defense of Berlin* (Baltimore: Johns Hopkins Press, 1963), pp. 121–3.

67 As early as 21 July Clay had argued that the augmented airlift could sustain Berlin indefinitely without extreme hardship, but the general feeling at that stage was that it would buy time to seek a diplomatic solution (Shlaim, *Berlin Blockade*, pp. 261–3). Bevin did not express his confidence publicly until 22 September, after the September increase in the airlift (Bullock, *Ernest Bevin*, pp. 606–7.)

68 Shlaim, *Berlin Blockade*, p. 354.

69 *Ibid.*, p. 353.

70 *Ibid.*, pp. 355, 366–9, 372–3.

71 *Ibid.*, pp. 360–1, 370–1; George F. Kennan, *Memoirs, 1925–1950* (London: Hutchinson, 1968), pp. 418–26.

72 Shlaim, *Berlin Blockade*, pp. 361–6.

73 *Ibid.*, pp. 374–7.

74 *Ibid.*, p. 380.

75 *Ibid.*, pp. 380–2, 334–8; Charles E. Bohlen, *Witness to History, 1929–1969* (London: Weidenfeld & Nicolson, 1973), pp. 283–5; Philip C. Jessup, 'Park Avenue Diplomacy – Ending the Berlin Blockade', *Political Science Quarterly*, 87 (1972), pp. 377–400.

76 Smith, *Clay Papers*, pp. 1045–6.

77 Shlaim, *Berlin Blockade*, p. 378.

78 A review of two of the main studies of Soviet policy in the crisis concludes that: 'What emerges is the frailty of the evidence on Soviet decision making' (Richard D. Anderson, Jr, 'Questions of Evidence and Interpretation in Two Studies of Soviet Decisions in the Berlin Crises', *Slavic Review*, 42 (1983), p. 677). The two works are Hannes Adomeit, *Soviet Risk Taking and Crisis Behavior: A Theoretical and Empirical Analysis* (London: George Allen & Unwin, 1982), and Robert M. Slusser, *The Berlin Crisis of 1961: Soviet–American Relations and the Struggle for Power in the Kremlin, June–November 1961* (Baltimore: Johns Hopkins University Press, 1973). More recently Michael Beschloss has noted that although 'oral and written reminiscences by Soviet figures' now offer new insights, they still cannot be checked

NOTES TO PAGES 205–7

against documentary sources. Michael R. Beschloss, *Kennedy v. Khrushchev: The Crisis Years 1960–63* (London: Faber and Faber, 1991), p. viii.

79 See, e.g., Desmond Ball, *Politics and Force Levels: The Strategic Missile Program of the Kennedy Administration* (Berkeley: University of California Press, 1980), pp. 93–8; Arnold L. Horelick and Myron Rush, *Strategic Power and Soviet Foreign Policy* (Chicago: University of Chicago Press, 1966).

80 Charles de Gaulle, *Memoirs of Hope: Renewal and Endeavor*, trans. Terence Kilmartin (New York: Simon and Schuster, 1971), pp. 199–269.

81 Harold Macmillan, *Riding the Storm, 1956–1959* (London: Macmillan, 1971), pp. 557–656; *Pointing the Way, 1959–1961* (London: Macmillan, 1972), pp. 61–115, 178–216; Stephen E. Ambrose, *Eisenhower*, vol. II. *The President 1952–1969* (London: George Allen & Unwin, 1984), pp. 511–80; George B. Kistiakowsky, *A Scientist at the White House* (Cambridge, MA: Harvard University Press, 1976), *passim*.

82 Nikita S. Khrushchev, 'On Peaceful Coexistence', *Foreign Affairs*, 38 (1959), pp. 1–18.

83 Jack M. Schick, *The Berlin Crisis, 1958–1962* (Philadelphia: University of Pennsylvania Press, 1971), pp. 7–10, 56–8; James L. Richardson, *Germany and the Atlantic Alliance: The Interaction of Strategy and Politics* (Cambridge, MA: Harvard University Press, 1966), pp. 53–5, 233–6.

84 Schick, *Berlin Crisis*, p. 4, citing the declaration by the US, Britain and France of 3 October 1954.

85 Schick, *Berlin Crisis*, offers the best overview; Richardson, *Germany*, pp. 264–300 a briefer narrative; the memoirs of Eisenhower and Macmillan offer valuable detail on the earlier phase, Honoré M. Catudal, *Kennedy and the Berlin Wall Crisis: A Case Study in US Decision Making* (Berlin: Berlin Verlag, 1980) the fullest account of American policy in the second phase, on which Walther Stützle, *Kennedy und Adenauer in der Berlin-Krise 1961–1962* (Bonn: Verlag Neue Gesellschaft, 1973) and Beschloss, *Kennedy v. Khrushchev*, pp. 174–353 are also comprehensive.

86 Schick, *Berlin Crisis*, pp. 10–17, 20–23. For the texts see United States Senate, Committee on Foreign Relations, *Documents on Germany, 1944–1961* (Washington, DC: Government Printing Office, 1961), pp. 348–63, 389–401.

87 Schick, *Berlin Crisis*, pp. 30–45; Townsend Hoopes, *The Devil and John Foster Dulles* (London: André Deutsch, 1974), pp. 465–9.

88 Schick, *Berlin Crisis*, pp. 63–4.

89 Dwight D. Eisenhower, *Waging Peace: The White House Years 1956–1961* (London: Heinemann, 1966), pp. 331, 340–2; Hoopes, *Devil*, pp. 469–71.

90 Macmillan, *Storm*, pp. 587–8, 647.

91 Bundy, *Danger and Survival*, p. 374. Bundy's sympathetic account of Eisenhower's thinking (pp. 371–4) may be contrasted with Schick's critique (*Berlin Crisis*, pp. 49–53).

92 Schick, *Berlin Crisis*, pp. 56–68; Macmillan, *Storm*, pp. 585–7, 639–40; *Pointing the Way*, pp. 64, 66, 82, 98–100, 103–4; Konrad Adenauer, *Erinnerungen, 1955–1959* (Stuttgart: Deutsche Verlags-Anstalt, 1967), pp. 468–71, 480–2.

93 Schick, *Berlin Crisis*, pp. 36–8.

94 *Ibid.*, pp. 58–63; Macmillan, *Storm*, pp. 589–635, 642–7; Eisenhower, *Waging Peace*, pp. 349–55.
95 Schick, *Berlin Crisis*, pp. 71–96; Richardson, *Germany*, pp. 269–71.
96 Schick, *Berlin Crisis*, p. 96.
97 *Ibid.*, pp. 88–9, 95; Eisenhower, *Waging Peace*, pp. 405–8, 411–12.
98 Schick, *Berlin Crisis*, p. 99.
99 Eisenhower, *Waging Peace*, pp. 448–9.
100 Khrushchev, 'Peaceful Coexistence'.
101 Schick, *Berlin Crisis*, pp. 107–11.
102 *Ibid.*, pp. 111–21; Ambrose, *Eisenhower*, pp. 513–15, 568–80; for more extensive accounts see David Wise and Thomas B. Ross, *The U-2 Affair* (London: Cresset Press, 1963); Michael R. Beschloss, *Mayday: Eisenhower, Khrushchev and the U-2 Affair* (New York: Harper & Row, 1986).
103 Schick, *Berlin Crisis*, pp. 121–2, 129–33.
104 These included an *aide-mémoire* to Bonn (17 February) and Khrushchev's conversations with US Ambassador Llewellyn Thompson in March and with Walter Lippmann in April (*ibid.*, pp. 139–40).
105 *Ibid.*, pp. 145–7; Catudal, *Wall Crisis*, pp. 99–118; Schlesinger, *A Thousand Days*, pp. 324–39; Theodore C. Sorensen, *Kennedy* (London: Hodder & Stoughton, 1975), pp. 584–6; Beschloss, *Kennedy v. Khrushchev*, pp. 182–236.
106 Bundy, *Danger and Survival*, pp. 371–8; Schick, *Berlin Crisis*, pp. 151–2, 154–6.
107 *Ibid.*, pp. 147–9; Catudal, *Wall Crisis*, pp. 43–4, 137–48, 172–5; Schlesinger, *Thousand Days*, pp. 344–8. Acheson differed from Clay in recommending an airlift as the initial response, but since it was expected that the Soviets might now obstruct an airlift, attention was focused on the next contingency, the two-division 'probe'. However, in some respects Acheson's advice led to greater caution in contingency planning. Under previous planning, in the event of the transfer of control over access to West Berlin to East German authorities, Western officers would not permit East Germans to process their transit documents, rendering a blockade likely at the outset. The US, and subsequently the other powers, accepted Acheson's advice that 'the issue over which the fight is made' should not be the stamping of documents but 'the persistent physical interference with military or civilian traffic ... whether by East Germans or Soviets' (Catudal, *Wall Crisis*, pp. 220–2).
108 Schlesinger, *Thousand Days*, pp. 348–52; Catudal, *Wall Crisis*, pp. 148–50.
109 Catudal's characterisation of the debate in terms of offensive or defensive hypotheses concerning Soviet motivation (*ibid.*, pp. 147–50) is unconvincing. For the general approaches to the handling of conflict, see Graham T. Allison, Albert Carnesale and Joseph S. Nye Jr. eds., *Hawks, Doves and Owls: An Agenda for Avoiding Nuclear War* (New York: Norton, 1985), pp. 206–22.
110 Catudal notes his 'deep suspicion' of contingency plans (*ibid.*, p. 151), one of many attitudes which he shared with Macmillan (Macmillan, *Pointing the Way*, p. 389, refers to the 'absurd' American contingency planning).
111 Schick, *Berlin Crisis*, pp. 149–54; Schlesinger, *Thousand Days*, pp. 353–4; Sorensen, *Kennedy*, pp. 591–2; Catudal, *Wall Crisis*, pp. 180–3, 191–6. As Catudal makes clear, the dual emphasis, on negotiation as well as the military buildup, was better perceived in Europe than in the US itself.

112 Schick, *Berlin Crisis*, p. 158; Richardson, *Germany*, p. 123.

113 *Ibid.*, p. 285; Catudal, *Wall Crisis*, p. 125.

114 *Ibid.*, pp. 210–11.

115 *Ibid.*, pp. 184–6, 208–12; Schick, *Berlin Crisis*, pp. 159–66; Adomeit, *Soviet Risk Taking*, pp. 203, 206–9. Adomeit refers to the 'plausible conjecture' that Ulbricht began to press Moscow for a decision on the border problem in March.

116 Catudal, *Wall Crisis*, pp. 200–3; Beschloss, *Kennedy v. Khrushchev*, pp. 264, 268–73.

117 Catudal reviews US expectations and concurring allied views (*Wall Crisis*, pp. 31–8, 216–19, 229–50).

118 *Ibid.*, p. 200.

119 Most accounts treat this as the crucial turning point in 1961, e.g. Schick, *Berlin Crisis*, pp. 184–6; Adomeit, *Soviet Risk Taking*, p. 214. Sorensen does not refer to it, while for Schlesinger, 'the crisis was suddenly over' (*Thousand Days*, p. 362).

120 Schick, *Berlin Crisis*, pp. 168, 179; Adomeit, *Soviet Risk Taking*, p. 212, and for other military measures at this point, pp. 242–3.

121 Schick, *Berlin Crisis*, pp. 179–81.

122 Adomeit, *Soviet Risk Taking*, p. 213; Sorensen, *Kennedy*, pp. 552–5.

123 For accounts of these differences see Schick, *Berlin Crisis*, pp. 181–4, 192–3, 198–205; Stützle, *Kennedy und Adenauer, passim*.

124 These attitudes are expressed especially clearly in Heinrich Krone, 'Aufzeichnungen zur Deutschland- und Ostpolitik, 1954–1969', in Rudolf Morsey and Konrad Repgen, eds., *Adenauer-Studien III* (Mainz: Matthias-Grünewald-Verlag, 1974), esp. pp. 160–174, and are reflected in certain passages of Adenauer's memoirs, e.g., Konrad Adenauer, *Erinnerungen, 1959–1963: Fragmente* (Stuttgart: Deutsche Verlags-Anstalt, 1968), pp. 119–20, 124–8.

125 Stützle, *Kennedy und Adenauer*, pp. 168–77; Krone, 'Aufzeichnungen', pp. 163–70, referring *inter alia* to suggestions prompted by the West German ambassador to Moscow, Hans Kroll, for direct bilateral talks, and Adenauer's suggestion of a ten-year moratorium on changes in the legal position of Berlin or Germany.

126 Schick, *Berlin Crisis*, pp. 190–2; Stützle, *Kennedy und Adenauer*, pp. 198–200; Sorensen, *Kennedy*, p. 596.

127 Schick, *Berlin Crisis*, pp. 193–203; Stützle, *Kennedy und Adenauer*, pp. 204–24.

128 Schick, *Berlin Crisis*, pp. 208–11; Stützle, *Kennedy und Adenauer*, pp. 226–9, 236.

129 *Ibid.*, pp. 240–1; Richardson, *Germany*, pp. 298–9.

130 Schick emphasises, rather, the costs of the negotiations (*Berlin Crisis*, pp. 45–9, 233–41).

10 Crises and the international system: arenas, alignments and norms

1 Kenneth N. Waltz, *Theory of International Politics* (Reading, MA: Addison-Wesley, 1979); Snyder and Diesing, *Conflict Among Nations*; Hinsley, *Power*

and Peace; Richard N. Rosecrance, *Action and Reaction in World Politics: International Systems in Perspective* (Boston: Little, Brown, 1963); Schroeder, 'The 19th-Century International System'; Gordon A. Craig and Alexander L. George, *Force and Statecraft: Diplomatic Problems of Our Time* (New York: Oxford University Press, 1983).

2 Waltz, *Theory*, p. 69.

3 Some passages in Waltz lend themselves to a more deterministic interpretation, however. For a critique of Waltz's theory, understood in this sense, see Peter Gellman, 'The Elusive Explanation: Balance of Power "Theory" and the Origins of World War I', *Review of International Studies*, 15 (1989), pp. 155–82.

4 Snyder and Diesing, *Conflict Among Nations*, p. 419.

5 *Ibid.*, pp. 429–50.

6 Schroeder, 'The 19th-Century International System'. Schroeder does not spell out his concept of structure, but it would be in accord with the conceptualisation of David Dessler, whose 'transformational model' of international structure treats rules and resources as components of a system's structure. See David Dessler, 'What's at Stake in the Agent–Structure Debate?', *International Organization*, 43 (1989), pp. 441–73.

7 The concept of the 'arena' discussed here is limited to the politico-military relations of the great powers, and does not refer to the global economic system. For a study which explores many of the dimensions of the transformation of the European system into the global system of the present time, see Hedley Bull and Adam Watson, eds., *The Expansion of International Society* (Oxford: Clarendon Press, 1984).

8 Snyder and Diesing, *Conflict Among Nations*, pp. 429–40.

9 The pattern of alignments changed radically during this period, from the Bismarckian system centred on Germany to the opposing coalitions of the later years. See, e.g., Craig and George, *Force and Statecraft*, pp. 35–47. The cases included in the present work illustrate only the second of these phases.

10 Snyder and Diesing, *Conflict Among Nations*, p. 433. This, of course, was not the only reason for Britain's intervention, which may have been prompted more by its immediate perception of German attitudes than by alignment calculations.

11 The analysis in this paragraph draws on comments by Glenn Snyder.

12 See, e.g., Edward Vose Gulick, *Europe's Classical Balance of Power: A Case History of the Theory and Practice of One of the Great Concepts of European Statecraft* (New York: Norton, 1967). The extent of their agreement should not be overstated: the term 'balance of power' is notoriously ambiguous, and its application in practice was subject to the pressures of competing interests, like the norms of the Concert of Europe, discussed below. Schroeder argues that the term 'political equilibrium' was used more frequently than 'balance of power', and normally used in a moral-legal sense which accorded with the conservative ideas of the period, rather than as a synonym for a territorial balance, although it sometimes also had the latter connotation. Paul W. Schroeder, 'The Nineteenth Century System: Balance of Power or Political Equilibrium?', *Review of International Studies*, 15 (1989),

pp. 135–53. Carsten Holbraad, *The Concert of Europe: A Study in German and British International Theory, 1815–1914* (London: Longman, 1970), distinguishes between conservative and balance of power theories of the Concert. It is clear that both ideas (equilibrium based on conservative solidarity, and a generally acceptable balance among the territories of the great powers) were present in 1815, and that the application of the balance came about through intense political conflict – but this is often true of the application of agreed general principles.

13 F. H. Hinsley, *Power and Peace*, pp. 225–6; Schroeder, *Austria*, pp. 404–6.

14 *Ibid.*, p. 405.

15 Hinsley, *Power and Peace*, pp. 256–7; see also James Joll, '1914: The Unspoken Assumptions', in H. W. Koch, ed., *The Origins of the First World War: Great Power Rivalry and German War Aims* (London: Macmillan, 1972), pp. 307–28.

16 Hinsley, *Power and Peace*, pp. 304–6. For a fuller discussion of the conflicting conceptions of the balance of power, see Ludwig Dehio, *Germany and World Politics in the Twentieth Century*, trans. Dieter Pevsner (London: Chatto & Windus, 1959), especially 'Ranke and German Imperialism', pp. 38–71.

11   The choice of goals: values, interests and objectives

1 Hans J. Morgenthau, *Politics Among Nations: The Struggle for Power and Peace*, 4th edn. (New York: Knopf, 1967), pp. 9, 25; Raymond Aron, *Peace and War: A Theory of International Relations* (New York: Doubleday, 1966), pp. 71–93.

2 Arnold Wolfers, *Discord and Collaboration*, (Baltimore: Johns Hopkins Press, 1962), pp. 73–7, 91–9; Alexander L. George and Robert O. Keohane, 'The Concept of National Interests: Uses and Limitations', in Alexander L. George, *Presidential Decisionmaking in Foreign Policy: The Effective Use of Information and Advice* (Boulder, CO: Westview, 1980), pp. 217–37.

3 The above argument is in terms of preferences among realistic outcomes. It would not be difficult to identify preferred aspirations, but these will have only a limited relationship to the goals which policy makers actually pursue.

4 For Eyre Crowe's memorandum, see G. P. Gooch and H. Temperley, eds., *British Documents on the Origins of the War, 1914–1918* (London: HMSO, 1928), vol. III, pp. 397–420. For Kennan's article: X, 'The Sources of Soviet Conduct', *Foreign Affairs*, 25 (1947), pp. 566–82.

5 Friedrich Kratochwil, 'On the Notion of "Interest" in International Relations', *International Organization*, 36 (1982), p. 8.

6 The present concept is closely related to Brodie's concept of 'vital interest', and to Morgenthau's contention that a policy is properly regarded as being in the national interest only if it can be shown to be necessary for the attainment of goals which, in terms of a hierarchy of national values, justify the ensuing costs. Brodie, discussing the changing character of the interests which American governments and public opinion have deemed vital, searches for criteria which would justify the use of that concept, and thus the risks and sacrifices of war. Used in this sense, the concept coincides with neither the crude 'objective' nor 'subjective' concepts of national interest. There can be no 'objective' national interest because there are always different conceptions of it. But not every expression of a decision maker's

preferences counts as a conception of the national interest: as Brodie insists, the criteria must be appropriate, the arguments weighty. Bernard Brodie, *War and Politics* (New York: Macmillan, 1973), pp. 341–74; Hans J. Morgenthau, 'Another Great Debate: The National Interest of the United States' in Stanley Hoffmann, ed., *Contemporary Theory in International Relations*, (Englewood Cliffs, NJ: Prentice-Hall, 1960), pp. 73–9. For objective and subjective theories of the national interest, see James N. Rosenau, 'National Interest', *International Encyclopedia of the Social Sciences* (New York: Macmillan & Free Press, 1968), vol. XI, pp. 34–40.

7 See Chapter 2 above.

8 See, e.g., Elster, 'Introduction', pp. 3–4.

12 Selective perception and misperception

1 For a discussion of the concept see Lebow, *Between Peace and War*, pp. 90–1. Snyder and Diesing, *Conflict Among Nations*, pp. 317–18, refer to problems of interpretation.

2 Jervis, *Perception and Misperception*, p. 176.

3 Jack S. Levy, 'Misperception and the Causes of War: Theoretical Linkages and Analytical Problems', *World Politics*, 36 (1983), pp. 76–99, at pp. 93–8; Jervis, *Perception and Misperception*, pp. 6–8; Ole R. Holsti, 'Foreign Policy Formation Viewed Cognitively', in Robert Axelrod, ed., *Structure of Decision: The Cognitive Maps of Political Elites* (Princeton: Princeton University Press, 1976), pp. 18–54.

4 Levy, 'Misperception', p. 80.

5 Temperley, *The Crimea*, p. 372.

6 Snyder and Diesing, *Conflict Among Nations*, pp. 315–39, 488.

7 *Ibid.*, pp. 488–9.

8 Arthur A. Stein, 'When Misperception Matters', *World Politics*, 34 (1982), pp. 505–26, at pp. 505–6.

9 Robert H. White, *Nobody Wanted War* (Garden City, NY: Doubleday/ Anchor, 1970); John G. Stoessinger, *Why Nations Go to War* (New York: St Martin's Press, 1974), esp. pp. 27–30, 223–30; Stephen Van Evera, 'Why Cooperation Failed in 1914', *World Politics*, 38 (1985), pp. 80–117.

10 Robert Jervis, *Perception and Misperception*; Lebow, *Between Peace and War*, esp. pp. 57–97.

11 Stein, 'When Misperception Matters', p. 506.

12 *Ibid.*

13 Snyder and Diesing, *Conflict Among Nations*, pp. 315–32, 488–9.

14 Levy, 'Misperception', pp. 83–6, 88–9.

15 *Ibid.*, pp. 86–7, 89–91.

16 Alan Bullock, *Hitler*, pp. 525–50.

17 Jervis, *Perception and Misperception*, pp. 343–55.

18 Snyder and Diesing, *Conflict Among Nations*, pp. 297–310, offer a systematic characterisation of hard line and soft line preferences and perceptions.

19 Jervis, *Perception and Misperception*, especially pp. 8–9, 356–81; see also Robert Jervis, 'Deterrence and Perception', *International Security*, 7 (Winter 1982–83), pp. 3–30, esp. pp. 29–30.

20 Lebow, *Between Peace and War*, pp. 222–8.
21 *Ibid.*, pp. 153–222.
22 See Jervis, *Perception and Misperception*, pp. 32–57, 343–55; Deborah Welch Larson, *Origins of Containment*, pp. 34–42.
23 Jervis, *Perception and Misperception*, p. 343.
24 Larson, *Origins of Containment*, pp. 342–54.
25 The open-endedness of this conclusion is in line with Jervis's comment that misperception does not lend itself to modeling or formalisation in the same way as, for example, bargaining. Robert Jervis, 'Models and Cases in the Study of International Conflict', *Journal of International Affairs*, 44 (1990), pp. 81–101 at pp. 87–8.

13 Crisis bargaining

1 Schelling, *Arms and Influence*, pp. 135–6.
2 Snyder and Diesing, *Conflict Among Nations*, pp. 38–9 and *passim*. In a later passage they distinguish between bargaining and several other types of interaction: negotiation for 'side-effects' and the two extremes of no perceived conflict and pure conflict, thus leaving nearly all conflict to be construed in terms of bargaining. *Ibid.*, pp. 476–7.
3 The term 'policy' presents the same problems. In everyday usage a government's actions are invariably described as its policy; only occasionally, in the event of spectacular incoherence, is the question raised whether it actually has a policy. In this way assumptions of rationality and goal-directedness are embedded in the language with which governmental behaviour is regularly described. This point was prompted by comments by Glenn Snyder.
4 Richard Smoke offers a similar view of the role of bargaining in the context of the escalation of crises and wars:

> The evidence gathered here suggests that, indeed, *the applicability of bargaining is a variable, not a constant*. It hardly ever vanishes entirely as long as there is some potential for an action-reaction cycle. However, it may be greatly reduced in importance, and become partly or wholly unconscious in decision-makers, if for any reason good or bad they minimise the danger of a prompt counteraction by the opponent. (Smoke, *War: Controlling Escalation*, pp. 242–3.)

5 For a discussion of bargaining along these lines, see David Baldwin, *Economic Statecraft* (Princeton: Princeton University Press, 1985), pp. 96–114.
6 For an extended discussion of the hostility spiral, see Jervis, *Perception and Misperception*, pp. 58–113.
7 Smoke, *War: Controlling Escalation*, pp. 23–6, 245–8.
8 *Ibid.*, pp. 252–64, 293–5.
9 Snyder and Diesing, *Conflict Among Nations*, p. 480.
10 For an extended discussion of these distinctions, see *ibid.*, pp. 88–129. Prisoner's Dilemma is depicted in the text; the other models are as follows:

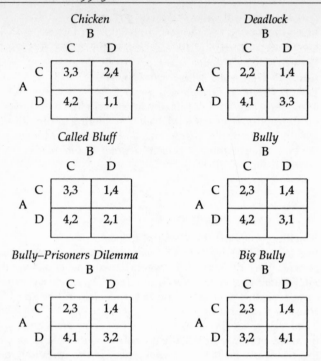

Each player (A and B) chooses a strategy (C or D, which may be understood as 'cooperate' and 'defect'). The payoffs, ranked from 4 (most preferred) to 1 (least preferred) depend on the players' combined choices, A's payoff being shown first. Figures as in Snyder and Diesing, *Conflict Among Nations*, pp. 43, 45–7. Copyright 1977 by Princeton University Press. Reproduced by permission of Princeton University Press.

11 *Ibid.*, pp. 39, 44, 86.
12 For an extended discussion, *ibid.*, pp. 88–106.
13 The table is based on *ibid.*, p. 482.
14 For Snyder and Diesing's interpretation of the case, see *ibid.*, pp. 111–13, 550–3.

14 Internal politics

1 For a brief comment on the 'state of the art' of theorising in this area, see Robert D. Putnam, 'Diplomacy and Domestic Politics: The Logic of Two-Level Games', *International Organization*, 42 (1988), pp. 427–60, at pp. 430–33.
2 The systems approach was developed by Gabriel A. Almond and G. Bingham Powell, *Comparative Politics: A Developmental Approach* (Boston: Little, Brown, 1966), and the associated Country Studies series, same publisher. The limited nature of the theoretical development since that period is indicated in Louis J. Cantori and Andrew H. Ziegler, Jr, eds. *Comparative Politics in the Post-Behavioral Era* (Boulder, CO: Lynne Rienner, 1988) and, with a somewhat different perspective, in Howard J. Wiarda, ed.,

New Directions in Comparative Politics (Boulder, CO: Westview, 1985), which notes the emergence of new 'paradigms' but concludes by endorsing the view that the general theories of the past have been replaced by 'islands of theory' in the present.

3 Putnam, 'Diplomacy and Domestic Politics'.

4 *Ibid.*, p. 460.

5 A further limitation of Putnam's model is its focus on formal negotiations in the economic issue area. Here the concept of winning the support of a coalition of interested parties is relatively straightforward, whereas in the national security issue area potential coalitions are much less well-defined, and many of the crucial actions are not part of a formal negotiation process. The concept of winning domestic support remains crucial, but the emphasis is largely on goals, symbols and images, for example, which set the parameters for potential bargaining.

6 Lebow, *Between Peace and War*, pp. 291–305.

7 Joll, *Origins of the First World War*, pp. 109, 116–17.

8 Lebow, *Between Peace and War*, pp. 169–92.

9 *Ibid.*, p. 293.

10 *Ibid.*, p. 305.

15   The outcome and the risk of war

1 Joll, *Origins of the First World War*, p. 204.

2 *Ibid.*, p. 205.

3 Waltz, *Theory*, pp. 68–9.

4 Snyder and Diesing, *Conflict Among Nations*, p. 525.

5 *Ibid.*, p. 488.

6 Karl Marx, *The Eighteenth Brumaire of Louis Bonaparte*, reprinted in Lewis S. Feuer, ed., *Marx and Engels: Basic Writings on Politics and Philosophy* (London: Collins Fontana Library, 1969), p. 360.

7 The issues are similar to those discussed in the debate on the causal significance of regimes: 'do regimes matter?' See Stephen D. Krasner, ed., 'International Regimes', special issue, *International Organization*, 36 (Spring 1982).

8 For this interpretation of Prisoner's Dilemma, following Snyder and Diesing, see Chapter 13 above.

16   Conclusions: theory and policy

1 For a discussion of this issue, see Ian Bell, 'Foreign Policy Analysis, International Relations Theory, and Social Theory: Critique and Reconstruction', Working Paper 1991/4, Department of International Relations, Australian National University, 1991, esp. pp. 7–8, 19–21. For policy studies, see the works on crises by Brecher and by Lebow, cited earlier, and in a different field, John Odell, 'Understanding International Trade Policies: An Emerging Synthesis', *World Politics*, 43 (1990), pp. 139–67.

2 See Alexander E. Wendt, 'The Agent–Structure Problem in International Relations Theory', *International Organization*, 41 (1987), pp. 335–70; David Dessler, 'What's at Stake in the Agent–Structure Debate?'.

3 For a brief account of structuration, see Wendt, 'Agent–Structure Problem', pp. 337–40; for a more extended exposition, Anthony Giddens, *The Constitution of Society: Outline of the Theory of Structuration* (Berkeley: University of California Press, 1984), pp. 1–40.

4 For the claim that the theory lacks empirical relevance, see Nicky Gregson, 'On the (ir)relevance of structuration theory to empirical research', in David Held and John B. Thompson, eds., *Social Theory of Modern Societies: Anthony Giddens and his Critics* (Cambridge: Cambridge University Press, 1989), pp. 235–48, and Giddens' response, *ibid.*, pp. 293–301.

5 Wendt, 'Agent–Structure Problem', p. 339.

6 Giddens formulates the point thus: 'In interpretative sociologies, action and meaning are accorded primacy in the explication of human conduct; structural concepts are not notably prominent, and there is not much talk of constraint. For functionalism and structuralism, however, structure (in the divergent senses attributed to that concept) has primacy over action, and the constraining qualities of structure are strongly accentuated'. Giddens, *Constitution of Society*, p. 2.

7 For a critique of Giddens' concept of structure see John B. Thompson, 'The theory of structuration', in Held and Thompson, eds., *Social Theory*, pp. 56–76, and for Giddens' response, *ibid.*, pp. 253–9.

8 This approach is developed by Dessler, 'Agent–Structure Debate?'.

9 See Wendt, 'Agent–Structure Problem', pp. 362–5.

10 Morton A. Kaplan, *System and Process in International Politics* (New York: Wiley, 1957), pp. 16–17; for this characterisation of the aim of neo-realist theory, see, e.g., Robert O. Keohane, 'Theory of World Politics: Structural Realism and Beyond', in Ada W. Finifter, ed., *Political Science: The State of the Discipline* (Washington, DC: American Political Science Association, 1983), pp. 508–9.

11 Martin Wight, 'Why is there no International Theory?' in Martin Wight and Herbert Butterfield, eds., *Diplomatic Investigations: Essays in the Theory of International Politics* (London: George Allen & Unwin, 1966), p. 33.

12 George and Smoke, *Deterrence in American Foreign Policy*, pp. 509–15, 616–42.

13 Snyder and Diesing, *Conflict Among Nations*, pp. 471, 480–4, 497–503.

14 The position taken here may be contrasted with that of Graham Allison, whose 'rational actor' is the 'unified national government', but who acknowledges as a 'variant of the classical model' that some analysts treat individual leaders or leadership cliques as the rational actors (see Chapter 2 above).

15 Jervis, 'Realism', p. 326.

16 Bruce Bueno de Mesquita, 'The Contribution of Expected Utility Theory to the Study of International Conflict', in Robert I. Rotberg and Theodore K. Rabb, eds., *The Origin and Prevention of Major Wars* (Cambridge: Cambridge University Press, 1989), p. 64.

17 Elster, *Sour Grapes*, p. 15.

18 Jervis, *Perception and Misperception*, p. 119.

19 As noted earlier, this is the broad finding of Snyder and Diesing's case studies, and also of the case studies undertaken as part of Michael Brecher's International Crisis Behavior Project.

20 The Eastern crisis provides a partial exception, but misconceptions were prominent in the following three cases (1853, 1870 and 1903) ending in war, the diplomacy of attrition in Agadir, the Pearl Harbor and the Berlin crises; the Sudeten crisis could, in these terms, be characterised as the diplomacy of cross-purposes.

21 For a conceptual discussion, see George and Keohane, 'Concept of National Interests'.

22 Elster, 'Introduction', p. 3.

23 George and Smoke, *Deterrence in American Foreign Policy*, p. 620.

24 Notably, in this subject area, the works of Snyder and Diesing and of Lebow, frequently cited above.

25 The reference is to Graham T. Allison, Albert Carnesale and Joseph S. Nye, eds., *Hawks, Doves and Owls*.

26 The role of national self-images is discussed in Lebow, *Between Peace and War*, pp. 192–222.

27 Metternich's complaint in 1840 was that both Palmerston and Thiers neglected this, bringing on a needless, but dangerous confrontation. For a general discussion, see Williams, *Crisis Management*, pp. 155–64, 200–1.

28 I. William Zartman, 'Alternative Attempts at Crisis Management: Concepts and Processes', in Winham, ed., *New Issues*, pp. 199–223.

29 Snyder and Diesing, *Conflict Among Nations*, pp. 489–93.

30 *Ibid.*, pp. 207–81, 489–91.

31 'Politics is a strong and slow boring of hard boards.' Max Weber, 'Politics as a Vocation', in H. H. Gerth and C. Wright Mills, eds., *From Max Weber: Essays in Sociology* (London: Routledge & Kegan Paul, 1948, reprinted 1982), p. 128.

32 Zartman, 'Alternative Attempts', p. 199.

SELECT BIBLIOGRAPHY

All references are included except those only to a single case study. These may be found in the notes to the respective chapters.

Abel, Elie. *The Missiles of October: The Story of the Cuban Missile Crisis*. London: MacGibbon & Kee, 1962.

Allison, Graham T. *Essence of Decision: Explaining the Cuban Missile Crisis*. Boston: Little, Brown, 1971.

Allison, Graham T., Albert Carnesale and Joseph S. Nye, Jr, eds. *Hawks, Doves and Owls: An Agenda for Avoiding Nuclear War*. New York: Norton, 1985.

Allison, Graham T. and Morton H. Halperin. 'Bureaucratic Politics: A Paradigm and Some Policy Implications', *World Politics*, 24 (Supplement, 1972), 40–79.

Almond, Gabriel A. and G. Bingham Powell. *Comparative Politics: A Developmental Approach*. Boston: Little, Brown, 1966.

Alperovitz, Gar. *Cold War Essays*. New York: Doubleday, 1970.

Aron, Raymond. *Peace and War: A Theory of International Relations*. New York: Doubleday, 1966.

Baldwin, David. *Economic Statecraft*. Princeton: Princeton University Press, 1985.

Bell, Coral. *The Conventions of Crisis: A Study in Diplomatic Management*. London: Oxford University Press, 1971.

Bell, Ian. 'Foreign Policy Analysis, International Relations Theory, and Social Theory: Critique and Reconstruction', Working Paper 1991/4, Department of International Relations, Australian National University, 1991.

Brecher, Michael. 'State Behavior in International Crises', *Journal of Conflict Resolution*, 23 (1979), 446–80.

Brecher, Michael, Jonathan Wilkenfeld and Sheila Moser. *Crises in the Twentieth Century*, vol. I, *Handbook of International Crises*. Oxford: Pergamon Press, 1988.

Brodie, Bernard. *War and Politics*. New York: Macmillan, 1973.

Buchan, Alastair. *Crisis Management: The New Diplomacy*. Boulogne-sur-Seine: Atlantic Institute, 1966.

Bueno de Mesquita, Bruce. *The War Trap*. New Haven: Yale University Press, 1981.

'The Contribution of Expected Utility Theory to the Study of International Conflict', in Robert I. Rotberg and Theodore K. Rabb, eds., *The Origin and Prevention of Major Wars*. Cambridge: Cambridge University Press, 1989.

412

Bull, Hedley. *The Anarchical Society: A Study of Order in World Politics*. London: Macmillan, 1977.

'The Great Irresponsibles? The United States, the Soviet Union and World Order', *International Journal*, 35 (1980), 437–47.

Bull, Hedley and Adam Watson, eds. *The Expansion of International Society*. Oxford: Clarendon Press, 1984.

Bullock, Alan. *Hitler: A Study in Tyranny*, revised edition. Harmondsworth: Penguin, 1962.

Bundy, McGeorge. *Danger and Survival: Choices About the Bomb in the First Fifty Years*. New York: Vintage Books, 1990.

Cantori, Louis J. and Andrew H. Ziegler, Jr, eds. *Comparative Politics in the Post-Behavioral Era*. Boulder, CO: Lynne Rienner, 1988.

Case, Lynn M. *French Opinion on War and Diplomacy During the Second Empire*. Philadelphia: University of Pennsylvania Press, 1954.

Chang, King-Yuh. 'Practical Suggestions for Crisis Management: An Inventory', in D. Frei, ed., *Managing International Crises*. Beverly Hills, CA: Sage, 1982.

Cohen, Eliot A. 'Why We Should Stop Studying the Cuban Missile Crisis', *The National Interest*, 2 (1986), 3–13.

Craig, Gordon A. and Alexander L. George. *Force and Statecraft: Diplomatic Problems of Our Time*. New York: Oxford University Press, 1983.

Dehio, Ludwig. *Germany and World Politics in the Twentieth Century*, trans. Dieter Pevsner. London: Chatto & Windus, 1959.

Dessler, David. 'What's at Stake in the Agent–Structure Debate?', *International Organization*, 43 (1989), 441–73.

Eberwein, Wolf-Dieter. 'Crisis Research – The State of the Art: A Western View', in Frei, ed., *International Crises and Crisis Management*.

Eckstein, Harry. 'Case Study and Theory in Political Science', in F. I. Greenstein and N. W. Polsby, eds., *Handbook of Political Science* (Reading, MA: Addison-Wesley, 1975), vol. VII.

Elster, Jon. *Sour Grapes: Studies in the Subversion of Rationality*. Cambridge: Cambridge University Press, 1983.

'Introduction', in Jon Elster, ed., *Rational Choice*. Oxford: Blackwell, 1986.

Fischer, Fritz. *War of Illusions: German Policies from 1911 to 1914*. London: Chatto and Windus, 1975.

Frei, Daniel, ed. *International Crises and Crisis Management: An East–West Symposium*. Farnborough: Saxon House, 1978.

Garst, Daniel. 'Thucydides and Neorealism', *International Studies Quarterly*, 33 (1989), 3–27.

Gellman, Peter. 'The Elusive Explanation: Balance of Power "Theory" and the Origins of World War I', *Review of International Studies*, 15 (1989), 155–82.

George, Alexander L. 'The Case for Multiple Advocacy in Making Foreign Policy', *American Political Science Review*, 66 (1972), 751–85.

'Case Studies and Theory Development: The Method of Structured, Focused Comparison', in P. G. Lauren, ed., *Diplomacy: New Approaches in History, Theory and Policy*. York: Free Press, 1979.

George, Alexander L., David K. Hall and William R. Simons. *The Limits of Coercive Diplomacy: Laos, Cuba, Vietnam*. Boston: Little, Brown, 1971.

413

George, Alexander L. and Robert O. Keohane. 'The Concept of National Interests: Uses and Limitations', in Alexander L. George, *Presidential Decisionmaking in Foreign Policy: The Effective Use of Information and Advice*. Boulder, CO: Westview, 1980.

George, Alexander L. and Richard Smoke. *Deterrence in American Foreign Policy: Theory and Practice*. New York: Columbia University Press, 1974.

Giddens, Anthony. *The Constitution of Society: Outline of the Theory of Structuration*. Berkeley: University of California Press, 1984.

Gilbert, Arthur N. and Paul G. Lauren. 'Crisis Management: An Assessment and Critique', *Journal of Conflict Resolution*, 26 (1980), 641–64.

Gottfried, Kurt, and Bruce G. Blair, eds. *Crisis Stability and Nuclear War*. New York: Oxford University Press, 1988.

'The Great War and the Nuclear Age', special issue, *International Security*, 9 (Summer 1984).

Gregson, Nicky. 'On the (Ir)relevance of Structuration Theory to Empirical Research', in Held and Thompson, eds., *Social Theory*.

Groom, A. J. R. 'Crisis Management in Long-Range Perspective', in Frei, ed., *International Crises and Crisis Management*.

Gulick, Edward Vose. *Europe's Classical Balance of Power: A Case History of the Theory and Practice of One of the Great Concepts of European Statecraft*. New York: Norton, 1967.

Halperin, Morton H. *Bureaucratic Politics and Foreign Policy*. Washington, DC: Brookings Institution, 1974.

Held, David, and John B. Thompson, eds. *Social Theory of Modern Societies: Anthony Giddens and his Critics*. Cambridge: Cambridge University Press, 1989.

Hermann, Charles F., ed. *International Crises: Insights from Behavioral Research*. New York: Free Press, 1972.

'Some Issues in the Study of International Crisis' in Hermann, ed., *International Crises*.

Hermann, Charles F. and Linda P. Brady. 'Alternative Models of International Crisis Behavior', in Hermann, ed., *International Crises*.

Hilsman, Roger. *To Move a Nation: The Politics of Foreign Policy in the Administration of John F. Kennedy*. Garden City, NY: Doubleday, 1967.

Hinsley, F. H. *Power and the Pursuit of Peace*. Cambridge: Cambridge University Press, 1963.

Holbraad, Carsten. *The Concert of Europe: A Study in German and British International Theory, 1815–1914*. London: Longman, 1970.

Holsti, Ole R. *Crisis, Escalation, War*. Montreal: McGill–Queen's University Press, 1972.

'Time, Alternatives and Communications: The 1914 and Cuban Missile Crises', in Hermann, ed., *International Crises*.

'Foreign Policy Formation Viewed Cognitively', in Robert Axelrod, ed., *Structure of Decision: The Cognitive Maps of Political Elites*. Princeton: Princeton University Press, 1976.

'Crisis Decision Making', in Philip E. Tetlock *et al.*, *Behavior, Society and Nuclear War*. New York: Oxford University Press, 1989.

414

Holsti, Ole R. and Alexander L. George. 'The Effects of Stress on the Performance of Foreign Policy Makers', *Political Science Annual*, 6 (1975), 255–319.

Ingle, Harold N. *Nesselrode and the Russian Rapprochement with Britain, 1836-1844*. Berkeley: University of California Press, 1976.

Jervis, Robert. *Perception and Misperception in International Politics*. Princeton: Princeton University Press, 1976.

'Deterrence and Perception', *International Security*, 7 (Winter 1982–83), 3–30.

'Realism, Game Theory, and Cooperation', *World Politics*, 40 (1988), 317–49.

'Models and Cases in the Study of International Conflict', *Journal of International Affairs*, 44 (1990), 81–101.

Joll, James. '1914: The Unspoken Assumptions', in H.W. Koch, ed., *The Origins of the First World War: Great Power Rivalry and German War Aims*. London: Macmillan, 1972.

The Origins of the First World War. London and New York: Longman, 1984.

Kaplan, Morton A. *System and Process in International Politics*. New York: Wiley, 1957.

Keiger, John F. V. *France and the Origins of the First World War*. London: Macmillan, 1983.

Kennedy, Robert. *Thirteen Days: The Missile Crisis*. London: Pan, 1969.

Keohane, Robert O. 'Theory of World Politics: Structural Realism and Beyond', in Ada W. Finifter, ed., *Political Science: The State of the Discipline*. Washington, DC: American Political Science Association, 1983.

Kinder, Donald R. and Janet A. Weiss. 'In Lieu of Rationality: Psychological Perspectives on Foreign Policy Decision Making', *Journal of Conflict Resolution*, 22 (1978), 707–35.

Kissinger, Henry A. *The White House Years*. Boston: Little, Brown, 1979.

Krasner, Stephen D., ed. 'International Regimes', special issue, *International Organization*, 36 (Spring 1982).

Kratochwil, Friedrich. 'On the Notion of "Interest" in International Relations', *International Organization*, 36 (1982), 1–30.

Larson, Deborah Welch. *Origins of Containment: A Psychological Explanation*. Princeton: Princeton University Press, 1985.

Lebow, Richard Ned. *Between Peace and War: The Nature of International Crisis*. Baltimore and London: Johns Hopkins University Press, 1981.

Nuclear Crisis Management: A Dangerous Illusion. Ithaca and London: Cornell University Press, 1987.

Levy, Jack S. 'Misperception and the Causes of War: Theoretical Linkages and Analytical Problems', *World Politics*, 36 (1983), 76–99.

'Preferences, Constraints and Choices in July 1914', *International Security*, 15 (Winter 1990/91), 151–86.

Luce, R. Duncan, and Howard Raiffa. *Games and Decisions*. New York: Wiley, 1957.

March, James, and Herbert Simon. *Organizations*. New York: Wiley, 1958.

Marx, Karl. 'The Eighteenth Brumaire of Louis Bonaparte', in Lewis S. Feuer, ed., *Marx and Engels: Basic Writings on Politics and Philosophy*. London: Collins Fontana Library, 1969.

415

Maxwell, Herbert. *The Life and Letters of George William Frederick, Fourth Earl of Clarendon*, 2 vols. London: Edward Arnold, 1913.

Milburn, Thomas. 'The Management of Crises', in Hermann, ed., *International Crises*.

Monger, George W. *The End of Isolation: British Foreign Policy 1900–1907*. London: Nelson, 1963.

Morgenthau, Hans J. 'Another Great Debate: The National Interest of the United States', in Stanley Hoffmann, ed., *Contemporary Theory in International Relations*. Englewood Cliffs, NJ: Prentice-Hall, 1960.

Politics Among Nations: The Struggle for Power and Peace, 4th edn. New York: Knopf, 1967.

Nesselrode, Anatol de. *Lettres et Papiers du Chancelier Comte de Nesselrode, 1760–1850*. Paris: A. Lahure, 1904–11), vols. VII, VIII, X.

Neuhold, Hanspeter. 'Principles and Implementation of Crisis Management: Lessons from the Past', in Frei, ed., *International Crises and Crisis Management*.

Nicholson, Michael. *Conflict Analysis*. London: English Universities Press, 1970.

Formal Theories in International Relations. Cambridge: Cambridge University Press, 1989.

Odell, John. 'Understanding International Trade Policies: An Emerging Synthesis', *World Politics*, 43 (1990), 139–67.

Putnam, Robert D. 'Diplomacy and Domestic Politics: The Logic of Two-Level Games', *International Organization*, 42 (1988), 427–60.

Richardson, James L. 'Crisis Management: A Critical Appraisal', in Winham, ed., *New Issues*.

'New Insights on International Crises', *Review of International Studies*, 14 (1988), 309–16.

Roberts, Jonathan M. *Decision-Making During International Crises*. London: Macmillan, 1988.

Robinson, James A. 'Crisis: An Appraisal of Concepts and Theories', in Hermann, ed., *International Crises*.

Rosecrance, Richard N. *Action and Reaction in World Politics: International Systems in Perspective*. Boston: Little, Brown, 1963.

Rosenau, James N. 'National Interest', *International Encyclopedia of the Social Sciences* (New York: Macmillan and Free Press, 1968), vol. XI.

Sagan, Scott D. '1914 Revisited: Allies, Offense and Instability', *International Security*, 11 (Fall 1986), 151–75.

Schelling, Thomas C. *The Strategy of Conflict*. Cambridge, MA: Harvard University Press, 1960.

Arms and Influence. New Haven: Yale University Press, 1966.

Schlesinger, Arthur M., Jr. *A Thousand Days: John F. Kennedy in the White House*. London: André Deutsch, 1965.

Schroeder, Paul W. *Austria, Great Britain and the Crimean War: The Destruction of the European Concert*. Ithaca: Cornell University Press, 1972.

Review of Holsti, *Crisis, Escalation, War*, in *Journal of Modern History*, 46 (1974), 537–40.

'The 19th-Century International System: Changes in the Structure', *World Politics*, 39 (1986), 1–26.

'The Nineteenth Century System: Balance of Power or Political Equilibrium?', *Review of International Studies*, 15 (1989), 135–53.

Shoemaker, Paul J.H. 'The Expected Utility Model: Its Variants, Purposes, Evidence and Limitations', *Journal of Economic Literature*, 20 (1982), 529–63.

Skocpol, Theda, and Margaret Somers. 'The Uses of Comparative History in Macrosocial Inquiry', *Comparative Studies in Society and History*, 22 (1980), 174–97.

Smoke, Richard. *War: Controlling Escalation*. Cambridge, MA: Harvard University Press, 1977.

Snyder, Glenn H. and Paul Diesing. *Conflict Among Nations: Bargaining, Decision Making, and System Structure in International Crises*. Princeton: Princeton University Press, 1977.

Starn, Randolph. 'Historians and "Crisis"', *Past and Present*, 52 (1971), 3–22.

Stein, Arthur A. 'When Misperception Matters', *World Politics*, 34 (1982), 505–26.

Steinbruner, John D. *The Cybernetic Theory of Decision: New Dimensions of Political Analysis*. Princeton: Princeton University Press, 1974.

Steiner, Zara S. *The Foreign Office and Foreign Policy*. Cambridge: Cambridge University Press, 1969.

Stoessinger, John G. *Why Nations Go to War*. New York: St Martin's Press, 1974.

Taylor, A. J. P. *The Struggle for Mastery in Europe, 1848-1918*. Oxford: Clarendon Press, 1954.

Temperley, Harold. *England and the Near East: The Crimea*. London: Longmans, Green & Co., 1936.

Thompson, John B. 'The Theory of Structuration', in Held and Thompson, eds., *Social Theory*.

Trachtenberg, Marc. 'The Meaning of Mobilization in 1914', *International Security*, 15 (Winter 1990/91), 120–50.

Van Evera, Stephen. 'Why Cooperation Failed in 1914', *World Politics*, 38 (1985), 80–117.

Vertzberger, Yaacov Y. I. *The World in Their Minds: Information Processing, Cognition and Perception in Foreign Policy Decisionmaking*. Stanford: Stanford University Press, 1990.

Waltz, Kenneth N. *Theory of International Politics*. Reading, MA: Addison-Wesley, 1979.

Weber, Max. 'Politics as a Vocation', in H.H. Gerth and C. Wright Mills, eds., *From Max Weber: Essays in Sociology*. London: Routledge and Kegan Paul, 1948, reprinted 1982.

Wendt, Alexander E. 'The Agent–Structure Problem in International Relations Theory', *International Organization*, 41 (1987), 335–70.

White, Robert H. *Nobody Wanted War*. Garden City, NY: Doubleday/Anchor, 1970.

Wiarda, Howard J., ed. *New Directions in Comparative Politics*. Boulder, CO: Westview, 1985.

Wiener, Anthony J. and Herman Kahn. *Crisis and Arms Control*. Harmon-on-Hudson, NY: Hudson Institute, 1962.

Wight, Martin. 'Why is There No International Theory?' in Martin Wight and

417

Herbert Butterfield, eds., *Diplomatic Investigations: Essays in the Theory of International Politics*. London: George Allen & Unwin, 1966.

Williams, Philip. *Crisis Management: Confrontation and Diplomacy in the Nuclear Age*. New York: Wiley, 1976.

Winham, Gilbert R., ed. *New Issues in International Crisis Management*. Boulder, CO: Westview, 1988.

'Conclusion', in Winham, ed., *New Issues*.

Wohlstetter, Roberta. *Pearl Harbor: Warning and Decision*. Stanford: Stanford University Press, 1962.

Wolfers, Arnold. *Discord and Collaboration*. Baltimore: Johns Hopkins University Press, 1962.

Woodward, Bob. *The Commanders*. New York: Simon and Schuster, 1991.

X, 'The Sources of Soviet Conduct', *Foreign Affairs*, 25 (1947), 566–82.

Young, Oran. *The Politics of Force*. Princeton: Princeton University Press, 1968.

Zartman, I. William. 'Alternative Attempts at Crisis Management: Concepts and Processes', in Winham, ed., *New Issues*.

INDEX

CAMBRIDGE STUDIES IN INTERNATIONAL RELATIONS